Lecture Notes in Computer Science 14890

Founding Editors

Gerhard Goos
Juris Hartmanis

Editorial Board Members

Elisa Bertino, *Purdue University, West Lafayette, IN, USA*
Wen Gao, *Peking University, Beijing, China*
Bernhard Steffen , *TU Dortmund University, Dortmund, Germany*
Moti Yung , *Columbia University, New York, NY, USA*

The series Lecture Notes in Computer Science (LNCS), including its subseries Lecture Notes in Artificial Intelligence (LNAI) and Lecture Notes in Bioinformatics (LNBI), has established itself as a medium for the publication of new developments in computer science and information technology research, teaching, and education.

LNCS enjoys close cooperation with the computer science R & D community, the series counts many renowned academics among its volume editors and paper authors, and collaborates with prestigious societies. Its mission is to serve this international community by providing an invaluable service, mainly focused on the publication of conference and workshop proceedings and postproceedings. LNCS commenced publication in 1973.

Patricia Santos · Claudio Álvarez ·
Davinia Hernández-Leo · Minoru Kobayashi ·
Gustavo Zurita
Editors

Collaboration Technologies and Social Computing

30th International Conference, CollabTech 2024
Barcelona, Spain, September 11–14, 2024
Proceedings

Editors
Patricia Santos ⓘD
Universitat Pompeu Fabra
Barcelona, Spain

Claudio Álvarez ⓘD
Universidad de los Andes
Santiago, Chile

Davinia Hernández-Leo ⓘD
Universitat Pompeu Fabra
Barcelona, Spain

Minoru Kobayashi ⓘD
Meiji University
Tokyo, Japan

Gustavo Zurita ⓘD
University of Chile
Santiago, Chile

ISSN 0302-9743   ISSN 1611-3349 (electronic)
Lecture Notes in Computer Science
ISBN 978-3-031-67997-1   ISBN 978-3-031-67998-8 (eBook)
https://doi.org/10.1007/978-3-031-67998-8

© The Editor(s) (if applicable) and The Author(s), under exclusive license to Springer Nature Switzerland AG 2024

This work is subject to copyright. All rights are solely and exclusively licensed by the Publisher, whether the whole or part of the material is concerned, specifically the rights of translation, reprinting, reuse of illustrations, recitation, broadcasting, reproduction on microfilms or in any other physical way, and transmission or information storage and retrieval, electronic adaptation, computer software, or by similar or dissimilar methodology now known or hereafter developed.
The use of general descriptive names, registered names, trademarks, service marks, etc. in this publication does not imply, even in the absence of a specific statement, that such names are exempt from the relevant protective laws and regulations and therefore free for general use.
The publisher, the authors and the editors are safe to assume that the advice and information in this book are believed to be true and accurate at the date of publication. Neither the publisher nor the authors or the editors give a warranty, expressed or implied, with respect to the material contained herein or for any errors or omissions that may have been made. The publisher remains neutral with regard to jurisdictional claims in published maps and institutional affiliations.

This Springer imprint is published by the registered company Springer Nature Switzerland AG
The registered company address is: Gewerbestrasse 11, 6330 Cham, Switzerland

If disposing of this product, please recycle the paper.

Preface

This volume contains the papers presented at the 30th International Conference on Collaboration Technologies and Social Computing. The conference was held during September 11–14, 2024, in Barcelona, Spain.

This year we received 36 submissions, including 26 full papers and 10 Work In Progress (WIP) contributions. Each paper was carefully reviewed by 3 to 5 Program Committee members in a double-blind process. As a result, the Program Committee Co-Chairs decided to accept 12 full papers, and 10 WIP papers. Among the WIP papers accepted, four correspond to full papers that were downgraded to WIP after review, while the remaining six were originally submitted as WIP. The accepted papers present relevant and interesting research works related to theory, models, design principles, methodologies, and case studies that contribute to a better understanding of the complex interrelations that exist at the intersection of collaboration and technology. The program also included two keynote presentations.

As editors, we would like to thank the authors of all submissions and the members of the Program Committee for their careful reviews. Our thanks also go to Universitat Pompeu Fabra and the Department of Engineering for hosting and supporting the conference through the celebration of its 25th anniversary and the Maria de Maetzu program (CEX2021-001195-M) and through projects of the TIDE research group funded by the Spanish Ministry (MICIU/AEI/10.13039/501100011033 PID2020-112584RB-C33) and the Catalan Government (SGR 00930, DHL-ICREA Academia). We thank Universidad de Chile for their support, including the Department of Management Control and Information Systems, and the Department of Computer Science. Our special thanks go to the Information Processing Society of Japan (IPSJ), for their sponsorship.

Finally, we would like to acknowledge the effort of the organizers of the conference, as well as thank the Steering Committee for the opportunity to organize the conference and the help provided in the process.

June 2024

Patricia Santos
Claudio Álvarez
Davinia Hernández-Leo
Minoru Kobayashi
Gustavo Zurita

Organization

General Chairs

Davinia Hernández-Leo   Universitat Pompeu Fabra, Spain
Minoru Kobayashi   Meiji University, Japan
Gustavo Zurita   Universidad de Chile, Chile

Program Co-chairs

Patricia Santos   Universitat Pompeu Fabra, Spain
Claudio Alvarez   Universidad de los Andes, Chile

Steering Committee

Nelson Baloian   Universidad de Chile, Chile
Ulrich Hoppe   RIAS Institute, Germany
Tomoo Inoue   University of Tsukuba, Japan
Minoru Kobayashi   Meiji University, Japan
Hideaki Kuzuoka   University of Tokyo, Japan
Hiroaki Ogata   Kyoto University, Japan

Program Committee

Ishari Amarasinghe   Radboud University, The Netherlands
Juan I. Asensio-Pérez   Universidad de Valladolid, Spain
Miguel L. Bote-Lorenzo   Universidad de Valladolid, Spain
Juan Felipe Calderón-Maureira   Universidad Andrés Bello, Chile
Hui-Chun Chu   Soochow University, Taiwan
Yannis Dimitriadis   University of Valladolid, Spain
Hironori Egi   University of Electro-Communications, Japan
Orlando Erazo   Universidad Técnica Estatal de Quevedo, Ecuador
Kinya Fujita   Tokyo University, Japan
Cédric Grueau   Setúbal Polytechnic University, Portugal
Yugo Hayashi   Ritsumeikan University, Japan
Naoko Hayashida   Fujitsu Laboratories Ltd., Japan

Atsuo Hazeyama	Tokyo Gakugei University, Japan
H. Ulrich Hoppe	RIAS Institute Duisburg, Germany
Satoshi Ichimura	Otsuma Women's University, Japan
Junko Ichino	Tokyo City University, Japan
Yuya Ieiri	Waseda University, Japan
Claudia-Lavinia Ignat	ETH Zurich, Switzerland
Indratmo Indratmo	MacEwan University, Canada
Tomoo Inoue	University of Tsukuba, Japan
Yutaka Ishii	Okayama Prefectural University, Japan
Kazuyuki Iso	NTT Corporation, Japan
Marc Jansen	University of Applied Sciences Ruhr West, Germany
Hideaki Kanai	Advanced Institute of Science and Technology, Japan
Ikkaku Kawaguchi	University of Tsukuba, Japan
Nobutaka Kawaguchi	Hitachi, Ltd., Japan
Minoru Kobayashi	Meiji University, Japan
Thomas Largillier	GREYC, Normandie
Liang-Yi Li	National Taiwan Normal University, Taiwan
Rene Lobo	Universitat Pompeu Fabra, Spain
Maíra Marques Samary	Boston College, USA
Sonia Guadalupe Mendoza Chapa	CINVESTAV, Mexico
Roc Meseguer	Universitat Politècnica de Catalunya, Spain
Marcelo Milrad	Linnaeus University, Sweden
Akihiro Miyata	Nihon University, Japan
Carmen Morgado	Universidade NOVA de Lisboa, Portugal
Mikihiko Mori	Mejiro University, Japan
Satoshi Nakamura	Meiji University, Japan
Hideyuki Nakanishi	Kindai University, Japan
Mamoun Nawahdah	Birzeit University, Palestine
Alexander Tobias Neumann	Aachen University, Germany
Arinobu Niijima	NTT Corporation, Japan
Sergio Ochoa	University of Chile, Chile
Masayuki Okamoto	Toyota Motor Corporation, Japan
Masaki Omata	University of Yamanashi, Japan
Gerald Oster	Université de Lorraine, France
Kouyou Otsu	Ritsumeikan University, Japan
Mondheera Pituxcoosuvarn	Ritsumeikan University, Japan
Elvira Popescu	University of Craiova, Romania
Matías Recabarren	Universidad de los Andes, Colombia
Armanda Rodrigues	Universidade NOVA de Lisboa, Portugal

Cristian Rusu	Pontificia Universidad Católica de Valparaiso, Chile
Nobuchika Sakata	Ryukoku University, Japan
Claudio Sapateiro	Instituto Politécnico de Setúbal, Portugal
Eliana Scheihing	Universidad Austral de Chile, Chile
Hidekazu Shiozawa	Tamagawa University, Japan
Marcus Specht	Delft University of Technology, The Netherlands
Masanori Sugimoto	Hokkaido University, Japan
Hideyuki Takada	Ritsumeikan University, Japan
Keisuke Tsunoda	NTT Corporation, Japan
Aurora Vizcaíno	Universidad de Castilla-La Mancha, Spain
Tzu-Yang Wang	Advanced Institute of Science and Technology, Japan
Benjamin Weyers	Trier University, Germany
Mika Yasuoka	Roskilde University, Denmark
Takashi Yoshino	Wakayama University, Japan
Takaya Yuizono	Advanced Institute of Science and Technology, Japan
Alejandro Zunino	CONICET-ISISTAN, Buenos Aires, Argentina
Gustavo Zurita	Universidad de Chile, Chile

Keynote Abstracts

Network Analysis Approaches in Research on Collaboration in Digital Communities - Evolution and Prospects

H. Ulrich Hoppe

RIAS Institute, Duisburg, Germany
uh@rias-institute.eu

Network models and network analysis techniques can reveal structural features of online communities and thus support a better understanding of community dependencies and processes [1]. This can help to make better informed decisions in community management and (self-)organization. Network analysis builds on a broad spectrum of mathematical and computational methods some of which, such as centrality measurement and community detection, have been widely adopted in application fields like CSCW, CSCL, and Learning Analytics [2, 3].

However, the adoption of network analysis methods is still selective and not much differentiated so that the potential is not fully realized. For example, in the case of community detection, the most frequently used approaches rely on modularity maximization [4] with variants that inherently do not allow for detecting overlaps between subcommunities as a property induced by the algorithm. Yet, overlaps are potentially very relevant when analyzing community structures under aspects of cooperativity [5]. Other techniques that have not been sufficiently exploited include role detection through positional analysis as well as the use of multi-mode network representations. In addition to providing examples of mainstream work, this talk intends to illustrate and exemplify this unused potential. Also, new challenges related to the combination of network analysis with Deep Learning approaches will be discussed.

References

1. Hoppe, H.U., Harrer, A., Göhnert, T., Hecking, T.: Applying network models and network analysis techniques to the study of online communities. In: Cress, U., Moskaliuk, J., Jeong, H. (eds.) Mass Collaboration and Education. Computer-Supported Collaborative Learning Series, vol. 16, pp. 347–366. Springer, Cham (2016). https://doi.org/10.1007/978-3-319-13536-6_17
2. Chen, B., Poquet, O.: Networks in learning analytics: where theory, methodology, and practice intersect. J. Learn. Analytics 9(1), 1–12 (2022)
3. Dado, M., Hecking, T., Bodemer, D., Hoppe, H.U.: On the adoption of social network analysis methods in CSCL research – a network analysis. In: Proceedings of CSCL 2017, International Society of the Learning Sciences (2017)

4. Chen, M., Kuzmin, K., Szymanski, B.K.: Community detection via maximization of modularity and its variants. IEEE Trans. Comput. Soc. Syst. **1**(1), 46–65 (2014)
5. Shahriari, M., Klamma, R., Jarke, M.: Dynamics of overlapping community structures with application to expert identification. In: Agarwal, N., Dokoohaki, N., Tokdemir, S. (eds.) Emerging Research Challenges and Opportunities in Computational Social Network Analysis and Mining. Lecture Notes in Social Networks, pp. 153–208. Springer, Cham (2019). https://doi.org/10.1007/978-3-319-94105-9_7

Leveraging Metaverse and Generative AI for Transformative Education

Minjuan Wang

The Education University of Hong Kong, Hong Kong SAR, China
mwang@sdsu.edu

Over the course of recent decades, eLearning has undergone a remarkable evolution, moving through distinct eras, each marked by its own epoch-defining technologies: from the "Age of Portals and Pages" (1994) to the "Age of Openness" (2001), from the "Age of MOOCs" (2008) to the dawning of the "Age of Personalization" in 2015 [1].

Fast forward to 2022 and 2023, and we have been standing at the threshold of the "Age of Metaverse and Generative AI." This is an era where the convergence of extended realities, metaverse platforms, and the ascent of Generative AI has ignited profound discussions worldwide regarding their implications for education and training [2]. These AI tools, exemplified by the likes of ChatGPT, Copilot and Gemini, can generate human-like text and multimedia content, which have the potential to transform various aspects of education and training.

Throughout these transformative ages, one pressing question has endured: Will Metaverse and Generative AI reshape education in the years to come? How can these innovative technologies be harnessed to design and deliver education and training experiences that are simultaneously user-centered and instructor-friendly?

In this keynote presentation, Dr. Wang will guide you through exemplary Metaverse platforms. You will have the opportunity to witness a 3D pedagogical framework—an ecosystem she co-created with her graduate students at San Diego State University [3]. She will then take you on an exciting tour of exemplary AI tools for designing instructional activities and for learning facilitation. Meanwhile, Generative AI introduces ethical dilemmas. This presentation will explore responsible AI use, privacy concerns, and bias mitigation.

References

1. Wang, M.J., Yu, H.Y., et al.: Constructing an edu-metaverse ecosystem: a new and innovative framework. IEEE Trans. Learn. Technol. **15**(6), 685–696 (2022). https://doi.org/10.1109/TLT.2022.3210828
2. Wang, M., Wang, M.J., et al.: Unleashing ChatGPT's power: a case study on optimizing information retrieval in flipped classrooms via prompt engineering. IEEE Trans. Learn. Technol. **17**, 629–641 (2024). https://doi.org/10.1109/TLT.2023.3324714

3. Bobko, T., Corsette, M., Wang, M.J., Springer, E.: Exploring the possibilities of edumetaverse: a new 3D ecosystem model for innovative learning. IEEE Trans. Learn. Technol. (2024). https://doi.org/10.1109/TLT.2024.3364908

Contents

Full Papers

LLM-Based Structuring of Oral Discussion in Workshop to Support
Collaboration Among Local Government and Simulated Citizens 3
  *Gen Sato, Shun Shiramatsu, Mizuki Hoshino, Shuhei Watanabe,
  Yu Haibo, and Takeshi Mizumoto*

A Metaverse-Based Virtual Office System with Overhearing Function
for Facilitating Smooth Joining in Ongoing Conversations 17
  Ryota Sugisawa and Kinya Fujita

Motivational Dynamics and Platform Design in Online Communities
of Teachers: A Multi-case Study 29
  *Patricia Santos, Nicolas Gutierrez-Paez, Davinia Hernández-Leo,
  Konstantinos Michos, and Mar Carrió*

Adaptation of a Self-determination Theory-Based Questionnaire
on Collaborative Classroom Dynamics 45
  *Khadija El Aadmi-Laamech, Patricia Santos,
  and Davinia Hernández-Leo*

Exploring Group Behavior and Discussion Productivity in Anonymous
Chatrooms for Ethical Decision-Making 61
  Claudio Álvarez, Gustavo Zurita, Antonio Farías, and Manuel Yunga

Extending an Intelligent Tutoring System for Oral Communication
with Peer Assessment Capabilities: An Evaluation Study 81
  Javier Ibarra, Claudio Álvarez, and Matías Recabarren

Dialogue Act Analysis of Facilitator-Children Multilingual
Communication 97
  Mizuki Motozawa, Yohei Murakami, and Mondheera Pituxcoosuvarn

Detecting Sports Spoiler Images on YouTube 114
  Yuichiro Kinoshita, Takumi Takaku, and Satoshi Nakamura

An Exploratory Study on Empathy and Online Discussions in Computer
Supported Collaborative Learning 129
  *Emily Theophilou, J. Roberto Sánchez-Reina, Valguima Odakura,
  and Davinia Hernández-Leo*

Interpreting Arrows in Mobile Robot-Human Encounters: The Influence
of Spatial Context and Presentation Timing 144
   Yo Kuwamiya, Atsuto Kurokochi, and Minoru Kobayashi

Quantitative Observation to Explore the Turn-Changing Mechanisms
of Conversations in Remote Meetings Accompanying Supplemental
Materials 161
   *Kenta Ohnaka, Taketo Imagawa, Kazuyuki Iso, Masayuki Ihara,
and Minoru Kobayashi*

Engagement Analysis of Speech Text from Activity Reports of a Distance
Project-Based Learning 177
   Kosuke Sasaki and Tomoo Inoue

Work in Progress Papers

Exploring Interest Similarity Features and Their Combinations
for Friendship Recommendation Without Cold Start 195
   Ana Beatriz Pires Quelhas, Natsuki Oka, and Kazuaki Tanaka

Stimulating Creative Hypothesis Discovery by Future Human-AI Teaming 203
   Soichiro Iga, Susumu Takatsuka, and Hiroki Tetsukawa

Using Word Games as Facilitator to Awareness Raising Communication
in Public Spaces 212
   Shinya Nishide and Takeshi Nishida

Enabling Mixed Genetic Algorithm for Automatic Group Formation
System 220
   Changhao Liang, Izumi Horikoshi, and Hiroaki Ogata

Make-Up FLOW: A Beauty YouTubers' Video Recommendation Method
Based on Make-Up Flowcharts 229
   Sayaka Takano and Satoshi Nakamura

Active Participation vs. Directed Observation in Collaborative 3D Virtual
Museums 237
   Gustavo Zurita, Joaquín Uribe, Nelson Baloian, and Valentina Aravena

Generative AI Chatbot in PyramidApp: Students' Behaviors and Design
Principles 248
   *Aldric Gutiérrez-Ferré, Davinia Hernández-Leo,
and J. Roberto Sánchez-Reina*

Generative AI Collaboration in the Orchestration of Supervised Classroom
Problem Solving 257
  Héctor Florido and Davinia Hernández-Leo

Development and Evaluation of Gamification-Based Addressing
Promotion System for Teaching Assistants 265
  Kanato Murobayashi, Takahiro Yoshino, and Hironori Egi

Boosting Non-Native Speaker Engagement: Simplifying Text with Large
Language Models 274
  Mondheera Pituxcoosuvarn and Yohei Murakami

Author Index 283

Full Papers

LLM-Based Structuring of Oral Discussion in Workshop to Support Collaboration Among Local Government and Simulated Citizens

Gen Sato[1(✉)], Shun Shiramatsu[1], Mizuki Hoshino[1], Shuhei Watanabe[1], Yu Haibo[1], and Takeshi Mizumoto[2]

[1] Nagoya Institute of Technology, Gokiso-cho, Showa-ku, Nagoya, Aichi 466-8555, Japan
g.sato.848@ict.nitech.ac.jp

[2] Hylable Inc., 2-203, Suzuoto Bldg., 2-26-12, Minami Otsuka, Toshima-City, Tokyo 170-005, Japan

Abstract. In oral discussions, such as workshops, notes and sticky notes are frequently used to record content of the utterances. However, the content of the discussion may not be accurately captured or be forgotten through manual writing. Although the results from speech recognition could be used, they are difficult to understand because they are redundant and consist of fillers. This study addresses this problem by recording the speech-recognition results into text, similar to writing on a sticky note. The text should be well-structured for participants to understand. The objective of this research is to develop a discussion structuring system for use in real time and demonstrate its utility as a substitute for notes. This system will enable users to easily reflect on the content and process of discussions. The large language model GPT-4 is used for paraphrasing speech-recognition results into simple sentences and structuring them. It will also be used for opinion generation to incorporate novel viewpoints to a target discussion. A discussion experiment using a prototype of this system was conducted for a workshop involving local government staff. It was shown that the system could serve as an alternative to sticky notes when people reflect on the discussions of the group and the artificial-intelligence-generated opinions from the system are effective in supporting discussion.

Keywords: Discussion support · Civic tech · Large language model · Semantic authoring

1 Introduction

In oral discussions, such as workshops, there are instances where dialogues become circular, preventing consensus formation, or past utterances and decisions being forgotten. To address this issue, we record discussion content on notes or sticky notes, yet there are occasions where the discussion content cannot be captured accurately or be forgotten. Therefore, it is important to automatically record the content and process of discussions, enabling participants to reflect on the discussions. Although speech recognition can be used, the results are redundant and consist of fillers because of colloquialisms. This study addresses this problem by recording the speech-recognition results into text, similar to writing on a sticky note. The text should be well-structured for participants to understand.

The objective of this research is to develop a discussion-structuring system for use in real time and demonstrate its utility as a substitute for sticky notes. This system will enable users to easily reflect on the content and process of discussions. To achieve this, we prototyped a discussion-structuring system on the basis the concept of semantic authoring [6]. The large language model GPT-4 [11], is used for paraphrasing speech-recognition results into simple sentences and structuring them. A previous study [16] developed methods for paraphrasing redundant audio-recognition results and paraphrasing them into expressions similar to those written on sticky notes using GPT-3's fine-tuning [3]. However, due to audio-recognition errors, these methods do not achieve a practical level accuracy. Additionally, the displayed texts had to be manually moved by an operator. Therefore, this research aims to resolve these issues by using GPT-4 and a discussion map based on semantic authoring.

Discussions cannot extend beyond the viewpoints of discussion participants. Therefore, we considered generating fictional personas in which artificial intelligence (AI) participates in the discussion and voices perspectives that were not present in the discussion up to that point in time.

This paper is organized as follows: Sect. 2 reviews related work. Section 3 explains the system we have developed. Section 4 shows the experimental setup. Section 5 explains the results and discussions. Section 6 concludes the paper.

2 Related Work

2.1 Semantic Authoring

Our prototype system uses "semantic authoring" [6] for structuring discussion context as it facilitates users' understanding of discussion. Semantic authoring is the process for structuring discussion context as a graph structure based on discourse relations [10] and ontology. Hasida [7] also developed an editor for semantic authoring based on the Personal Life Repository. The difference between semantic authoring and similar structuring methods for discussions such as argument mapping, concept mapping, mind mapping [4], or argumentation frameworks [12] is diversity of relation labels. With semantic authoring, several discourse, logical, and dialogical relations are annotated to the edges of the graph.

Shiramatsu et al. [13] applied semantic authoring to discussions and conducted case studies to support consensus building on the basis of evidence. They also studied structuring discussion processes and the application of discussion facilitation using semantic authoring [14].

2.2 Structuring Discussions

Our system employs Miro [2], an online whiteboard for visualizing a structure of spoken discourse. Research on the structuring of discussions [8,9] is useful for quickly and intuitively understanding the flow of discussions. Yoshimura et al. [16] proposed fine-tuned models to paraphrase texts and a method for extracting related texts to structure discussions in real time. Tomobe et al. [15] proposed a method for semi-automatically structuring meeting minutes to support knowledge discovery.

There have been several studies on structuring discussions; however, there have been few studies using semantic authoring and on developing applications for discussion facilitation. We aim to use semantic authoring for our discussion-structuring system and enable collaboration between the system and discussion participants.

3 Prototype System

3.1 Overview

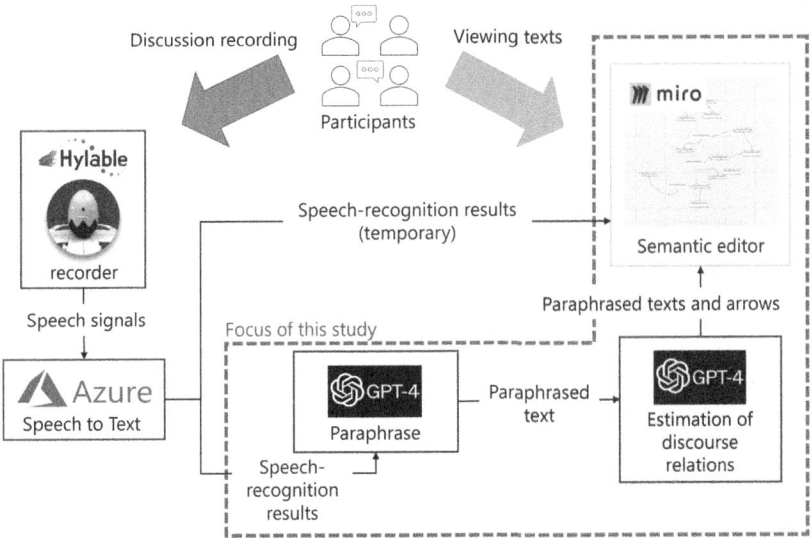

Fig. 1. Structure of prototype system

The structure of our prototype system is shown in Fig. 1. The speech signals obtained using a recorder are converted into speech-recognition results using Microsoft Azure's Speech to Text. The speech-recognition results are temporarily displayed on Miro using REST API of Miro and separately paraphrased to concise texts using GPT-4. Discourse relations are estimated among the paraphrased texts using GPT-4. Paraphrased texts become nodes similar to sticky notes, and discourse relations become arrows and displayed on Miro using the REST API of Miro. Users can view the speech-recognition results and the paraphrased texts on the monitor.

Figure 2 illustrates user experience of the system. In the initial state, there is an area on the left displaying the speech-recognition results and an area on the right displaying the discussion map (Fig. 2(a)). As the discussion begins, the speech-recognition result of each utterance is written on blue cards and displayed on an area called "the speech-recognition results display area" (Fig. 2(b)). Approximately one minute later, paraphrased texts and arrows are displayed on an area called "structured area" (Fig. 2(c)). The speech-recognition results disappear after a certain time, whereas the discussion map remains (Fig. 2(d)).

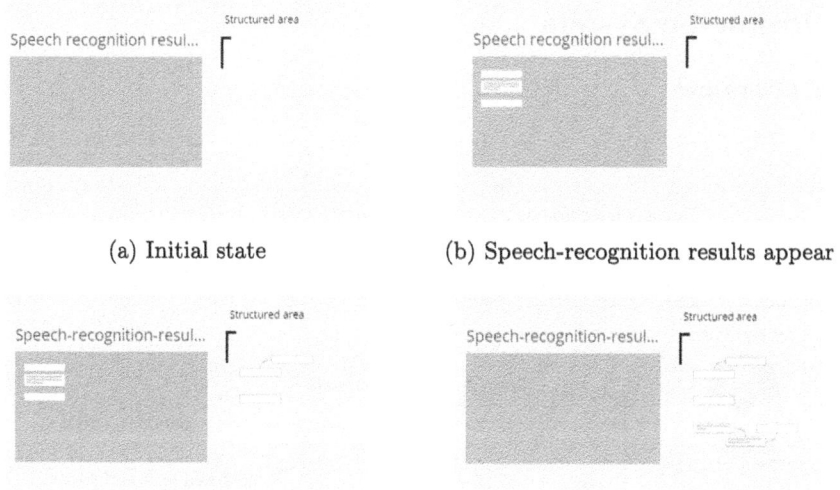

(a) Initial state (b) Speech-recognition results appear

(c) Paraphrased texts and arrows appear (d) Speech-recognition results disappear

Fig. 2. User experience of system

Table 1 shows the differences between Yoshimura's system and our system. We utilize the GPT-4, incorporating features such as an estimation of discourse relations and connections using arrows. This enhancement improves the accuracy of paraphrasing and enables the automatic placement of paraphrased nodes. Consequently, users no longer need to manually move nodes, which enhances convenience.

Table 1. The differences between Yoshimura's system and our system

	Yoshimura's method	Our method
Large-language-model(LLM)	GPT-3	GPT-4
Paraphrase of speech-recognition-results	✓	✓
Display of text	✓	✓
Estimation of discourse relation	✗	✓
Connections using arrows	✗	✓

3.2 Prompt Design

GPT-4 paraphrases speech-recognition results and estimates discourse relationships following the system structure (Fig. 1). In this section, we introduce prompts to clearly give commands for paraphrasing and estimating discourse relations.

Listing 1.1 shows prompts in the paraphrase of statements. In this study, we paraphrased target utterances containing preceding context that proved effective in the discussion-structuring system proposed by Yoshimura. We also attempted paraphrasing speech-recognition results using few-shot learning because speech-recognition errors need to be corrected. The input for GPT-4's text generation consists of a prompt, single target utterance, and the preceding context up to one minute prior, and the output consists of concise paraphrasing.

Listing 1.1. Prompts in the paraphrasing of statements (translated from Japanese)

```
# Situation
- You are using voice recognition for workshop conversations, which may
    include recognition errors and be verbose.
- Therefore, you're correcting the voice recognition while trying to record
    it on sticky notes.
- The prompt input includes not only the target utterance to be recorded on
    the sticky notes but also the preceding context.

# Instructions
1. If there are any recognition errors in the given voice-recognition results
    , correct them and paraphrase only the target utterance into a concise
    expression suitable for writing on a sticky note.
    - Use the preceding context only to supplement meaning, and concisely
        paraphrase only the target utterance.
    - Remove fillers, back-channels, and greetings.
2. If the paraphrased expression consists of fillers, back-channels,
    greetings, or meaningless expressions, output null for "concise
    paraphrasing".

# JSON Output Format
{
    "concise paraphrasing": "..."
}

# Paraphrasing Examples
(three examples are shown here)
```

Listing 1.2 shows prompts in the estimation of discourse relations. We used the discourse-relation labels (Table 2) proposed by Hashida because estimating discourse relations requires classifying these relations into multiple labels. The input for GPT-4's text generation consists of a prompt, several recent candidate texts, and one target text, and the output consists of a discourse label and number of candidate texts.

Listing 1.2. Prompts in estimating discourse relations (translated from Japanese)

```
# Situation
- Conversations from a workshop are being transcribed onto sticky notes.
- Sticky notes that have a discourse relation with each other are connected
  with arrows to structure the discussion.
- The input prompt includes the target text and multiple candidate texts.

# Instructions
- Select the number of candidate texts that have the most discourse relations
    to the target text from multiple candidate texts.
    - Choose the most appropriate label for the discourse relation.
    - If there is no text with a discourse relation, output null.

# Discourse-relation Labels
(discourse-relation labels are shown here)

# JSON Output Format
{
    "candidate text number": number,
    "discourse relation": "..."
}
```

Table 2. List of discourse-relation labels

Logical conjunction	Label	Logical conjunction	Label	Logical conjunction	Label
Meronymy	Equal	Copulative conjunction	Causes	Dialogue	Response
	Part		Conclusion		Approval
	Member		Triggers		Disapproval
	Example		Purpose		Solution
Positive conjunctive	Addition		Conditional	Time relations	Before
	Specific		Foreground		Sametime
	Content	Adversative	Conflict		Situation
Negative conjunctive	Contrast		Unconditional	Other relation	Object
	Disjunction		Compromise		
	Dissimilar				

3.3 Algorithm for Determining Node Coordinates

It is necessary to determine the coordinates of the nodes when displaying nodes on an editor. The conditions for determining coordinates include adaptability to semantic authoring and the availability to update in real time. In this study, we developed an algorithm to determine new node coordinates (Algorithm 1) by referencing nodes already displayed on Miro on the basis of these conditions.

Algorithm 1. Node-addition Algorithm

Require: $viewport, source\_x, source\_y$
Ensure: True and coordinates of the new node if addition is successful, False and invalid coordinates if it fails
    if $source\_x \geq \text{len}(viewport) - 1$ **then**
        return false, $-1, -1$
    end if
    $next\_x \leftarrow source\_x + 1$
    for $delta\_y$ in range(len($viewport[next\_x]$)) **do**
        $y\_coords \leftarrow [source\_y + delta\_y, source\_y - delta\_y]$
        for y in y_coords **do**
            if $0 \leq y < \text{len}(viewport[next\_x])$ and $viewport[next\_x][y] == 0$ **then**
                $viewport[next\_x][y] \leftarrow 1$
                return true, $next\_x, y$
            end if
        end for
    end for
    return false, $-1, -1$

The algorithm generates a hierarchical graph from left to right, conceptualizing a 2D array as its coordinate system. Separately, nodes determined to have no discourse relationship with other nodes are displayed at the bottom of the screen. However, this coordinate system is finite and has the disadvantage of extending monotonously to the right. Therefore, we plan to explore and improve methods to address these issues.

3.4 Opinion Generation of Fictional Personas

We conducted discussion experiment using our prototype discussion-structuring system. To broaden the perspectives of the discussion participants, we included an AI in the discussion that would voice perspectives that were not previously present in the discussion.

Given the prior context of the discussion, a fictional persona was generated using GPT-4. The generated AI opinions are based on the created persona. Opinions are generated in response to a prior opinion; the following three types of opinions were generated from one persona.

1. A surprising response about one prior opinion, from a different point of view from the previous discussions
2. An evaluation of one prior opinion that the persona agrees with and the reasons for it
3. An evaluation of one prior opinion that the persona disagrees with and the reasons for it

To make the persona feel more familiar, an image of the person is generated using DALL-E 3 [1]. A detail node about the persona, three different opinion nodes, and an image of the person are posted on Miro. Note that at the time of conducting the experiment, operator manipulation was required to adjust the timing of opinion generation, position of the nodes, and post the image.

4 Demonstration Experiment

To evaluate the discussion-structuring system, we conducted a discussion experiment involving the system being used in a workshop held at Nagoya City Hall. The main objective of the workshop was sharing ideas for public-private partnerships to increase KANKEI JINKO, i.e., people who do not live in the target region but regularly engage with the region. The discussion experiment was conducted with 24 personnel working at Nagoya City Hall or with local governments around Nagoya. They were divided six groups each consisting of four people. Monitors and recorders were placed on desks and operators operated Miro to make it easier for the participants to see their opinions (Fig. 3). We created three display areas on Miro because the workshop was divided into three sessions: first session of 20 min, second session of 15 min, and third session of 15 min.

Fig. 3. Discussion participants in workshop

The participants were public officials, and there were no individuals from private enterprises. Therefore, the personas to be generated were "simulated citizens". Persona and opinion generation was conducted a few times during the discussion experiment. The results were checked by the participants during the break between the second and third sessions. A subjective evaluation of the system was conducted using a questionnaire including items based on a 7-point scale and those that were open-ended and given to the participants after the discussion experiment. The number of questionnaires collected was 22.

5 Results and Discussion

5.1 Examples of Discussion-Structuring System

Figure 4 shows examples of our discussion-structuring system during the experiment. Figure 4(a) shows that the nodes connected with arrows are quite dense, and the discussion is structured using semantic authoring. Continuous nodes that are not connected to any of the others were found in several places, which is not semantic authoring. Figure 4(b) is an example of paraphrasing; recognition errors in one target utterance remained even after paraphrasing. Figure 4(c) is an example of estimating discourse relations. 'Equal' is suitable as a two-node discourse relation, but ideally the right node should be "Form a related population through tourism and the transportation environment" and the label 'Specific'.

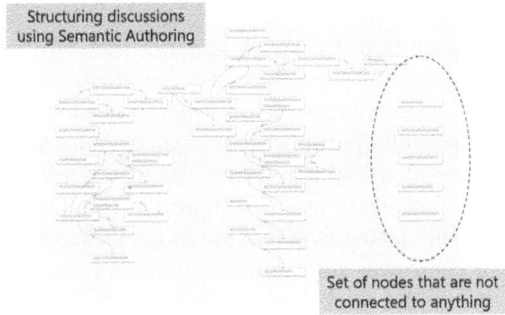

(a) Excerpts displayed on Miro during discussion experiment

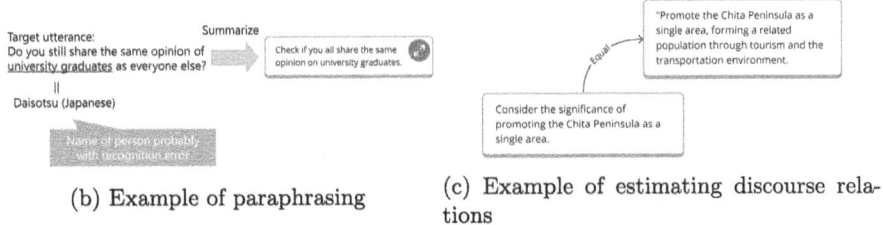

(b) Example of paraphrasing

(c) Example of estimating discourse relations

Fig. 4. Examples of discussion-structuring system (translated from Japanese)

5.2 Questionnaire Results (7-Point-Scale Items)

Figure 5 indicates the result of the questionnaire item "Was the discussion structuring-system useful during the reflection and overall sharing sessions of the workshop?". Eighteen participants answered with a score of 5 or more, which is 81% of the total. During this workshop, there was an opportunity to reflect on what they had said during the discussion and during the plenary sharing at the end of the workshop. A participant who answered with a score of 2 said "I am not used to using this system, so I could not see the way like sticky notes." Discussion participants were not fully briefed on how to use the system.

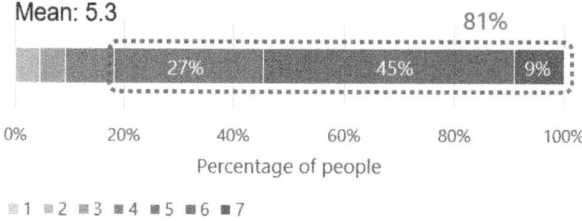

Fig. 5. Scores on usefulness of system for reflection

Figure 6 shows the results of the questionnaire item "Automatic paraphrasing will likely replace handwritten sticky notes." and Fig. 7 shows the results of the questionnaire item "How much did you feel you needed to manually correct things that were automatically paraphrased?". Mann-Whitney U tests were conducted on the two items at a 5% significance level to determine whether there is a difference between this study and Yoshimura's [16]. The former resulted in a p-value of 0.078 and the latter in a p-value of 0.246, indicating no significant differences. Although there was no significant difference in the functionality of the system as a substitute for sticky notes, the mean values increased compared with Yoshimura's experiment, suggesting that our discussion-structuring system could function as a replacement for sticky notes. However, the item on the need for modification did not change much from Yoshimura's research. The reason could be attributed to the fact that our system operates automatically, whereas in Yoshimura's research, the operator had to manually select which nodes to keep.

These results indicated that our discussion-structuring system could be helpful as a substitute for sticky notes when reflecting on group discussions. However, since the displayed statements require correction, viewing the discussion maps of other groups could lead to misunderstandings.

5.3 Questionnaire Results (Open-Ended Items)

In the open-ended items of the questionnaire, six respondents mentioned that "I could focus on the discussion without spending time on notes." The participants were keenly taking notes before the workshop began. It is conceivable that they are accustomed to spending time taking notes in their regular duties. Therefore, our discussion-structuring system could reduce this burden, ensure discussion time, and improve quality of discussion. This applies not only to the local government personnel who were the participants in this experiment, but also to anyone who regularly take notes.

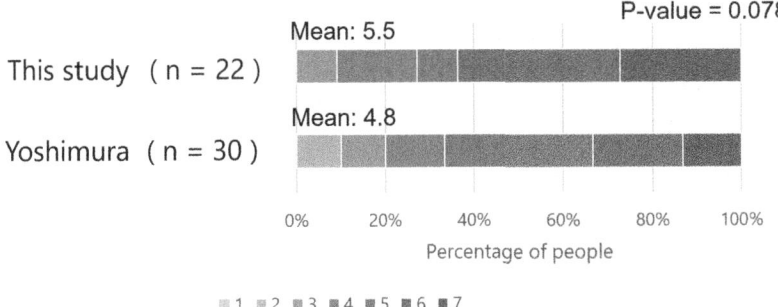

Fig. 6. Scores on functionality of system as substitute for sticky notes

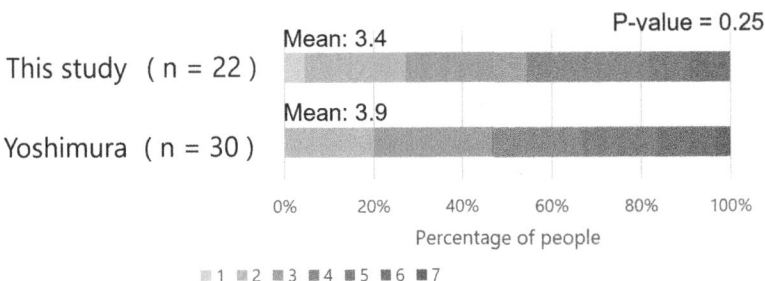

Fig. 7. Scores on need for modification

Three respondents to the open-ended items expressed that "without the function to paraphrase nodes, it is difficult to review the content of the discussion." The average number of nodes output to Miro was 120 per group, with 60% of these nodes connected with arrows through semantic authoring. This means that an average of 48 nodes per group were not connected to any other node. While semantic authoring makes understanding the content easier, having many nodes displayed or having many independent nodes can make it difficult to grasp the discussion content. Figuring out all the nodes in Fig. 4(a) is also a challenge. Hence, it will be necessary for us to analyze the necessity of the displayed nodes and the validity of the independent nodes. It also became clear that our discussion-structuring system will require not only the function to display statements but also the capability to succinctly structure the discussion content. We can consider using hypergraph [5] to achieve this function and capability.

5.4 Results of Opinion Generation

An example of a simulated citizen and opinions is shown in Fig. 8. Food product designer Misaki Sato gave a low evaluation of the opinion, "The return gifts for the hometown tax donations are all brown and plain." It was suggested that this could be due to a contradiction with her design philosophy. In response to this opinion, the discussion participants remarked, "The idea that we should

Fig. 8. Example of simulated citizen and a opinion generation (translated from Japanese, node is being edited for size and location)

not forget the philosophy of the creator was missing from the group discussion, but we realized that it was an important point to consider." Fig. 9 indicates the result of the questionnaire item "Did the AI-generated opinions help facilitate discussion?". Eighteen participants answered with a score of 5 or more, which is 81% of the total. Therefore, simulated citizens can be helpful in facilitating the discussion and give perspectives that were not present in the discussion.

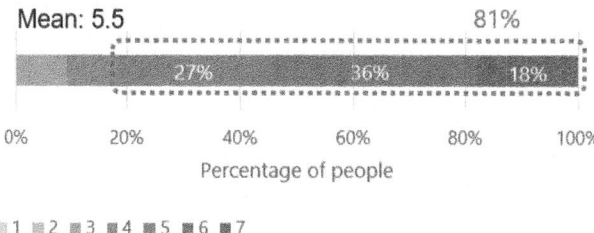

Fig. 9. Scores on usefulness of system for simulated citizen's opinion (7-point scale)

5.5 Limitations

The system has two limitations. First, the system does not have a function for managing multiple sticky notes. The number of them increases as the discussion time and activity increase. In such a situation, the users will have difficulty understanding the discussion overview. Therefore, the system needs a function that organizes sticky notes to maintain simplicity. Second, the number of experiments cannot claim the system's effectiveness in various situations. We need to evaluate the system in a wide range of situations involving different participants and for various purposes.

6 Conclusion

We developed a discussion-structuring system with the aim that can be a substitute for sticky notes. We carried out prompt engineering and constructed an algorithm for determining node coordinates. We conducted a demonstration experiment of a prototype discussion-structuring system involving local government staff and simulated citizens. It was shown that the discussion-structuring system could serve as a substitute for sticky notes when reflecting on group discussions, and that the system has the potential to keep participants focused on the discussion and enhance the quality of discussion. Generated opinions of the simulated citizens were also effective in supporting discussion. The need for a feature to succinctly structure discussion content was identified.

For future work, we aim to continue the development of the discussion-structuring system to enable collaboration between participants and AI to completely correct speech-recognition errors.

Acknowledgements. This work was supported by NEDO (JPNP20006) and JST CREST (JPMJCR20D1). We thank Division for the Promotion of Metropolitan and Wide-Area Government, City of Nagoya.

References

1. Dall·e 3. https://openai.com/dall-e-3. Accessed 31 Mar 2024
2. Miro. https://miro.com/online-whiteboard/. Accessed 6 Mar 2024
3. Brown, T.B., et al.: Language models are few-shot learners. arXiv e-prints arXiv:2005.14165 (2020)
4. Davies, M.: Concept mapping, mind mapping and argument mapping: what are the differences and do they matter? High. Educ. **62**, 279–301 (2011)
5. Feng, Y., You, H., Zhang, Z., Ji, R., Gao, Y.: Hypergraph neural networks (2019)
6. Hasida, K.: Semantic authoring and semantic computing. In: Sakurai, A., Hasida, K., Nitta, K. (eds.) JSAI 2003-2004. LNCS (LNAI), vol. 3609, pp. 137–149. Springer, Heidelberg (2007). https://doi.org/10.1007/978-3-540-71009-7_12
7. Hasida, K.: Decentralized, collaborative, and diagrammatic authoring. In: Sakurai, A., Hasida, K., Nitta, K. (eds.) The 3rd International Workshop on Argument for Agreement and Assurance (2017)
8. Konat, B., Lawrence, J., Park, J., Budzynska, K., Reed, C.: A corpus of argument networks: Using graph properties to analyse divisive issues. In: Calzolari, N., et al. (eds.) Proceedings of the Tenth International Conference on Language Resources and Evaluation (LREC'16), pp. 3899–3906. European Language Resources Association (ELRA), Portorož (2016). https://aclanthology.org/L16-1617

9. Matsumura, N., Kato, Y., Osawa, Y., Ishizuka, M.: Understanding and identifying issues through visualization of discussion structures. Intell. Inf. **15**(5), 554–564 (2003)
10. Moser, M., Moore, J.D.: Toward a synthesis of two accounts of discourse structure. Comput. Linguist. **22**(3), 409–419 (1996). https://aclanthology.org/J96-3006
11. OpenAI: Gpt-4 technical report (2023)
12. Sadiq, A.T., Abdulah, H.S., Kareem, A.T.: Argumentation frameworks-a brief review. Int. J. Online Biomed. Eng. **18**(2), 1–16 (2022)
13. Shiramatsu, S., Igarashi, Y.: A preliminary consideration toward evidence-based consensus building through human-agent collaboration on semantic authoring platform. In: Proceedings of the 15th International Conference on Knowledge, Information and Creativity Support System (11 2020)
14. Shiramatsu, S., Onochi, M., Suenaga, A.: Considering methods for structuring and facilitating discussion based on semantic authoring. In: Proceedings of the Type 2 Workshop of the Artificial Intelligence Society (SWO-054), p. 03 (2021). https://doi.org/10.11517/jsaisigtwo.2021.SWO-054_03
15. Tomobe, H., Nagao, K.: Activation support for communications by descriptions of relation between minutes. In: Proceedings of the National Conference of the Artificial Intelligence Society JSAI05, pp. 137–137 (2005)
16. Yoshimura, Y., Shiramatsu, S.: Structuring Discussion using Speech Recognition and GPT-3 in Face-to-face Workshops. Unpublished thesis, Nagoya Institute of Technology (2023)

A Metaverse-Based Virtual Office System with Overhearing Function for Facilitating Smooth Joining in Ongoing Conversations

Ryota Sugisawa and Kinya Fujita(✉)

Tokyo University of Agriculture and Technology, Koganei 184-8588, Japan
kfujita@cc.tuat.ac.jp

Abstract. In remote work environments, communication deficits pose significant challenges. To address this issue, metaverse-based virtual office systems have been developed. However, while these virtual offices provide spaces for conversation, they do not fully resolve communication deficits. Therefore, we focused on the barrier encountered when joining in ongoing conversations and developed a virtual office system with an overhearing function. Additionally, to address the anxiety induced by being overheard conversations, we implemented a feature to distort conversational audio. Evaluation experiments confirmed that unprocessed raw audio overhearing effectively facilitates smooth joining in conversations. On the other hand, overhearing with distorted audio, while mitigating users' anxiety about being overheard to some extent, resulted in a compromise in the smoothness of conversation joining as a trade-off. Consequently, the need for additional system enhancements aimed at further reducing user resistance while facilitating smoother joining in conversations through overhearing became apparent.

Keywords: Remote Work · Virtual Office · Overhearing · Metaverse

1 Introduction

Amidst the global COVID-19 pandemic, information-sharing systems such as remote conference systems, chat systems, and file-sharing platforms have played a significant role in sustaining business continuity. Given their advantages in terms of time efficiency and cost-effectiveness, remote work is anticipated to persist in the future.

However, remote work has been identified as facing a significant challenge in terms of communication deficiencies. Communication deficiency could potentially weaken intra-team connectivity [1], diminish the sense of belonging [2], increase feelings of social isolation [3], and consequently impair work efficiency.

Therefore, to alleviate communication deficiencies in remote work environments, metaverse-based virtual office systems have been investigated. Sohlenkamp et al. [4] developed DIVA, a system presenting a virtual office in a simple 2D interface. Honda et al. [5] developed Valentine, a 3D virtual office system. Currently, various virtual office systems are commercially available [6, 7]. While these systems provide spaces for remote teams to converse, they have not completely resolved deficiency in communication. One contributing factor is the difficulty in gauging the appropriate timing for initiating conversations. To address this issue, efforts have been made to implement awareness-sharing functionalities that enable remote team members to infer each other's work statuses [8].

Another challenge is the difficulty in joining in ongoing conversations. In a metaverse where multiple users communicate concurrently, conversation audio is typically controlled based on the proximity between avatars, allowing for multiple voice conversations to take place simultaneously. Systems such as Valentine [5], Gather [6], DIVE [9], and MASSIVE [10] have implemented an on/off control mechanism, where conversations become possible as users approach a certain distance. Conversely, an analog control mechanism has been introduced, where audio volume varies based on the distance between avatars [7, 11]. While distance-based analog control is an intuitive approach, conversing with multiple users at different distances can result in varying voice volumes, making it challenging to discern. Hence, the majority of the virtual office systems still utilize the on/off control mechanism. While on/off control is advantageous in terms of ease of use and prevention of unintended volume fluctuations, users outside the conversation range have no means to listen to the ongoing conversations. Consequently, users outside the conversation are unable to discern the content and atmosphere before joining, which may lead to unintentional inadequate participation or hesitation in joining.

Therefore, aiming to allow users outside the conversation to read the atmosphere and content of ongoing conversations, thus assisting them in determining the optimal timing to join, this study proposes a virtual office system integrating an on-demand overhearing function.

The structure of this paper is as follows: Sect. 2 discusses the requirements and implementation of the virtual office system with overhearing function. Section 3 details the procedures, conditions, and evaluation items for the verification experiment of the implemented system. Section 4 presents the results of the verification experiment. Section 5 explores the effects of the overhearing function and audio distortion, discusses future challenges, and addresses the limitations of this research. Section 6 concludes this study.

2 Virtual Office System with Overhearing Function

In this section, we first outline the system requirements (Sect. 2.1), followed by a detailed description of the implementation method for the overhearing function adopted in this study (Sect. 2.2).

2.1 Requirements

To foster common understanding and discussion across the team, it is desirable to involve additional members in ongoing conversations. On the other hand, the joining of additional individuals in certain types of conversations, such as rebukes, is undesirable. Hence, many office workers read the atmosphere of the conversation in advance and only join when they judge it is acceptable to join the conversation. Consequently, in virtual offices as well, it is desired to provide workers means to adequately judge the acceptability of ongoing conversations. Thus, the requirement for individuals joining in a conversation (hereinafter referred to as 'joiners') is as follows:

(rq.1) Ability to determine the appropriateness of joining in the conversation before actually joining.

On the other hand, from the perspective of those engaged in the conversation, uncontrolled disclosure of conversation content to outside individuals is clearly unacceptable. In addition to the content of the conversation, the anonymity of the listener can also be a cause of anxiety for participants. Therefore, both the ability to restrict the disclosure of information and the capability to identify the listeners are required. The requirements for individuals accepting additional participants in a conversation (hereinafter referred to as 'joinee') are as follows:

(rq.2) Ability to restrict the disclosed information.
(rq.3) Ability to identify the listeners.

Therefore, the system is required to balance and accommodate those conflicting requirements between joiners and joinees.

2.2 Implementation of the Overhearing Function

To address both requirements rq.1 and rq.2, this study implemented an overhearing function. This functionality allows users to listen to designated conversation audio through mouseover interaction, without joining in the conversation, as illustrated in Fig. 1. Since overhearing function is intentionally activated on-demand, it thus allows restricting the content being heard to a certain extent.

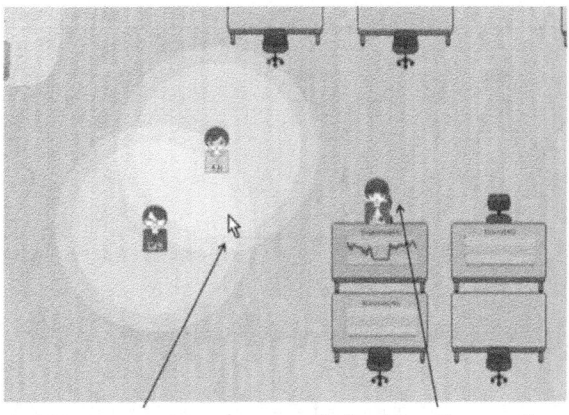

Fig. 1. Activation of overhearing function.

Furthermore, to meet the requirement outlined in rq.3 for joinees, the name of the overhearing user and an ear icon were displayed to those being overheard, as shown in Fig. 2.

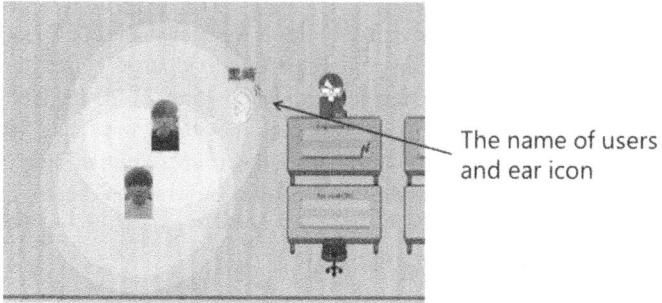

Fig. 2. Screen of a user while being overheard.

To meet requirement rq.1, we also implemented a function to visualize turn-taking, as shown in Fig. 3. Since an increase in conversation activity leads to more speech overlaps and turn-takings [12], visualization of turn-taking is expected to assist overhearing users in reading the atmosphere of the conversation. In the base virtual office system [8], the conversation range is displayed as a white circle. Therefore, visualization of turn-taking was implemented by sinusoidally oscillating the color intensity of the circle for active speaker exclusively.

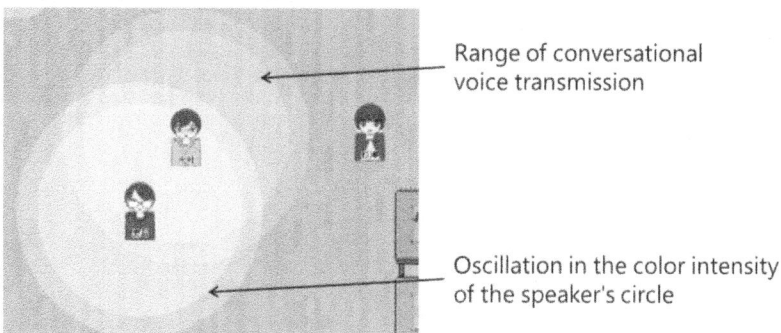

Fig. 3. Visualization of turn-taking.

Although on-demand overhearing and displaying the name of overhearing user could relieve the anxiety of the users being overheard, it may not completely remove it. On the other hand, it has been noted that the internal state of a speaker, such as emotion, can affect speaking voice [13]. Therefore, we attempted to modulate the voice to a degree where the content becomes unintelligible, while preserving non-verbal cues such as intonation and pitch. This modification involved a band-pass filter (passband: 220–260 Hz) and a distortion filter (distortion level = 0.4).

The virtual office system with the aforementioned overhearing function was implemented using Unity. The system architecture is shown in Fig. 4. The modules supporting conversation joining are highlighted with double lines. The Conversation manager/Overhear controller receives the positions of all users from the Virtual space server and controls the creation and deletion of conversation groups. When users join in a conversation, their video and audio are shared with other participants through the Video and audio sharing server.

When the Conversation manager/Overhear controller receives a mouseover signal from a client, it identifies the requesting user and the group being moused over. If the user is not participating in the conversation, the overhearing function is activated. Once activated, overhearing users can listen to either distorted or undistorted audio depending on the settings of the audio distortion feature. At the same time, overhearing users are displayed to users being overheard, as shown in Fig. 2.

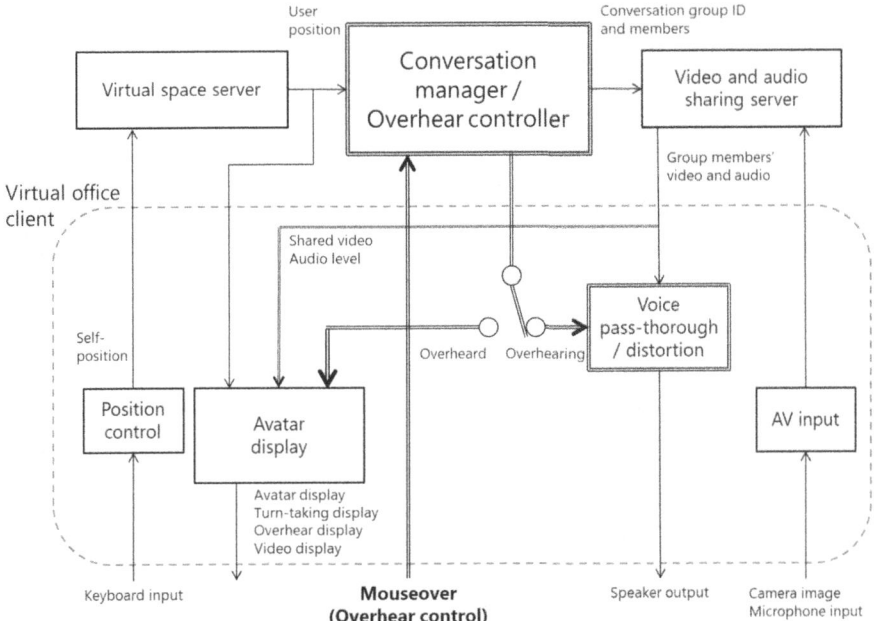

Fig. 4. Block diagram of the virtual office system with overhearing function.

3 Verification Experiment

This section discusses the verification experiment for the developed system. First, an overview of the experiment is provided (Sect. 3.1). Next, the experimental conditions (Sect. 3.2) and procedures (Sect. 3.3) are detailed. Finally, the evaluation items are presented (Sect. 3.4).

3.1 Overview

We conducted a verification experiment to assess the ease of reading conversational atmosphere and the anxiety related to being overheard in conversation by integrating the overhearing function into the virtual office system. The participants in the experiment were 12 university or graduate school students affiliated with our university. The experiment was conducted with approval from the university's ethics committee.

The participants were divided into four groups. In real office settings, team members are typically acquainted with each other. Therefore, each group of three participants was composed of individuals who were already familiar with one another. Each group participated in a set of four 15-min conversation sessions under four different conditions. Two out of three participants were instructed to initiate the conversation first, while the remaining participant was instructed to observe the conversation using the function provided, depending on the condition, and then join the conversation later.

After each conversation task in the respective condition, participants provided subjective evaluations regarding their perception of the conversation atmosphere, anxiety about being overheard, and other relevant factors.

3.2 Experimental Conditions

The four experimental conditions are listed in Table 1. Two conditions involved the overhearing function, while the other two did not. In the NV (No Voice) condition, where the overhearing function was absent, conversation audio was inaudible until joining in the conversation. In the AWV (Always Voice) condition, conversation audio was consistently audible, even to the individuals not joining.

Conversely, the two conditions with the overhearing function allowed not-joining users to hear conversation audio upon mouseover interaction, either through unprocessed raw audio in the OHV (Overhearing Voice) condition or distorted audio in the OHDV (Overhearing Distorted Voice) condition. In these two conditions, the names of overhearing participants were displayed on the conversation participants' screens, as illustrated in Fig. 2. The turn-taking visualization feature was enabled across all four conditions.

Table 1. Experimental conditions. NV, AWV, OHV, and OHDV represent No Voice, Always Voice, Overhearing Voice, and Overhearing Distorted Voice conditions, respectively.

Conditions	Overhearing function	Conversation audio
NV	Not available	Not available
AWV		Always available
OHV	Available	Raw audio
OHDV		Distorted audio

3.3 Experimental Procedure

The experimental procedure is shown in Fig. 5. Initially, participants were instructed to utilize the virtual office system for five minutes under each of the four conditions (amounting to a total of 20 min) to familiarize themselves with its functionalities and operations.

Subsequently, participants were assigned one of two roles in the conversation: one participant acted as the joiner, while the other two acted as the joinees. They engaged in the conversation tasks under each of the four aforementioned conditions. After each conversation, they were prompted to provide subjective evaluations based on the five criteria described in the following subsection.

Here, the topics of the conversation (e.g., seriousness or complexity) might influence the impression (awkwardness, etc.) upon joining. Therefore, joinees were instructed to engage in conversation with alternating topics including casual topics, discussions, and serious ones.

Joiners were requested to join at least once during the 15-min conversation session. Additionally, they were instructed to listen or observe the conversation before joining, utilizing the implemented features, and to determine the appropriate timing.

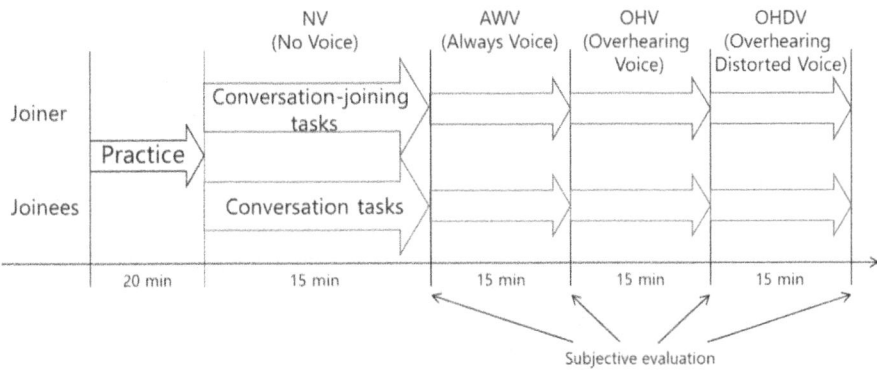

Fig. 5. Experimental procedure.

3.4 Evaluation Items

Table 2 presents the subjective evaluation items prompted to the joiners. The first two items relate to the ease of joining the conversation, while the third item addresses the side effects of overhearing. Similarly, Table 3 lists the items evaluated by the joinees. The first item concerns the smoothness of accepting the joiner, while the second focuses on the side effect of overhearing.

All items were evaluated using a 5-point Likert scale.

Table 2. Subjective evaluation items and questions for joiner.

Joiner	
Evaluation items	Questions
Sense of reading the atmosphere of conversation	How well were you able to sense the atmosphere of the conversation?
Smoothness while joining in	How smoothly were you able to join the conversation?
Hesitation for listening	How much hesitation did you feel about overhearing the conversation?

Table 3. Subjective evaluation items and questions for joinee.

Joinee	
Evaluation items	Questions
Smoothness while being joined in	How smoothly were you able to accept the joiner?
Anxiety about being listened	How much anxiety did you feel about being overheard?

4 Result

The subjective scores evaluated by the joiners and joinees are summarized in Fig. 6 and 7, respectively. Each of the four colored bars in the graphs illustrates the distribution of the subjective scores corresponding to the conversation conditions.

In terms of the ease of feeling atmosphere and smoothness of joining, as depicted in Fig. 6(a) and (b), as well as Fig. 7(a), the AWV condition, where conversation audio is continuously audible, received high scores of 4 or 5 across the participants. It is evident that listening to the conversation content before joining significantly improves the ease and smoothness of joining ongoing conversations compared to the NV condition, where no audio is accessible prior to joining. However, as shown in Fig. 7(b), it also leads to a concurrent increase in joinees' anxiety levels.

The OHV condition, which allows overhearing raw conversation audio, was valued almost as highly as the AWV condition in terms of ease and smoothness of joining. Furthermore, as shown in Fig. 7(b), joinees' anxiety was reduced compared to the AWV condition. These results suggest that on-demand overhearing, where conversation audio is shared only when required, assists smooth participation in conversation with less anxiety compared to the continuous overhearing. However, as revealed in Fig. 6(c), explicit interaction for overhearing unexpectedly imposed hesitation for joiners.

The OHDV condition, which allows overhearing distorted audio, was rated higher than the NV condition in terms of the ease of feeling atmosphere and smoothness of joining. This suggests that distorted audio, while not providing a complete understanding of the conversational content, still assists reading the atmosphere and determining the timing to join. However, relatively lower scores compared to the OHV condition indicate that its functionality is limited compared to the overhearing with raw audio. Regarding the hesitation of joiners and anxiety of joinees, as shown in Fig. 6(c) and Fig. 7(b), we expected that distorting audio would alleviate them; however, the effect remained ambiguous.

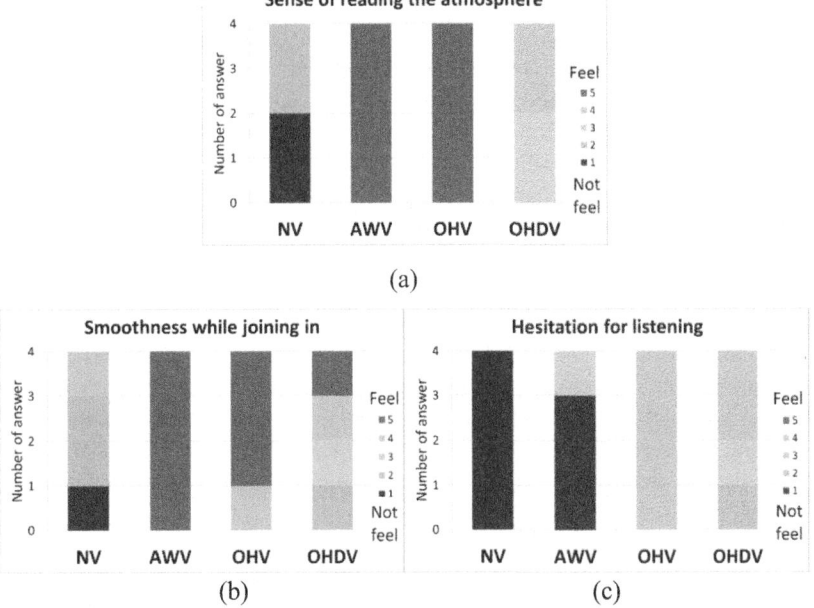

Fig. 6. Subjective scores of joiners on; (a) Sense of reading the atmosphere, (b) Smoothness while joining in, and (c) Hesitation for listening. The four bars from left to right represent NV (No Voice), AWV (Always Voice), OHV (Overhearing Voice), and OHDV (Overhearing Distorted Voice).

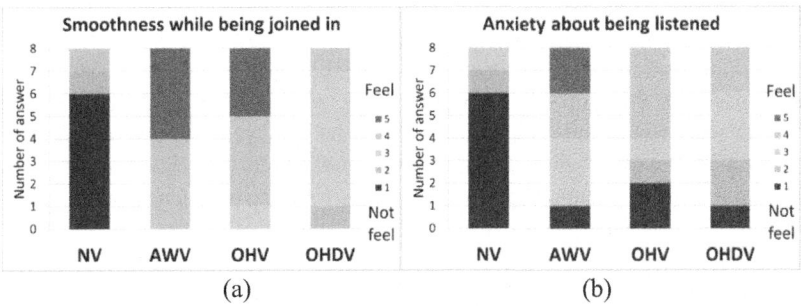

Fig. 7. Subjective scores of joinees on; (a) Smoothness while being joined in and (b) Anxiety about being listened. The four bars from left to right represent NV (No Voice), AWV (Always Voice), OHV (Overhearing Voice), and OHDV (Overhearing Distorted Voice).

5 Discussion

The conditions with overhearing function through raw conversation audio (AWV, OHV) enabled smoother joining in conversations for both joiners and joinees, com-pared to the condition where no audio was audible before joining (NV). Moreover, while the AWV condition increased anxiety among joinees compared to the NV con-dition, the increase in anxiety in the OHV condition was less than in the AWV condi-tion, indicating a mitigating effect of the on-demand overhearing function on anxiety. Considering a previous study reporting that transition to open-plan office decreased face-to-face communication [14], coupled with the increased anxiety in the AWV condition, it seems that an environment where conversation audio is consistently audible may not be suitable for actual remote work scenarios. Consequently, it is concluded that the on-demand overhearing function holds promise in facilitating smooth joining of additional individuals into a conversation while alleviating the increased anxiety experienced by already-participating users.

On the other hand, overhearing function, whether with raw or distorted audio, induced a certain level of hesitation among joiners. The conceivable cause of this hesitation is that intentional mouseover operation led them to feel like they are illegally eavesdropping on the conversation. Therefore, improvement to the system is required for mitigating this interfering sense. One potential improvement is to modify the ear icon displayed to something less reminiscent of eavesdropping. Another approach could be to incorporate animations that avatars move closer to the conversation group upon initiating overhearing, signaling interest in the conversation.

The distortion of overhearing audio reduced the anxiety among joinees to some extent compared to the overhearing of raw audio; however, it compromised the ability for smooth participation in compensation. This fact certifies that understanding the conversation content is essential for smooth joining in conversation. However, such a requirement from joiners conflicts with that from joinees for reducing the overheard contents. Therefore, for instance, a system could be improved to provide distorted audio when the overhearing function is activated, and switch to raw audio only when permitted by joinees. Further improvement is required to achieve smooth joining in conversation while mitigating the anxiety among joinees and the hesitation among joiners.

Furthermore, we also need to consider the potential impact of the relationship among the participants on their anxiety regarding being overheard. In this study, validation experiments were conducted with groups of students who were already well-acquainted with each other. The results indicated no significant difference in the sense of resistance, i.e. hesitation among joiners and anxiety among joinees, between raw and distorted audio. However, it is anticipated that in situations where group members hold different positions (e.g., supervisor and subordinate) or are not familiar with each other, raw audio overhearing may evoke a stronger sense of resistance. In contrast, distorted audio overhearing, which obscures the conversation, is expected to elicit less resistance than raw audio.

The limitations of this study include the small sample size in the verification experiment, limited variation in the relationship among participants, and the potential influence of order effects. Future evaluations of the improved system should take these factors into account.

6 Conclusion

In this study, we developed a virtual office system with an overhearing function, aimed at alleviating psychological barriers when joining ongoing conversations within teleworking environments, using a metaverse-based platform. The verification experiment confirmed that the overhearing function facilitates smooth joining in conversations. The findings also suggested that distorting the overhearing audio reduces hesitation among joiners as well as anxiety among joinees; however, it could potentially disrupt the smoothness of conversation joining. Therefore, further improvements to the system, especially the exploration of overhearing functionalities that mitigate resistance for both joiners and joinees while facilitating smooth conversation engagement are desired.

Acknowledgments. This work was partly supported by funds from the Japan Society for the Promotion of Science (KAKENHI).

Disclosure of Interests. The authors have no competing interests to declare that are relevant to the content of this article.

References

1. Yang, L., et al.: The effects of remote work on collaboration among information workers. Nature Hum. Behav. **6**, 43–54 (2022)
2. Mann, S., Holdsworth, L.: The psychological impact of teleworking: stress, emotions and health. N. Technol. Work. Employ. **18**(3), 196–211 (2003)
3. Boell, S.K, Campbell, J., Dubravka, C.K., Cheng, J.E.: Advantages, challenges and contradictions of the transformative nature of telework: a review of the literature. In: Proceedings of the Nineteenth Americas Conference on Information Systems, (2013)
4. Sohlenkamp, M., Chwelos, G.: Integrating communication, cooperation, and awareness: the DIVA virtual office environment. In: Proceedings of the 1994 ACM Conference on Computer Supported Cooperative Work, pp. 331–343 (1994)
5. Honda, S., Tomioka, H., Kimura, T., Oosawa, T., Okada, K.I., Matsushita, Y.: A company-office system "Valentine" providing informal communication and personal space based on 3D virtual space and avatars. Inf. Softw. Technol. **41**(6), 383–397 (1999)
6. Gather. https://www.gather.town/. Accessed 3 Apr 2024
7. SpatialChat. https://www.spatial.chat/. Accessed 3 Apr 2024
8. Kurosaki, K., Sugisawa, R., Fujita, K.: Development of virtual office system with aware-ness-sharing function to facilitate communication among remote team members. In: Kurosu, M., Hashizume, A. (eds.) HCII 2023, vol. 14012, pp. 408-419. Springer, Cham. (2023). https://doi.org/10.1007/978-3-031-35599-8_27
9. Carlsson, C., Hagsand, O.: DIVE a multi-user virtual reality system. In: Proceedings of IEEE Virtual Reality Annual International Symposium, pp. 394–400 (1993)
10. Greenhalgh, C., Benford. S.: MASSIVE: a collaborative virtual environment for teleconferencing. ACM Trans. Comput.-Human Interact. **2**(3), 239–261 (1995)
11. Nakanishi, H., et al.: Freewalk: supporting casual meetings in a network, Proceedings of the 1996 ACM Conference on Computer Supported Cooperative Work, pp. 308–314 (1996)
12. Nishimura, R., Kitaoka, N., Nakagawa, S.: Analysis of factors to make prosodic change in spoken dialog. J. Phonetic Soc. Jpn. **13**(3), 66–84 (2009)

13. Bezooyen, R.V.: Characteristics and Recognizability of Vocal Expressions of Emotion; Foris Publications (1984)
14. Kim, J., de Dear, R.: Workspace satisfaction: the privacy-communication trade-off in open-plan offices. J. Environ. Psychol. **36**, 18–26 (2013)

Motivational Dynamics and Platform Design in Online Communities of Teachers: A Multi-case Study

Patricia Santos[1](✉), Nicolas Gutierrez-Paez[1], Davinia Hernández-Leo[1], Konstantinos Michos[2], and Mar Carrió[3]

[1] Engineering Department, Universitat Pompeu Fabra, Barcelona, Spain
{patricia.santos,nicolas.gutierrez,
davinia.hernandez-leo}@upf.edu
[2] Institute of Education, University of Zurich, Zurich, Switzerland
konstantinos.michos@ife.uzh.ch
[3] Institute of Science Education, Universitat Politècnica de Catalunya, Barcelona, Spain
mar.carrio@upc.edu

Abstract. A multi-case study with three online communities that use customized instantiations of the Integrated Learning Design Environment (ILDE) platform is presented to explore and understand how teachers' motivations to participate in OCs are related to their perceptions about incentives and features implemented in OC supporting platforms. Data was collected following a mixed-method approach. A cross-case analysis, including a correlation analysis of teachers' motivations and their perception about different incentive mechanisms, suggests that there is a relationship between these factors. Teachers' main motivation is to gain knowledge, and they perceive recommendation systems, tutorials, news sections and social features as the most interesting features to be implemented in an OC of teachers. In contrast, they consider reputation as the least important motivator, and they do not perceive features such as users' rankings or contributors' acknowledgement sections as important. These results contribute to the improvement of the supporting platforms for OC of teachers and the integration in teaching practice.

Keywords: Online Communities · Teachers · Motivation · Incentives · Self-determination theory · Case study

1 Introduction

Online communities (OCs) have several applications in the domain of Education with a special focus on teacher professional development (TPD) [2, 17] The development of OC of teachers enables diverse collaborative actions such as knowledge exchange, practice reflection, sharing of educational resources, emotional support, generation of content, editing/reviewing existing content or consuming content (lurkers) [8, 19, 30] Due to the dependency on community members for the generation of new content, a challenge for OCs' developers focuses on encouraging and sustaining users' participation.

To understand how and why users participate in an OC, several theories and frameworks have been developed. It has been proven that the willingness to participate in a certain type of activity within an OC is highly related to the users' motivations [20]. For OC's developers, these motivations give insights about the incentive mechanisms that should be implemented in a specific community and how they should be personalized to increase interest and participation [33]. The motivations of teachers to participate in different OCs have been widely studied [15, 16, 32]. Likewise, other studies have explored the design principles required for a supporting platform in an OC of teachers based on theories of participation [31], based on the use given by the participants [13], or by analyzing the social impacts of the platform [18, 28]. Nevertheless, it is still necessary to specifically understand the relation of teachers' motivations with the different incentives and features to be implemented in OC platforms to define design principles, and to foster the building and supporting of the community.

This research centers on analyzing the motivations driving participants in teachers' online communities and their implications for platform design. To grasp teachers' specific utilization of an online community and demonstrate the application of design principles, our study is situated within the context of the Integrated Learning Design Environment (ILDE) platform [11]. Previous studies of teacher behavior in learning design communities have shown the benefits and challenges of using ILDE for TPD [1], how it can support co-design [21], community building and interactions [22], and how it facilitates teacher individual and collective, data-informed reflections on their classroom practice [23]. However, none of these studies explored members' motivation to participate in the OC in relation to their perceptions about the different community functionalities of the ILDE and other related learning design platforms. This research establishes the relation between the participants' motivations and how they are fostered and enhanced through the features and incentives implemented in an OC aimed to support teachers' collaborative practices. Thus, this study aims to answer the following research questions: (RQ1) Is there a relation between users' motivations and the perceived value of functionalities for the participants of an OC of teachers? (RQ2) Does teachers' perceived motivation provide information for platform designers about the most valuable functionalities?

2 Materials and Methods

A multi-case study analysis [29] is performed to answer the research questions. Case studies are appropriate when the study aims to explore contemporary phenomena or issues in natural settings [24]. Three case studies were defined to answer the research questions. Even when the data sources used in every case study can differ from each other due to the circumstances related to time or accessibility constraints, the cross-case analysis compares both qualitative and quantitative measurable effects [12, 29]. The main cases studied in this paper use the ILDE platform, specifically the ILDE+, which is a minimum viable product (MVP) based on ILDE for an OC of teachers [9, 10]. ILDE+ platform has been instantiated to support two different learning contexts with similar characteristics. Thus, this study describes both contexts as separate case studies. Likewise, another case study was conducted with a group of teachers that were familiar with the traditional ILDE platform. The initial case study was conducted with two schools that were already familiar with the use of the traditional ILDE platform. This case study allowed us to validate and refine the non-exhaustive list of participation incentives for the main case study as well as to validate the required features in an MVP version of the ILDE. The first main case study was conducted in the context of 'Makers in the classroom' project [9], which focus on an OC of in-service teachers and the second in the context of the project called 'Teachers in network' [10], which is a community of pre-service teachers. In both cases the aim of the communities was focused on exploring, contributing, and sharing learning resources according to the topics covered by the communities.

2.1 Data Collection Instruments

Data has been collected from different sources following a mixed-method methodology [4], and has proven to be useful to study teacher and learning communities [22, 34]. Quantitative analysis with descriptive and inferential statistics was conducted using RStudio. Qualitative analysis was conducted using the open coding method [3] for the analysis of the open-ended responses of the questionnaires and group discussions to identify the main topics of teachers' responses. All participants were informed about the purpose of the research and gave their informed consent to participate.

The variables measured through questionnaires are presented in Table 1, where the generalized versions of the questions are presented, but slight modifications were made to adapt them to the context of every case study.

To collect information about participants' motivations (see variable Motivations to participate in Table 1, following a format of Likert scale questions: 1- Not important at all; 5- Very important), factors were adapted from the motivational model used by Nov et al. [26, 27] the Self-determination theory [7] and the Technology Acceptance Model [6], as described by Gutierrez-Paez et al. [9, 10]. Participants' perceptions regarding the importance of functionalities in OCs were measured using a non-exhaustive list of direct and indirect incentives that are commonly used in OCs to engage participation (see variable Perceived value of common participation incentives in online communities in Table 1; following a format of Likert scale questions: 1- Not important at all; 5- Very important). Additionally, open-ended questions (marked with an *) regarding the positive aspects and the limitations of the ILDE+ platform were incorporated into the questionnaires, in order to collect qualitative data regarding functionalities and incentives that are not contemplated in the non-exhaustive list (see variable Positive and negative aspects about platform in Table 1; following a format of Likert scale questions: 0- Not useful at all; 4- Very useful).

Table 1. Variables measured in the case studies.

Measured variables	Code	General version
Motivations to participate		*Indicate the perceived level of importance for each of the following statements to motivate you to participate in an online community of practice:*
Enjoyment	FUN	*Have fun while exploring and sharing learning designs*
Knowledge gain	KNO	*Learn and improve my knowledge about learning designs*
Reputation	REP	*Make my learning designs known to the community*
Collective motives	COM	*Collaborate with the aim of contributing to the development of the teaching community*
Social interaction	SOI	*Meet people and groups who share my opinions and ideas about learning designs*
Facilitate community activities using technology	SIM	*Being able to easily share, explore, and comment on my learning designs and other learning designs across the community*
Perceived value of common participation incentives in online communities		*From the list of some functionalities that can be implemented in an online community, please indicate the level of importance that every functionality has according to your interests within the community*
	GLR	*Global rankings for users/designs based on community statistics*
	RES	*Recommender systems with suggestions about designs or users to follow*
	STA	*User/community statistics*
	ACK	*Featured users acknowledgment sections*
	NEW	*Section with relevant news for the community members*
	BAD	*Badges for users/designs' reputation*
	CHA	*Collaborative/Competitive challenges to engage contributions*
	TUT	*Tutorials and guides to comment, share or create designs within the community*
	*	*Which functionalities would you like to have in the ILDE+ platform?*

(*continued*)

Table 1. (*continued*)

Measured variables	Code	General version
Perception about platform functionalities		***Indicate the usefulness of each funtionality of the ILDE+ platform:***
	TEM	*Template for new project creation*
	FIB	*Filter bar for exploring available designs in the platform*
	COM	*Comment option for designs*
	COD	*Projects' co-design option*
	COF	*Community features (like, views, follow buttons)*
Positive and negative aspects about platform	PA*	*Which positive aspects would you highlight from ILDE+ ?*
	NA*	*Which limitations do you think ILDE+ has?*

3 Results

3.1 Initial Case Study: ILDE Experienced Users

In this case a single questionnaire was used to know teachers' perceptions about ILDE, their motivations to participate in the community ($\alpha = 0.78$), their perceptions about the non-exhaustive list of common participation incentives used in OCs ($\alpha = 0.83$) and open-ended questions regarding the positive aspects and aspects to improve within ILDE+. A total of 18 participants (13 female, 5 male) responded to the questionnaire.

The analysis of the motivations to participate in an OC for sharing and exploring learning designs and experiences (18 valid answers, Fig. 1a) showed that gaining knowledge (Median: $M_{KNO} = 4$, Mode: $Mo_{KNO} = 4$) is the main motivation, followed by social interaction ($M_{SOI} = 3$, $Mo_{SOI} = 3$). On the other hand, the least important motivator for participants is to have fun (FUN), followed by the reputation (REP1 and REP2). Interestingly, reputation is slightly more important in local contexts (REP2) than in global contexts (REP1), which indicates that participants feel more confidence and value recognition in their local communities. For the other case studies, we focused on the global contexts since our interest is an open OC, and not local sub-communities.

An extended list of incentives was presented to participants: Global rankings item (GLR) was divided into most used designs ranking (GLR1), most commented designs ranking (GLR2), best rated designs ranking (GLR3) and most active members ranking (GLR4). User and community statistics item (STA) was also divided into users' statistics (STA1), designs' statistics (STA2), subgroups' (such as schools) statistics (STA3) and community statistics (STA4). Acknowledgements section (ACK) item was divided into users' public acknowledgment section (ACK1) and designs' public acknowledgement section (ACK2). News section item (NEW) was divided into news sections managed by administrators (NEW1) and forums and blogs as news section (NEW2).

The results of user perception about the common incentives (Fig. 1b) show that participants prefer incentives such as tutorials and guidelines for creating better designs and discussions within the OC (TUT), recommender systems with customized suggestions about designs or users to follow (RES) or sections with relevant news for OC members (NEW). On the other hand, incentives based on statistics (STA) are perceived as less important for participants, followed by the incentives based on recognition such as users' and designs' rankings (GLR), progress badges (BAD) and acknowledgment sections (ACK).

Regarding the perception about rankings, there is a clear difference between the importance given to rankings based on automatic data collection such as views, comments, and user activity (GLR1, GLR2 and GLR4) and community-based rankings (GLR3), since participants give more importance to the latter. The respondents also considered that public acknowledgment of designs (ACK2) is slightly more important than the public acknowledgement of users (ACK1). Furthermore, around half of the participants perceived the different public statistics for users and designs that can be presented in an OC (STA1, STA2, STA3, STA4) as not important or slightly important. These results suggest that respondents do not perceive as important all the automatic information that could be collected through their use of the OC platform and the feedback it could provide.

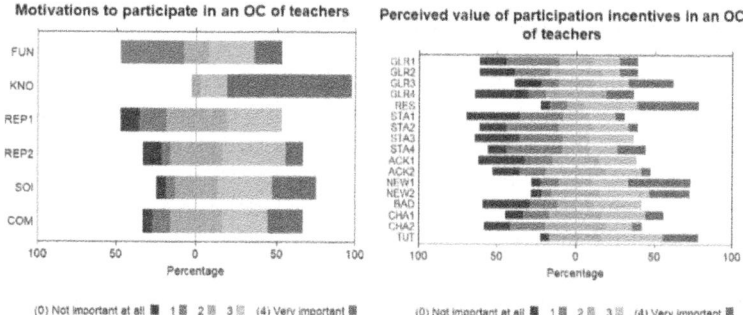

Fig. 1. (a) Motivations to participate in an OC of teachers. (b) Perceived value of participation incentives in an OC of teachers.

A content analysis for the open-ended questions revealed that most participants find the full version of ILDE platform (with multiple learning design tools integrated) too complex. For instance, a participant expressed: "(…) it would be very good to have an environment with a search engine for resources, by subjects, levels, etc. (…) and then we could deepen everything we wanted in each of the projects (statistics, timing, objectives, etc.). It is important to facilitate the search and to have more dynamism to contact with the community". Other users emphasized the need of having more resources to explore and to learn more from them ("I haven't used the platform to search other teachers' designs due to the lack of designs for my subjects"). As positive aspects, they highlighted the different design templates ("You can create designs using different tools such as ldFeedback, PyramidApp, google forms, etc.") and the possibility of duplicating a design ("(…) the duplicate feature for designs allows to review and use them again, facilitating and incentivizing their use"). Additionally, participants mentioned the difficulty of using a new tool such as ILDE as a key factor to participate in the community. Thus, for the other case studies a new motivational factor was included when participants were asked about their motivations: Facilitate community activities using technology (SIM), understood as the introduction of an online tool into the existing process of creating, exploring and sharing learning designs.

3.2 Case Study 1: Makers in the Classroom

The methodology to collect data in this case study was the following: first, participants filled a pre-questionnaire (N = 252) to gather information regarding their motivations to participate in an OC ($\alpha = 0.88$) and the perceived value of a non-exhaustive list of common participation incentives used in OCs ($\alpha = 0.90$). Then, participants received the training regarding 'Maker' methodology, and then they were introduced to ILDE+ (participants were not previously familiar with it) as a tool for sharing and exploring 'Maker' resources and designs, as well as to connect with other members of the community. Then, participants filled a post-questionnaire (N = 84) regarding their perception about some of the functionalities implemented and open-ended questions regarding the positive aspects and aspects to improve within the ILDE+ platform.

Even though most of the participants of this case study were in-service teachers (N = 196), there was a group of pre-service teachers that participated in the MOOC (N = 13), as well as other users' profiles (N = 33), e.g., content editors, project managers and psychologists. Using the kruskal-wallis test, no significant differences between the three profiles were found for any of the collected data.

A total of 252 participants (46 male, 191 female, 15 prefer not to say/no answer) responded to the pre-questionnaire and 100 (16 male, 72 female, 12 prefer not to say/no answer) to the post-questionnaire. The post-questionnaire was distributed after the completion of the training session which resulted in a lower response rate.

The analysis of the motivations (242 valid answers) to participate in an OC for sharing and exploring their 'Maker' educational activities designs (Fig. 2a) showed that participants' main motivation is to gain knowledge ($M_{KNO} = 3$, $Mo_{KNO} = 4$), enjoyment ($M_{FUN} = 3$, $Mo_{FUN} = 3$) and collective motives ($M_{COM} = 3$, $Mo_{COM} = 2$). The least important motivation according to the respondents is reputation ($M_{REP} = 2$, $Mo_{REP} = 2$).

A similar analysis for the perceived importance of the common incentives used in OCs of teachers (242 valid answers, Fig. 2b) showed that participants prefer indirect incentives that help them improve their knowledge, such as sections with relevant news for OC members ($M_{NEW} = 3$, $Mo_{NEW} = 2$), recommender systems with customized suggestions about designs or users to follow ($M_{RES} = 3$, $Mo_{RES} = 3$) or tutorials and guidelines for creating better designs and discussions within the OC ($M_{TUT} = 3$, $Mo_{TUT} = 3$). On the other hand, incentives focused on user recognition such as users' and designs' rankings ($M_{GLR} = 1$, $Mo_{GLR} = 1$), progress badges ($M_{BAD} = 2$, $Mo_{BAD} = 2$) or acknowledgements sections ($M_{ACK} = 2$, $Mo_{ACK} = 2$) are perceived as less important for participants. External incentives such as contests or challenges to increase contributions are considered important if they encourage collaboration (CHA1) over competition (CHA2).

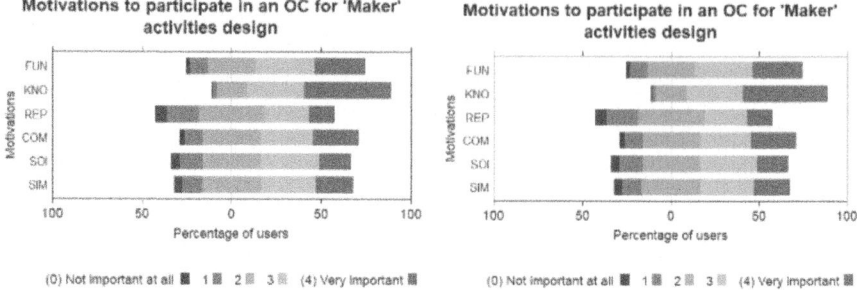

Fig. 2. (a) Motivations to participate in an OC for 'Maker' activities design. (b) Perceived value of participation incentives in an OC for 'Maker' activities design.

A content analysis for the open-ended questions revealed that one of the most positive aspects of the platform according to participants is the sharing feature (sharing and exploring designs and experiences within a community of teachers). One participant summarized this positive aspect as "The possibility of being part of a space where different teachers can give their point of view on educational experiences with maker methodology that we share among ourselves".

The content analysis also revealed that the main problem reported by the participants was the lack of knowledge and available resources and time. One participant mentioned that the main limitation for participating in an OC for such as ILDE+ is the "lack of time for teacher training" and "lack of resources in school". Likewise, other participants mentioned the available options for searching designs within the platform as a limitation ("I think it would be positive for ILDE to have the option to classify the experiences according to the comments and ratings it receives(…)"). Another identified limitation was the time and effort required to introduce a technological tool as ILDE+ in a school environment.

3.3 Case Study 2: Teachers in Network

This case study helped to complement the analysis regarding the perception of preservice teachers and to deepen in the analysis of users' perception about the implemented functionalities of the ILDE+ platform. To collect data, a similar methodology as the one used in the case study 1 was conducted during two academic periods (first academic period with 40 participants, second academic period with 51 participants). The process to collect data was similar for both periods: participants filled a pre-questionnaire (N = 91) about their motivations to participate in such communities ($\alpha = 0.82$). Then, they performed an activity in which they used the ILDE+ instantiation (participants were not previously familiar with it) to explore previously uploaded designs and then to create their own designs. At the end of the activity, participants filled a post-questionnaire (N = 91) with open-ended questions regarding the positive aspects and aspects to improve within the platform.

Due to the COVID-19 crisis, some methodological aspects differ from both periods. During the first period (October 2019 - March 2020), a focus group (with 40 participants) was conducted to know participants' perceptions about the platform and about the participation incentives that could be implemented, as well as to deeply discuss the positive and negative aspects of the ILDE+ platform. During this focus group, a researcher participated as an observer, taking field notes. For the second period (October 2020 – May 2021) participants were asked through the questionnaires about their perceived value of a non-exhaustive list of common participation incentives used in OCs (N = 51, α = 0.82). Using the kruskal-wallis test, no significant differences were found for the answers to the questions that were asked in both periods. For that reason, this data was analysed together.

A total of 91 participants (31 male, 56 female, 4 prefer not to say/no answer) responded to the pre-questionnaire. And 78 (30 male, 47 female, 1 prefer not to say/no answer) to the post-questionnaire. In this case, the post-questionnaire was also distributed after the completion of the training phase which resulted in a lower response rate.

The analysis of the motivations (91 valid answers) to participate in an OC for sharing and exploring their educational activities designs (Fig. 3a) showed that participants main motivation is to gain knowledge ($M_{KNO} = 4$, $Mo_{KNO} = 4$), followed by facilitate community activities using technology ($M_{SIM} = 4$, $Mo_{SIM} = 4$). Most of the respondents have indicated that reputation ($M_{REP} = 2$, $Mo_{REP} = 2$) is the least important motivation to participate in such an OC.

The analysis for the perceived importance of the incentives used in OCs of pre-service teachers (51 valid answers, Fig. 3b) showed again that participants prefer indirect incentives that help them improve their knowledge, i.e. sections with relevant news for OC members ($M_{NEW} = 3$, $Mo_{NEW} = 4$), recommender systems with customized suggestions about designs or users to follow ($M_{RES} = 3$, $Mo_{RES} = 3$) or tutorials and guidelines for creating better designs and discussions within the OC ($M_{TUT} = 3$, $Mo_{TUT} = 2$). In this case study, incentives focused on user recognition such as users' and designs' rankings ($M_{GLR} = 1$, $Mo_{GLR} = 1$), progress badges ($M_{BAD} = 1$, $Mo_{BAD} = 1$) and acknowledgements sections ($M_{ACK} = 2$, $Mo_{ACK} = 1$) are perceived as less important for participants.

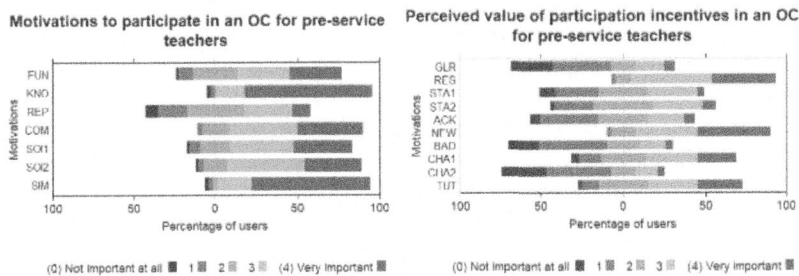

Fig. 3. (a) Motivations to participate in an OC for didactic units and classroom activities design sharing. (b) Perceived value of participation incentives in an OC for pre-service teachers (Only second period).

A content analysis was made with the open-ended answers: positive aspects of ILDE+, aspects to improve and desired features to be implemented in future platform releases. For each question, a manual coding was performed, and general topics were defined. Regarding the positive aspects, participants highlighted the simplicity of the platform and that it is easy to use (8 responses). Likewise, 6 responses were related to the ability of exploring other teachers' ideas and the available filtering options. As for the limitations, since this is a completely new ILDE+ instantiation, users indicated that there were a limited number of resources available during the training session (few resources, empty metadata associated to the available resources, etc.). Furthermore, some minor bugs with the saving options as well as the functioning of the search bar were reported by users in the open-ended answers. The analysis of the desired features showed that even when users do not consider social interaction as the main motivator, most of them would like to have social network features such as forums or private chats to discuss about available resources and to contact directly with their owners.

During the focus group session, participants deepened on the positive aspects of the platform, as well as the limitations and the desired features. One of the most important discussed topics was the best way to display and recommend designs for users. Participants acknowledged the importance of rankings to explore the most useful designs and the best contributors, even when reputation is not a motivator for them. They also indicated that the template for uploading designs is too long and they did not fill it entirely, but they acknowledged the importance of the metadata collected through the template to explore and discover other users' resources. Again, another important issue mentioned by participants is the available resources. The quantity and the quality of the resources affect users' perception of usefulness of the platform. Thus, a set of initial resources is needed, as well as a content reviewer (manual or automatic) to remove or filter useless designs.

3.4 Cross-Case Analysis and Discussion

A cross-case analysis was conducted to determine similarities and differences among the three case studies about teachers' motivations to participate in online OCs. A summary of this analysis is presented (Table 2). Regardless of whether the community is for pre- or in-service teachers, users' main motivation to participate in such types of OC is the willingness to improve their skills and extend their knowledge through the exploration and sharing of learning designs (intrinsic motivation), as well as to help and contribute to the community goals, which is in line with previous research [14, 16, 32]. Likewise, teachers rated higher the features and incentives related to search, filtering and tutorials, as well as social features and statistics that provide knowledge exchange for participants and interesting ways to discover resources and community members.

As for the reputation, results showed that most of the participants do not consider it as an important motivator to participate and contribute to an OC of teachers (in Table 2, REP has the lowest positive percentage, as well as the highest negative percentage) and they perceive incentives focused on user recognition (global rankings, badges, etc.) as less important. Nevertheless, the focus group performed within the participants of the case study 2 showed that reputation is important as an instrument for exploring and discovering useful resources and community members. Several studies have provided evidence of the importance of reputation systems in OCs [5, 25], as reputation is highly associated with leadership and trust among community members. In our study, despite reputation was rated generally as the least important motivator, 36 out of 351 participants (10.2%) among the three case studies rated reputation higher than other motivations, which suggests an indirect measurement of leadership among the study participants.

Table 2. Comparison of positive (Likert scores 3 and 4) and negative (Likert scores 0 and 1) perceived importance of motivations among the three case studies.

	Perceived importance	FUN	KNO	REP	COM	SOI	SIM
ILDE experienced users	**Positive**	44,4%	94,4%[a]	33,3%[b]	50,0%	61,1%	—
	Negative	38,9%[d]	0,0%[c]	27,8%	16,7%	11,1%	—
Makers in the classroom	**Positive**	60,0%	78,5%[a]	36,1%[b]	51,7%	48,8%	51,2%
	Negative	11,7%	2,9%[c]	24,9%[d]	13,2%	18,5%	16,6%
Teachers in network	**Positive**	55,0%	95,0%[a]	27,5%[b]	82,5%	72,5%	95,0%
	Negative	15,0%	5,0%	27,5%[d]	0,0%[d]	8,8%	5,0%

[a] Highest positive percentage among the different motivations
[b] Lowest positive percentage among the different motivations
[c] Lowest negative percentage among the different motivations
[d] Highest negative percentage among the different motivations

Another interesting result from the motivations is how participants perceived the need of a technological tool to facilitate community activities as a key motivator to be part of an OC of teachers. In the initial case study participants' answers to open-ended questions confirmed that even when the original ILDE platform provides valuable tools for designing and sharing learning resources, most of the respondents indicated that they faced issues with the interface and the complexity to create, share and explore resources, which directly affects their motivation to participate in the community. Results of the two main case studies also showed that facilitating community activities with technology is a key motivator for participants in an OC of teachers, even when it is not the most important motivator. Thus, usability is a key factor that affects participation, but it does not motivate participants by itself.

As for the features to incentivize teachers' participation, the results indicate that special attention should be paid to the design of features regarding search and filtering, as well as social features that provide knowledge exchange for participants (e.g., news bulletins, blogs, forums, chats, etc.). Similarly, social statistics are valuable features for users since they provide interesting ways to discover resources and community members (most viewed resource, most liked resource, user with most contributions, etc.).

Regarding the RQ1 (Is there a relation between teachers' motivations and the perceived value of functionalities for the participants of an OC of teachers?) a correlation analysis was conducted to determine the relationship between motivations and the different functionalities for incentivizing participation in the initial case study, the case study 1 and the second period of the case study 2. Based on the statistically significant correlation coefficients ($p < 0.05$), for each incentive the motivations were arranged from highest to lowest. Then, a comparison was made between the case studies. A summary of the most relevant results is presented in Table 3. On the one hand, there is a positive correlation between gaining knowledge (KNO) and some of the best rated incentives, i.e., tutorials (TUT) and recommendation systems (RES). Likewise, social interaction (SOI) and collective motives (COM) are also correlated with incentives such as user/community statistics (STA) and tutorials (TUT), respectively. On the other hand, the lowest rated motivation, reputation (REP), has a correlation with incentives such as rankings (G–LR), public acknowledgement (ACK), Badges (BAD), challenges (CHA) and user/community statistics (STA).

Table 3. Correlation analysis of incentives and motivations. All correlations presented are statistically significant (p-value < 0.05) and have the highest correlation for each combination motivation-incentive.

Incentives:		GLR	RES	STA		ACK	NEW	BAD	CHA	TUT	
Motivations:		REP	KNO	SOI	REP	REP	COM	REP	REP	KNO	COM
ILDE experienced users	Kendall τ_B	0,46–0.61	0,56	0,55–0,60	0,50–0,65	0,67	0,48	0,63	0,49–0,65	0,46	–
	Spearman p	0.55–0,71	0,60	0,67–0,72	0,58–0,72	0,75	0,54	0,71	0,56–0,73	0,49	–
Makers in the classroom	Kendall τ_B	0,29	0,47	0,30–0,38	0,32–0,36	0,34	0,41	0,32	0,27–0,30	0,49	0,41
	Spearman p	0,33	0,53	0,36–0,45	0,37–0,42	0,39	0,47	0,37	0,32–0,35	0,54	0,47
Teachers in network	Kendall τ_B	0,25	–	0,25	0,30	0,26	0,27	0,32	0,32–0,33	0,29	0,26
	Spearman p	0,30	–	0,29	0,36	0,30	0,31	0,39	0,38–0,39	0,32	0,29

Regarding the RQ2 (Do teachers' motivations provide information for platform designers about the most valuable functionalities?), results of perceived motivations of participants offered valuable information to refine and enhance the ILDE+ platform. For instance, a Twitter embedded timeline was inserted to make users aware of new useful information. Likewise, a news section was added, where platform administrators can add short articles with external links to relevant information for the community members such as events or meetings. Additionally, based on the feedback obtained from the participants of the focus group in the case study 2, the community features of the platform were refined, as social interaction is important for community members, and filters for exploring designs and members were added (based on likes, comments, views, and followers). These community features were used to add a list of featured designs to the home section of the platform, which is automatically updated based on the comments, visualizations and likes each design has. As for improving the usability and making the designs' sharing process simpler, the title and a short description became mandatory in the creation template to upload a design and a progress indicator will be added to show each member how complete a design is (based on the template fields). This will reduce the number of designs without any metadata and will give initial feedback to the users about the completeness of their own designs (and hence, about the usefulness within the community).

4 Conclusions and Future Work

This paper focused on the use of OCs by teachers, through the analysis of an existing platform called ILDE+. Three case studies were analyzed to understand the relation between participants' motivations and the perceived importance of features and incentives to be implemented in an OC of teachers aimed to support collaborative practice. The initial case study was a community of 18 teachers of two Catalan schools that were already familiar with the ILDE platform and have used it for creating, exploring, and sharing learning designs (ILDE experienced users), and allowed us to validate the design requirements for an MVP supporting platform of an OC of teachers. It also provided useful feedback to improve the instruments used in the two main case studies. The first main case study was a community of 252 participants, mainly in-service teachers, that participated in a MOOC and a face-to-face training, in which an ILDE+ instantiation was introduced for creating, sharing, and exploring 'Maker' LDs. The second case study was a community of 91 students of a pre-service science teacher master course, where an independent ILDE+ instantiation was introduced as a tool for exploring and sharing didactic units and or classroom activities designs.

The findings of this study have implications for the design of online communities for teachers and for the development of features and incentives that can motivate teachers to participate and contribute to these communities. According to the collected data, teachers' main motivation is the possibility of improving their knowledge (KNO), as well as to interact and exchange knowledge and experience with other teachers (SOI), which agrees with previous research. Connected with our RQ1 on the connection between teachers' motivations and the perceived value of functionalities, our results indicate that the most important features to implement in an online community (OC) for teachers are indirect incentives that enhance their knowledge. These include tutorials and guidelines for creating better designs and fostering discussions within the community (TUT), recommender systems offering customized suggestions about designs or users to follow (RES), and a section with relevant news for OC members (NEW).

Participants also highlighted the importance of social features that facilitate knowledge exchange, such as blogs, forums, and chats. Social statistics were also deemed important as they help discover new resources and foster collaboration by identifying active community members (e.g., most viewed resource, most liked resource, user with the most contributions, etc.). The results of this multi-case study suggest a relationship between teachers' motivations to participate in an OC and the desired features. Is crucial to collect this type of data and share it with platform developers to incentivize participation (RQ2). Therefore, implications for platform developers of OCs for teachers should focus on prioritizing design requirements and features based on motivational factors. Implementing the suggested social features, which consider teachers' motivations, can enhance other online communities of teachers beyond ILDE+, and the findings can be applied to broader educational contexts. This integration will result in a more effective use of technology for sharing knowledge and learning designs, facilitating collaborative practice, and enhancing teacher professional development.

In this study the surveys were not mandatory, and fewer participants completed the second survey. Moreover, since new instances of ILDE+ were used for two of the case studies (still not populated with generated content), participants' perception was affected by the limited number of initial resources, as well as by the number of incomplete resources. Likewise, the results of this research are strongly connected to the context in which the analysis was conducted, making them difficult to generalize to other communities.

Future research will include user evaluation experiments to validate the usefulness of the features implemented in the ILDE+ platform based on the results of this study. Likewise, the analysis of log data collected from user behaviour within the platform will provide stronger results regarding the importance of the different features of an OC, as well as will allow us to define clear metrics to assess different types of participation. Future work should also include additional instruments, e.g., user data analytics, to contrast participants' self-reported motivations with behaviours, to understand motivational drivers more in depth.

Acknowledgments. This work was supported in part by PID2020-112584RB-C33 funded by MCIN/AEI/https://doi.org/10.13039/501100011033, the Ramón y Cajal programme (P. Santos) and ICREA under the ICREA Academia programme (D. Hernández-Leo, Serra Hunter).

Disclosure of Interests. No potential conflict of interest was reported by the authors.

References

1. Asensio-Pérez, J.I., et al.: Towards teaching as design: exploring the inter-play between full-lifecycle learning design tooling and Teacher Professional Development. Comput. Educ. **114**, 92–116 (2017). https://doi.org/10.1016/j.compedu.2017.06.011
2. Cho, H., Stefanone, M., & Gay, G.: Social information sharing in a CSCL community. In Computer Support for Collaborative Learning, pp. 43–50. Routledge (2023)
3. Corbin, J., Strauss, A.: Basics of Qualitative Research: TECHNIQUES and Procedures for Developing Grounded Theory, 4th edn. Sage publications, Thousands Oaks (2014)
4. Creswell, J.W., Plano Clark, V.L.: Designing and Conducting Mixed Methods Research. SAGE Publications, Thousands Oaks (2017). https://us.sagepub.com/en-us/nam/designing-and-conducting-mixed-methods-research/book241842
5. Cruz, C.C.P., Motta, C.L.R., Santoro, F.M., Elia, M.: Reputation model in communities of practice: a case study. In: 2008 12th International Conference on Computer Supported Cooperative Work in Design, pp. 777–782 (2008). https://doi.org/10.1109/CSCWD.2008.4537077
6. Davis, F.D.: Perceived usefulness, perceived ease of use, and user acceptance of information technology. MIS Q. **13**(3), 319–340 (1989). https://doi.org/10.2307/249008
7. Deci, E.L., Ryan, R.M.: The «What» and «Why» of goal pursuits: human needs and the self-determination of behavior. Psychol. Inq. **11**(4), 227–268 (2000). https://doi.org/10.1207/S15327965PLI1104_01
8. Duncan-Howell, J.: Teachers making connections: online communities as a source of professional learning. Br. J. Edu. Technol. **41**(2), 324–340 (2010). https://doi.org/10.1111/j.1467-8535.2009.00953.x
9. Gutierrez-Paez, N., Santos, P., Hernández-Leo, D.: Understanding participants' motivational factors for the design of a teacher community platform. In: 2021 International Conference on Advanced Learning Technologies (ICALT), pp. 132–134 (2021). https://doi.org/10.1109/ICALT52272.2021.00047

10. Gutiérrez-Páez, N.F., Santos, P., Hernández-Leo, D., Carrió, M.: Designing a pre-service teacher community platform: a focus on participants' motivations. In: De Laet, T., Klemke, R., Alario-Hoyos, C., Hilliger, I., Ortega-Arranz, A. (eds.) EC-TEL 2021. LNCS, vol. 12884, pp. 352–357. Springer, Cham (2021). https://doi.org/10.1007/978-3-030-86436-1_34
11. Hernández-Leo, D., et al.: An integrated environment for learning design. Front. ICT **5**, 9 (2018). https://doi.org/10.3389/fict.2018.00009
12. Hernández-Leo, D., Jorrín-Abellán, I.M., Villasclaras-Fernández, E.D., Asensio-Pérez, J.I., Dimitriadis, Y.: A multicase study for the evaluation of a pattern-based visual design process for collaborative learning. J. Vis. Lang. Comput. **21**(6), 313–331 (2010). https://doi.org/10.1016/j.jvlc.2010.08.006
13. Hernández-Leo, D., Moreno, P., Chacón, J., Blat, J.: LdShake support for team-based learning design. Comput. Hum. Behav. **37**, 402–412 (2014). https://doi.org/10.1016/j.chb.2012.05.029
14. Hew, K.F., Hara, N.: Empirical study of motivators and barriers of teacher online knowledge sharing. Educ. Tech. Res. Dev. **55**(6), 573 (2007). https://doi.org/10.1007/s11423-007-9049-2
15. Hofer, S.I., Nistor, N., Scheibenzuber, C.: Online teaching and learning in higher education: lessons learned in crisis situations. Comput. Hum. Behav. **121**, 106789 (2021)
16. Hur, J.W., Brush, T.A.: Teacher participation in online. Communities **41**(3), 279–303 (2009). https://doi.org/10.1080/15391523.2009.10782532
17. Kirschner, P.A., Lai, K.W.: Online communities of practice in education. Technol. Pedagogy Educ. **16**(2), 127–131 (2007). https://doi.org/10.1080/14759390701406737
18. Laurillard, D., Kennedy, E., Charlton, P., Wild, J., Dimakopoulos, D.: Using technology to develop teachers as designers of TEL: evaluating the learning designer. Br. J. Edu. Technol. **49**(6), 1044–1058 (2018). https://doi.org/10.1111/bjet.12697
19. Macià, M., García, I.: Informal online communities and networks as a source of teacher professional development: a review. Teach. Teach. Educ. **55**, 291–307 (2016). https://doi.org/10.1016/j.tate.2016.01.021
20. Malinen, S.: Understanding user participation in online communities: a systematic literature review of empirical studies. Comput. Hum. Behav. **46**, 228–238 (2015). https://doi.org/10.1016/j.chb.2015.01.004
21. Marín, V.I., Asensio-Pérez, J.I., Villagrá-Sobrino, S., Hernández-Leo, D., García-Sastre, S.: Supporting online collaborative design for teacher professional development. Technol. Pedagogy Educ. **27**(5), 571–587 (2018). https://doi.org/10.1080/1475939X.2018.1547787
22. Michos, K., Hernández-Leo, D.: Supporting awareness in communities of learning design practice. Comput. Hum. Behav. **85**, 255–270 (2018). https://doi.org/10.1016/j.chb.2018.04.008
23. Michos, K., Hernández-Leo, D.: CIDA: a collective inquiry framework to study and support teachers as designers in technological environments. Comput. Educ. **143**, 103679 (2020). https://doi.org/10.1016/j.compedu.2019.103679
24. Mohammadi, F., Abrizah, A., Nazari, M., Attaran, M.: What motivates high school teachers to use web-based learning resources for classroom instruction? an exploratory case study in an Iranian smart school. Comput. Hum. Behav. **51**, 373–381 (2015). https://doi.org/10.1016/j.chb.2015.05.016
25. Muller, P.: Reputation, trust and the dynamics of leadership in communities of practice. J. Manag. Gover. **10**(4), 381–400 (2006). https://doi.org/10.1007/s10997-006-9007-0
26. Nov, O., Anderson, D., Arazy, O.: Volunteer computing: a model of the factors determining contribution to community-based scientific research. In: Proceedings of the 19th International Conference on World Wide Web, pp. 741–750 (2010). https://doi.org/10.1145/1772690.1772766
27. Nov, O., Arazy, O., Anderson, D.: Technology-mediated citizen science participation: a motivational model. In: Proceedings of the International AAAI Conference on Web and Social Media (2011). http://citeseerx.ist.psu.edu/viewdoc/summary?doi=10.1.1.366.3430

28. Rodríguez-Triana, M.J., Prieto, L.P., Ley, T., de Jong, T., Gillet, D.: Social practices in teacher knowledge creation and innovation adoption: a large-scale study in an online instructional design community for inquiry learning. Int. J. Comput.-Support. Collab. Learn. **15**(4), 445–467 (2020). https://doi.org/10.1007/s11412-020-09331-5
29. Stake, R.E.: Multiple Case Study Analysis. Guilford press, New York (2013)
30. Sun, N., Rau, P.P.-L., Ma, L.: Understanding lurkers in online communities: a literature review. Comput. Hum. Behav. **38**, 110–117 (2014). https://doi.org/10.1016/j.chb.2014.05.022
31. Tekkumru-Kisa, M., Schunn, C.: Integrating a space for teacher interaction into an educative curriculum: design principles and teachers' use of the iPlan tool. Technol. Pedagogy Educ. **28**(2), 133–155 (2019). https://doi.org/10.1080/1475939X.2019.1595707
32. Tseng, F.-C., Kuo, F.-Y.: A study of social participation and knowledge sharing in the teachers' online professional community of practice. Comput. Educ. **72**, 37–47 (2014). https://doi.org/10.1016/j.compedu.2013.10.005
33. Vassileva, J.: Motivating participation in social computing applications: a user modeling perspective. User Model. User-Adap. Inter. **22**(1), 177–201 (2012). https://doi.org/10.1007/s11257-011-9109-5
34. Zydney, J.M., deNoyelles, A., Kyeong-Ju Seo, K.: Creating a community of inquiry in online environments: an exploratory study on the effect of a protocol on interactions within asynchronous discussions. Comput. Educ. **58**(1), 77–87 (2012). https://doi.org/10.1016/j.compedu.2011.07.009

Adaptation of a Self-determination Theory-Based Questionnaire on Collaborative Classroom Dynamics

Khadija El Aadmi-Laamech[✉], Patricia Santos, and Davinia Hernández-Leo

Universitat Pompeu Fabra, 08018 Barcelona, Spain
{khadija.elaadmi,patricia.santos,davinia.hernandez-leo}@upf.edu

Abstract. In this paper we explore the adaptation and validation of a scale on the collaborative classroom dynamics that impact students' well-being. We leverage the Self-Determination Theory to understand such well-being impacts, as well as use the Basic Psychological Need satisfaction as a means to improve collaborative classroom dynamics. Therefore, the aim of this work is to generate an SDT-based instrument that evaluates the collaborative classroom dynamics from a well-being perspective. For that, we make use of an existing scale where learning and collaboration are also present (BPNSS-Work scale) and adapt it to the context of education. The scale is adapted and validated to meet the needs of students, pointing out the similarities and differences between the scale used in the work context versus the educational one. The work follows the process and employed methodology in order to achieve the validation. We discuss the potential of the resulting scale: for the teacher, it serves to support classroom management (redesigning activities, interactions between groups), and for the students, it serves (alongside with the resulting recommendations) to support their well-being and self-regulation.

Keywords: CSCL · Self-Determination Theory · Collaboration · Well-being · Scale adaptation · Scale validation

1 Introduction

Collaboration in Technology-Enhanced Learning (TEL) settings, particularly in education, plays a pivotal role in shaping students' learning experiences and overall development. The emphasis on fostering a collaborative environment is rooted in the understanding that such dynamics significantly influence students' academic performance, personal growth, and psychological well-being [1, 2]. In this context, the application of Self-Determination Theory (SDT) to educational settings has been a topic of considerable interest. SDT, which focuses on the inherent human needs (also known as basic psychological needs– BPNs) for autonomy, competence, and relatedness, has been extensively reviewed and applied in various contexts, including technology use and education [3, 4, 15]. Furthermore, the SDT has also been a staple in understanding student behavior and engagement levels during their learning, creating a link between classroom dynamics and need satisfaction [15]. And satisfying (or frustrating) the needs of autonomy, competence and relatedness have been observed to directly impact well-being [3].

SDT instruments have been leveraged to measure and understand technology interactions in CSCL environments from a well-being perspective. For instance, in previous work [5] we used the instruments proposed by [3] in order to understand technology interactions from a well-being perspective at the interface level of a CSCL tool. However, the used SDT instruments only provide ways to measure interactions within the virtual environment, and do not provide a way to measure the interactions of collaborative dynamics in class (i.e. those occurring outside the virtual collaborative environments). In this line, [6] and colleagues critically point out that the nature of interaction (within a virtual environment) varies based on the specific learning environment, suggesting that the dynamics of collaboration can differ depending on several factors: not only the technology used, but also the structure of the learning activity as well as the characteristics of the learners involved. The collaborative process further varies when other complex forms of interaction are taken into account (i.e. socio-emotional forms of interaction). Balancing the different interactions helps achieve a successful collaboration [6].

The aim of this paper is to contribute with an instrument that helps with the understanding of the collaborative dynamics that happen outside the virtual environment, while using the virtual environment –specifically from a well-being perspective. We explore the adaptation of an existing SDT-based scale developed for assessing collaborative dynamics in similar environments to educational settings, where learning is also present (i.e. work) as a novel approach to addressing the observed gap. This adaptation is grounded in the similarities of collaborative practices in both educational (CSCL) and professional (Computer Supported Collaborative Work - CSCW) collaborative settings (both approaches support collaborative learning, foster knowledge construction, and facilitate diverse activities within dynamic, structured virtual learning environments [7]). And also due to lack of SDT-based scales that target collaboration in our context (i.e. education). By leveraging an existing and validated SDT-based scale that focuses on collaboration (i.e. Basic Psychological Need Satisfaction Scale - Work or BPNSS-Work) [10–13] this study aims to provide new insights into the collaborative nature of classroom environments, especially those dynamics that go beyond the context in which digital collaboration directly takes place (i.e. technological collaborative interfaces), from a well-being perspective. This approach is exploratory, aiming to help bridge the technological and non-technological collaborative dynamics in schools.

What sets this work apart from other collaborative dynamics instruments, is that it does not only focus on the collaborative dynamics, rather it is leveraged from a psychological well-being perspective as well (i.e. basic psychological need satisfaction), thanks to the SDT. As pointed out by [23], the SDT can aid in understanding several behaviors and motivational factors related to the CSCL nature, such as the learner's level of contribution through their level of self-determination [24], and positive student engagement [25] through autonomy support [26], between others. Therefore, the ultimate goal is to provide practitioners and educators with an instrument that helps shape students' learning experiences within CSCL environments, taking into account their well-being (i.e., BPNs fulfillment or frustration) throughout the entire collaborative process.

2 Methodology

Below there is a representation (Fig. 1) of the followed adaptation and validation process (1st outcome) [8, 9] as well as the recommendations generated as a tool to help educators with the collaborative process (2nd outcome). The process for the first outcome is divided in three main phases: 1. Design of the scale, 2. Validation of the scale and 3. Reliability analysis of the scale. As for the process for the second outcome, it was a standalone workshop. Each outcome as well as phases had their respective methods and profile plus number of participants. In the following subsections, we detail and justify each one of the phases, the methods utilized and the profiles of the participants.

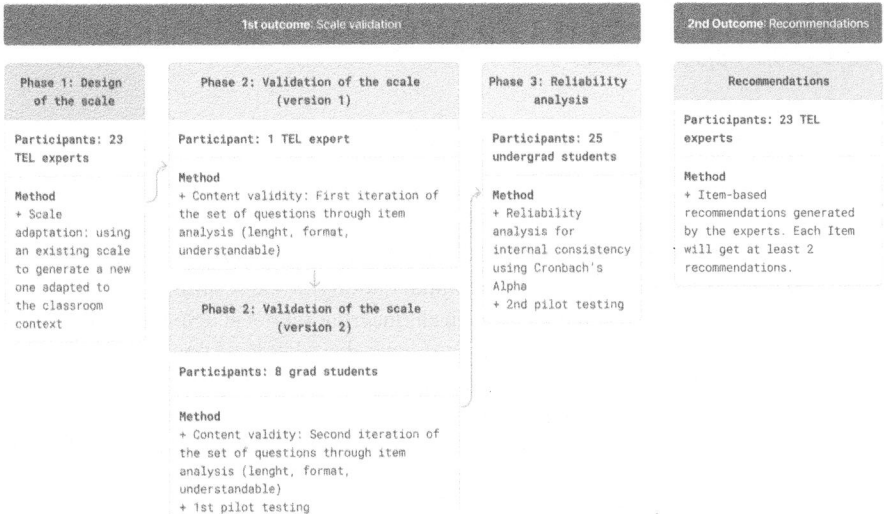

Fig. 1. Outcomes, methods, participants and phases of the development of the scale

2.1 Phase 1. Design of the Scale

Phase 1 consisted of a 60-min workshop. The participating profiles are seasoned experts in various subfields of TEL. A breakdown of the different profiles and their respective areas of expertise can be found in the supplementary material [22]. The main objective of this workshop was to evaluate and adapt the original BPNSS-Work scale's questions [10–13], transitioning them from a work environment to a classroom setting. Each two sets of experts were assigned specific questions related to each one of the Basic Psychological Needs (BPNs). The workshop duration was of 60 min, with the initial 40 min allocated for the review and adaptation of the questions. The remaining 20 min were dedicated to generating a first list of recommendations (see phase 4) aimed at assisting both students and teachers in enhancing the students' classroom dynamics when utilizing this scale. Every question resulting from the adaptation process was associated with a minimum of two practical recommendations.

2.2 Phase 2. Validation of the Scale and 1st Pilot

The second phase (validation) was carried out with one main purpose: Content validity. Content validity assesses if the questionnaire fully represents the concept we are measuring. This often involves expert reviews where subject matter experts evaluate each item for relevance, clarity, and completeness. This phase was carried out twice: first with a TEL expert seasoned in CSCL research, and second with a group of 8 grad students. The TEL expert helped guide the first tweaking to the scale, giving feedback where needed. Afterwards, students were presented with the set of questions reviewed by the TEL expert. Aside from reviewing the questions, students were also asked to fill out the scale as a 1st pilot testing of the scale, since administering the questionnaire to a small, representative sample of the target population helps identify any issues with the questionnaire's clarity, length, and format. The obtained feedback from the students was used to further adjust the scale.

2.3 Phase 3. Reliability Analysis and 2nd Pilot

A reliability analysis followed the validation process, helping ensure the questionnaire is consistent in its measurement. We carried out an internal consistency analysis using Cronbach's alpha, which checks how well the items measuring the same construct correlate with each other. In order to test the initial validity of the resulting questionnaire, we recruited a sample of 25 students from an engineering school at a Spanish University. The condition of recruitment is that they must have shared at least one course together, in this case "Introduction to Information and Communication Technologies" course. We also carried out a 2nd piloting in order to detect any underlying issues that might have been overlooked in the previous phases. The piloting involved asking students if questions are clear enough and understandable.

2.4 Preliminary Recommendations

The group of experts recruited in phase 1 were also asked to generate a list of recommendations of the initial items generated after the first review of the scale. Even though the resulting recommendations might require further tweaking in order to fully adapt them to the current scale (and the final version after future iterations), these first recommendations path a way in which the scale can not only measure classroom dynamics, but also assist in diagnosing them whenever students do not score in the scale in a desirable way.

3 Results

3.1 Results of Phase 1: Design of the Scale

In Tables 1, 2 and 3, we can see the original questions of the BPNSS-Work [10–13], and their adapted version into classroom dynamics. All items maintain the same BPN as well as the type of scoring of the original scale. Reversed items are marked with a "(–)".

Table 1. Autonomy: Original scale items and Adapted scale items

Original BPNSS-Work item	Adapted item for classroom dynamics
I feel like I can make a lot of inputs to deciding how my job gets done. (A1)	I feel like I can influence how the learning activities are done
I feel pressured at work. (A2), (−)	I feel under pressure during classroom activities
I am free to express my ideas and opinions on the job. (A3)	I am free to express my ideas and opinions during classroom activities
When I am at work, I have to do what I am told. (A4), (−)	During classroom activities, I have to do exactly what the teachers say
My feelings are taken into consideration at work. (A5)	In the classroom, my feelings are taken into consideration
I feel like I can pretty much be myself at work. (A6)	I feel like I can pretty much be myself in the classroom
There is not much opportunity for me to decide for myself how to go about my work. (A7), (−)	There is not much opportunity for me to decide how I complete my learning activities

Table 2. Competence: Original scale items and Adapted scale items

Original BPNSS-Work item	Adapted item for classroom dynamics
I do not feel very competent when I am at work. (C1), (−)	I do not feel very competent in my abilities during classroom activities
People at work tell me I am good at what I do. (C2)	My classmates and teachers tell me I am good at doing my classwork
I have been able to learn interesting new skills on my job. (C3)	I have been able to learn interesting skills during my classroom activities
Most days I feel a sense of accomplishment from working. (C4)	Most days, I feel a sense of accomplishment from participating in class
On my job I do not get much of a chance to show how capable I am. (C5), (−)	During class, I do not get much of a chance to show how capable I am
When I am working, I often do not feel very capable. (C6), (−)	During class, I often do not feel very capable about my abilities

3.2 Results of Phase 2: Validation Process and 1ˢᵗ Pilot Testing

The results of the pilot testing phase shed light on the formulation of some items. The student answers (P) are represented in the figure below (Fig. 2) as a heatmap: green represents that the question is "easy to understand", red represents that the question is "hard to understand", and yellow represents "not sure". Students were also able to provide comments where they saw fit.

Table 3. Relatedness: Original scale items and Adapted scale items

Original BPNSS-Work item	Adapted item for classroom dynamics
I really like the people I work with. (R1)	I really like my classmates
I get along with people at work. (R2)	I get along with my classmates
I pretty much keep to myself when I am at work. (R3), (−)	I pretty much keep to myself during classroom activities
I consider the people I work with to be my friends. (R4)	I consider my classmates to be my friends
People at work care about me. (R5)	My classmates care about me
There are not many people at work that I am close to. (R6), (−)	There are not many classmates that I am close to
The people I work with do not seem to like me much. (R7), (−)	My classmates do not seem to like me much
People at work are pretty friendly towards me. (R8)	My classmates are pretty friendly towards me

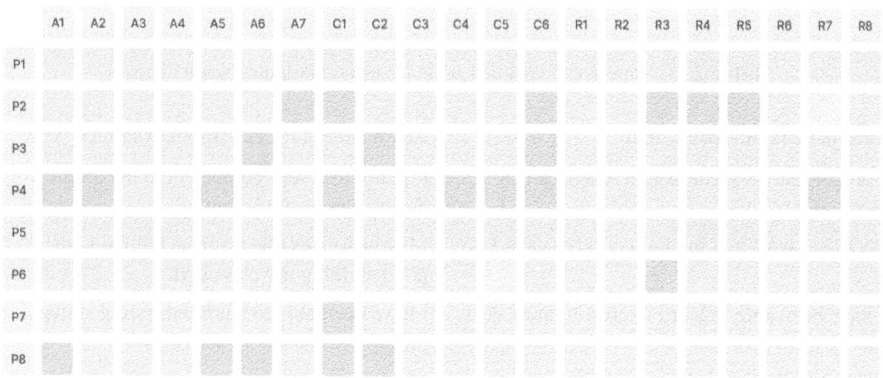

Fig. 2. Students' validation results

The most critical takeaways from the results are items C1 (I do not feel very competent in my abilities during classroom activities) and C6 (During class, I often do not feel very about my abilities). Both these items were the hardest to understand. Interestingly, both these items represent a similar question, and both were formulated in a negative voice. As for C3, students discussed the possibility of adding an item for knowledge (theoretical) and not just skills (practical), since it made more sense to have both variants in an educational setting. In the same line, they also discussed whether it would be important to separate between classmates and teachers (C2 "My teachers and classmates tell me I am good at doing my classwork"). Autonomy (A) items and relatedness (R) items were the least problematic when it came to understanding, relatedness items being the easiest to understand.

Another critical observation that was made is the use of "classroom" instead of "course". The latter word makes the question more specific context-wise, rather than using a generic word like "classroom". Also, instead of keeping the capabilities of students limited to a generic word like "class" (i.e. item C1 and C6), it would be better to make it context specific, such as "learning activities".

Below (Table 4) there is a list of the changes we did to the current items. It is important to point out that the problematic items (such as C1 and C6) were also kept, with the condition of changing the negative formulation of item C6 into a positive one, which will help us understand whether the problem lies in the formulation of the question or the nature of the question.

Table 4. List of changed items

Changed items	C2.1 "My teachers tell me I am good at doing my classwork"
	C2.2 "My classmates tell me I am good at doing my classwork"
	C3.1 "I have been able to learn interesting skills during my course activities"
	C3.2 "I have been able to learn interesting knowledge during my course activities"
	C1. "I did not feel very competent in my abilities during the learning activities." (-)
	C6. "During my learning activities, I felt capable about my abilities."

3.3 Results of Phase 3: Reliability Analysis and 2nd Pilot Testing

We used JASP software to calculate the reliability of all groups of items of the scale (i.e. Relatedness, Autonomy and Competence). The initial results are as follows (Tables 5, 6 and 7).

First of all, Relatedness items were the least problematic out of the three BPNs. They have an excellent reliability score (0.9), meaning that the items consistently measure the need of relatedness.

As for Autonomy items, the score is questionable and below the acceptable threshold of 0.7. However, dropping items A4 and A1 resulted in a score of 0.7. Nonetheless, Autonomy items seem to still require some work and tweaking in order to reliably measure the construct of Autonomy.

Finally, for competence items there is a similar trend to Autonomy items. Considering Competence already had some issues initially during the pilot session with items C1 and C6, the same issue still prevails with item C6, the one that was changed to a positive formulation. Which means that the nature of the question itself was the problem and not the original negative formulation (Refer to Table 2). If C6 is dropped, the reliability of the scale can be adjusted to 0.674, Though it is still not within the acceptable threshold of 0.7. Therefore, the competence scale still requires some changes and pilots.

As for items C2.1 and C2.2, there is a slight difference between student feedback and teacher feedback: the student peers seem to be the ones that engage in giving (positive) feedback about their work to each other (i.e. telling them how good they are when

Table 5. Relatedness items

Frequentist Scale Reliability Statistics

Estimate	Cronbach's α
Point estimate	0.900

Frequentist Individual Item Reliability Statistics

Item	If item dropped Cronbach's α
QR1	0.881
QR2	0.884
QR3 (−)	0.898
QR4	0.871
QR5	0.872
QR6 (−)	0.897
QR7 (−)	0.894
QR8	0.894

Note. The following items were reverse scaled: QR3 (−), QR6 (−), QR7 (−).

Table 6. Autonomy items

Frequentist Scale Reliability Statistics

Estimate	Cronbach's α
Point estimate	0.666

Frequentist Individual Item Reliability Statistics

Item	If item dropped Cronbach's α
QA1	0.692
QA2 (−)	0.618
QA3	0.636
QA4 (−)	0.640
QA5	0.626
QA6	0.615
QA7 (−)	0.576

Note. The following items were reverse scaled: QA7 (−), QA4 (−), QA2 (−).

performing an activity). Teachers on the other hand do not tend to engage so much in such behaviors, at least in the context this test was carried out (higher education).

Finally, for items C3.1 and C3.2 there is not that much of a difference, indicating that students do not tend to differentiate between the skills and knowledge they learn in their course.

Table 7. Competence items

Frequentist Scale Reliability Statistics

Estimate	Cronbach's α
Point estimate	0.657

Frequentist Individual Item Reliability Statistics

	If item dropped
Item	Cronbach's α
QC1 (-)	0.602
QC2.1	0.656
QC2.2	0.609
QC3.1	0.605
QC3.2	0.610
QC4	0.651
QC5 (-)	0.592
QC6	0.674

Note. The following items were reverse scaled: QC1 (-), QC5 (-).

As for the results of the 2nd piloting, students did not report any issues with the content or understanding of the items.

3.4 Results of Phase 4: Preliminary Recommendations

As we adjusted the questionnaire set of questions, we worked in parallel with the group of experts to generate a set of recommendations tailored to each question of the scale. The purpose of these recommendations is to be given to whoever takes the questionnaire, as a means to improve their BPNs, if needed. The list of recommendations is the following (adapted to the final questionnaire [22]):

Autonomy. A1. 1 Redesigned Activity with Options: 1. Offer a list of diverse ideas on how to contribute, respecting varying cultural expectations. 2. Provide prompts or triggers tailored to different cultural perspectives to assist students in generating inputs effectively.

A2. 1 Understanding and Adapting to Student Pressure: 1. Evaluate whether the level of pressure is perceived as positive or negative and identify the timing of the pressure. 2. As educators, delve deeper into the situation to gain a comprehensive understanding. 3. Explore varied student reactions to pressure and tailor plans to accommodate different profiles. **A2. 2 Adapting Teaching Strategies:** 1. Consider reducing overall workload to alleviate pressure. 2. Foster a relaxed atmosphere in the classroom to create a conducive learning environment. 3. Decrease the emphasis on grades in relation to specific activities to alleviate performance-related stress.

A3. 1 Fostering Trust in the Classroom: 1. Create a trustworthy atmosphere through engaging activities such as games, icebreakers, or physical activities. 2. Encourage anonymous expression of ideas to promote openness without fear of judgment. 3.

Provide a private platform for students to write and share their thoughts, ensuring confidentiality. 4. Actively promote constructive criticism as a means to enhance learning and collaboration within the classroom.

A4.1 Navigating Task Instructions: 1. Seek to understand the reasons behind students not following instructions, fostering open communication. 2. Enhance clarity in task instructions by providing precise and clear descriptions to minimize confusion. 3. Evaluate the relevance and impact of tasks on grading to ensure alignment with learning objectives and fair assessment.

A5.1 Group Feedback on Classroom Atmosphere: 1. Integrate an anonymous group feedback mechanism, such as a class mood tool, to gauge the overall mood and sentiments of the students. 2. Demonstrate empathy towards students, acknowledging and understanding their feelings. 3. Create an environment where students feel safe expressing their emotions without the fear of punishment, fostering open communication and emotional well-being.

A6.1 Fostering Collaboration in a Positive Atmosphere: 1. Implement trust-building exercises to enhance collaboration and a positive atmosphere. 2. Pay attention to cultural values to ensure inclusivity and respect for diversity. 3. Recognize that promoting well-being might extend beyond the teacher's competence and involve external units responsible for the system's overall health. A6.2 Creating Inclusive Environments: 1. Strive to create an inclusive environment where all students feel valued and respected. 2. Adopt a friendly and informal demeanor to facilitate approachability and open communication within the collaborative setting.

A7.1 Providing Options for Students: 1. Increase flexibility in task execution, allowing students to choose methods that align with their learning styles. 2. Introduce individual activities, recognizing diverse learning preferences and providing personalized experiences. 3. Offer the option for students to select project tasks, promoting autonomy and engagement in their learning journey.

Competence. C1.1 Key points for academic success: 1. Seek help from teachers or classmates when needed. 2. Practice similar activities at home to reinforce learning. 3. Review course materials regularly. 4. Overcome shyness; ask questions and express concerns openly. 5. Actively participate in class discussions; raise your hand. 6. Take notes on challenging concepts for reflection. 7. Utilize teacher's office hours for clarification. 8. Collaborate with competent classmates for mutual understanding. 9. Consider taking online courses to reinforce specific skills or competencies.

C2.1 and C3.1 Key points for handling feedback: 1. View comments as opportunities for improvement. 2. Detach personal feelings from feedback; see it as constructive. 3. Acknowledge and reflect on the effort invested in the task. 4. Seek guidance from teachers or classmates on areas for improvement. 5. Don't worry unless explicitly told by the teacher about a problem. 6. If you believe in your capabilities, request personalized feedback for clarification and understanding.

C4.1 Key points for proactive engagement in your education: 1. Communicate your interests to the teacher; express preferences. 2. Suggest methodology changes if you have alternative recommendations. 3. Inform the teacher about your preferred resources and learning methods. 4. Regularly review the syllabus to ensure alignment with course expectations. 5. If unsure, engage with the teacher to clarify any gaps in understanding.

6. Connect the course goals with your professional aspirations for a meaningful learning experience.

C5.1 Key points for effective studying: 1. Maintain a positive mindset; not every day is equally productive. 2. Recognize the importance of rest; sometimes, revisiting later is more effective. 3. Identify challenging issues and communicate them to the teacher. 4. Acknowledge that concepts vary in difficulty; allocate time accordingly. 5. Organize and study in advance for better preparation. 6. Plan your schedule to ensure ample time for homework, enhancing its quality. 7. Seek a second opinion from classmates or the teacher before submitting homework for improved accuracy and understanding.

C6.1 Key points for active participation in the classroom: 1. Engage in activities and volunteer for various tasks. 2. Inform the teacher about your diverse interests and willingness to contribute. 3. Communicate openly about needing more time when necessary. 4. Overcome shyness; express your ideas freely, understanding that mistakes contribute to learning. 5. Offer to volunteer for course-related activities if possible. 6. Strategically showcase your capabilities by selecting opportunities that align with your strengths. 7. Support your classmates in course activities, fostering a collaborative learning environment.

Relatedness. R1.1 Addressing challenges in group dynamics. Scenario 1: Feeling Disconnected in a Group: 1. Consider switching to another group. 2. Initiate conversations with new people. 3. Showcase your abilities or offer assistance to foster connections with classmates. **Scenario 2: Addressing a Student Issue in a Group:** 1. Privately talk with the student to understand the situation. 2. Based on the discussion: 2a: In case of toxic behaviors, engage with classmates to address the issue. 2b: In other situations, discuss the matter with the teacher for additional perspectives and support.

R2.1 Addressing Personal Behaviors: 1. Reflect on your own behaviors; consider adjustments where possible to contribute positively to the learning environment. 2. Encourage open communication with classmates to enhance mutual understanding and a positive atmosphere. **R2.2 Promoting Collaboration:** 1. Engage in team-building activities and collaborative projects to create opportunities for working together with fellow students. 2. If there's a conflict with a specific classmate, express concerns to teachers, and avoid being paired with them in assignments to ensure a more comfortable learning experience.

R3.1 Fostering Social Connections: 1. Aim to have a daily conversation with someone to build connections and a sense of community. 2. Appreciate opportunities for collaborative work, allowing for shared learning experiences and teamwork. **R3.2 Respecting Personal Boundaries:** 1. Acknowledge that not everyone may feel comfortable with constant socialization. 2. Understand that forcing social interactions can be counterproductive, and it's important to respect individual preferences and comfort levels.

R4.1 Building Connections Outside the Classroom: 1. Endeavor to meet someone in informal settings like the cafeteria or campus square to broaden social connections beyond the classroom. 2. Initiate conversations about shared hobbies to find common interests and foster connections. **R4.2 Perspective on Friendship in University:** 1. In a university setting, the emphasis on friendships may differ, and it's not necessarily viewed as problematic. 2. Acknowledge that, in the university environment, as long as individuals get along well, the necessity of formal friendships might be less emphasized compared to other academic stages.

R5.1 Self-Reflection on Authenticity: 1. Reflect on whether you authentically express yourself to others, ensuring genuine connections. **R5.2 Encouraging Interaction:** 1. If you find yourself not engaging with classmates, challenge yourself to interact more actively with them. 2. Feel free to share your feelings with classmates; it can lead to open communication and a supportive environment.

R6.1 Building Outside-Class Connections: 1. Take the initiative to meet classmates in casual settings outside the classroom for a more relaxed interaction. **R6.2 Enhancing Collaboration:** 1. Advocate for more collaborative activities to create additional chances for interaction and teamwork. 2. Explore and adopt suggested approaches to connect with classmates, similar to the concepts presented in R6 and R9.

R7.1 Personal Reflection: 1. Take a moment to consider if there are valid reasons or evidence behind your thoughts on a particular matter. **R7.2 Observing and Addressing Behavior:** 1. If a fellow student seems to exhibit problematic behavior, approach them with observations or engage in a conversation. If toxicity is identified, you can consult a teacher to offer advice or provide support. 2. In the absence of toxic behavior, actively create opportunities for networking, fostering positive connections among students.

R8.1 Expanding Social Connections in Class: 1. Take a moment to recognize if there are individuals in the classroom whom you haven't engaged in conversation with. 2. The same principles of R7 can be applied.

4 Discussion

The adaptation of the scale brought quite some challenges and insightful takeaways. We revolve our discussion around two main themes, each discussing the two contributions of this paper:

First Contribution: Scale validation and differences in collaboration between work and education contexts. Even though learning and collaboration are two essential outcomes in both work and education within CSCL and CSCW environments [7], their objectives differ to some extent. For instance, [14] discusses even though CSCL and CSCW both build on shared theories of cognition, but their implications may vary for students versus professionals. Examples of these differences can be found in the way students may understand or formulate a question, and we found four critical ones: **1. Context**: The context of the original BPNSS-Work scale fully takes place in the workplace, but when adapting the questions to an educational context, various options come up. Two of these options are observed during the validation process, which are the classroom context and the course context. These two contexts may vary depending on the educational level [20, 21] (e.g. secondary education vs higher education), where a classroom setting makes more sense to secondary education setting (where students belong to one classroom during the school term), and a course makes more sense in higher education settings (where students rotate classes as well as peers depending on which course they are taking). Therefore, in further evaluations of the scale it is important to differentiate between this type of contexts, providing practitioners with the option to adapt the scale depending on their own educational context. **2. Skills vs knowledge**:

The second difference lies in skill building vs knowledge building. While skill building is vital in both work and education settings, knowledge building is also a prominent outcome in educational settings [17]. **3. Autonomy in work vs education**: The third difference lies in item A4 ("When I am at work, I have to do what I am told" adapted to "During classroom activities, I have to do exactly what the teachers say"). This item can become problematic since in the original scale it counts as a negative impact item. But for students, listening to what the teacher says is perceived as something positive, a notion also supported by [18]. This is especially important in how professionals and students might perceive the figures of authority within their respective contexts: in education, students' perception of interpersonal teacher behavior is a crucial regulator for both students' and teacher well-being [19], especially when the teacher's communication style and skills are perceived by the students as positive [18]. Furthermore, dropping this item from the adapted scale resulted in a lower internal consistency, which might point out a difference in the autonomy perception in education vs work settings. **4. Wording**: Similar to the first point, the wording of some items might slightly change depending on the educational context. For instance, course-work vs learning activities. Both might be similar but have different implications depending on the educational context the scale might be used in (e.g. secondary education vs higher education). This point also includes the need to balance out negatively formulated items vs positively formulated questions.

Second Contribution: Recommendations. As for the second contribution regarding the recommendations, even though these are still in preliminary stages, it is important to keep in mind that the implications observed in the first contribution also apply to the recommendations, especially the implications regarding the Context and the Wording.

These implications shed light on which areas to work on in the future iterations that are needed to further validate the scale.

The resulting questionnaire, considering all these implications, can be found in the supplementary material [22].

5 Conclusions and Future Work

This work explored two main contributions: first, the adaptation of a SDT-based scale that helps with the understanding of the collaborative classroom dynamics from a well-being perspective, and the second contribution revolves around potential recommendations that can be used as a tool to support the well-being of the students taking the questionnaire of the first contribution. In the first contribution we explored the validation process of the scale, as well as the potential drawbacks and differences that might arise when adapting a scale, even when the context is similar. Future work regarding this first contribution includes further iterations taking into account the four main implications considered in the discussion section.

As for the second contribution, and connected with the first one, it opens the opportunity to be implemented as learning analytics in TEL systems, where the idea behind taking the questionnaire is to not only diagnose students' well-being during collaborative classroom dynamics, but also provide ways in which they can improve them. Furthermore, this paper provides the scale with all variables, metrics and associated recommendations in order to be implemented for data collection and analysis in CSCL environments. Moreover, offering the recommendations and generating them automatically after taking the questionnaire could offer advantages such as monitoring the classroom dynamics during the duration of the course, providing both the teachers and students tools for individual and classroom self-regulation during their collaborative process [16]. In this regard, this paper presents all the necessary validation work beforehand, crucial for ensuring the proper implementation of such a tool.

In considering the potential of the scale from the perspective of teachers, leveraging the scale opens up avenues for refining classroom management techniques from a well-being perspective. By utilizing the insights provided by the scale, teachers can tailor activities to better suit the BPNs and collaborative dynamics of their students, ultimately creating a more engaging and productive learning environment [15]. Moreover, the scale serves as a tool for educators to enhance interactions between student groups. By understanding the dynamics and preferences of different groups, teachers can facilitate collaboration and teamwork, fostering a sense of community within the classroom [15].

On the student side, the scale and its resulting recommendations play a crucial role in promoting well-being and self-regulation in a collaborative environment. By providing students with personalized feedback and strategies for improvement (i.e. recommendations), the scale empowers them to take ownership of their learning journey. This not only enhances academic performance but also cultivates essential learning and well-being skills such as self-regulation in the classroom [16].

Acknowledgments. This work was supported in part by PID2020-112584RB-C33 funded by MCIN/AEI/https://doi.org/10.13039/501100011033, the Ramón y Cajal programme (P. Santos) and ICREA under the ICREA Academia programme (D. Hernández-Leo, Serra Hunter).

Disclosure of Interests. The authors report no conflicts of interest.

References

1. Mullins, D., Rummel, N., Spada, H.: Are two heads always better than one? differential effects of collaboration on students' computer-supported learning in mathematics. Int. J. Comput.-Support. Collab. Learn. **6**, 421–443 (2011). https://doi.org/10.1007/s11412-011-9122-z
2. Laal, M., Ghodsi, S.: Benefits of collaborative learning. Procedia Soc. Behav. Sci. **31**, 486–490 (2012). https://doi.org/10.1016/J.SBSPRO.2011.12.091
3. Peters, D., Calvo, R.A., Ryan, R.M.: Designing for motivation, engagement and wellbeing in digital experience. Front. Psychol. **9**, 300159 (2018)
4. Deci, E.: Motivation and education: the self-determination perspective (2008). https://doi.org/10.1080/00461520.1991.9653137
5. Hakami, E., El Aadmi-Laamech, K., Hakami, L., Santos, P., Hernández-Leo, D., Amarasinghe, I.: Students' basic psychological needs satisfaction at the interface level of a computer-supported collaborative learning tool. In: Wong, L.H., Hayashi, Y., Collazos, C.A., Alvarez, C., Zurita, G., Baloian, N. (eds.) Collaboration Technologies and Social Computing. CollabTech 2022. LNCS, vol. 13632, pp. 218–230. Springer, Cham (2022). https://doi.org/10.1007/978-3-031-20218-6_15

6. Vuopala, E., Hyvönen, P., Järvelä, S.: Interaction forms in successful collaborative learning in virtual learning environments. Act. Learn. High. Educ. **17**, 25–38 (2016). https://doi.org/10.1177/1469787415616730
7. Stahl, G.: Groupware Goes to School, pp. 7–24 (2002). https://doi.org/10.1007/3-540-46124-8_2
8. Moliner, L., Alegre, F., Cabedo-Mas, A., Chiva-bartoll, O.: Social well-being at school: development and validation of a scale for Primary Education students. Front. Educ. **6**, 800248 (2021)
9. Arsalani, N., Fallahi-Khoshknab, M., Ghaffari, M., Josephson, M., Lagerstrom, M.: Adaptation of questionnaire measuring working conditions and health problems among Iranian nursing personnel. Asian Nurs. Res. **5**(3), 177–182 (2011)
10. Deci, E.L., Ryan, R.M.: The "what" and "why" of goal pursuits: human needs and the self-determination of behavior. Psychol. Inq. **11**, 227–268 (2000)
11. Deci, E.L., Ryan, R.M., Gagné, M., Leone, D.R., Usunov, J., Kornazheva, B.P.: Need satisfaction, motivation, and well-being in the work organizations of a former eastern bloc country: a cross-cultural study of self-determination. Pers. Social Psychol. Bull. **27**(8), 930–942 (2001). https://doi.org/10.1177/0146167201278002
12. Ilardi, B.C., Leone, D., Kasser, R., Ryan, R.M.: Employee and supervisor ratings of motivation: main effects and discrepancies associated with job satisfaction and adjustment in a factory setting. J. Appl. Soc. Psychol. **23**, 1789–1805 (1993)
13. Kasser, T., Davey, J., Ryan, R.M.: Motivation, dependability, and employee supervisor discrepancies in psychiatric vocational rehabilitation settings. Rehabil. Psychol. **37**, 175–187 (1992)
14. Stahl, G.: Theories of collaborative cognition: foundations for CSCL and CSCW together, pp. 43–63 (2013). https://doi.org/10.1007/978-1-4614-1740-8_3
15. Jang, H., Kim, E.J., Reeve, J.: Why students become more engaged or more disengaged during the semester: a self-determination theory dual-process model. Learn. Instr. **43**, 27–38 (2016)
16. Boekaerts, M., Corno, L.: Self-regulation in the classroom: a perspective on assessment and intervention. Appl. Psychol. **54**(2), 199–231 (2005)
17. Méhaut, P., Winch, C.: The European qualification framework: skills, competences or knowledge? Eur. Educ. Res. J. **11**(3), 369–381 (2012)
18. Andersen, J., Norton, R., Nussbaum, J.: Three investigations exploring relationships between perceived teacher communication behaviors and student learning. Commun. Educ. **30**, 377–392 (1981). https://doi.org/10.1080/03634528109378493
19. Petegem, K., Aelterman, A., Rosseel, Y., Creemers, B.: Student perception as moderator for student wellbeing. Soc. Indic. Res. **83**, 447–463 (2007). https://doi.org/10.1007/S11205-006-9055-5
20. Lam, B., Kember, D.: The relationship between conceptions of teaching and approaches to teaching. Teach. Teach. **12**, 693–713 (2006). https://doi.org/10.1080/13540600601029744
21. Axmedov, M.M., Hojikarimova, G.T., Boybabayev, R.H., Safarova, G.M.: Supporting innovative approaches in the education system. Academicia: Int. Multidisc. Res. J. **11**(1), 38–41 (2021). https://doi.org/10.5958/2249-7137.2021.00001.X
22. El Aadmi-Laamech, K., Santos Rodriguez, P., Hernández-Leo, D.: Supplementary material - Adaptation of a self-determination theory-based questionnaire on collaborative classroom dynamics. Zenodo (2024). https://doi.org/10.5281/zenodo.11370809
23. Rienties, B., Giesbers, B., Tempelaar, D., Lygo-Baker, S., Segers, M., Gijselaers, W.: The role of scaffolding and motivation in CSCL. Comput. Educ. **59**(3), 893–906 (2012)
24. Chen, K.C., Jang, S.J., Branch, R.M.: Autonomy, affiliation, and ability: relative salience of factors that influence online learner motivation and learning outcomes. Knowl. Manag. E-Learn. Int. J. **2**(1), 30–50 (2010)

25. Beers, P.J., Boshuizen, H.P., Kirschner, P.A., Gijselaers, W.H.: The analysis of negotiation of common ground in CSCL. Learn. Instr. **17**(4), 427–435 (2007)
26. Chen, K.C., Jang, S.J.: Motivation in online learning: testing a model of self-determination theory. Comput. Hum. Behav.Behav. **26**(4), 741–752 (2010)

Exploring Group Behavior and Discussion Productivity in Anonymous Chatrooms for Ethical Decision-Making

Claudio Álvarez[1(✉)], Gustavo Zurita[2], Antonio Farías[2], and Manuel Yunga[3]

[1] Facultad de Ingeniería y Ciencias Aplicadas, Universidad de los Andes, Santiago, Chile
calvarez@uandes.cl
[2] Facultad de Economía y Negocios, Departamento de Control de Gestión y Sistemas de Información, Universidad de Chile, Santiago, Chile
{gzurita,anfari}@fen.uchile.cl
[3] Universidad Técnica Particular de Loja, Loja, Ecuador
mayunga@utpl.edu.ec

Abstract. Discussing ethical dilemmas is a common practice in teaching professional ethics. Technology-supported collaboration scripts facilitate case analysis activities by providing features like automatic grouping of participants based on specific criteria and anonymous chatrooms for discussing controversial or sensitive ethical issues without fear of judgment or criticism. However, the group behavior in this context, particularly that of participants with minority viewpoints, needs a thorough investigation to understand whether anonymity and chat communication alone lead to productive discussions. In this study, we analyzed the behavior of 258 students from various higher education programs at a Latin American University while discussing an ethical dilemma and striving for a consensus on its resolution. We aimed to identify recurring group behaviors regarding discussion productivity, characterize them, and determine the most frequent. We also examined the behavior patterns of students holding minority positions within these groups. Our findings suggest that anonymity does not inherently foster productive discussions, as the most common group behavior patterns tend towards quick consensus building around the first decision proposed by a peer. Additionally, while we observed various behaviors among minority peers, they often conformed to the majority stance. We discuss the potential causes of these phenomena, the implications for designing environments for such applications, and the prospect of developing AI-based agents and facilitators to enhance discussions.

Keywords: Group Behavior · Anonymous Discussions · Ethics · Groupware

1 Introduction

Teaching ethics in educational contexts often faces the challenge of fostering discussion processes about moral dilemmas [1]. EthicApp emerges as an innovative tool that integrates individual and anonymous collaborative work phases in its script [2–8] and seeks to support discussion processes based on case-based learning [2]. Through EthicApp, ethical dilemmas can be addressed in a structured manner, promoting the exposure of students' viewpoints and more affluent, more diverse deliberation, mainly when conducted among small peer teams through mechanisms of anonymous chat communication. However, the influence of anonymity in these learning dynamics is a territory that requires exploration in this context, especially regarding conformity, minority behavior, equity, and the quality of group decisions. In this context, it is crucial to investigate the efficacy of anonymous chat to reach a reflective and well-founded ethical consensus, which responds to the dichotomous nature of the presented dilemmas and reflects a nuanced understanding of the complexities of the ethical decisions involved.

Using anonymous chat as a means of decision-making in small groups within educational settings presents unique challenges regarding participant dynamics, communication quality, and consensus-building effectiveness. It is essential to evaluate whether anonymity promotes more honest and equitable participation or decreases individual accountability and potential negative dynamics among participants. Additionally, whether anonymous chat allows for a deep and meaningful discussion of the presented ethical dilemmas or encourages superficial and detached responses should be considered.

Potential issues in anonymous chat interactions include the possibility that anonymity can enhance or detract from the quality of dialogue. For example, it may encourage the expression of controversial opinions or lead to trivial consensus due to a lack of personal identification [3]. Conformity dynamics can result in group members following dominant voices without visible identifiers [4]. Additionally, anonymous chat might facilitate or obscure conflict management, preventing honest dialogue and problem-solving [5]. Finally, anonymity can impact the participation of minority voices, either promoting equity in participation or reinforcing majority dominance [6, 7].

Using anonymous chat for group decision-making in educational contexts is a potentially powerful but double-edged tool. On the one hand, it can stimulate more accessible and equitable participation without the inhibitions often associated with personal identification. On the other hand, there is a risk that anonymity may promote irresponsibility, uncritical conformity, or even negative behaviors. Given this duality, exploring how these dynamics manifest in practice and the net balance regarding communication quality, dialogue effectiveness, and equity in participation is a highly relevant aspect with implications for the design of online learning environments for ethics education.

The following research questions are proposed:

- **RQ1**: In the context of anonymous chat interaction in small groups with EthicApp, how often do productive discussion dynamics manifest?
- **RQ2**: In the decision-making process of small groups using anonymous chat on EthicApp, what recurring patterns of communication (productive or not) emerge, and how do these relate to the effectiveness of the decision process?
- **RQ3**: What is the behavior of minorities compared to majorities in small groups (of 3 members) in the decision-making process in this context of anonymous discussions?

2 Social Influence and Moral Conformity

Moral judgments are social, and discussions with others continually shape them [8]. Humans are social beings who live in communities, work in social environments, and interact through social media. As such, they are constantly subject to social influences. People often adjust high cognitive aspects of their behavior, including preferences, judgments, and attitudes, to conform to others to gain affiliation, maintain a positive self-concept, or obtain rewards [9].

Many scholars have studied this effect since Solomon Asch's seminal studies in 1956 [10]. Different experiments have demonstrated conformity effects in scenarios ranging from judgments regarding the acceptability of torture [11] and decency violations [12] to risk-taking behaviors involving monetary decisions [13]. A domain that has gained increasing attention from researchers regarding the conformity effect is the context of moral decision-making [14]. People make ethical decisions daily, and their choices in such contexts may be susceptible to influence from their peers, a phenomenon commonly referred to as the moral conformity effect. Investigating whether people conform to the ethical opinions of others is interesting, as moral questions might not always have an obvious correct answer [15].

To explore moral conformity, scholars have examined social influence on ethical decision-making. This line of research delves into understanding how external influences, such as social norms and peer opinions, shape individuals' moral reasoning and behavior [16]. Kundu and Cummins [14] used a variation of the Asch paradigm, questioning if moral decisions are prone to conform to majority views. Involving 33 participants, the study compared moral judgments made individually and within a group, using a Likert scale for responses. Results showed significant conformity, with social pressure altering the permissibility of actions.

Recent research has focused on moral conformity in online environments [9, 15], spurred by the increased online interaction among younger generations and amplified by the COVID-19 pandemic. Utilizing a modified Solomon Asch paradigm on Zoom, a study involving 120 participants assessed responses to moral dilemmas in both individual and group contexts [17]. The findings reveal a notable moral conformity effect, with participants aligning with the group consensus in half of the dilemmas. Additionally, scholarship in the past two decades has explored the interplay between anonymity and conformity. This suggests that anonymity influences conformity depending on whether individuals are in a group setting or acting alone [9].

Kelly et al. experimented to study whether moral conformity can be extended to anonymous online settings [15]. In this experiment, 302 participants were tasked with completing an online survey while presenting statistical information regarding the frequency of a particular response chosen by others. The results confirm the influence of social norms on moral conformity, even in anonymous online environments. Participants tended to perceive actions as more acceptable when most previous respondents also deemed the action acceptable, and conversely, for actions judged as unacceptable.

In summary, the literature suggests that people always conform to others' opinions across different contexts, even in anonymous online situations [9]. This is particularly interesting in higher education settings because of the permanent growth of online courses and the growing emphasis on collaborative and interactive learning experiences online, so studies investigating the social influences within this domain are welcomed [18]. In collaborative learning environments - a common feature in undergraduate programs nowadays - this is especially important because the observed tendency to conform may undermine the work productivity of students. Moreover, anonymous collaborative learning activities may enhance conformity by reducing individuals' sense of accountability [18] or fostering depersonalization [19].

3 Exploratory Study

3.1 Educational Context and Sample Description

This study was conducted with teachers and student samples from Universidad Técnica Particular de Loja (UTPL), a private higher education institution located in Loja, Ecuador. Students from a general ethics training course, part of the institution's cross-disciplinary training program, participated, resulting in the enrollment of students from 15 different majors, including Biology, Biochemistry, Physiotherapy, Medicine, Nursing, Business Administration, Economics, Finance, Gastronomy, Telecommunications, Environmental Engineering, Educational Psychology, and Clinical Psychology. The student sample from the course numbered 445, mostly aged between 20 and 24 years. The intervention involved ten different teachers and one coordinating teacher.

3.2 Materials

This section will describe the materials used for this research: the teaching support application EthicApp, the case study used, and the script of the designed pedagogical activity.

EthicApp. It is a collaborative application that includes functionalities for designing and executing collaborative learning activities supporting decision-making, such as those required in ethical teaching situations or teaching various contents that use the case-based learning methodology and where students are required to engage in processes of reflection and discussion. EthicApp was developed based on the analysis of literature on how to support ethical teaching [2, 20–22] and has been applied to date under different purposes, configurations, and research objectives, such as promoting ethical discussions [23], assessing ethical discernment under incentives in business students [24], fostering reflection and reasoning in role-playing contexts [25], reducing the cognitive load of teachers by providing automated content analysis of student responses [26], evaluating whether reflective questions and social interaction can influence ethical reasoning initially guided by intuition [27], integrating implicit Human-Computer Interaction (iHCI) to enhance student participation in ethical case discussions [28], and studying the influence of peers in ethical education using rankings in a group setting [29]; all of the above, with different cohorts of students, degrees, and universities.

EthicApp allows the specification of a series of phases with questions to be answered individually and collaboratively, embodying in each phase aspects required to facilitate reflection and discussion. It provides functionalities for synchronous communication via anonymous chat so that students can openly express their points of view without being subject to value judgments from their peers, thereby potentially reducing any anxiety that might arise; however, it also considers that participants might conform due to anonymity.

EthicApp supports collaborative and individual learning in in-person and virtual settings, accommodating case-based discussions with synchronous or asynchronous options [1, 2]. It caters to ethical dilemmas or content from any subject area, prompting students to decide on specific dichotomous issues. Configurable for 2 to any number of participants, it groups students based on random or previous response similarity or diversity. Teachers can craft questions that delve into the nuances and complexities of cases, demanding students to make choices on a semantic differential scale of 2 to n points. These questions can be tailored to extract nuanced positions or preferences, and students may provide justifications to satisfy specific educational objectives. EthicApp also features a teacher's dashboard for activity monitoring, with the application accessible on various devices, including smartphones, tablets, laptops, and PCs.

Sebastian Case. The pedagogical activity supporting ethical teaching considers a dichotomous ethical case, named 'Sebastian Case.' The case centers on Sebastian, a university student confronting the possibility of failing an accounting course. The ramifications of failure are severe: it could derail his academic progress and lead to financial strife for his family, who depend on a scholarship for his tuition. Faced with such stakes, Sebastian reaches out to his best friend, the narrator of the case, in search of assistance to pass his exam, hinting at cheating as a solution. Raised with a strong emphasis on hard work and honesty by his family, Sebastian finds himself at a moral crossroads, contemplating actions that conflict with his upbringing. Meanwhile, the narrator, Sebastian's confidant, is torn. While understanding Sebastian's predicament, he is troubled by the suggestion of dishonesty, especially given his own negative experiences with the consequences of such actions. This ethical case underscores the clash between one's principles and the formidable external pressures that can drive students to consider compromising their values when faced with critical challenges.

Activity Script. Table 1 describes the script for the pedagogical activity, supported by EthicApp, which comprises 5 phases, each with a question to be answered individually or collaboratively based on a Rating Scale (RS) from 1 to 4 and its respective justification in some of these phases. A scale ranging from 1 to 4 was chosen to force an answer toward one of the poles. The poles of the RS present the dichotomous ethical decision of "Helping Sebastian with his exam" or "Not helping him with his exam," with the selection being intentional due to the type of questions in each phase.

In **phase 1**, students encounter a vignette summarizing the "Sebastian Case" without knowing its details. They are required to respond to a question individually within 30 s to capture their initial intuition.

In **phase 2**, after reading a one-page case description, students re-answer the same question individually in 30 s, engaging their initial reasoning with more context.

Phase 3 involves a vignette presenting two specific viewpoints of the case. It prompts students to select a stance on the Response Spectrum (RS) and justify their choice in detail within 5 min, preparing them for peer discussions in the next phase.

In **phase 4**, EthicApp creates diverse three-member teams based on differing phase 3 responses to facilitate collaborative answer formation via anonymous chat, fostering debate and consensus-building. The intention of this and previous phases is for the

Table 1. Activity Script.

P			M	J	T
p1	In	Complete the rating scale			
	Q	Sebastian, a very good friend of yours, needs to pass the Accounting course to stay in the program. He's really struggling and asks you to help him with the online exam. **What would you do?**	I	N	30s
	RS	I help him answer the exam (1) (2) (3) (4) I don't help him answer the exam			
p2	In	Read the "Sebastian Case"	I		3m
	In	Complete the rating scale			
	Q	Sebastian, a very good friend of yours, needs to pass the Accounting course to stay in the program. He's struggling and asks you to help him with the online exam. **What would you do?**	I	N	30s
	RS	I help him answer the exam (1) (2) (3) (4) I don't help him answer the exam			
p3	In	Respond to the rating scale in detail, providing arguments that justify your response			
	Q	**On one hand,** Sebastian needs to pass the exam, and I owe him a lot for his loyalty and friendship. He and his family even took me in for a few months during the pandemic. If he doesn't finish the course well, he'll have serious financial problems to continue studying. **On the other hand,** Sebastian and I have been critical of those who cheat or copy to progress in our courses. We always fight against those who try to take shortcuts. We put in a lot of effort to pass our courses and genuinely want to be good professionals. **Given Sebastian's situation, my decision would be:**	I	Y	5m
	RS	I help him answer the exam (1) (2) (3) (4) I don't help him answer the exam			
p4	In	Agree among all of us on the response, discussing anonymously via chat aspects you have already considered or others you have not considered in the previous questions. Everyone must choose the same numerical value in the response, even though each person can provide different justification arguments			
	Q	**Given Sebastian's situation, my decision would be:**	C	Y	15m
	RS	I help him answer the exam (1) (2) (3) (4) I don't help him answer the exam			
p5	In	Considering all of the above and especially after agreeing on the response with your peers, you can again give your individual response			
	Q	**Given Sebastian's situation, my decision would be:**	I	Y	5m
	RS	I help him answer the exam (1) (2) (3) (4) I don't help him answer the exam			

Notation. Px = phase x. M = Modality (p1 to p5 refer to phase 1 to phase 5). In = Instructions. Q = Question. RS = Rating Scale. M = Modality. J = Justification. I = Individual. C = Collaborative. T = Time (m, minutes; s, seconds). Y = Yes. N = No.

student to consider different stances of the case to foster discussion with their peers in the next phase. Furthermore, to answer the research questions, the responses provided by the students in phases 3 and 4 were analyzed.

Phase 5 allows students to independently articulate their final decision, informed by their initial responses and insights from the collaborative deliberations.

3.3 Measures and Analyses

Data Collection. This includes the students' responses to phase 3 of the instructional design, which are individual responses before group discussion, encompassing the numerical value each student marked on a four-point semantic differential scale ranging from "help" (1) to "not help" (4) for Sebastian. Additionally, each participant's numerical responses from phase 4 and a complete transcript of their anonymous chat conversation are included. Finally, the individual response following the group discussion corresponding to phase 5 is also incorporated.

Analysis of Group Discussion Behavior. To address research questions RQ1 and RQ2, an initial search for productive discussion behaviors within groups was conducted, utilizing a complete transcript of the chat rooms during student activities. EthicApp automatically generated this transcript, which the authors of this study subsequently reviewed. Based on the transcripts, the authors determined the presence of specific recurring patterns in the sample, the most frequent being a rapid consensus among participants regarding the first option presented by one of them, with little to no debate of ideas. Based on this observation, a prompt was formulated by the present authors (see Table 2) to perform a semi-automated analysis of all chat room transcripts using OpenAI's completions API (https://platform.openai.com/docs/api-reference) with the Large Language Model (LLM) "gpt-4-turbo-preview". The prompt underwent numerous iterations of trial and error before reaching its optimal form. The authors deemed the prompt satisfactory when the model reliably identified groups following rapid consensus or exhibiting unproductive discussion patterns and those engaging in productive discussions. The client code was written in R version 4.3.1, using the 'openai' package. The authors manually verified the analyses produced by the model for each group to ensure consistency with the actual discussions in each chat room. The authors discerned the patterns of group discussion from these automated analyses.

Analysis of Minority Behavior. To focus on RQ3, we analyzed the behavior of minority peers based on the data generated by groups of three in phase 4. This is because groups of two and four peers are less common, as they are only formed with the remaining students after forming groups of three. To understand the frequency with which groups decide considering the majority stance, the minority stance, or the middle ground, we constructed a two-dimensional heatmap data representation. The heatmap cells display the number of groups transitioning from a particular state of peer responses in phase 3 (e.g., $<1,1,4>$) to another state of responses in phase 4 (e.g., $<2,2,2>$). Minority participants were determined for each group in phase 3, considering the absolute difference between the chosen response in phase 3 and the group average in phase 3 as a metric. If this difference exceeds the group's standard deviation, the response (and the peer who generated it) is considered a minority. Then, the map is analyzed cell by cell to determine the nature of the decision taken by the group; that is, whether the group in phase 4 leans towards reaching a consensus that consists of opting for the majority response or whether the group decides to negotiate an intermediate stance, or if the group ends up leaning towards the minority stance. Cases where groups in phase 4 do not reach an agreement are also recorded. To delve deeper into the behavior of minority participants, the present authors developed a second prompt for the same language model mentioned above (see Table 3). Based on this prompt, chat message transcripts, and LLM responses, the authors of this study seek to identify different patterns of minority behavior and their frequency in the sample.

Table 2. Prompt utilized with the LLM to analyze groups' discussion behavior.

LLM Prompt #1 – Analysis of group discussion behavior
"I have a csv file containing the transcription of an anonymous chat conversation where people are discussing an ethical dilemma; whether to help or not help a friend at risk of failing a university subject and losing their higher education funding to take an online exam. The csv file has the following columns: user_id: identifier of the user who sends the message message: text of the chat message The people in the group must agree to mark the same value on a semantic differential scale with values 1 (help the friend) and 4 (do not help the friend) The participants can see the response they individually gave to the question about helping or not helping in a previous phase before the chat discussion In many groups that we have observed, there is a pattern: One of the contributors proposes a decision to the rest (numerical value and/or explanation about it), and the rest join in without counter-arguing or debating, that is, there is practically no conflict and no clash of ideas. Can you determine if this group follows this pattern? I will give you the content of the csv file next: [FILE_CONTENTS]"

Finally, to determine if the discussion in phase 4 influences minority and non-minority participants differently, we visualize the decision paths of both types of participants in phases 3, 4, and 5 using Sankey diagrams.

3.4 Procedure

To facilitate the educational activity, necessary configurations were made one week before setting up 11 identical work sessions in EthicApp. Also, this week, students from different sections were asked to create their accounts in EthicApp. The educational activity for each session was carried out for 50 to 60 min throughout a week, with the 11 sessions spread out at different times on the days of that week. At the start of each session, in the first few minutes, the activity's objective was explained to the students, along with a general description of the phases that the students would follow in sequence.

Then, everyone was asked to be connected to the session so that the activity could begin once it was verified that all were connected, as it requires synchronous execution. If there were any doubts about how to carry out the activity, the teacher provided direct assistance to the student, with very few situations requiring assistance. The 11 sessions were carried out by each of the authors of this article, using the role of the teacher in EthicApp. At the end of each session, students were asked to express their comments on the EthicApp application, the Sebastian Case, and any other issues or comments they wanted to make.

Table 3. Prompt utilized with the LLM to analyze minority participants' behavior.

LLM Prompt #2 – Analysis of minority participant behavior
"I have a csv file containing the transcription of an anonymous chat conversation where individuals discuss an ethical dilemma; whether to help or not help a friend who is at risk of failing a university course and losing funding for their higher education, in taking an online exam. The csv file has the following columns: user_id: identifier of the user who generates the message: text of the chat message sel_a3: individual decision of the person regarding the ethical dilemma, delivered before the discussion via chat with others. The individual decision is on a semantic differential scale with values 1 (help the friend) and 4 (do not help the friend) minority: a binary variable (values TRUE/FALSE) identifying whether the person has held a minority position in the group according to the sel_a3 variable As a result of the chat conversation, individuals in the group must agree to mark the same value on a semantic differential scale with values 1 (help the friend) and 4 (do not help the friend) If there is a participant marked as a minority in the group (that is, minority with a TRUE value), please determine whether the participant defended their point of view in the discussion, influenced what was decided by the group, or simply conformed to what was proposed by the other participants I will give you the content of the csv file below: [FILE_CONTENTS]"

4 Results

4.1 Participation

The Fig. 1 summarizes students' participation in the EthicApp activity based on the number of answers submitted. The intersections depicted between phases represent the number of students who submitted responses across all the included phases. Participation in phase 4 was significantly lower, which could be attributed to the ambiguity some cohorts experienced regarding whether each group member was required to submit a response upon consensus or if a single representative's response per group would suffice. Additionally, chat data for phase 4 was recorded for 383 participants, indicating that 51 participants engaged in the discussion but did not submit their responses (with only 332 responses recorded) despite being active in the anonymous chat.

Only complete cases were considered for the subsequent analyses. Specifically, this includes 258 participants (forming 86 groups of three in phase 4), and each member submitted a response in all activity phases and participated in the chat discussion.

4.2 Group Chat Behavior Patterns

Based on the semi-automated analysis of 86 groups using an LLM with the prompt in Table 2, four patterns of group discussion were identified, as listed in Table 4. The first two are characterized by low productivity, and the last two are characterized by higher productivity, considering that some groups reached consensus (pattern 3) while others did not (pattern 4). It was determined that the pattern of group discussion behavior 1, that is, the least productive discussion, was the most frequent (Fig. 2). Only in a minority of the groups was conflict, debate, and exchange of positions in reaching a group agreement.

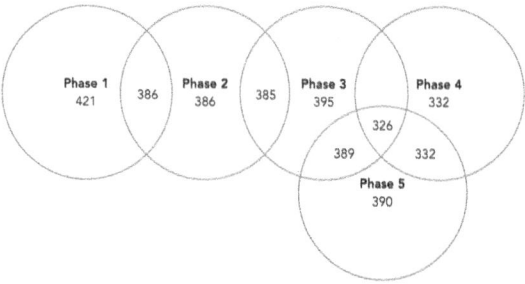

Fig. 1. Venn diagram illustrating students' participation (i.e., number of responses submitted) in the activity supported by EthicApp.

Table 4. Group discussion patterns found through LLM-supported chat transcript analysis.

GPAT	Description	LLM Sample Response
1	In the discussion, someone proposes a solution, and all others adhere without opposition or discussion of their viewpoints	"Yes, this group follows the pattern. Initially, there is debate, but in the end, one person proposes a concrete decision ("put yes") and the rest agree without further significant discussions, opting for unanimity in the final decision."
2	In the discussion, someone proposes a decision that is weakly questioned by others, but it ultimately prevails	"Yes, this group follows the pattern. One user proposes a decision (value 2) and, although there is some discussion, the others end up conforming without much confrontation, all agreeing to mark the value 2."

(*continued*)

Table 4. (*continued*)

GPAT	Description	LLM Sample Response
3	The group engages in a debate with arguments and counterarguments on different stances regarding the case before reaching a joint decision	"This group does not follow the pattern observed in other groups. Here, there is a debate with the exchange of opinions and different aspects are considered before making a collective decision. They reach a consensus after discussing and not merely by following a proposal without questioning it."
4	The group engages in a debate with arguments and counterarguments on different stances regarding the case without reaching a joint decision	"This group does not follow the pattern observed in other groups, as there is a debate with the exchange of opinions and arguments before making a final decision. There is no observed unanimous decision or conformity without discussion."

Notation. GPAT = Group discussion pattern.

To exemplify the behavior of groups with low and high productivity, we present a stage-by-stage analysis of chat transcripts from groups with these characteristics: discussion patterns 1 and 3.

Table 5 displays the stage-by-stage conversation analysis of a group matching discussion pattern 1. Participants in phase 3 had chosen < 1, 1, 4 > values on the semantic differential scale. This set-up represented a minority versus majority relationship with completely opposing decisions. According to the analysis in Table 5, in phase 4, there was a complete lack of commitment from the minority participants to their stance, which was not to help Sebastian. Instead, the participants agreed to help and chose the value 1 as the joint response without any debate. The conversation was excessively relaxed, and the participants were more engaged in joking than discussing.

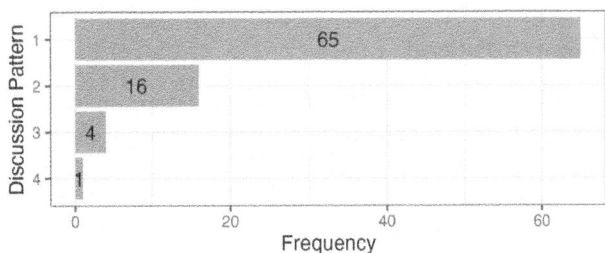

Fig. 2. Frequency of group discussion patterns observed.

Contrastingly with the previous case, Table 6 exemplifies the conversation analysis of a group matching pattern 3, however, in which there was no minority versus majority configuration. Instead, all participants had different stances, as in phase 3, with < 1, 2, 3 > values on the semantic differential scale. In phase 4, they engage in a highly productive discussion, in which they also coordinate and self-regulate effectively. They start by introducing themselves to each other and presenting the dilemma. Then, they analyze their prior evaluations and discrepancies in viewpoints. Following that, they discuss reasons and seek consensus, negotiating a middle ground. They agree on the implications of their decision. The group responds with a 3, justifying their decision based on ethical behavior and the support of the peer to prepare for their exam rather than direct exam intervention.

Table 5. Example of a group with discussion pattern 1. MR = Message number range.

Peer Responses in phase 3: < 1,1,4 >		Group Response in phase 4: 1
Analysis of Dialogue in phase 4		
Stage	MR	Relevant Actions
Initial Inquiry and Quick Agreement	1–4	The conversation begins with a question about whether to help or not help Sebastian, and the participants quickly agree, showing an initial consensus without much debate
Decision on the Response	5–10	Participants joke and decide to rate their willingness to help with the highest score, discussing briefly how to phrase their argument
Finalization and Validation	11–17	The group confirms their decision and finalizes their response, ensuring that everyone is on the same page
Casual Banter and Closure	18–25	The conversation shifts to casual banter, signaling that the decision-making process is over, and the group is relaxed

4.3 Minority Behavior Patterns

Based on the analysis of the behavior of minority peers using an LLM with the prompt in Table 3, a typology of five patterns was found with increasing defense of the minority participant's position and the degree of convincing other peers to adopt it (Table 7).

The heatmap shown in Fig. 3 displays in each cell the number of groups transitioning from a given response configuration in phase 3 (horizontal axis) to another (or the same) response configuration in phase 4 (vertical axis). Note that groups in the heatmap are only those with a peer with a minority response in phase 3 (51 groups). Responses cast by a minority participant are highlighted with an asterisk (*) character in phase 3's response configurations (e.g., < 1,1,3* >). An orange border surrounds cells in the heatmap to indicate that the group inclines towards the majority stance in their decision (e.g., consider transition < 1*,3,3 > to < 3,3,3 >). The green border color indicates that the group negotiates an intermediate stance (e.g., < 1*,3,3 > to < 2,2,2 >), and the

Table 6. Example of a group with discussion pattern 3. MR = Message number range.

Peer Responses in p3: < 1,2,3 >		Group Response in phase 4: 3
Analysis of Dialogue in phase 4		
Stage	MR	Relevant Actions
Introduction and Presentation of Dilemma	1–5	Users greet each other and introduce the need to reach a consensus on Sebastian's case
Initial Assessment and Discrepancy in Opinions	6–14	Participants reveal their initial assessments showing a wide disparity in viewpoints, indicating different evaluation criteria and personal justifications
Discussion of Reasons and Search for Consensus	15–28	Group members ask for explanations about the given ratings and discuss potential approaches to help Sebastian, focusing on preparation rather than taking the exam for him
Negotiation Towards a Middle Ground Consensus	29–40	The group leans towards a consensus by considering a "middle ground" in their evaluations, discussing an ethical compromise that avoids direct help in the exam but supports in preparation
Final Agreement and Conclusion	41–69	After a deeper discussion about values and the implications of their decisions, the group finally agrees on a rating of 3, justifying it in terms of personal values and support in preparation rather than direct exam intervention

blue border color suggests that the group inclines towards the minority stance (e.g., < 1,2,4* > to < 3,3,3 >).

From the heatmap, it is evident that the most frequent behavior of minority peers is to conform to the majority viewpoint. It is less common for a minority peer to influence their peers. Even less frequent is the negotiation of a middle ground. It is also noteworthy that in many cases, groups do not agree in phase 4, as observed in the heterogeneous response configurations on the vertical axis of the heatmap.

Figure 4 shows the frequency with which different minority behavior patterns listed in Table 7 were observed in the sample. In most cases, minority participants conform to the majority's stance. In contrast, in a minority of cases, patterns 4 and 5 are matched, meaning that the minority peer defends their stance persistently.

Figure 5 illustrates the evolution of responses from participants with minority and majority positions within their respective groups, considering phases 3 and 5 (a and b) and incorporating phase 4 (c and d). It can be observed that responses tend to stay consistent for non-minority participants, indicating that group discussion does not significantly alter

Table 7. Minority participant behavior patterns found through LLM-supported chat transcript analysis, and sample responses from the LLM corresponded to each pattern.

MPAT	Description	LLM Sample Response
1	There is no evident effort to defend his/er position, and s/he conforms to the majority	"The participant marked as a minority (user_id: 7989) defended their point of view (consistently voting for option 4, not to help the friend) in the discussion. However, they did not influence the group's final decision, as the group ultimately decided to help (value 1). It was observed that the minority participant did not change their initial position but nevertheless accepted the group's decision without further strong argumentation, integrating with conciliatory responses such as "Haha okay" and ":)"
2	There is some effort to defend his/her position, but ultimately s/he conforms to the majority	The minority participant (user_id 7994) initially defended their point of view (message: "4"), trying to influence the group's decision. However, in the end, they conformed to the group's decision, which was to choose value 2. This suggests that the minority participant did not manage to influence the final decision of the group, ending up accepting the majority decision
3	He/she is persistent in defending their position but end up negotiating a middle ground with the rest	The participant marked as a minority (8163) defended their perspective in the discussion, attempting to sway the group toward a stance closer to their own (from 1 to 2). Despite initially disagreeing with the others (positions at 3), the group ultimately adjusted their collective decision toward a middle ground (2), indicating that the minority participant had an influence on the final decision
4	He/she is persistent in defending their position and maintain it, regardless of what the others decide	The participant marked as a minority (user_id 8135) actively defended their point of view on helping their friend. They presented arguments focused on loyalty, reciprocal aid, and the importance of friendship, even suggesting that they could teach the friend afterward to ensure their understanding in the future. Although it cannot be determined with certainty if this changed the group's decision based solely on this information, it is evident that they maintained their position and argued in its defense, trying to influence others to shift their perspective toward helping

(*continued*)

Table 7. (*continued*)

MPAT	Description	LLM Sample Response
5	He/she is persistent in defending their position and manage to convince the others to respond as they do	The minority participant (8173) defended their point of view in the discussion, influenced the group's decision (moving them towards an intermediate stance, marked as 3 on the scale), and did not simply conform to the proposals of the others

Notation. MPAT: Minority behavior pattern.

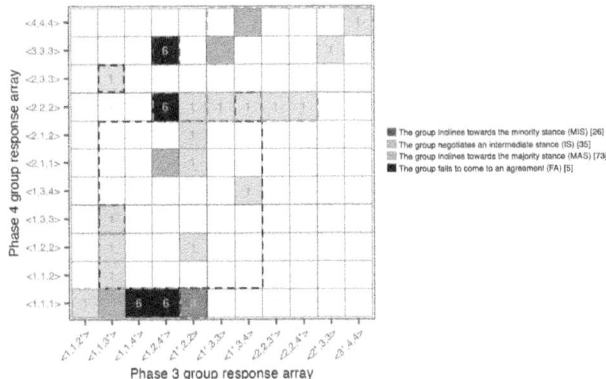

Fig. 3. Group transition map based on decisions in activities 3 and 4.

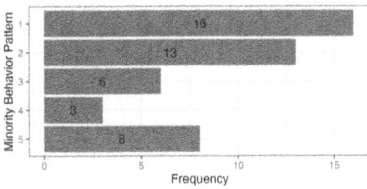

Fig. 4. Frequency of minority behavior patterns observed.

their stance in phase 5 as much as it does for minority participants. Minority participants are often seen to change stance during phase 5, influenced by the discussion (and the review of peers' responses) in phase 4. For example, in Fig. 5 (b), it is noticeable how most minority participants who had chosen option 4 in phase 3 shifted their position, with some even flipping to value 1. Likewise, in Fig. 5 (d), it is evident that minority participants conform to the majority decision and even maintain this stance in phase 5.

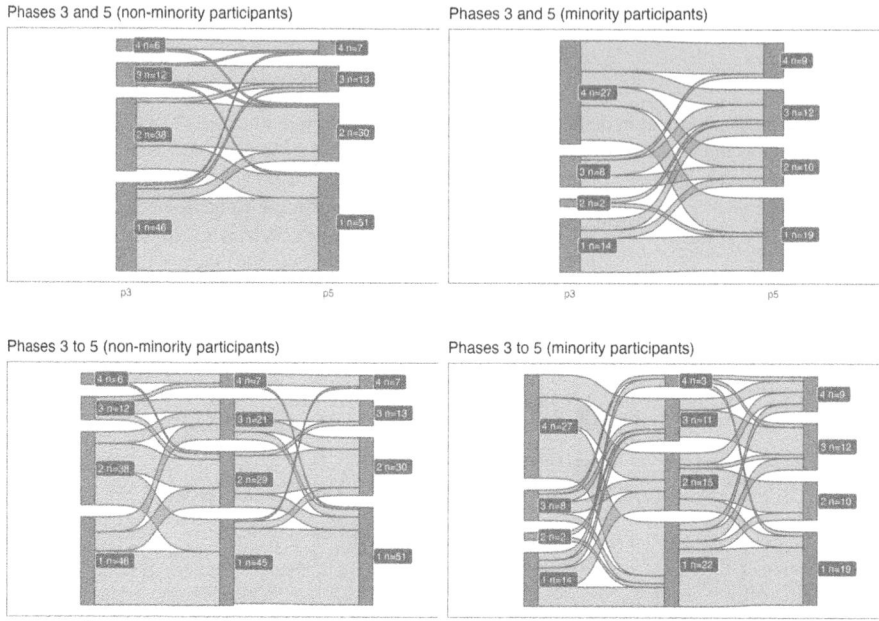

Fig. 5. Decision-making paths of non-minority and minority students before/after of phase 4 (top correlograms), and including the group discussion phase 4 (bottom correlograms).

5 Discussion

Regarding our first research question (RQ1), our analyses revealed that participants in anonymous chat rooms often quickly aligned with the initial decision presented in the conversation, exhibiting minimal conflict and generally weak or no opposition or discussion of their viewpoints. Thus, under the context studied, productive discussions were infrequently observed. In total, four group discussion patterns were found, which responds our second research question (RQ2). The third and fourth group discussion patterns can be considered of productive discussion, however, these only amounted to 5.8% of total observation (which further responds RQ1). These findings highlight the persistent influence of conformity effects across various decision-making domains, including moral judgment [9]. Lastly, regarding our third research question (RQ3), five behavioral patterns of decreasing conformity were found regarding participation of subjects holding minority positions, of which the two most prevalent were those in which subjects acted with the highest conformity, with 63% of observations. Lowest conformity patterns 4 and 5 were observed in 23.9% of analyzed groups. These findings may be attributed to the depersonalizing effect of online interactions. The absence of physical presence and the anonymity provided by the medium can reduce personal accountability and encourage the adoption of group norms [19].

The online setting of our study—characterized by anonymity and lack of direct interpersonal cues—likely contributed to a reduced sense of individual responsibility, thereby facilitating greater conformity. This is supported by research suggesting that anonymity can amplify conformity by diminishing self-regulation and fostering a more robust identification with the group [18]. These factors may explain why participants were more inclined to conform without substantial resistance, aligning with findings from other studies that have noted increased conformity in anonymous or depersonalized settings [15].

Given these observations, it is necessary to investigate further how online educational platforms can be designed to mitigate conformity issues and engage participants in genuine and productive debates. Educators and designers of online learning environments should consider these dynamics to foster environments that enhance learning and support the development of independent moral judgment. In turn, the influence of social norms on moral conformity, even in anonymous online environments, suggests a need for educational interventions that explicitly address the ethical dimensions of conformity and decision-making [30]. The design of learning environments for collaborative analysis of ethical situations mediated by anonymous chat communication could benefit from integrating artificial intelligence technologies, particularly LLMs. Recent research has shown how LLMs can facilitate group conversations [31]. Furthermore, as the research methodology in the present study has demonstrated with the post hoc processing of chat transcripts, using LLMs to monitor and analyze interactions in real time would enable the identification of unproductive patterns such as premature consensus or superficial argumentation. Upon recognizing these patterns, AI agents can tactfully intervene, posing challenging questions or requesting further elaboration to enhance the dialogue. Such AI facilitators can encourage a more reflective and reasoned discourse by prompting participants to support their views with evidence or explore alternative perspectives. This approach enriches the educational experience and promotes more deliberate and ethical group engagement. Crucially, deploying AI-driven scaffolding must be carefully managed to balance constructive guidance with respecting participant autonomy.

6 Conclusions

In this article, we present research on the effects of using anonymous chat for small group discussions in ethical decision-making. In this context, we set out to determine the frequency with which productive discussion dynamics occur in groups, the emerging patterns of group discussion behavior, and the behavior of minorities about majorities in the decision-making process. In total, four significant patterns of group discussion behavior were identified, and it was determined that under the conditions of anonymity in which discussions took place, the less productive patterns, such as rapid consensus around the first alternative proposed by one of the participants, were the most frequent behaviors among collaborators. In a minority of the groups, a healthy level of conflict was observed, with the individual responsibility of the participants to hold authentic positions and negotiate a joint solution with others.

On the other hand, regarding the behavior of minorities, it was possible to identify five patterns with decreasing levels of conformity. The dominant behavior of peers with minority positions was to align with the majority. Furthermore, a few participants with minority positions persevered in defending their stance and questioned the majority's position. We have discussed possible causes of the moral conformity phenomena encountered, explaining them based on the deindividuation in anonymous discussions, the lack of accountability for changing individual stances, and the lack of individual responsibility. However, the anonymous environment does fulfill its purpose of allowing debate without collaborators feeling inhibited from expressing their genuine points of view and positions on controversial ethical matters.

As for future work, the dysfunctional discussion patterns found in this research could be reversed by developing AI agents and facilitators to detect unproductive dialogue in groups and guide participants in decision-making.

Acknowledgments. Special thanks to all teachers and students who participated in this study at UTPL, Ecuador.

References

1. Mulhearn, T.J., et al.: Review of instructional approaches in ethics education. Sci. Eng. ethics. **23**, 883–912 (2017)
2. Thiel, C.E., et al.: Case-based knowledge and ethics education: improving learning and transfer through emotionally rich cases. Sci. Eng. Ethics **19**, 265–286 (2013)
3. Lapidot-Lefler, N., Barak, A.: Effects of anonymity, invisibility, and lack of eye-contact on toxic online disinhibition. Comput. Hum. Behav. **28**(2), 434–443 (2012)
4. Postmes, T., Spears, R., Lea, M.: Breaching or building social boundaries? SIDE-effects of computer-mediated communication. Commun. Res. **25**(6), 689–715 (1998)
5. Cialdini, R.B., Goldstein, N.J.: Social influence: compliance and conformity. Annu. Rev. Psychol. **55**, 591–621 (2004)
6. Lee, E.J.: Deindividuation effects on group polarization in computer-mediated communication: the role of group identification, public-self-awareness, and perceived argument quality. J. Commun. **57**(2), 385–403 (2007)
7. Haines, R., Cao, L., Haines, D.: Participation and persuasion via computer-mediated communication: anonymous versus identified comments. In: Proceedings of the International Conference on Information Systems, ICIS 2006, Milwaukee, Wisconsin, USA, December 10–13 (2006)
8. Keshmirian, A., Deroy, O., Bahrami, B.: Many heads are more utilitarian than one. Cognition **220**, 104965 (2022)
9. Marton-Alper, I., Sobeh, A., Shamay-Tsoory, S.: The effects of individual moral inclinations on group moral conformity. Curr. Res. Behav. Sci. **3**, 100078 (2022)
10. Goodmon, L.B., et al.: The power of the majority: social conformity in sexual harassment punishment selection. J. Appl. Soc. Psychol. **50**(8), 441–455 (2020)
11. Aramovich, N.P., Lytle, B.L., Skitka, L.J.: Opposing torture: moral conviction and resistance to majority influence. Soc. Influence **7**(1), 21–34 (2012)
12. Alshaalan, H., Gummerum, M.: Conformity on moral, social conventional and decency issues in the United Kingdom and Kuwait. Int. J. Psychol. **57**(2), 261–270 (2022)
13. Jiang, Y., et al.: People conform to social norms when gambling with lives or money. Sci. Reports **13**(1), 853 (2023)
14. Kundu, P., Cummins, D.D.: Morality and conformity: the Asch paradigm applied to moral decisions. Soc. Influence **8**(4), 268–279 (2013)
15. Kelly, M., et al.: Moral conformity in online interactions: rational justifications increase influence of peer opinions on moral judgments. Soc. Influence **12**(2–3), 57–68 (2017)

16. Bostyn, D.H., Roets, A.: Trust, trolleys and social dilemmas: a replication study. J. Exp. Psychol. Gen. **146**(5), e1 (2017)
17. Paruzel-Czachura, M., Wojciechowska, D., Bostyn, D.: Online moral conformity: how powerful is a group of strangers when influencing an individual's moral judgments during a video meeting? Curr. Psychol. **43**(7), 1–11 (2023). https://doi.org/10.1007/s12144-023-04765-0
18. Beran, T., et al.: Conformity of responses among graduate students in an online environment. Internet High. Educ. **25**, 63–69 (2015)
19. Chan, T.K., et al.: Bystanders join in cyberbullying on social networking sites: the deindividuation and moral disengagement perspectives. Inf. Syst. Res. **34**(3), 828–846 (2023)
20. Felton, E.L., Sims, R.R.: Teaching business ethics: targeted outputs. J. Bus. Ethics **60**, 377–391 (2005)
21. Johnson, J.F., et al.: Case-based ethics education: the impact of cause complexity and outcome favorability on ethicality. J. Emp. Res. Hum. Res. Ethics **7**(3), 63–77 (2012)
22. Hess, J.L., Fore, G.: A systematic literature review of US engineering ethics interventions. Sci. Eng. Ethics **24**, 551–583 (2018)
23. Alvarez, C., Zurita, G., Baloian, N., Jerez, O., Peñafiel, S.: A CSCL script for supporting moral reasoning in the ethics classroom. In: Nakanishi, H., Egi, H., Chounta, I.A., Takada, H., Ichimura, S., Hoppe, U. (eds.) CRIWG+CollabTech 2019. LNCS, vol. 11677, pp. 62–79. Springer, Cham (2019). https://doi.org/10.1007/978-3-030-28011-6_5
24. Alvarez, C., Zurita, G., Farias, A.: A collaborative pedagogical activity design for teaching ethics in a business school. In: EDULEARN21 Proceedings. IATED (2021)
25. Alvarez, C., et al.: A social platform for fostering ethical education through role-playing. Factoring Ethics Technol. Policy Making Regul. AI **107** (2021)
26. Alvarez, C., Zurita, G., Carvallo, A., Ramírez, P., Bravo, E., Baloian, N.: Automatic content analysis of student moral discourse in a collaborative learning activity. In: Hernández-Leo, D., Hishiyama, R., Zurita, G., Weyers, B., Nolte, A., Ogata, H. (eds.) CollabTech 2021. LNCS, vol. 12856, pp. 3–19. Springer, Cham (2021). https://doi.org/10.1007/978-3-030-85071-5_1
27. Álvarez, C., et al.: Scaffolding of intuitionist ethical reasoning with groupware: do students' stances change in different countries? In: Wong, L.H., Hayashi, Y., Collazos, C.A., Alvarez, C., Zurita, G., Baloian, N. (eds.) Collaboration Technologies and Social Computing: 28th International Conference, CollabTech 2022, Santiago, Chile, November 8–11, 2022, Proceedings, pp. 261–278. Springer International Publishing, Cham (2022). https://doi.org/10.1007/978-3-031-20218-6_18
28. Alvarez, C., Zurita, G., Baloian, N.: Applying the concept of implicit HCI to a groupware environment for teaching ethics. Pers. Ubiquit. Comput. **26**, 1373–1391 (2022). https://doi.org/10.1007/s00779-020-01495-z
29. Álvarez, C., Zurita, G., Carvallo, A.: Analyzing peer influence in ethical judgment: collaborative ranking in a case-based scenario. In: Hideyuki Takada, D., Marutschke, M., Alvarez, C., Inoue, T., Hayashi, Y., Hernandez-Leo, D. (eds.) Collaboration Technologies and Social Computing: 29th International Conference, CollabTech 2023, Osaka, Japan, August 29–September 1, 2023, Proceedings, pp. 19–35. Springer Nature Switzerland, Cham (2023). https://doi.org/10.1007/978-3-031-42141-9_2

30. Garcia, R.J., Shaw, E.V., Scurich, N.: Normative and informational influence in group decision making: effects of majority opinion and anonymity on voting behavior and belief change. Group Dyn. Theor. Res. Pract. **25**(4), 319 (2021)
31. Mao, M., et al.: Multi-user chat assistant (MUCA): a framework using LLMS to facilitate group conversations. arXiv preprint arXiv:2401.04883 (2024)

Extending an Intelligent Tutoring System for Oral Communication with Peer Assessment Capabilities: An Evaluation Study

Javier Ibarra[1], Claudio Álvarez[1,2], and Matías Recabarren[1(✉)]

[1] Universidad de los Andes, Chile. Facultad de Ingeniería y Ciencias Aplicadas, Santiago, Chile
mrecabarren@miuandes.cl
[2] Universidad de los Andes, Chile. Centro de Investigación en Educación y Aprendizaje, Santiago, Chile

Abstract. The ability to succinctly and effectively communicate complex ideas is increasingly recognized as a critical skill for engineering professionals, defining a realm of ill-defined learning tasks. The elevator pitch, particularly, serves as a prime example of this necessity. This study explores the extension of the EPIC intelligent tutoring system, originally designed to enhance oral communication skills in development and performance of elevator pitches through individual learning, by integrating collaborative capabilities with a focus on peer-assessment. A pilot study with 24 engineering students was conducted to assess the user experience, usability and learning outcomes. Results indicate that students' experience and usability perceptions are generally positive. Moreover, students who positively rated the peer-assessment functionalities showed marked improvements in their abilities to deliver effective elevator pitches. Pedagogical implications and design criteria aiming to improve students' valuation of collaborative work are discussed.

Keywords: Intelligent Tutoring System · Oral Communication · Peer-Assessment

1 Introduction

Intelligent Tutoring Systems (ITS) aim to provide learners with immediate and personalized instruction or feedback through computer programs, without requiring human intervention [1]. These systems have been used in various learning domains, such as geometry, mathematics, algebra, physics, and computer science [2], demonstrating their effectiveness for teaching [2,3].

The promising results of ITS in traditional domains have motivated the development of these tools for teaching more complex or "ill-defined domains" [4], such as essay writing [5]. Tasks in ill-defined domains are characterized by one or more of the following features: 1) incomplete or vague task instructions, 2) high complexity in establishing objective criteria to verify task completion, and 3) lack of clear strategies to solve tasks in each of their steps [4].

In asynchronous online learning, where students work independently and at their own pace, significant challenges can arise, especially within ill-defined domains where tasks lack clarity and solutions are not immediately apparent [4]. To succeed in these environments, learners will often need to deploy their executive functions and metacognitive strategies up to levels that can be highly demanding [6], and draw upon an array of knowledge, skills, and methods accumulated throughout their educational journey. This process often requires learners to make multiple attempts, and success is not guaranteed if they cannot find an effective resolution strategy given their current competency levels.

The ability to succinctly and effectively communicate complex ideas is increasingly recognized as a critical skill for engineering professionals, defining a realm of ill-defined learning tasks. The elevator pitch, particularly, serves as a prime example of this necessity [7]. It is a concise presentation of an idea, designed to capture a listener's interest within a brief time frame, showcasing the imperative for engineers to master synthetic communication. This skill is not limited to the relevance of the communicated content but also encompasses its efficient delivery [8]. Such capability is crucial for engineers who frequently need to convey complex technical concepts to a varied audience, including stakeholders without a technical background. Despite its significance, there is a noticeable lack of research on intelligent tutoring systems aimed at cultivating this specific oral communication skill. A recent review by Chen et al. underscores this gap [9], indicating a need for innovative educational tools that can effectively teach oral communication skills, including the elevator pitch, thereby augmenting the communicative competence of engineering students.

To address these challenge of improving oral communication skills in engineering education, educational environments must provide robust support mechanisms. One relevant way to accomplish this is through the role of peer collaboration and social support networks [10,11]. Creating opportunities for learners to engage with peers, share strategies, and offer mutual support can alleviate the isolation often experienced in asynchronous learning settings and contribute to a more engaging and effective learning experience.

In this research, we focus on enhancing the capabilities of EPIC [12], an intelligent tutoring system initially designed for individual use by students to teach oral communication skills. We extend the tutor with support for collaboration, incorporating peer-assessment features to enable students to learn from the feedback provided by others. Moreover, the design offers learners opportunities for vicarious learning through evaluating the work of their peers. We propose the design of the tutor, along with a case study involving engineering students where we evaluate their user experience, usability, and self-learning perception.

2 Literature Review: Intelligent Tutoring Systems with Collaboration Capabilities

Intelligent Tutoring Systems (ITS), traditionally designed to provide adaptive, personalized learning experiences to individuals, are increasingly being integrated into CSCL environments to augment this collaborative learning process [13,14]. ITS bring the precision of artificial intelligence to model individual learning paths and problem-solving processes, offering tailored support that resembles the assistance provided by a human tutor [9]. When applied within CSCL settings, ITS can significantly enhance the collaborative experience by providing adaptive feedback not only to individual learners but also within the group context. This integration supports the group dynamics and helps maintain a productive level of interaction, ensuring that the collaboration effectively contributes to the learning objectives of each participant [15].

The confluence of ITS and CSCL represents a promising research area in educational technology, where the adaptive and intelligent capabilities of ITS are employed to foster not just individual learning but also to enhance collaborative skills and group learning outcomes. This synergy has the potential to transform traditional learning environments by making them more responsive to the complexities of group dynamics and the specific needs of learners within a collaborative setting. By focusing on the intersection of these two areas, researchers and practitioners can develop more sophisticated systems that support a wide range of learning activities, thus addressing the nuanced demands of modern educational contexts.

Several notable studies exemplify the integration of CSCL with ITS. Tchounikine [16] emphasized the necessity for technological platforms that provide adaptive guidance and feedback, leveraging ITS to tailor support based on detailed interaction analysis. Virvou's work [17] introduced systems that merge adaptive capabilities with error diagnosis and collaborative modules, facilitating asynchronous communication in multiple languages. However, this integration was not fully explored within an ITS environment. Furthermore, Epstein [18] employed text-mining tools within an ITS to enhance learner interaction, although the focus shifted towards external web resources rather than fostering intrinsic collaborative learning.

Olsen et al. [13] investigate the effects of collaborative learning using an ITS in elementary school settings, specifically in the domain of learning fractions. The research focused on both procedural and conceptual knowledge acquisition within this subject area. The results indicated that collaborative learning environments supported by ITS could achieve similar learning gains to individual learning approaches, but with fewer problems solved. This suggests a potential efficiency in learning, as students reach equivalent educational outcomes with fewer direct interventions. This finding underscores the utility of collaborative ITS in fostering effective learning interactions and supporting the cognitive development of younger students in both individual and collaborative settings, particularly in mathematics education.

Chopade's [19] research on enabling ITS to facilitate collaborative problem solving utilized a combination of log data, eye-tracking, and audio/video recordings to enhance the collaborative experience. This approach exemplifies the trend of achieving collaboration outside the conventional ITS environments. Haq et al. [14] present a comprehensive framework for Intelligent Tutoring Supported Collaborative Learning (ITSCL), which aims to seamlessly integrate the capabilities of ITS and CSCL platforms. ITSCL distinguishes itself by supporting three types of interactions: learner-tutor, learner-learner, and group of learners-ITS, thereby enabling dynamic knowledge exchange and collaborative problem-solving among students. It was implemented within the domain of computer science education, specifically focusing on programming concepts.

The integration of ITS and CSCL environments has remained underexplored in supporting learning within ill-defined domains [9]. Tasks in these domains are often marked by incomplete or vague instructions, complexity in establishing objective criteria for task completion, and the absence of clear strategies for solving tasks step-by-step [4]. The domain of oral communication, and particularly, that of the 'Elevator Pitch' [8], is an ill-defined task domain, which has been addressed in ITS, primarily through environments designed to enhance oral communication performance skills [12,20]. However, there appears to be no existing learning environment in the literature that combines ITS with scripted collaboration to support the mastery of developing and performing an elevator pitch. In this study, we aim to propose a collaboration model that extends the capabilities of an ITS developed by the present authors, EPIC [12], to support oral communication performance for elevator pitches. We implemented collaboration features based on this model within the ITS and conducted a pilot study to evaluate the tool with a cohort of engineering students at a Latin American university.

3 EPIC Tutor Overview and Collaboration Features

3.1 Overview

The EPIC tutor supports three distinct learning designs for individual elevator pitch training, namely, designs A, B, and C, offering a spectrum of options that facilitate a range from focused practice to diverse and reinforced learning experiences [12]. Design A endorses an iterative and concentrated methodology: learners are immersed in a singular task of developing and refining an elevator pitch, with each iteration accompanied by detailed, attribute-specific feedback, culminating in a comprehensive review upon the completion of all iterations.

Design B is based on five sequential tasks across two different categories; the first compels the learner to conceive an elevator pitch from a given topic, with a strict word limit of 120 to 140 words. The second category tasks the learner with the refinement and oral presentation of an elevator pitch initially provided as written text by the ITS, thereby emphasizing delivery over creation.

Design C parallels Design B in terms of the main tasks but interlaces them with subdomain tasks. These interspersed tasks are of two types: the first type includes quizzes with five multiple-choice questions that test comprehension of the attributes essential to an effective elevator pitch. The second type comprises emulation quizzes with five questions, where learners must identify and emulate high-quality attributes from exemplary pitches. This design allows learners to hone specific facets of oral communication by choosing to engage in one to four supplementary tasks, thereby enriching their learning trajectory with targeted practice on the finer points of pitch delivery and content.

EPIC is designed to be used asynchronously. It is implemented as a conversational robot (chatbot) based on Telegram, a cross-platform instant messaging application. Through a Telegram frontend, the ITS provides the learner with all the instructions for carrying out the activities, provides feedback on their performance, among other actions. The learner develops their elevator pitch independently of the application. They then use Telegram to record and send their elevator pitch as a voice note. This allows for massive and autonomous use of the ITS.

The underlying tutor model of EPIC is constraint-based, that is, a set of constraints defines what is acceptable or unacceptable regarding learner's oral communication performance. Constraints are modeled as five quality attributes of oral presentation, in the elevator pitch delivery:

1. Long silences or fillers: Quantity of voice fillers (e.g. "uhmmm") and long pauses.
2. Passion: Sentiment expressed by transcription and voice recording.
3. Clarity: Number of words in the recorded speech that are transcribed (i.e., with Google's GCloud Speech to Text API) with a confidence above 0.8 within a range from 0 to 1.
4. Speech rate: Total words over voice-recording duration in minutes.
5. Useful words: the amount of words do not correspond to stopwords.

The above-listed attributes are operationalized as constraints based on ranges of their acceptable values. Each quality attribute of the oral delivery of an elevator pitch achieves three discrete ratings: poor, acceptable, and good. On the other hand, the tutor models the learner's state based on the same constraints as the domain model, recording which constraints the student has satisfied and which ones violated in their oral delivery of an elevator pitch. Thus the student model in the tutor is based in the domain model.

3.2 Collaboration Capabilities

The integration of collaborative learning into the EPIC tutor is manifested through the newly introduced Design D (see Fig. 1), which builds on the pedagogical strengths of the existing models while introducing a collaboration script to deepen learning outcomes. This design unfolds in three stages, beginning with individual work based on Design C's structure, but with a focus on iterative

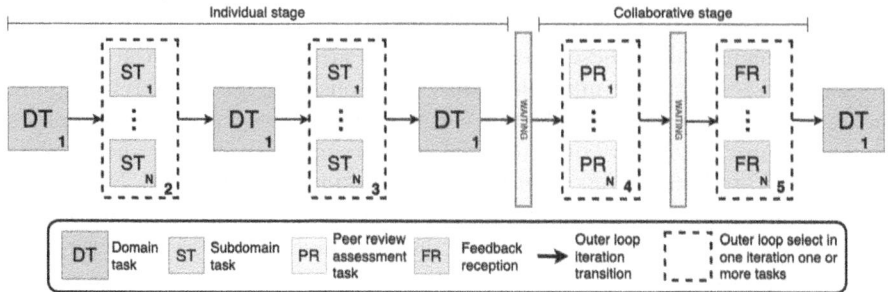

Fig. 1. EPIC outer loop with the addition of the collaborative stage

refinement of a single elevator pitch akin to Design A. Between each pitch iteration (the domain task), students engage in one to four subdomain tasks akin to quizzes, echoing the structure of Design C.

For the collaborative stage, groups of four to five students are formed. Group formation occurs at a synchronization milestone, where students who have completed the individual stage are initially grouped, with subsequent participants joining as they finish their individual tasks. While this may reduce individual autonomy temporarily, it allows obtaining a diversified group composition.

The core of the collaborative phase involves a peer evaluation process where students assess each other's elevator pitches against the attributes previously worked on individually. This serves a dual purpose: it reinforces the evaluator's understanding of these attributes and provides the evaluated with additional, diverse feedback. The peer evaluation workflow is illustrated in Fig. 2, which captures the sequence of activities in this phase.

Following peer feedback on each attribute of the elevator pitches, students receive an overview of how their pitch was assessed by their peers, as well as feedback on their performance as evaluators. This comparative analysis fosters reflection and learning from the peer review process, which can be visualized in Fig. 2.

The final stage sees students revisiting the domain task, armed with insights from both the ITS and their peers, to submit their refined elevator pitch. The group formation is managed by a scheduled task designed to ensure a balanced and effective distribution of participants, aligning skills, knowledge, and profiles within the collaborative setting.

4 Evaluation Study

4.1 Educational Context and Sample Description

The study was conducted within the context of an entrepreneurship and innovation course in the software industry, enrolling senior computer engineering students at a Latin American university, ages 22 to 25. The course had a total enrollment of 24 students, among which only three were women.

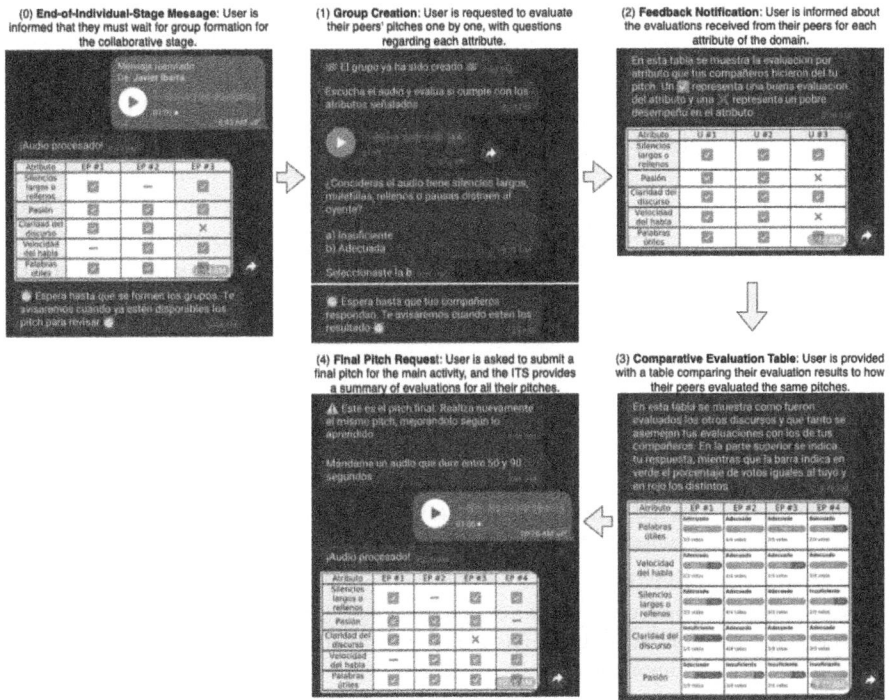

Fig. 2. Sequence of the collaborative peer-assessment workflow in EPIC, based on actual screenshots in Spanish language from the ITS as utilized in the present study.

4.2 Procedure

Students were tasked with designing an elevator pitch for a project they had been developing throughout the course. The primary goal of these pitches was to persuade an accelerator to provide funding for their projects, simulating a real-world scenario where clear, concise, and compelling pitches are crucial for securing investment.

After crafting their pitches, students were required to practice and refine them using EPIC with Design D. Their final submission to the ITS was considered their official course assignment submission. Following the collaborative phase facilitated by EPIC's Design D, students were invited to participate in a survey. This survey aimed to collect feedback on their experiences and learning outcomes from using EPIC. Participation in the survey was optional. The students were informed about the context of the study and the voluntary nature of their participation at this stage.

4.3 Measures

Upon completion of the activity, a questionnaire was administered to the students to assess various aspects of their experience. They were asked to evaluate: (1) their overall experience using the tool, (2) the usability of the tool using the System Usability Scale (SUS), and (3) their self-perceived learning. This self-perception covered both the domain-specific attributes defined for the pitch and, more specifically, the contribution they believed the collaborative phase made to their learning. Table 1 provides detailed descriptions of the items included in the questionnaire, offering a comprehensive overview of the areas of interest covered by the study.

Table 1. Table captions should be placed above the tables.

Variable	Item	Response scale
Experience score	What grade would you give your overall experience with the use of the tool?	1 to 7
Usability	System usability scale [21] (SUS, 10 items)	0 to 100
Self-perception of learning	Indicate your level of agreement: Evaluating other pitches helped me better understand the importance of the attributes.	Likert-5
	Indicate your level of agreement: The evaluation my peers made of my pitch helped me improve it.	Likert-5
	For each of the attributes worked with the tool, how much do you consider you knew about the topic BEFORE using it.	1 to 7
	For each of the attributes worked with the tool, how much do you consider you know about the topic AFTER using it.	1 to 7

Additionally, user behavior during the collaborative phase was measured, focusing primarily on the timing of their interactions with the ITS. A key behavior metric was the duration taken by users to conduct their first evaluation of a pitch. This measure was intended to determine whether users were fully listening to the pitches before proceeding with their evaluations. Moreover, the evaluation of each pitch by EPIC, according to the domain model, was recorded, providing a detailed account of the ITS's assessment of each user-submitted pitch.

5 Results

This section presents the results of the intervention that was carried out, including only those results of the students who voluntarily accepted their participation in the study. The results are divided between the users' experience, and those related to learning. There were 18 students who completed the use of EPIC including the collaborative phase and who also completed the final questionnaire.

5.1 User Experience and Behavior

Upon evaluating the overall user experience with EPIC, students provided an average rating of 4.94 out of 7. This score reflects a positively received user experience across the board. In addition to this general assessment, the System Usability Scale (SUS) offered further insights into the tool's usability, yielding an average score of 67.9. The distribution of SUS scores, showed in Fig. 3, aligns with the "moderately acceptable" usability range [22]. This indicates that while the tool is considered usable and meets a satisfactory level of user experience, there are opportunities for improvement to achieve higher usability standards.

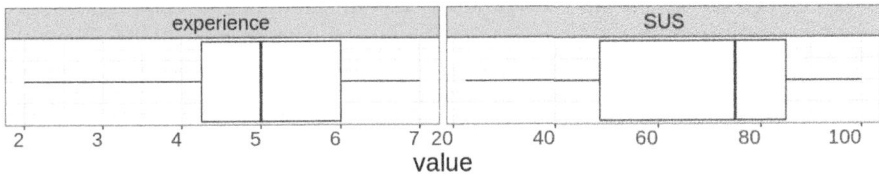

Fig. 3. Distribution of the results for the overall evaluation of the ITS usage experience and for the SUS.

The analysis extended to how students engaged with peer review, specifically measuring the time taken from when a fellow student's pitch was presented to them until they evaluated its first attribute. This was designed to gauge whether students devoted sufficient time to listen to the pitch attentively and make a meaningful assessment. Consequently, a benchmark of 50 s was established as the minimum valid time, reflecting the expected minimum duration of a pitch. The distribution of these times is depicted in Fig. 4 through a histogram, revealing that 26% of the evaluations for the first attribute were completed before reaching the minimum pitch duration. In particular, 3 students spent less than 50 s listening to all the pitches they had to review.

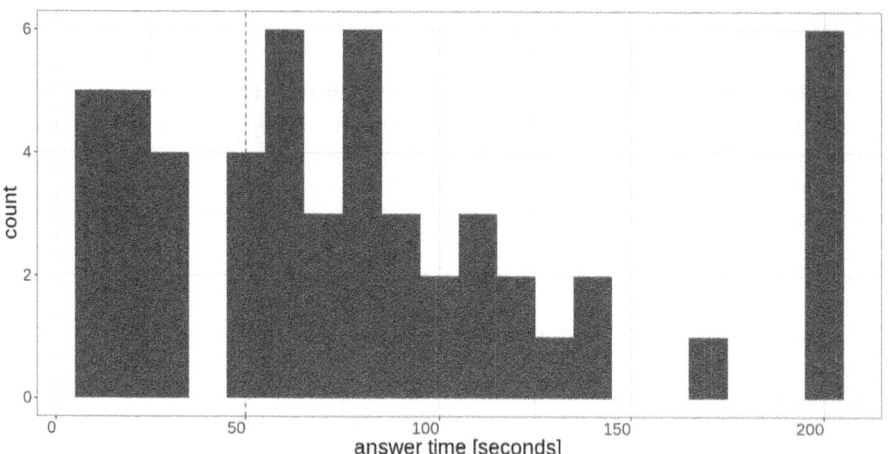

Fig. 4. Time for first response in peer review. The red line represents the minimum expected duration for a pitch (50 s (Color figure online)).

5.2 Learning

To assess perceived learning, students were surveyed about their knowledge regarding each of the five attributes both before and after using EPIC. Figure 5 illustrates the distribution of responses provided. Although there is an observed improvement in the average knowledge level across all five attributes, none of the increases reached statistical significance. This outcome can likely be attributed to the small sample size of participants, which may limit the power of the study to detect significant changes (Fig. 5).

Students were also asked to evaluate the specific contribution of the collaborative phase to their learning. This included both their assessment of their peers' pitches and the feedback received from peers on their own pitches. As illustrated in Fig. 6, 50% of students agreed or strongly agreed that reviewing other pitches aided their understanding of the attributes being taught. In contrast, only 28% felt that the feedback from their peers on their own pitch contributed to their learning. This discrepancy highlights the varied impact of different collaborative learning activities, suggesting that while peer evaluation can enhance understanding of key concepts for some, the feedback received may not always be perceived as beneficial to one's own learning process.

Based on the domain utilized in the ITS, a scoring system was established reflecting the achievement level for each of the five considered attributes, with -1 indicating a low level, 0 a medium level, and 1 a high level for each attribute. Therefore, the attribute score is obtained by summing the values for each. This scoring was applied to students' pitches at three points in time: at the beginning of their EPIC usage (ep1), after completing the individual stage (ep3), and after submitting their pitch following peer evaluations (ep4). Figure 7 displays the distribution of these scores across the three stages. A significant increase was

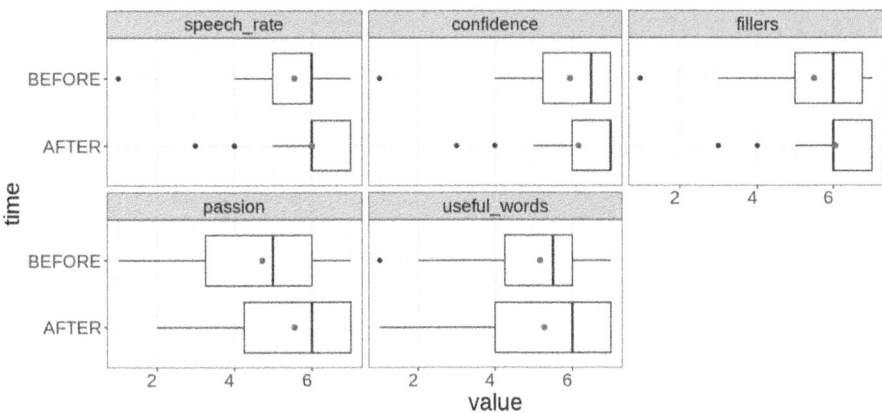

Fig. 5. Distribution of responses for self-perception of knowledge by attribute before and after using EPIC.

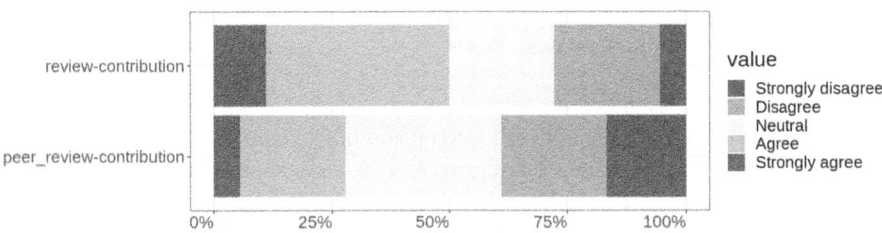

Fig. 6. Distribution of responses for items on self-perception of contribution of the peer-review process to learning.

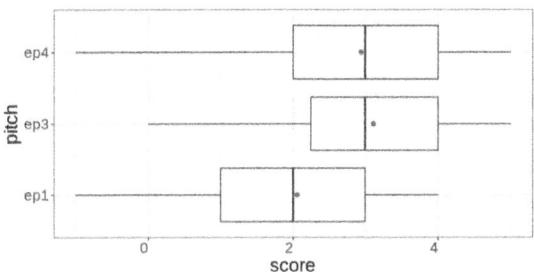

Fig. 7. Distribution of the scores for the pitches in three moments of use of the ITS: ep1 = initial pitch, ep3 = pitch at the end of the individual stage, ep4 = pitch after the collaborative stage.

observed from ep1 (average 2.06) to ep3 (average 3.11) (p = .001), while there was no significant change between ep3 and ep4 (average 2.94).

Exploring the lack of variation in scores following participation in the collaborative stage, Fig. 8 was created to analyze the evolution of these scores for each

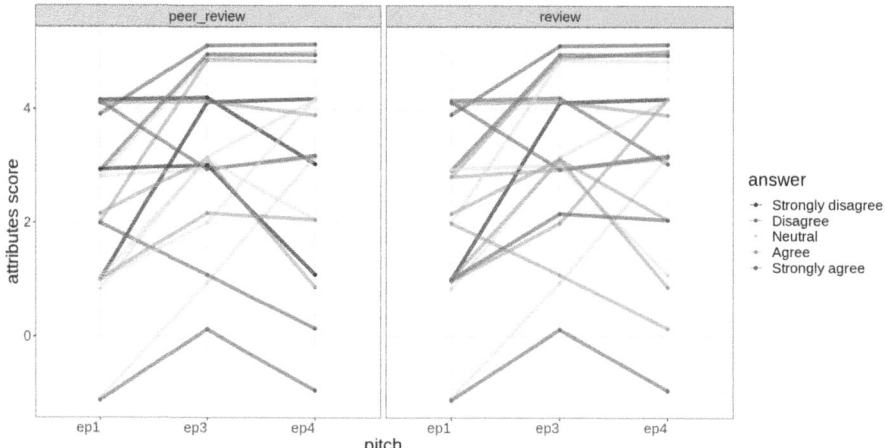

Fig. 8. Evolution of each student's pitch scores in three stages of their use of EPIC, based on their response regarding the contribution of each review activity, highlighting the negative contribution responses.

student, correlating it with their self-perception of the contribution from the two actions involved in this stage. The figure reveals that those who disagreed with the positive impact of the collaborative stage actions did not improve their scores during this phase. Similarly, none of the students who completed any evaluation without meeting the minimum expected time showed improvement in their final pitch; in fact, 56% of them saw a decrease in their scores. Conversely, in the group that completed all their evaluations within valid times, 33% improved in their last pitch, and only one student from this group experienced a decline.

6 Discussion

The results have shown that students tend to prefer evaluating others over receiving feedback from their peers. This can be partially attributed to the format of the feedback provided by the tutor, which is highly structured and quantitative, articulated in numerical scales, without the inclusion of qualitative assessments.

There are several important aspects of feedback, as identified by Nelson & Schunn [23], which are limited in delivery through the designed modality. For instance, factors such as the precise identification of issues, including their location in the speech or content, and thus the specificity of the feedback, are constrained within the used reporting format. Additionally, the use of affective language in feedback can lead to improvements in motivation, and this is not possible through the structured feedback format featured by the tutor. In contrast, when a student evaluates the work of their peers, they make a conscious effort to identify weaknesses according to different evaluation criteria, leading to a more intensive use of their perceptual abilities and executive functions. This is likely the reason why students value providing feedback more than receiving it in the experience offered by EPIC's Design D.

These findings carry pertinent implications for learning. According to Nelson & Schunn [23], feedback can differentially impact learning and performance. Learning refers to the knowledge acquired through transfer tasks, such as preparing various elevator pitches, while performance relates to improvements observed in repetitive tasks, like repeatedly training a specific elevator pitch. Feedback lacking explanations may boost performance but not necessarily foster deeper learning, and the use of examples can affect both learning and performance. To enhance the educational value of feedback, the tutor's feedback could be extended to include time references (markers) in relation to the recording being evaluated. These markers could include comments providing qualitative assessments in written or recorded formats, offering a more informative type of feedback. This approach would not only help students improve their skills in crafting and delivering an elevator pitch but also deepen their understanding of content and performance nuances.

We observed that the improvement in students' delivery of their elevator pitches following peer evaluation was correlated with their assessment of the peer evaluation activity itself. Specifically, students who negatively rated the collaborative phase did not improve their performance and, in some cases, it actually deteriorated. This phenomenon could be linked to a lack of engagement or motivation among these students, the causes of which warrant further investigation. However, the reasons might be associated with their experience and usability evaluations. Results in the lower quartiles for experience scores and the System Usability Scale (SUS) indicate that a significant number of students encountered difficulties using the tool or had a less satisfactory experience with it, which could have influenced their engagement with both the task of training on the elevator pitch and the evaluation of their peers' work. Despite the tool being based on an instant messaging interface - a platform with which students are generally familiar - the fact that it is a mobile application should not cause us to overlook potential issues such as connectivity quality, which can affect performance when uploading audio for processing.

Furthermore, it is important to consider the potential impact of errors perceived by students in the evaluation process conducted by the EPIC system. Afzal et al. [24] highlighted that errors made by tutors can significantly affect students' engagement and motivation. In the context of EPIC, where the evaluation of elevator pitches involves subjective elements and nuanced criteria, students may perceive discrepancies or inaccuracies in the feedback provided by the system or by their peers. This perception of errors could undermine students' trust in the system's assessment capabilities and diminish their motivation to engage fully with the feedback process. Particularly in ill-defined domains, where the criteria for evaluation may not be clearly defined or understood by students, the presence of perceived errors could exacerbate feelings of frustration or confusion. Therefore, addressing these concerns and ensuring the accuracy and reliability of the evaluation process are paramount to maintaining students' motivation and engagement with the EPIC system.

7 Conclusions and Future Work

In this research, we present the development and evaluation of new collaborative capabilities based on peer assessment integrated into the EPIC tutor for learning oral communication skills focused on the 'Elevator Pitch' exercise. The tutor offers mass usability by being self-service and incorporating peer assessment in small groups created on demand. Moreover, it is used by students asynchronously, both for generating elevator pitches and for peer assessment, which is advantageous from the perspective of the freedom and autonomy it provides to students to practice their skills.

A pilot study with a sample of 24 engineering students has shown that the features of peer assessment integrated into the EPIC tutor are highly valued by the students, and that those who benefited most from the intervention are those who evaluated the peer assessment capabilities most positively. Based on the experience and literature, it is possible to define design criteria aimed at improving the format of feedback delivered to students by their peers, incorporating qualitative elements to enhance the informative nature of the comments, their specificity, the ability to locate issues and problems, and the use of affective language that can contribute to greater student motivation. In the future, our efforts will be directed towards enhancing feedback elaboration, designing the necessary interactions and means for the conversational interface on which the tool is based, and conducting further evaluations with larger samples to address common usability and experience issues.

References

1. Almasri, A., Ahmed, A.: Intelligent tutoring systems survey for the period 2000–2018. Int. J. Acad. Eng. Res. (IJAER) **3**(5), 21–37 (2019)
2. Kulik, J.A., Fletcher, J.D.: Effectiveness of intelligent tutoring systems: a meta-analytic review. Rev. Educ. Res. **86**(1), 42–78 (2016)
3. VanLehn, K.: The relative effectiveness of human tutoring, intelligent tutoring systems, and other tutoring systems. Educ. Psychol. **46**(4), 197–221 (2011)
4. Fournier-Viger, P., Nkambou, R., Nguifo, E.M.: Building intelligent tutoring systems for ill-defined domains. In: Nkambou, R., Bourdeau, J., Mizoguchi, R. (eds) Advances in Intelligent Tutoring Systems. Studies in Computational Intelligence, vol 308, pp. 81–101. Springer, Berlin, Heidelberg (2010).
5. Butterfuss, R., Roscoe, R.D., Allen, L.K., McCarthy, K.S., McNamara, D.S.: Strategy uptake in writing pal: adaptive feedback and instruction. J. Educ. Comput. Res. **60**(3), 696–721 (2022)
6. Meijs, C., Gijselaers, H.J., Xu, K.M., Kirschner, P.A., De Groot, R.H.: The relation between cognitively measured executive functions and reported self-regulated learning strategy use in adult online distance education. Front. Psychol. **12** (2021)

7. House, R., Livingston, J., Summers, S., Watt, A.: Elevator pitches, crowdfunding, and the rhetorical politics of entrepreneurship. In: 2016 IEEE International Professional Communication Conference (IPCC), pp. 1–4. IEEE (2016)
8. Margherita, A., Verrill, D.: Elevator pitch assessment model: a systematization of dimensions in technology entrepreneurship presentations. IEEE Trans. Prof. Commun. **64**(4), 304–321 (2021)
9. Chen, X., Zou, D., Xie, H., Cheng, G., Liu, C.: Two decades of artificial intelligence in education. Educ. Technol. Soc. **25**(1), 28–47 (2022)
10. Hernández-Sellés, N., Muñoz-Carril, P.C., González-Sanmamed, M.: Computer-supported collaborative learning: an analysis of the relationship between interaction, emotional support and online collaborative tools. Comput. Edu. **138**, 1–12 (2019)
11. Qureshi, M.A., Khaskheli, A., Qureshi, J.A., Raza, S.A., Yousufi, S.Q.: Factors affecting students' learning performance through collaborative learning and engagement. Interact. Learn. Environ. **31**(4), 2371–2391 (2023)
12. Recabarren, M., Correa, V., Álvarez, C., Milrad, M.: Comparison of different pedagogical designs for an ITS: the case of oral speech as an ill-defined domain. In: Milrad, M., et al. Methodologies and Intelligent Systems for Technology Enhanced Learning, 13th International Conference, MIS4TEL 2023. Lecture Notes in Networks and Systems, vol. 764, Springer, Cham (2023)
13. Olsen, J.K., Belenky, D.M., Aleven, V., Rummel, N.: Using an intelligent tutoring system to support collaborative as well as individual learning. In: Trausan-Matu, S., Boyer, K.E., Crosby, M., Panourgia, K. (eds.) ITS 2014. LNCS, vol. 8474, pp. 134–143. Springer, Cham (2014). https://doi.org/10.1007/978-3-319-07221-0_16
14. Haq, I.U., Anwar, A., Basharat, I., Sultan, K.: Intelligent tutoring supported collaborative learning (itscl): a hybrid framework. Int. J. Adv. Comput. Sci. Appl. **11**(8) (2020)
15. Magnisalis, I., Demetriadis, S., Karakostas, A.: Adaptive and intelligent systems for collaborative learning support: a review of the field. IEEE Trans. Learn. Technol. **4**(1), 5–20 (2011)
16. Tchounikine, P., Rummel, N., McLaren, B.M.: Computer supported collaborative learning and intelligent tutoring systems. In: Advances in intelligent tutoring systems, pp. 447–463. Berlin, Heidelberg: Springer Berlin Heidelberg (2010). https://doi.org/10.1007/978-3-642-14363-2_22
17. Virvou, M., Alepis, E., Troussas, C.: User modeling on communication characteristics using machine learning in computer-supported collaborative multiple language learning. In: 2012 IEEE 24th International Conference on Tools with Artificial Intelligence, Vol. 1, pp. 1088–1093. IEEE (2012)
18. Epstein, D., da Costa Pinho, I., Acosta, O.C., Reategui, E.: Inquiry-based learning environment using intelligent tutoring system. In: 2013 IEEE Frontiers in Education Conference (FIE), pp. 1072–1074. IEEE (2013)
19. Chopade, P., Khan, S., Stoeffler, K., Edward, D., Rosen, Y., von Davier, A.: Framework for effective teamwork assessment in collaborative learning and problem solving. In: Proceedings of the 19th International Conference on Artificial Intelligence in Education (AIED 2018), pp. 48–59. IOS Press (2018)
20. Schneider, J., Börner, D., Van Rosmalen, P., Specht, M.: Can you help me with my pitch? Studying a tool for real-time automated feedback. IEEE Trans. Learn. Technol. **9**(4), 318–327 (2016)
21. Brooke, J.: SUS: A quick and dirty usability scale. Usability Eval. Ind. **189** (1995)
22. Bangor, A., Kortum, P.T., Miller, J.T.: An empirical evaluation of the system usability scale. Int. J. Human-Comput. Interact. **24**(6), 574–594 (2008)

23. Nelson, M.M., Schunn, C.D.: The nature of feedback: how different types of peer feedback affect writing performance. Instr. Sci. **37**, 375–401 (2009)
24. Afzal, S., Shashidhar, V., Sindhgatta, R., Sengupta, B.: Impact of tutor errors on student engagement in a dialog based intelligent tutoring system. In: Nkambou, R., Azevedo, R., Vassileva, J. (eds.) ITS 2018. LNCS, vol. 10858, pp. 267–273. Springer, Cham (2018). https://doi.org/10.1007/978-3-319-91464-0_26

Dialogue Act Analysis of Facilitator-Children Multilingual Communication

Mizuki Motozawa[✉][ID], Yohei Murakami[ID], and Mondheera Pituxcoosuvarn[ID]

Ritsumeikan University, Osaka, Japan
is0380sr@ed.ritsumei.ac.jp, {yohei,mond-p}@fc.ritsumei.ac.jp

Abstract. Multilingual communication among children is beneficial for cultivating an attitude that respects cultural diversity at an early age. Improvements in translation accuracy by neural machine translation can enhance children's mutual understanding. However, a significant challenge remains in involving children who speak low-resource languages (with limited language resources) in multilingual communication due to poor translation quality in those languages, resulting in a low number of utterances from the children. Meanwhile, facilitators play an important role in encouraging children's dialogue. Therefore, we have analyzed the facilitator's dialogue acts in a children's intercultural workshop to clarify which acts can promote their utterances. Specifically, we annotated all facilitator utterances with a dialogue act corresponding to each instance of children's language use in the actual multilingual dialogue log. Subsequently, we tallied the number of responses to each dialogue act. With this data, we compared the number of children's responses for each dialogue act across languages, analyzed the number of children's responses in each language for each dialogue act, and examined the patterns of change in dialogue acts for language pairs where translation was involved. The analysis finds that although no act has significant differences in the number of responses across different languages, the facilitator's utterance act changes caused by machine translation can result in a difference in the number of children's responses.

Keywords: intercultural collaboration · multilingual communication · machine translation · dialogue act

1 Introduction

"Quality Education" is one of the Sustainable Development Goals. This goal emphasizes the importance of respecting cultural diversity in today's increasingly globalized society. The summer school "KISSY" is organized by the non-profit organization Pangaea and represents a novel initiative aimed at fostering the instillation of such attitudes during childhood. The children from different countries discuss the solutions to international problems in KISSY. These children do not share a common language because they speak different languages.

Using machine translation is beneficial for their communication. Furthermore, adult facilitators participate to support children's discussions in KISSY. These facilitators ask questions and give instructions to children to elicit their ideas and opinions. In this way, children's discussions are supported in various ways in KISSY. However, the number of utterances by children speaking low-resource languages(LRL) was still fewer than in other languages [13]. The accuracy of machine translation was relatively lower for low-resource languages due to the lack of resources such as dictionaries and corpora. Therefore, it was difficult to participate in the discussion for children who speak LRL. The previous research focused on the facilitator's dialogue acts and analyzed how each dialogue act influenced the number of children's responses [11]. The dialogue act refers to the intentions conveyed by the utterances, the functions of utterances, and the actions carried out by the utterance [15,18]. The results of previous research clearly indicate differences in children's responses based on the strength of the facilitator's directives. Nevertheless, children's responses are influenced by the translated facilitator's messages because communication in KISSY uses machine translation. Therefore, this study focuses on the dialogue acts that children perceive and clarified the facilitation of the response of children in LRL by the field analysis. In addition, the effect of machine translation on the dialogue act is clarified. Specifically, the dialogue log data obtained in KISSY were annotated with dialogue acts, and significant differences in response counts among dialogue acts and languages were analyzed. Additionally, the dialogue acts were compared before and after translation.

The following sections include existing research and hypotheses in Sect. 2, field collection of dialogue log data in Sect. 3, annotations to the log data in Sect. 4, analysis methods and their results in Sect. 5, and a discussion of the results in the final section.

2 Difficulties in Machine Translation-Mediated Communication

2.1 Polysemy

Polysemy often causes three types of mistranslation: asymmetry, inconsistency, and transitivity[19,20]. Asymmetry means that machine translation translates the same polysemy differently between an utterance from the sender and a response from the addressee. Inconsistency indicates that machine translation translates the same polysemy differently between utterances from the same sender. Transitivity elucidates that machine translation translates the same polysemy differently from the sender to two addressees in three-way communication. However, In this research the focus is not on polysemy but the influence of machine translation on dialogue acts.

Table 1. Examples of Conversation

Speaker(Language)	Message
Facilitator(Japanese)	Do you have any ideas?
Child(Japanese)	serve sweets to entertain
Child(Khmer)	yes i have
Child(Japanese)	Play with words

2.2 Dialogue Acts

Machine translation is particularly beneficial for facilitating multilingual communication among children because they lack a common language. Moreover, The neural machine translation advent recently [1] has substantially enhanced translation accuracy [17]. Despite this, actual multilingual communication still leads to misunderstandings. Examples of such cases are presented in Table 1. This excerpt represents a segment of the children's actual communication. This example shows the different responses to the facilitator's same utterance. Japanese children responded with their ideas because they recognized that they were being asked for their ideas, while Khmer children responded with whether or not they had an idea because they recognized the message in the literal sense of the word. Thus, the intended meanings of the received utterances varied across the children's languages. On the other words, the dialogue act perceived by each language user was different. The existing research on dialogue support focuses on dialogue acts and proposes dialogue roles for the listener by analyzing dialogue act patterns that facilitate easier speaking for the other person [8]. The adjacent pairs are pairs of utterances consisting of an utterance and its corresponding response [14]. These are categorized based on the type of response prompted by the type of utterance. These studies have uncovered the effects of dialogue act on responses in the same language. However, the effects of dialogue acts in multilingual communication are not clear. In addition, these studies focused on the dialogue act uttered by the speaker. Although the utterances are translated in multilingual communication, so it is important to determine which dialogue act the listener receives. Therefore, this research focused on the dialogue acts received by the listener side and analyzed when the dialogue acts received how these affect the responses in each language. Additionally, we compared the responses by not only the dialogue act in each language but also between languages in each dialogue act. Furthermore, the impact of machine translation on the dialogue act was analyzed because the same utterance was recognized in different dialogue acts depending on the language from observations of actual communication.

2.3 Reseach Question

This research focuses on the dialogue acts perceived by children, aiming to clarify the following three points.

RQ1 Do children's ease of response differ depending on the dialogue acts? If they do differ, which dialogue acts make it easier for children to respond?

RQ2 Does the ease of response for children differ depending on the languages they use? If they do differ, for which language does each dialogue act make it easier for children to respond?

RQ3 Does the dialogue act change before and after translation by machine translation? If they do differ, in which language pairs does the dialogue act change, and how does it change?

3 Field Analysis

3.1 KISSY(Kyoto International Summer School for Youth)

KISSY is a summer school organized by the non-profit organization Pangaea. Children from various countries participated in the KISSY. They are divided into groups to discuss solutions to international issues and then create clay animations depicting their ideas. An adult facilitator participated in each group to support children's discussions. During discussions, group members sit together at the same desk, face each other, and communicate using a communication tool for multilingual text chats. Face-to-face communication is also possible when children speak the same language. For instance, minimal conversations occurred, such as confirming the discussion content. Some non-facilitator adult staff members also participated in KISSY to assist children with tasks, such as typing and using communication tools.

3.2 Multilingual Communication Tool

Communication in KISSY utilizes a chat-based multilingual communication tool with Language Grid [4,5]. Language Grid is a platform that offers translation services that combine unique dictionaries and machine translation. Using this information, a Pangea-specific dictionary and machine translation were developed. This promotes the accuracy of translation and ensures the smooth communication of Pangaea activities [12]. Figure 1 shows the user interface (UI) of the multilingual communication tool used in KISSY. This is for English users, where utterances by other language users are translated into English and displayed. At the top, the facilitator's photo, name, utterance, and current discussion theme are displayed. On the lower side, each child's photo, name, and country flag were displayed in areas framed in red. On either side, each child's utterances were displayed in areas framed in black. The color bar below each child's photo indicates the relative number of utterances for that child. This is a user interface design aimed at increasing awareness of the number of utterances. Furthermore, using this tool, users can use "Picton," as in pictograms. This was developed by Pangaea to help children communicate their feelings without language barriers [9,16].

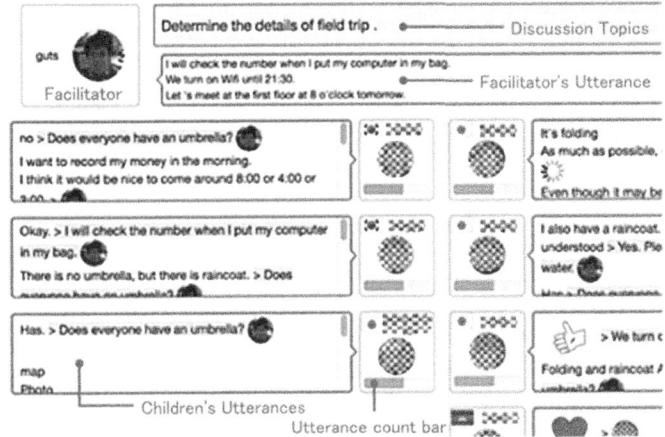

Fig. 1. Communication Tool UI(Photo offered by NPO Pangaea)

Table 2. Breakdown for Each Group.

Team	Role	Japan(ja[1])	Kenya(en[1])	Georgia(ka[1])	Cambodia(km[1])
Team A	Facilitator	1(ja)			
	Children	5(ja)	1(en)		1(km)
Team B	Facilitator	1(en)			
	Children	5(ja)	1(en)		1(en)
Team C	Facilitator		1(en)		
	Children	5(ja)		1(en)	1(km)
Team D	Facilitator				1(en)
	Children	5(ja)		1(en)	1(en)

[1] ja: Japanese, en: English, ka: Georgian, km: Khmer

3.3 Participants

At KISSY, 28 children from third grade to junior high school and four adult facilitators participated. Their nationalities were diverse, including Japanese, Kenyan, Georgian, and Cambodian. Khmer is spoken by Cambodians and is one of the LRL. Participants were divided into four groups, with efforts made to minimize differences related to nationality and language. Each group was composed of seven children and one facilitator. Table 2 shows the breakdown of the number of participants by nationality, native language, and language used in each group. Each group had one child of Cambodian. However, two of them used Khmer, while the other two used English. Also, the facilitators of Team A used Japanese, and others used English.

Table 3. Examples of Dialogue in Log Data

Speaker(Language[1])	Message
Facilitator(ja)	Do you have an idea for a solution for migrants to spend a pleasant time at school?
Child A (ja)	talk
Child B (en)	they should be given teachers that understands there language or even google translate
Child A (ja)	Play together
Child B (en)	what do you mean by play together (*Child A*)
Child C (ja)	Create a country-specific class
Child B (en)	we adopt the system of international schools

[1] ja: Japanese, en: English, km: Khmer

3.4 Dialogue Data

This research analyzed actual dialogue log data collected from the communication tool used in KISSY. This was a dialogue log from four groups, including 155 facilitator utterances and 777 children's utterances, and does not include oral dialogue. Table 3 shows a part of the dialogue logs. The names of the children in this table were anonymized. This is a situation in which a discussion is held on the topic "How can we accept immigrant children in our schools?". These utterances are English dialogue logs, and utterances in languages other than English were translated into English. In addition to English, Japanese and Khmer dialogue data were used in this study.

4 Utterance Annotation

Annotation is necessary for the quantitative analysis of each facilitator's utterances in the dialogue log. The following section describes the tag set used for annotation and the annotation procedure for each language.

4.1 Tag Set Based on Utterance Act

We used the tag set defined in ISO/DIS 24617-2 [2], an international standard for dialogue annotation in this research. In this tag set, five basic dialogue acts were used, along with four subdivisions of "Directive." Only the "Directive" subdivision was utilized for analysis, as it is considered important to encourage the children's response by the facilitator [11].

Table 4 shows definitions for each of the five basic categories, distinguished by the intention of the utterance. Additionally, Table 5 shows definitions for each of the subdivisions of "Directive," distinguished by the method or strength of the directive.

Table 4. Tag Definition of Basic Dialogue Act

Dialogue Act	Classification Tag Definition
Information-Providing	The utterance of a dialogue act in which the speaker aims to inform the listener of certain information. Example: "Our presentation title is ○○."
Information-Seeking	The utterance in which the speaker questions the listener to get the information that he is looking for. Example: "What are your ideas?"
Directive	The utterance in which the speaker puts pressure on the addressee to perform a certain action. Example: "Please tell me your ideas."
Commissive	The utterance in which the speaker commits oneself to perform a certain action. Example: "I will inform you about tasks in today."
Dimension-Specific	The utterance in which the speaker performs social obligations, for example, greeting, expressing her/his gratitude, and apologizing. Example: "Thank you.", "I am happy.", "Hello!"

Table 5. Tag Definition of Subtype of "Directive"

Dialogue Act	Classification Tag Definition
Request	The directive in which the speaker performed to make the addressee conditional on the addressee's consent to perform the action. Example: "Please tell me your ideas."
Instruct	The directive in which the speaker performed to make the addressee regardless of consent to perform the action. Example: "Tell idea."
Suggestion	The utterance in which the speaker performed to make the addressee consider the performance of a certain action. Example: "Let's all share our opinions"
Address Offer	The utterance which the speaker performed indicates the possibility that listeners perform the action that the speaker offered to perform. Example: "Yes, please." (Response to the "Shall we do ○○?")

4.2 Annotation Process

The facilitator's utterances in the dialogue logs were annotated in Japanese, English, and Khmer, using the tag set described in the previous section. Annotations were performed by annotators proficient in each language: four Japanese speakers, four English speakers, and three Khmer speakers. Several annotators were annotated in each language to avoid any bias. The annotators used an annotation manual and form to annotate consistently [10]. The annotators followed the manual and tagged each facilitator utterance with the dialogue act and confidence level (on a 5-point scale). The results of annotations were checked for the degree of agreement between annotators for each language and a Kappa coefficient to verify credibility. The annotators were provided with all dialogue logs, including the facilitator's utterances and the children's responses, and were instructed to decide which dialogue act was most appropriate, taking into account the context.

These Kappa values were evaluated using Landis' criteria [7]. The Kappa coefficient and evaluation are 0.518(moderate) for Japanese, 0.660(substantial) for English, and 0.727(substantial) for Khmer. Subsequently, unmatched annotations among the annotators were identified and tagged according to the confidence level of each annotator. For instance, if three annotators tag an utterance as (Suggestion, 1), (Information-Seeking, 4), and (Suggestion, 2), the highest total confidence level is 4 for "Information-Seeking." Thus, the tagging for this utterance is determined to be "Information-Seeking."

5 Analysis of Dialogue Acts

5.1 Comparison of Responses Among Dialogue Acts

"Directive" and "Information-Seeking" are dialogue acts designed to prompt responses from listeners. Therefore, the analysis focused on "Request," "Instruct," "Suggestion," "Address Offer," and "Information-Seeking," comparing the number of children's responses to each. This analysis aimed to determine whether these dialogue acts influence the number of children's responses and, if so, which ones. The following outlines the counting method for children's responses, the analysis techniques used, and the results obtained.

Tabulation of Children's Responses to Each Dialogue Act. Each facilitator's utterance was paired with the children's responses to it, taking into account the context. Based on this, the number of expected responses, responses, and non-responses to each facilitator's utterance are tallied. The number of expected responses, responses, and non-responses to each facilitator's utterance are tallied. The expected response count represents the number of children who received the utterance. Among these, the number of children who responded was counted as the response count, and the number of children who did not respond was counted as the non-response count. These counts were tabulated by dialogue act and language. For instance, if there were five Japanese children in the group and among three children responded to the utterance, the expected response is 5, the response is 3 and the non-response is 2. Table 6 shows the counting results. The discussion themes and facilitators' nationalities/languages vary between each group. However, the tabulation by group was not separated. This decision was

Table 6. Aggregation Number of Children's Responses in Each Utterance Type.

Utterance Acts	Japanese		English[1]		Khmer	
	Response	Non-Response	Response	Non-Response	Response	Non-Response
Information-Seeking	16	54	13(4,3)	38(8,11)	8	12
Request	50	130	2(0,1)	9(1,3)	0	1
Instruct	1	24	4(1,2)	16(4,4)	0	1
Suggestion	3	52	2(0,0)	12(6,4)	0	7

[1] All English User(Georgian English User, Cambodian English User)

based on our belief that there were no significant differences in facilitation methods. Facilitators had previously received training on the same facilitation methods and were provided with the KISSY program, resulting in similar schedules for their discussions. The data of "Address Offer" was omitted as it had a zero value in all languages. The data for Georgian and Cambodian English users are shown next to the data for English users in parentheses. English is not their native language. They may have translated between English and their native language in their minds, resulting in the conversion of the dialogue act. Therefore, their data were compared using Fisher's exact test with the data from Kenya. The results showed no significant differences. In essence, non-native English speakers may have translated messages between English and their native language in their minds, but their influence on the interpretation of the dialogue act was minimal. For this reason, the English user's data were tabulated without separated between native and non-native.

Statistical Test. Based on Table 6, we detected significant differences using Fisher's exact test (at the 5% level of significance). The test was selected based on the expected values. The data for "Request" and "Instruct" for Khmer were extremely low, each being only one. Hence, when analyzing the data for Khmer, only "Information-Seeking" and "Suggestion" were used. A p-value < 0.05, indicates that any of the dialogue acts influence the responses. In this case, we also conducted a residual analysis (at the 5% significance level) using adjusted residuals to identify which dialogue acts exhibited significant differences. If the residual value surpasses 1.96, the difference is considered significant. A significant difference in response values indicates that the dialogue act encourages children to respond. Conversely, if there is a significant difference in non-response values, it essentially suppresses the children's responses. Table 7 shows the results of each analysis. The results revealed significant differences in the data for the Japanese children, whereas there were no significant differences in the data for the English and Khmer children. In particular, "Request" utterances facilitated Japanese children's responses, whereas "Instruct" and "Suggestion" inhibited their responses. In the results for Khmer children's data, the small sample size could have influenced. Therefore, the actual measurements were compared. From Table 6, the Khmer children did not respond to any of the "Suggestion" utterances but did respond to some of the "Information-Seeking" utterances. There-

Table 7. Analysis Results for RQ1.

Language	p-value[2]	Results of Residual Analysis[3]
Japanese	$p < .001$ **	Request(+), Instruct(−), Suggestion(−)
English	$p = .905$ ns	–
Khmer	$p = .068$ ns	–

[2] ns:$p \geq .050$, *:$p < .050$, **:$p < .010$
[3] (+) Significant in Number of Responses, (−) Significant in Number of Non-Responses

fore, it is possible that "Information-Seeking" encouraged responses from children using Khmer. The variation in analytical results across languages suggests that dialogue acts may influence responses differently, depending on the language. On the other hand, it is also potential that factors other than the dialogue act influenced the number of responses. For example, there are differences in children's motivation to participate in KISSY or their ability to verbalize or type. Participation in KISSY was voluntary, unlike in compulsory school classes, so its influence is considered minimal. Additionally, the children received support from facilitators or other staff for verbalization and typing, which may have affected response speed, but had little impact on the value of responses.

5.2 Comparison of Responses Among Languages

The results of RQ1 suggested the possibility that the dialogue acts facilitating responses differed depending on the language used by the children. Therefore, the purpose of RQ2's analysis is to clarify the following two goals: 1. Whether the ease of responding differs across languages depending on the dialogue act. 2. if so, which language the children used. Specifically, the comparison of response numbers across languages for each dialogue act was conducted. Initially, a cross-tabulation table was created based on the data from Table 6, depicting the counts of responses and non-responses in each language for each dialogue act. Subsequently, statistical tests were conducted using these tables. The following is a description of the test methods used in the analysis and their results.

Statistical Test. Using the cross-tabulation tables generated in the preceding section, we conducted a significant difference detection for each table using Fisher's exact test or chi-square test(at the 5% level of significance). The decision to use either test was based on the expected value calculated from each value. As in the analysis of RQ1, only "Information-Seeking", "Request", "Instruct" and "Suggestion" were included in the analysis. The data for the "Request" and "Instruct" in Khmer were extremely low. Consequently, the data for these two dialogue acts were exclusively analyzed for the data for Japanese and English. The analysis results indicated that there was no significant difference in the data of responses for any of the dialogue acts. It suggested that there was no significant difference in the number of children's responses based on the language used.

In other words, it was not the case that children who used Japanese responded particularly more to "Request" than children using other languages.

5.3 Consistency of Dialogue Acts Through Translation

From the results of RQ1, a significant difference was observed in the number of responses of Japanese children between each dialogue act. However, the results of RQ2, this effect was not specific to Japanese language users. The analysis of RQ1 and RQ2 without considering translation. This suggests that the intervention of machine translation may have affected the dialogue acts and caused differences in the number of each dialogue act received depending on the language. Therefore, the purpose of RQ3 was to clarify the effect of translation on dialogue acts. Concretely, the number of each perceived dialogue act in each language was compared and the changes in dialogue acts before and after translation were analyzed. First, the received dialogue acts were aggregated in each language. Table 8 was created based on this aggregation. The data of "Address Offer" was omitted because it was not observed in any language. Then, the significant differences were detected using Fisher's exact test. The obtained result showed a p-value less than 0.001, indicating a significant difference. Subsequently, the residual analysis with adjusted residuals (at the 5% level of significance) was also compared to which language perceives more or less of each dialogue act. The signs in Table 8 represent the results of this analysis. This indicates whether the difference is positive or negative. The positive sign indicates that the dialogue act was received more frequently compared to other languages, while the negative sign indicates that it was received less frequently compared to other languages. The results for "Request" indicate Japanese user perceived this dialogue act more often than others. This can be related to the results of RQ1. The Children Japanese used were given more opportunities to respond to the "Request" messages compared to others.

This result implies that the dialogue act might have been altered through machine translation. Next, the impacts of machine translation on the dialogue acts were analyzed. Specifically, the language pairs where translation intervened were identified, and the occurrences of dialogue acts that differed between pre- and post-machine translation were tabulated. McNemar test was performed using the result of tabulation. The following sections provide details on the counting method of the pre and post-translation dialogue act combinations, the analysis method, and the results.

McNemar Test. The tables that differentiate changes in dialogue acts before and after the translation of each dialogue act were created for each Language pair (Table 9 to Table 11). The language pairs are Japanese to English, English to Japanese, and English to Khmer. The distinguished patterns include "No Change", "Change to Other Dialogue Act", "Change from Other Dialogue Act" and "Other". The "Address Offer" was omitted from the analysis because of not observed in any language pair. Following this, the McNemar test (at a significance level of 5%) was conducted using each prepared table. Table 12 shows the

Table 8. Number of Occurrences of Each Utterance Type.

Language	IP[1]	IS[1]	Request	Instruct	Suggestion	Commissive	DS[1]
Japanese	32	14 (−)	36 (+)	5	11	2	19 (+)
English	35	37 (+)	7 (−)	14 (+)	10	12 (+)	4 (−)
Khmer	46 (+)	34	4 (−)	2	9	3	15

[1] IP: Information-Providing, IS: Information-Seeking, DS: Dimension-Specific

Table 9. Tabulation for Japanese to English Translation Pairs.

	Dialogue Act	After Translation						
		IP[1]	IS[1]	Request	Instruct	Suggestion	Commissive	DS[1]
Before Translation	IP	16	1	0	0	1	0	0
	IS	0	10	1	0	1	0	0
	Request	0	15	5	4	0	0	0
	Instruct	0	0	0	3	0	0	0
	Suggestion	0	0	0	3	3	1	0
	Commissive	0	0	0	0	0	1	0
	DS	1	1	1	0	0	0	10

[1] IP: Information-Providing, IS: Information-Seeking, DS: Dimension-Specific

Table 10. Tabulation for English to Japanese Translation Pairs.

	Dialogue Act	After Translation						
		IP[1]	IS[1]	Request	Instruct	Suggestion	Commissive	DS[1]
Before Translation	IP	27	0	0	1	0	0	3
	IS	0	9	12	1	0	0	0
	Request	0	0	1	0	0	0	0
	Instruct	1	0	6	1	1	0	0
	Suggestion	0	0	0	1	6	0	0
	Commissive	0	0	0	0	0	2	0
	DS	0	0	0	0	0	0	4

[1] IP: Information-Providing, IS: Information-Seeking, DS: Dimension-Specific

results of the utterance acts for which there were significant differences. These revealed significant differences in certain dialogue acts within each language pair. Specific details of the results for each language pair are provided in the following section.

Results for Japanese-to-English Language Pairs The dialogue acts of "Information-Seeking," "Request," and "Instruct" were affected by translation. The dialogue acts of "Information-Seeking" and "Instruct" were changed from different ones after translation. Conversely, the dialogue act of "Request" was changed to others by translation. Referring to Table 9, "Request" most frequently changed to "Information-Seeking", followed by "Instruct". In addition,

Table 11. Tabulation for English to Khmer Translation Pairs.

	Dialogue Act	After Translation						
		IP[1]	IS[1]	Request	Instruct	Suggestion	Commissive	DS[1]
Before Translation	IP	44	0	1	0	0	1	2
	IS	4	42	1	2	0	0	0
	Request	5	0	2	0	1	0	0
	Instruct	9	1	4	2	3	0	0
	Suggestion	7	0	0	0	5	0	0
	Commissive	1	0	0	0	0	3	0
	DS	0	0	0	0	0	0	14

[1] IP: Information-Providing, IS: Information-Seeking, DS: Dimension-Specific

Table 12. Result of McNemar Test.

Language Pair	Dialogue Act	p-value[2]	Type of Change[3]
Japanese to English	Information-Seeking	.001*	(−)
	Request	<.001**	(+)
	Instruct	.023*	(−)
English to Japanese	Informaiton-Seeking	<.001**	(+)
	Request	<.001**	(−)
English to Khmer	Information-Providing	<.001**	(−)
	Instruct	.001**	(+)

[1] ns: $p \geq .050, * : p < .050, ** : p < .010$
[2] (+):Change to other dialogue acts, (-):Change from other dialogue acts

"Information-Seeking" was most frequently changed from "Request". This observation suggests the tendency for the dialogue act of "Request" to transform towards "Information-Seeking" and "Instruct" when translating from Japanese to English.

Results for English-to-Japanese Language Pairs The dialogue acts of "Information-Seeking" and "Request" were impacted by translation. The dialogue act of "Information-Seeking" changed to different ones after translation, whereas "Request" changed from different ones. Referring to Table 10, "Information-Seeking" most often changed to "Request". Moreover, "Request" most regularly changed from "Information-Seeking". This observation implies the dialogue act of "Information-Seeking" shift to "Request" when translation between English to Japanese.

Results for English-to-Khmer Language Pairs The dialogue acts of "Information-Providing" and "Instruct" were influenced by translation. The dialogue act of "Information-Providing" was altered from different ones by translation. On the other hand, the dialogue act of "Instruct" was altered to different ones. Referring to Table 11, "Instruct" was most commonly changed to "Information-

Providing" after translation. Furthermore, "Information-Providing" was most commonly changed from "Instruct" by translation. This observation indicates the dialogue act of "Instruct" to transform to "Information-Providing" when translation between English to Khmer.

6 Discussion

The analysis results revealed consistent patterns of changes in the dialogue acts across language pairs involving Japanese and English, regardless of the language before translation. Specifically, the combination of "Information-Seeking" (English) - "Request" (Japanese) and "Instruct" (English) - "Request" (Japanese). Table 13 provides some examples. The two messages in Example 1 of this table appear to convey similar meanings; however, the recognized dialogue acts differed in each language. Therefore, we interviewed the annotators in each language about how they interpreted them. Japanese annotators perceived that they were being asked about their ideas, while English annotators perceived that they were being asked whether they had ideas. This suggests that children using Japanese may perceive such utterances as indirect requests, while children using English may perceive them as direct requests. The two messages in Example 2 of Table 13 were interpreted as strongly commanding requests in English, while they are recognized as polite requests using expressions that include "please" in Japanese. This suggests that the level of politeness may have changed due to translation. The result of the Japanese-English language pairs indicated a shift between dialogue acts designed to elicit responses from the other person. On the other hand, when translating from English to Khmer, "Instruct" changed to "Information-Providing". The dialogue act of "Instruct" involves requesting a response from the other person, whereas the purpose of "Information-Providing" is to convey information to the other party and does not necessitate a response. When such a change in dialogue act occurs, children using Khmer may not respond. Example 3 of Table 13 provides an example. In English, this utterance was understood as a direct request for an idea, while in Khmer, it was perceived simply as conveying the fact that they wanted an idea. Furthermore, many of these changes were often spoken by facilitators using English.

For these reasons, it is suggested that indirect requests may be causing changes in the dialogue acts due to translation. In addition, children tend to find it easier to comprehend direct requests compared to indirect requests [3]. Also, indirect requests also demand a higher cognitive processing load for comprehension than standard utterances [6]. Therefore, the indirect requests may still be difficult for children to understand, even if there is no change in dialogue acts. Taking this factor into account, in multilingual group work, it's crucial to avoid indirect requests like "Do you have any ideas?". Direct requests such as "Please, give me your idea." should used. In addition, designing a machine translation that is not only fluent and adequate but can maintain the same dialogue act is also beneficial.

Table 13. Examples of changed dialogue acts.

	Language	Message(Dialogue Act)
Example 1:	Japanese	Do you have any ideas on solutions for accepting immigrants into schools?[1](Request)
	English	Do you have an idea for a solution to accept immigrants in school?(Information-Seeking)
Example 2:	English	Tell me your position(Instruct)
	Japanese	Please tell me your position[1](Request)
Example 3:	English	About how the story ends. I want the original blue team idea! (Instruct)
	Khmer	I want the blue team's original idea. How to end the story![1] (Information-Providing)

[1] The original statement was translated back into English

7 Conclusion

In multilingual communication using machine translation for children, a challenge arises due to fewer responses from those with low-resource languages(LRL). Thus, this research focused on the dialogue acts perceived by the receiver and analyzed the facilitator's dialogue acts to encourage responses from LRL children. As a result, there were differences in the dialogue act that encouraged the children's responses by language. Nevertheless, this effect is not specific to a language. This suggests that the intervention of machine translation may have affected the dialogue acts. Therefore, the effect of translation on the dialogue acts was analyzed. In consequence, in the case of translation from English to Khmer, "Instruct" transformed into "Information-Providing". The purpose of "Information-Providing" is to provide information only and does not require a response. Therefore, changing the dialogue act inhibits to response of LRL children. Moreover, most of this conversion involved indirect expressions. Hence, in multilingual communication facilitated by machine translation, encouraging children's responses through direct requests. Finally, the following two points should be clarified in future work. The first is to conduct controlled experiments on the actual efficacy of promoting participant responses because the findings from this study were acquired through field analysis. The second is the analysis that uses the logs of oral dialogue to clarify whether regarding observed trends in this study are limited to text chats with machine translation.

Acknowledgments. This research was partially supported by a Grant-in-Aid for Scientific Research (B) (21H03561, 2021-2024), a Grant-in-Aid for Early-Career Scientists(21K17794, 2021-2024) from the Japan Society for the Promotion of Sciences(JSPS), Society for the Advancement of Science and Technology at Ritsumeikan.

References

1. Bahdanau, D., Cho, K., Bengio, Y.: Neural machine translation by jointly learning to align and translate. In: 3rd International Conference on Learning Representations (2015)
2. Bunt, H., et al.: ISO 24617-2: A semantically-based standard for dialogue annotation. In: Proceedings of the Eighth International Conference on Language Resources and Evaluation, pp. 430–437 (2012)
3. Elrod, M.M.: Children's understanding of indirect requests. J. Genet. Psychol. **148**(1), 63–70 (1987)
4. Inaba, R., Murakami, Y., Nadamoto, A., Ishida, T.: Multilingual communication support using the language grid. In: Ishida, T., Fussell, S.R., Vossen, P.T.J.M. (eds.) IWIC 2007. LNCS, vol. 4568, pp. 118–132. Springer, Heidelberg (2007). https://doi.org/10.1007/978-3-540-74000-1_9
5. Ishida, T., Murakami, Y., Lin, D., Nakaguchi, T., Otani, M.: Language service infrastructure on the web: the language grid. IEEE **51**(6), 72–81 (2018)
6. Gibbs Jr, R.W.: Contextual effects in understanding indirect requests. Discourse Process. **2**(1), 1–10 (1979)
7. Landis, J.R., Koch, G.G.: The measurement of observer agreement for categorical data. Biometrics **33**(1), 159–174 (1977)
8. Meguro, T., Higashinaka, R., Dohsvoberto, Byron, D., Young, S., Purver, M.: Analysis of listening-oriented dialogue for building listening agents. In: Proceedings of the SIGDIAL 2009 Conference, pp. 124–127. Association for Computational Linguistics (2009)
9. Mori, Y., Takasaki, T., Ishida, T.: Patterns in pictogram communication. In: Proceedings of the 2009 International Workshop on Intercultural Collaboration, pp. 277–280 (2009)
10. Motozawa, M., Murakami, Y., Pituxcoosuvarn, M.: Annotation references for facilitation analysis in intercultural collaboration. In: Cross-Cultural Design. Applications in Business, Communication, Health, Well-being, and Inclusiveness. pp. 157–172. Springer International Publishing (2022)
11. Motozawa, M., Murakami, Y., Pituxcoosuvarn, M., Takasaki, T., Mori, Y.: Conversation analysis for facilitation in children's intercultural collaboration. In: Proceedings of the 20th Annual ACM Interaction Design and Children Conference, pp. 62–68. Association for Computing Machinery (2021)
12. Murakami, Y., Ishida, T., Nakaguchi, T.: Infrastructure for language service composition. In: 2006 Semantics, Knowledge and Grid, Second International Conference on, pp. 5–5 (2006)
13. Pituxcoosuvarn, M., Ishida, T., Yamashita, N., Takasaki, T., Mori, Y.: Machine translation usage in a children's workshop. In: Egi, H., Yuizono, T., Baloian, N., Yoshino, T., Ichimura, S., Rodrigues, A. (eds.) CollabTech 2018. LNCS, vol. 11000, pp. 59–73. Springer, Cham (2018). https://doi.org/10.1007/978-3-319-98743-9_5
14. Schegloff, E.A., Sacks, H.: Opening up closings, vol. 8, pp. 289–327. Semiotica (1973)
15. Searle, J.: Speech acts. Cambridge University Press (1969)
16. Takasaki, T., Mori, Y.: Design and development of a pictogram communication system for children around the world. In: Ishida, T., Fussell, S.R., Vossen, P.T.J.M. (eds.) IWIC 2007. LNCS, vol. 4568, pp. 193–206. Springer, Heidelberg (2007). https://doi.org/10.1007/978-3-540-74000-1_15

17. Tu, Z., Lu, Z., Liu, Y., Liu, X., Li, H.: Modeling coverage for neural machine translation. In: Proceedings of the 54th Annual Meeting of the Association for Computational Linguistics (Volume 1: Long Papers), pp. 76–85 (2016)
18. Vanderveken, D.: Meaning and Speech Acts, vol. 1. Cambridge University Press, Principles of Language Use (1990)
19. Yamashita, N., Inaba, R., Kuzuoka, H., Ishida, T.: Difficulties in establishing common ground in multiparty groups using machine translation. In: Proceedings of the SIGCHI Conference on Human Factors in Computing Systems, pp. 679–688. Association for Computing Machinery (2009)
20. Yamashita, N., Ishida, T.: Effects of machine translation on collaborative work. In: Proceedings of the 2006 20th Anniversary Conference on Computer Supported Cooperative Work, pp. 515–524. Association for Computing Machinery (2006)

Detecting Sports Spoiler Images on YouTube

Yuichiro Kinoshita[✉], Takumi Takaku, and Satoshi Nakamura

Meiji University, 4-21-1 Nakano, Nakano-Ku, Tokyo, Japan
zirogingin@gmail.com

Abstract. Spoilers of sports matches reduce the enjoyment of time-shifted viewing. On YouTube, users who like sports often inadvertently know the outcomes of matches by seeing thumbnails of recommended sports videos. Therefore, this paper focused on YouTube video thumbnails and verified the possibility of detecting images that contain spoiler information on YouTube. We constructed a dataset of sports spoiler images comprising 4,531 thumbnails from baseball, soccer, and basketball. In addition, we proposed three detection methods: the Image-Recognition method using optical character recognition (OCR), emotion assessment, and posture assessment; the Vision-Direct method using the OpenAI Vision API only; and the Vision-Text method that judges using the spoiler dictionary for an image's description by the OpenAI Vision API. We evaluated the accuracy of these methods, and our results indicated that the Vision-Text method achieved an accuracy of 85% in detecting spoiler images. Furthermore, the evaluation results indicated that the Vision-Text method might be the most effective for detecting spoiler images in baseball and soccer. In contrast, the Vision-Direct method seems to be the most effective in basketball.

Keywords: Spoilers · Sports images · YouTube · ChatGPT

1 Introduction

Watching sports matches is popular all over the world, and one of the reasons for this is that the unpredictability of the results evokes excitement [1]. For this reason, many people prefer to watch matches in real time, but time differences or personal reasons often make this impractical. In such cases, recording or rebroadcasting matches offer alternatives for enjoying the matches at one's own convenience. However, when intending to watch a match later, people may inadvertently encounter information about the sports match through social networking services, video-sharing sites, and news sites before watching the match. This information about sports match outcomes is called a *spoiler*, and spoilers reduce tension and enjoyment when watching sports [2].

To prevent sports spoilers, Nakamura et al. [3] proposed a method for blocking spoilers on the web by ambiguating textual information about sports matches. Sasano et al. [4] detected tweets containing spoilers of baseball games using a personalized support vector machine. These studies focused on spoilers in text, but sports spoilers also exist in images. For instance, Fig. 1 is a soccer image without direct information about the winner or loser, but fans may predict the match outcome from the players' facial expressions. Previous studies targeted textual spoilers and no methods for preventing spoilers through images have been proposed.

People can encounter spoiler images under various circumstances. For instance, while using social networking services to catch up with friends or searching for videos on video-sharing sites, people might inadvertently discover the results of sports matches through images posted on social networking services or by seeing thumbnails of recommended videos (see Fig. 2). In this study, we focus on spoilers given through thumbnails on YouTube because avoiding spoilers on YouTube is difficult due to its recommendation algorithm. For example, if a user often watches sports videos, YouTube is likely to recommend sports content even when watching different content types. Consequently, users may encounter sports spoilers through the thumbnails of these recommended videos. Therefore, preventing image-based spoilers on YouTube is important for those who wish to enjoy sports matches without spoilers.

This paper verified the possibility of detecting spoiler images to prevent spoilers through images. We constructed a dataset of sports spoiler images and analyzed their features. Furthermore, we proposed three methods for detecting spoiler images and evaluated the performance of our methods.

The contributions of this paper are as follows:

(1) We categorized spoiler images into two types, direct and indirect spoilers, and defined spoiler images as images that enable the prediction of match outcomes based on preliminary investigation.
(2) We constructed a dataset of sports spoiler images consisting of 4,531 thumbnails extracted from YouTube videos of baseball, soccer, and basketball and annotated by three collaborators.
(3) We achieved 85% accuracy in detecting spoiler images by describing an image as a text and matching the words with our spoiler dictionary.

2 Related Work

2.1 Spoilers

Leavitt et al. [5] investigated the impact of spoilers on the enjoyment of novels and found that spoilers do not necessarily reduce enjoyment. In contrast, Rosenbaum et al. [6] discovered that people not accustomed to reading novels tend to find stories with spoilers more appealing, whereas avid readers prefer stories unspoiled. In addition, Levine et al. [7] showed that encountering spoilers before reading a novel can diminish its attractiveness. Maki et al. [8] investigated the effects of spoilers depending on the reading progress and found that while spoilers do not change the degree of reading enjoyment, they reduce interest in continuing to read the story.

Tsang et al. [9] revealed that spoilers reduce the willingness to watch a movie. Johnson et al. [10] showed that while spoilers diminished enjoyment in comedy movies, they increased enjoyment in fantasy and thriller genres. Li et al. [11] investigated the influence of spoilers on box office revenue and its variation over time, finding that spoilers negatively impacted box office revenue only within the first six days after a movie's release.

Fig. 1. An image that provides insights to predict the match result.

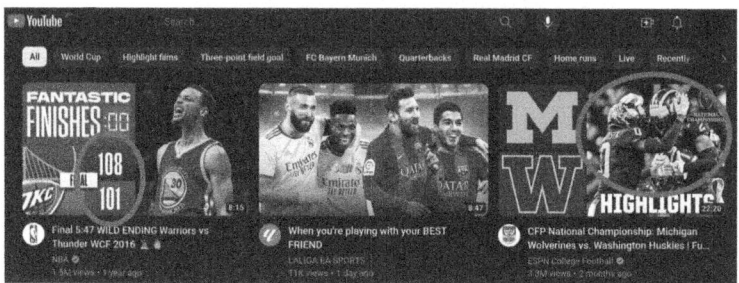

Fig. 2. Encountering spoiler images on YouTube.

In sports, Shiratori et al. [2] indicated that spoilers reduce both tension and enjoyment when watching matches. This paper focused on sports spoilers through images.

Regarding the detection of spoilers, Boyd-Graber et al. [12] developed an automatic spoiler detector for social media posts. Golbeck [13] proposed a method to block spoilers related to dramas and sports on Twitter by automatically adding various words to a block list. Nakamura et al. [14] implemented a system that blocks web content, such as sports match results, book reviews, and movie reviews, based on the distribution time of the content. In addition, Wan et al. [15] created a large-scale dataset of book reviews and developed an end-to-end neural network architecture for detecting spoilers in those reviews. Hijikata et al. [16] identified sentences that include story plots in reviews of comics, novels, and movies. They improved the accuracy of identifying story plots by using both contextual and word information.

In sports spoilers, Nakamura et al. [3] proposed a method to block them by making the textual information on websites ambiguous. Jeon et al. [17] also detected Twitter posts containing spoilers about soccer. This paper verified the feasibility of detecting spoiler images in sports to prevent spoilers through images.

2.2 Classification of Sports Images and Videos

Li et al. [18] developed an automatic framework to categorize sports genres, achieving an average accuracy rate of 83% across all 14 sports. Farhad et al. [19] utilized the VGG16 transfer learning model to classify images from 18 sports, achieving 93% accuracy. Podgorelec et al. [20] created a dataset of images from four similar sports and proposed an effective method for their classification. In addition, Rafiq et al. [21] utilized a pretrained AlexNet Convolutional Neural Network for the classification of five different

Fig. 3. (a) A direct spoiler image, (b) an indirect spoiler image.

scenes in cricket videos, achieving an accuracy of 99%. Hao et al. [22] successfully identified fine-grained player movements within soccer and basketball highlight reels and demonstrated the potential for classifying detailed scenes such as scoring and fouls.

There has been considerable research on sports image and video classification. While there is the possibility of applying methods from previous research on sports scene classification to detect spoiler images, no method for detecting sports spoiler images has been proposed. This paper analyzes the features of sports spoiler images and proposes methods for their detection.

3 Sports Spoiler Images

3.1 Types of Spoilers

This paper defines sports spoilers as information that enables users to predict match outcomes and reduces their tension and enjoyment of watching recorded matches. Such information can be conveyed not only through text but also through images. For example, Fig. 3 (a) shows the final score of a basketball game, and Fig. 3 (b) captures the scene of players celebrating in a baseball game, indirectly indicating which team won. Thus, due to the difference in the importance of the information conveyed by spoiler images, we categorize sports spoiler images into direct and indirect ones and analyze their features in detail.

We define direct and indirect spoiler images as follows:

- Direct spoiler images: Images that display words related to winning or losing, or the match's final score, directly revealing the match's outcome.
- Indirect spoiler images: Images that allow people to predict the match's outcome based on the players' demeanor.

3.2 Preliminary Investigation of Spoiler Label Annotation

Since there are various types of spoilers, the criteria for determining spoilers vary among individuals. For instance, some consider only showing the final results of a match to be a spoiler, while others perceive that giving information about a player's performance could be a spoiler, too. To reduce the inconsistency in annotation due to different personal criteria, we conducted a preliminary investigation to unify the criteria for determining spoilers.

Fig. 4. Examples of images labeled both *"Would not reduce enjoyment for viewers"* and *"Would definitely reduce enjoyment for viewers"*.

We defined spoiler images as images containing information that could spoil viewers' enjoyment of watching the recorded or delayed broadcasting match. Following our definition, three annotators—two authors and one graduate student who regularly watches sports—annotated images using a web system that we designed. Among the three annotators, one regularly watches baseball, another watches baseball, soccer, and basketball, and the third watches soccer, basketball, and American football. They annotated images by choosing one from three levels of spoilers:

- Would not reduce enjoyment for viewers.
- Might reduce enjoyment for viewers.
- Would definitely reduce enjoyment for viewers.

To verify whether our spoiler image definition standardized spoiler criteria among annotators, we sampled 50 YouTube thumbnails from each of five sports (baseball, soccer, basketball, American football, and volleyball), totaling 250 images, for annotation.

The annotation results revealed an agreement rate of 0.54 among the three annotators. We attributed this low rate to the inadequacy of our definition and the unsuitability of some images as target data. We analyzed images that had greatly divergent labels (both *"Would not reduce enjoyment for viewers"* and *"Would definitely reduce enjoyment for viewers"*) and found many of them were thumbnails of video compilations of individual players' highlights (see Fig. 4). This was because videos focusing on individual players often covered performances across multiple matches, such as monthly or season highlights, leading to differences in determining whether they constituted spoilers among the annotators.

From these observations, we believed that our definition of spoiler images required modification to reduce subjectivity in annotation. Furthermore, video thumbnails that focus on individual players should be excluded from the dataset.

4 Dataset

4.1 Target Images

Based on the results of our preliminary investigation, we constructed a dataset of sports spoiler images. This paper focused on five popular sports: baseball, soccer, basketball, American football, and volleyball. We also targeted the following YouTube channels covering all teams' matches, including official sports leagues and tournament channels. We collected video thumbnails from these sources using the YouTube Data API.

- Baseball: MLB
- Soccer: Bundesliga, FIFA, LALIGA EA Sports, Series A
- Basketball: FIBA – The Basketball Channel, March Madness, NBA, WNBA
- American football: ESPN College Football, NFL
- Volleyball: Power Volleyball, Volleyball World

We excluded thumbnails of videos shorter than one minute from our collection target, as many did not relate to the matches' content. We obtained approximately 2,000 images per sport from the above 13 YouTube channels, totaling 10,150 images.

4.2 Spoiler Label Annotation

We revised the definition of spoiler images to images that enabled the prediction of match outcomes. This more precise definition would improve the agreement rate for spoiler annotations. We also modified the levels of spoilers as follows:

- Match outcomes cannot be predicted.
- Match outcomes can be somewhat predicted.
- Match outcomes are clearly predicted.

Additionally, we removed images that focused on individual players and those with low relevance to the match content from the dataset. As a result, the total number of images was reduced to 7,185. Table 1 shows the number of images per sport.

To verify that the label agreement rate among the three annotators would improve, we randomly sampled 100 images from 7,185 images and conducted annotation. The annotators were the same as those mentioned in Sect. 3.2. As a result of annotation, the agreement rate was improved to 0.87. Based on this result, we determined that the definition of spoiler images and the target images were appropriate, and we annotated the remaining 7,085 images.

Each of the three annotators annotated all 7,185 images using our annotation system (see Fig. 5), resulting in the final label agreement rate of 0.78.

4.3 Proportion of Spoiler Images

To determine the correct labels, we assigned scores according to the level of spoilers:

- 0 points to *Match outcomes cannot be predicted.*
- 1 point to *Match outcomes can be somewhat predicted.*
- 2 points to *Match outcomes are clearly predicted.*

Table 1. Number of images and proportion of spoiler images per sport.

	Baseball	Soccer	Basketball	American Football	Volleyball
Number of images	1,506	1,620	1,405	1,328	1,326
Proportion of spoilers	0.19	0.58	0.20	0.08	0.11

An image was determined as a spoiler if it received a total spoiler label score of 2 or more from the three annotators and as a non-spoiler if the total score was less than 2.

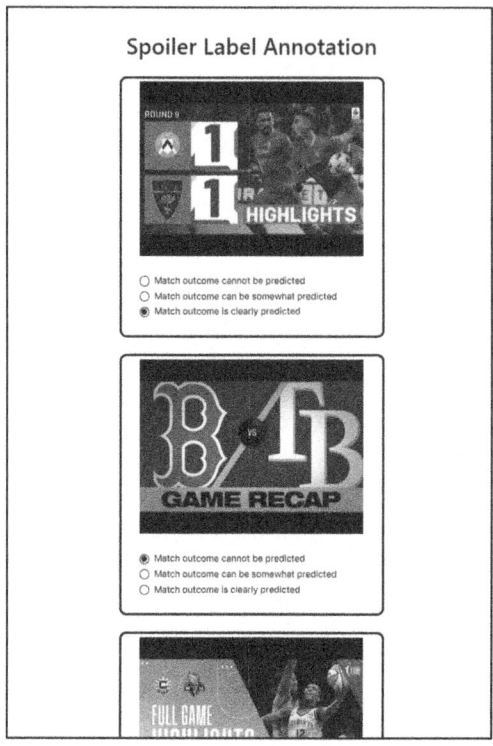

Fig. 5. The spoiler label annotation system.

Following this scoring method, the proportion of spoiler images in our dataset was 0.24. Table 1 indicates that soccer had the highest number of spoiler images, whereas American football and volleyball had significantly fewer. Due to the scarcity of spoiler images in American football and volleyball, we focused on detecting spoilers in the 4,531 images from baseball, soccer, and basketball.

Fig. 6. Examples of spoiler images.

Fig. 7. Examples of non-spoiler images.

Table 2. Proportion of direct and indirect spoiler images per sport.

	Baseball	Soccer	Basketball
Direct spoilers	0.05	0.03	0.30
Indirect spoilers	0.95	0.97	0.70

4.4 Features of Spoiler Images

Figure 6 illustrates examples of spoiler images, while Fig. 7 shows examples of non-spoiler images. Many direct spoiler images displayed the match's final score, whereas images that included words related to the outcome, such as *win* or *lose*, were less frequent. Indirect spoiler images often focused on players' expressions and poses, indicating their joy. In contrast, non-spoiler images typically depicted only team logos, focused equally on players from both teams, and captured moments not crucial to the match outcome.

Based on the definition in Sect. 3.1, we manually classified spoiler images into direct and indirect spoilers. The classification results showed that the proportion of direct and indirect spoilers varied across sports (see Table 2). Basketball had a higher proportion of direct spoilers compared to other sports, while baseball and soccer had a lower proportion of direct spoilers.

We visually investigated all spoiler images and identified the following features:

- The final match outcome is displayed.
- Players' expressions include smiling or shouting.
- Players strike poses that express joy or excitement.
- Players from the same team gather to celebrate.

Table 3. Portion of the manually created spoiler dictionary.

Common	Baseball	Soccer	Basketball
happy, success, excite, shout, joy, smile, positive, win, celebrate, embrace	jump, run, big	goal, slip, dive, lead, kneel	fantastic, ending, dramatic, advance

Table 4. Portion of the manually created non-spoiler dictionary.

Common	Baseball	Soccer	Basketball
altercation, brawl, confront, dispute		contest	split-screen, divide, separate, composition

5 Detection Methods

Based on the features of spoiler images described in Sect. 4.4, this paper proposes the following three methods for detecting spoiler images:

- **Image-Recognition method:** This method employs OCR, emotion assessment, and pose assessment for detecting spoiler images. It uses OCR to identify scores and words associated with match outcomes, emotion assessment to detect facial expressions like smiles or shouting, and pose assessment to recognize poses expressing joy or excitement. An image is classified as a spoiler if any of these features are detected. This method leverages the Google Cloud Vision API for OCR and emotion assessment, and YOLOv8 for pose assessment.
- **Vision-Direct method:** This method employs AI to detect spoiler images. It uses the OpenAI Vision API (using the gpt-4-vision-preview model), configuring the prompt to: *Please analyze this YouTube video thumbnail and determine if it is a spoiler or non-spoiler image. Define a spoiler image as one that reveals the outcome of an event, characterized by the presence of a score or result-related words, players exhibiting emotions of joy or triumph, such as smiling or cheering poses. If the image is a spoiler, respond with 'Spoiler.' If it is a non-spoiler, respond with 'Non-spoiler.' Do not output any other words.* This method uses the API's responses directly as the detection result.
- **Vision-Text method:** This method converts images into text and detects spoiler images based on the textual content. It uses the OpenAI Vision API (using the gpt-4-vision-preview model) to verbalize images and configure the prompt to: *This image is a thumbnail for a YouTube video. Please describe this image.* This method obtains descriptions of the input image and determines whether the image is a spoiler by checking if words in the description match those in a spoiler or non-spoiler dictionary (see Tables 3 and 4). We created the dictionaries by sampling 100 spoiler images and 100 non-spoiler images, respectively, and examining frequently occurring words related to spoiler and non-spoiler features. The dictionaries were constructed by combining words commonly associated with spoiler or non-spoiler features across three sports (baseball, soccer, basketball) and those specific to individual sports. The total number of words in the spoiler dictionary is 82, while the total number in the non-spoiler dictionary is 19. Additionally, this method excludes sentences that mention logos or designs to avoid false positives, particularly the risk of images without players being incorrectly identified as spoilers (see Table 5).

Table 5. An example of OpenAI Vision API's output in the Vision-Text method. Even in images without any people, words in the spoiler dictionary (in this case, *excitement*) appeared.

Input image	Output text
	The image you've provided appears to be a graphic design representing a sports event. This is a thumbnail for a YouTube video about a basketball game. It features the FIBA U20 European Championship logo, suggesting that this is an event for under-20 basketball teams in Europe. The text "FULL GAME QUARTER-FINALS" prominently displayed indicates that the video includes the full coverage of a quarter-final match of the championship. On the left side, there is a basketball with the French flag design, which implies that the French team is one of the competitors in this game. On the right side, there's another basketball with the colors of the Lithuanian flag, representing Lithuania as the other competing team. The background is dark blue with dynamic blue lines and shapes, giving a sense of motion and **excitement** which is often associated with sporting events. It's designed to attract viewers interested in watching the full game from the championship's quarter-finals between the two national teams.

6 Evaluation

We assessed the performance of the three methods using the constructed dataset. We employed accuracy, recall, precision, and F1 score as evaluation metrics. In this study, accuracy refers to the proportion of images correctly classified as either spoiler or non-spoiler. Recall indicates the proportion of actual spoilers that are accurately identified, and precision indicates the proportion of identified spoilers that were actually spoilers. Although both precision and recall are important evaluation metrics, this paper particularly emphasizes recall, given the importance of blocking all spoiler information.

Table 6 shows the results of detecting spoiler images using the entire dataset. The Image-Recognition method achieved the highest recall at 0.90, but its precision was the lowest at 0.39. This indicates that the Image-Recognition method determined many

Table 6. Spoiler detection results for the entire dataset.

	Image-Recognition	Vision-Direct	Vision-Text
Accuracy	0.50	0.83	0.85
Recall	0.90	0.72	0.80
Precision	0.39	0.75	0.76
F1 score	0.55	0.74	0.78

images to be spoilers. The Vision-Text method reached a recall of 0.80 and the highest F1 score of 0.78. The Vision-Text method seems to be the most effective for detecting spoiler images. Additionally, the Vision-Direct method showed a recall of 0.72 and an F1 score of 0.74, indicating its potential effectiveness in spoiler detection.

Table 7. Spoiler detection results for baseball.

	Image-Recognition	Vision-Direct	Vision-Text
Accuracy	0.48	0.79	0.86
Recall	0.88	0.71	0.71
Precision	0.25	0.47	0.61
F1 score	0.39	0.57	0.65

Table 8. Spoiler detection results for soccer.

	Image-Recognition	Vision-Direct	Vision-Text
Accuracy	0.69	0.77	0.81
Recall	0.90	0.69	0.83
Precision	0.67	0.89	0.84
F1 score	0.77	0.78	0.83

Table 9. Spoiler detection results for basketball.

	Image-Recognition	Vision-Direct	Vision-Text
Accuracy	0.30	0.92	0.89
Recall	0.92	0.86	0.81
Precision	0.21	0.79	0.69
F1 score	0.35	0.82	0.75

Tables 7, 8, and 9 show the detection results for each sport. In baseball and soccer, the Image-Recognition method achieved the highest recall, while the Vision-Text method reached the highest F1 score. Due to the low precision of the Image-Recognition method, the Vision-Text method appears to be the most effective for detecting spoiler images in baseball and soccer. In basketball, although the Image-Recognition method showed the highest recall, its precision was significantly low. On the other hand, the Vision-Direct method achieved the highest F1 score. Consequently, the Vision-Direct method seems to be the most accurate for spoiler detection in basketball.

These findings suggest that the effectiveness of detection methods can vary depending on the sport.

7 Discussion

7.1 Differences in Detecting Accuracy Across Sports

Across all three detection methods, we observed significant differences in recall and precision among the sports. These differences can largely be attributed to the unique characteristics of each sport, especially in scoring frequency. Specifically, soccer is a sport where scoring is less frequent compared to baseball and basketball, making each point highly significant. As a result, many soccer images depicting scoring moments were annotated as spoilers in our dataset. In contrast, images from baseball and basketball capturing scoring moments were often annotated as non-spoilers because annotators needed to consider additional factors, such as the timing of the score within the match and the number of points scored in the play. This gap led to differences in recall and precision by sport.

7.2 Causes of Misdetection by Each Method

The Image-Recognition method detected poses expressing joy or excitement based on simple spatial relationships, such as wrists and elbows positioned above the shoulders, leading to false positives and reduced precision (see Fig. 8 (a)). Additionally, although this method achieved high recall across all sports, it also produced false negatives due to limited accuracy in emotion assessment (see Fig. 8 (b)).

The Vision-Direct method appears to be effective in detecting spoiler images, as indicated by an F1 score of 0.74 for the entire dataset. In this method, we configured the OpenAI Vision API to provide only detection results. Consequently, we were unable to clarify the specific causes of misdetection (see Fig. 9). Modifying the prompt to include reasons for the detection outcomes could help reveal the causes of misdetection.

The Vision-Text method seems to be the most accurate in detecting spoiler images, but there were some false positives due to reliance on word matching (see Fig. 10 (a)). Specifically, an image was determined as a spoiler if any word from the spoiler dictionary (see Table 3) appeared even once, which led to reduced precision. Furthermore, we found that false negatives occurred due to excluding sentences mentioning logos or designs during preprocessing (see Fig. 10 (b)). Concretely, this exclusion led to the omission of some sentences that referenced scores or match outcomes, resulting in false negatives.

7.3 Future Work

Our detection results might have been influenced by the features of the thumbnails from the YouTube channels used for data collection. Therefore, we aim to expand the dataset of sports spoiler images. Specifically, we plan to increase the variety of sports used for spoiler detection and collect images from sports news sites and social networking services.

Fig. 8. Examples of misdetection in the Image-Recognition method: (a) False positive due to simplistic pose detection, (b) False negative due to incorrect emotion assessment.

Fig. 9. Examples of misdetection in the Vision-Direct method: (a) False positive, (b) False negative. The causes of misdetection could not be identified.

Fig. 10. Examples of misdetection in the Vision-Text method: (a) False positive due to word matching, (b) False negative due to exclusion of sentences mentioning designs.

Additionally, we aim to improve the accuracy of the Vision-Direct and Vision-Text methods. For the Vision-Direct method, we plan to adjust the prompt to output not only the detection results but also the reasons behind the decisions. This adjustment seeks to uncover the causes of misdetection, and we believe that fine-tuning the prompt based on these causes can enhance detection accuracy. As for the Vision-Text method, we expect that accuracy will increase by including sentences that mention designs and by evaluating the number and frequency of words from the spoiler or non-spoiler dictionary in OpenAI Vision API's responses to determine spoiler images.

8 Conclusion

In this paper, to prevent sports spoilers through images, we verified the feasibility of detecting spoiler images. We specifically focused on YouTube thumbnails for sports content, defining spoiler images as images that enable the prediction of match outcomes. We constructed and analyzed a dataset of sports spoiler images and proposed three detection methods.

Upon evaluating the performance of our methods with the entire dataset, the Vision-Text method appears to be the most effective for detecting spoiler images. However, the most effective method and detection accuracy might vary depending on the sport type.

Our future work will aim to include a wider range of sports and expand the dataset by collecting images from various media, including news sites and social networking services. Additionally, we intend to enhance the detection accuracy of both the Vision-Direct and Vision-Text methods.

Acknowledgments. This work was partly supported by JSPS KAKENHI Grant Number JP22K12338.

References

1. Bernhardt, P.C., Dabbs, J.M., Jr., Fielden, J.A., Lutter, C.D.: Testosterone changes during vicarious experiences of winning and losing among fans at sporting events. Physiol. Behav. **65**(1), 59–62 (1998)
2. Shiratori, Y., Maki, Y., Nakamura, S., Komatsu, T.: Detection of football spoilers on Twitter. In: Egi, H., Yuizono, T., Baloian, N., Yoshino, T., Ichimura, S., Rodrigues, A. (eds.) CollabTech 2018. LNCS, vol. 11000, pp. 129–141. Springer, Cham (2018). https://doi.org/10.1007/978-3-319-98743-9_11
3. Nakamura, S., Komatsu, T.: Study of information clouding methods to prevent spoilers of sports match. In: Proceedings of the International Working Conference on Advanced Visual Interfaces, pp. 661–664 (2012)
4. Sasano, I., Morisawa, K., Hirakawa, Y.: Personalized spoiler detection in tweets by using support vector machine. J. Adv. Technol. Eng. Res. **5**(5), 219–226 (2019)
5. Leavitt, J.D., Christenfeld, N.J.S.: Story spoilers don't spoil stories. Psychol. Sci. **22**(9), 1152–1154 (2011)
6. Rosenbaum, J.E., Johnson, B.K.: Who's afraid of spoilers? Need for cognition, need for affect, narrative selection and enjoyment. Psychol. Pop. Media Cult. **5**(3), 273–289 (2016)
7. Levine, W.H., Betzner, M., Autry, K.S.: The effect of spoilers on the enjoyment of short stories. Discourse Process. **53**(7), 513–531 (2016)
8. Maki, Y., Shiratori, Y., Sato, K., Nakamura, S.: A consideration to estimate spoiling pages in comics. In: International Symposium on Affective Science and Engineering, vol. ISASE2018, pp. 1–6 (2018)
9. Tsang, A.S.L., Yan, D.: Reducing the spoiler effect in experiential consumption. Assoc. Consum. Res. North Am. Adv. **36**, 708–709 (2009)
10. Johnson, B.K., Rosenbaum, J.E.: (Don't) tell me how it ends: spoilers, enjoyment, and involvement in television and film. Media Psychol. **21**(4), 582–612 (2018)
11. Li, Y., Luo, X.R., Li, K., Xu, X.: Exploring the spoiler effect in the digital age: evidence from the movie industry. Decis. Support Syst. **157**, 113755 (2022)

12. Boyd-Graber, J., Glasgow, K., Zajac, J.S.: Spoiler alert: machine learning approaches to detect social media posts with revelatory information. Proc. Assoc. Inf. Sci. Technol. **50**(1), 1–9 (2013)
13. Golbeck, J.: The Twitter mute button: a web filtering challenge. In: Proceedings of the SIGCHI Conference on Human Factors in Computing Systems, pp. 2755–2758 (2012)
14. Nakamura, S., Tanaka, K.: Temporal filtering system to reduce the risk of spoiling a user's enjoyment, In: Proceedings of the 12th International Conference on Intelligent User Interfaces, pp. 345–348 (2007)
15. Wan, M., Misra, R., Nakashole, N., McAuley, J.: Fine-grained spoiler detection from large-scale review corpora. In: Proceedings of the 57th Annual Meeting of the Association for Computational Linguistics, pp. 2605–2610 (2019)
16. Hijikata, Y., Iwai, H., Nishida, S.: Context-based plot detection from online review comments for preventing spoilers. In: 2016 IEEE/WIC/ACM International Conference on Web Intelligence (WI), pp. 57–65 (2016)
17. Jeon, S., Kim, S., Yu, H.: Spoiler detection in TV program tweets. Inf. Sci. **329**, 220–235 (2016)
18. Li, L., Zhang, N., Duan, L., Huang, Q., Du, J., Guan, L.: Automatic sports genre categorization and view-type classification over large-scale dataset. In: Proceedings of the 17th ACM International Conference on Multimedia, pp. 653–656 (2009)
19. Farhad, M.Y., Hossain, S., Tanvir, M.D.R.K., Chowdhury, S.A.: Sports-Net18: various sports classification using transfer learning. In: 2020 2nd International Conference on Sustainable Technologies for Industry 4.0 (STI), pp. 1–4 (2020)
20. Podgorelec, V., Pečnik, Š, Vrbančič, G.: Classification of similar sports images using convolutional neural network with hyper-parameter optimization. Appl. Sci. **10**(23), 8494 (2020)
21. Rafiq, M., Rafiq, G., Agyeman, R., Choi, G.S., Jin, S.: Scene classification for sports video summarization using transfer learning. Sensors **20**(6), 1702 (2020)
22. Hao, Y., Zhang, H., Ngo, C., Liu, Q., Hu, X.: Compact bilinear augmented query structured attention for sport highlights classification. In: Proceedings of the 28th ACM International Conference on Multimedia, pp. 628–636 (2020)

An Exploratory Study on Empathy and Online Discussions in Computer Supported Collaborative Learning

Emily Theophilou[1]([✉]) [iD], J. Roberto Sánchez-Reina[1] [iD], Valguima Odakura[2] [iD], and Davinia Hernández-Leo[1] [iD]

[1] TIDE, ICT Department, Universitat Pompeu Fabra, Barcelona, Spain
emily.theophilou@upf.edu
[2] Universidade Federal da Grande Dourados - UFGD, Dourados, Brazil

Abstract. Empathy, the ability to understand and share the feelings of others, is integral to effective communication and social interaction. In collaborative learning environments, empathy assumes even greater significance as it facilitates idea exchange and problem-solving among students. While previous studies have explored the role of empathy in collaboration, research focusing specifically on its impact on Computer-Supported Collaborative Learning (CSCL) remains limited. Therefore, this study aims to investigate the relationship between students' levels of affective and cognitive empathy and their chat discussion behavior within a CSCL environment. An exploratory descriptive study with 188 students from Spain (N = 133) and Brazil (N = 55) (M_{age} = 15.7 years) examined how affective and cognitive empathy influence student's online discussion within a CSCL environment. This study provides initial insights into the relationship between empathy and online collaboration. The findings indicate a positive correlation between students' levels of Perspective Taking and messages oriented to socialization. While, groups with higher max values under cognitive and affective empathy demonstrated a positive correlation with task-oriented messages. This study provides novel insights into the emergence of empathy within CSCL environments and has implications for the design of online collaborative learning platforms and educational technologies.

Keywords: Computer Supported Collaborative Learning · Online Discussion · Chat · Empathy

1 Introduction

Empathy is a complex human ability that allows us to connect with others. It allows us to not only understand and share the feelings of others but also respond appropriately to their viewpoints and beliefs [1, 2]. This multifaceted ability extends beyond the emotional realm as it allows us to step into the shoes of others, simulating their "mental states" to gain insight into their experiences, intentions, and needs [1, 3]. Empathy is a multifaceted concept, but it can be divided into two key dimensions [4]. The first dimension is referred to as affective empathy, reflecting our emotional response to another person's feelings. This might involve feeling sad when someone else is sad, or happy when they are happy. The second dimension is referred to as cognitive empathy, which involves understanding how others think and feel. This allows us to see the world from their perspective.

In the realm of social interactions, empathy plays a pivotal role in effective interpersonal communication. Empathy can reduce prejudice between groups [5] and even de-escalate tense situations, potentially preventing violence [6]. It enables individuals to understand others' perspectives, leading to increased social communication and cohesion [1]. Cognitive empathy becomes a powerful conflict resolution tool. Collaborators who consider each other's viewpoints naturally exchange more information, leading to a deeper understanding and better recall [7]. The ability to take perspective, fostered by empathy, makes it a crucial tool for conflict resolution [8]. These findings collectively underscore the pivotal role of empathy in fostering positive social interactions and implementing effective communication strategies.

Empathy is not only essential for positive social interactions, but also a crucial component in the collaborative learning process. Through effective communication fostered by empathy, students can exchange ideas and perspectives, leading to the generation of novel and innovative solutions to complex problems. Research by Xiang and Jing [9] supports this notion, demonstrating that individuals with higher empathic abilities can lead group dynamics more effectively resulting in more frequent communication among group members. A study by Falk and Johnson [10] suggests that groups actively taking the perspective of another student produce more creative solutions, exhibit greater cooperation, and experience increased trust and satisfaction among members. Building on these findings, Mouw et al. [11] identified distinct profiles of cooperative behavior based on student interactions during collaboration. They explored the role of perspective-taking abilities in these profiles, but interestingly, individual perspective-taking skills did not directly predict them. However, they found differences in cooperative behaviors based on group composition where groups with overall stronger perspective taking abilities were more likely to exhibit a "hard-workers" profile, characterized by leading the cooperative process, planning, task focus, and minimal off-task communication. This aligns with further research by Wei and Jing [9], which showed that groups with highly empathetic leaders, who presumably possess strong perspective-taking skills, achieved better learning outcomes compared to those with random leaders. These findings indicate that individual perspective-taking abilities may not directly predict collaborative behaviors; however, it appears to be a key driver of successful group learning on the group level. Groups with strong overall empathy, or those led by highly empathetic individuals, exhibit more effective communication, collaboration and achieve better outcomes.

Affective empathy, the ability to share the emotional experience of others, also plays a crucial role in fostering prosocial behaviors during collaboration. Affective empathy allows us to share the emotions of others, ranging from feeling compassionate to someone in grief to simply acknowledging their distress leading to a deeper emotional connection and concern for their well-being [15, 27]. This emotional connection fuels a desire to help and fosters a sense of concern for others' well-being and can increase congruence, the ability to be open, non-judgmental, and honest within a group [28]. In collaborative settings, affective empathy allows us to recognize and respond to the emotions of our peers. This can involve feelings of concern or a desire to help, fostering a more supportive and positive environment [26]. By fostering emotional connection and concern for others, affective empathy can create a more positive and supportive collaborative environment, ultimately promoting prosocial behaviors that benefit the collaborative process.

However, online environments present a challenge as the absence of nonverbal cues can lead to misunderstandings and misinterpretations of emotions and intentions [29]. Additionally, anonymity can further embolden negative behavior towards peers, especially for those with lower empathy [30, 31]. Research in the domain of Computer-Supported Collaborative Learning (CSCL) frequently overlooks the impact of interpersonal and socio-emotional skills [14], failing to explore how these factors could potentially impede the learning process [23]. This neglect exists despite studies indicating how student characteristics like gender and culture can influence collaboration within CSCL environments [12, 13]. Moreover, while discussion analysis within CSCL environments often show diverse types of interactions occurring [19, 25] they often overlook how students' interpersonal skills such as empathy could have influenced in fostering these interactions [14]. Despite the link established between strong interpersonal skills and collaboration, a knowledge gap remains regarding how these skills are fostered within CSCL groups [24] and the role of empathy remains underexplored [14]. This lack of understanding presents a significant gap, as empathy is a crucial aspect of human communication and can significantly impact how students collaborate and learn in CSCL settings.

Subsequently, the main objective of this study is to investigate the relationship between students' level of affective and cognitive empathy and the quality of collaboration within a CSCL environment. Hence the following research question is formulated: How do students' levels of affective and cognitive empathy influence their online discussion within a CSCL environment?

By addressing this research question, the study aims to shed light on the influence of perspective-taking and empathy on collaboration quality in CSCL activities through an exploratory study. Drawing from previous work [10, 11], we hypothesize a positive association between students' cognitive empathy abilities and task-oriented messages within a CSCL setting (H1). This expectation arises from the idea that strong perspective-taking allows individuals to grasp others' viewpoints, leading to more active contributions in collaborative problem-solving within CSCL environments. Furthermore, we hypothesized a positive association between students' affective empathy abilities and positive socialization messages within a CSCL setting (H2). This hypothesis is grounded in the notion that individuals with elevated affective empathy tend to foster a supportive and amicable atmosphere [15], thereby promoting interactions characterized by encouragement, and motivation among peers.

This initial exploration will pave the way for future research to examine potential causal links and inform the design of interventions that can enhance perspective-taking and empathy skills within CSCL environments.

2 Methodology

2.1 Participants and Setting

The present study was conducted as part of a Media Literacy workshop held in schools from Barcelona (Spain) and Dourados (Brazil). A total of 203 high school students participated in the workshops (Spain, N = 142, Brazil, N = 61). After data collection and cleaning, the final sample of the study consisted of 188 students (Boys N = 105, 55.9%, Girls, N = 74, 39.4%, Other/Not specified N = 9, 4.8%, M_{Age} = 15.7, Age_{Rank} 13 to 17 years, Spain, N = 133, Brazil, N = 55). In accordance with the university's ethical board guidelines, all participants included in the study were briefed on the research objectives of the workshop and provided their consent for participation by digitally signing a form. For underage participants, parental consent was additionally obtained.

2.2 Procedure, CSCL Environment and Materials

A Media Literacy workshop to strengthen adolescents' empathy towards cyberbullying scenarios in social media platforms was the setting of the study. The intervention saw the development of a Computer Supported workshop assisted with a Virtual Learning companion [17] in a narrative-scripted environment [16]. As part of the instructed activities, students were directed to a collaborative online activity within the PyramidApp tool to engage in discussion about cyberbullying and reflect on the educational material covered during the session (see Fig. 1 for procedure).

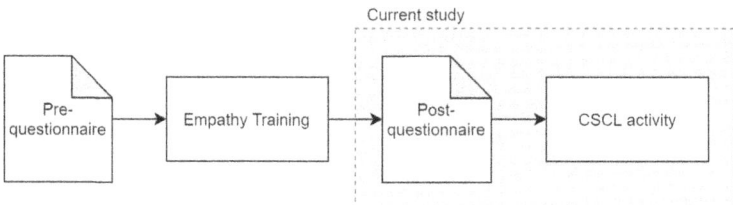

Fig. 1. Procedure of the study. Data collection for this study occurred within the gray area.

The PyramidApp is a web-based CSCL tool that follows the pyramid collaborative learning flow pattern [18], enabling students to construct improved answers synchronously through online discussion. This tool divides collaboration into distinct phases, facilitating students' interaction towards solving a problem collectively. In the initial phase, students are tasked with providing individual answers. Once all submissions are received, the system organizes students into small groups, allowing them to view and rate each other's answers. Moving to the answer-improving stage, students engage in discussions aimed at collectively refining their answers. Following this phase, students are grouped into larger cohorts, fostering further discussions and enabling voting for the best answers to achieve a consensus by the activity's conclusion. Within the CSCL tool a group awareness tool was enabled to promote student participation [19].

Aligned with the main objectives of the workshop, students were introduced to the following collaborative task within the PyramidApp tool: "Bullying is a growing problem in schools. In your opinion, what type of bullying affects children and young people the most: bullying (for example, at school) or cyberbullying (i.e. Internet harassment)? Why do you think that?". The prompt encouraged students to reflect on the previously covered material and provided them with opportunities to engage in conversations where they could share their opinions.

The PyramidApp activity involved a single level of collaboration: students initially provided individual answers and subsequently, were grouped into teams of similar numbers of students to engage in discussions to reach a consensus answer to the question. Based on the criteria of Velazaman et al. [20], students' participation in the PyramidApp was anonymized to foster collaboration and interaction.

2.3 Measures

Sociodemographic: To report demographic data, students reported their (male/female/diverse/no answer) and age as part of initial pre-questionnaire.

Empathic Concern: To measure the students affective empathy, the Empathic Concern subscale from the Interpersonal Reactivity Index [2] was utilized. This subscale focuses on "others-oriented" feelings of sympathy and concern for others, which can indicate the students abilities to sympathize with their peers. It consists of seven items, such as "I try to look at everybody's side of a disagreement before I make a decision". Participants rated their agreement with each item on a 5-point Likert scale, ranging from 1 (does not describe me well) to 5 (describes me very well).

For this study, we aimed to measure affective empathy as the ability to understand and share the feelings of others. Therefore, we excluded the Personal Distress subscale of the Interpersonal Reactivity Index, which assesses one's own emotional discomfort in response to another's emotions.

Perspective-Taking: To measure participants' cognitive empathy, the Perspective-Taking subscale from the Interpersonal Reactivity Index [2] was implemented. This subscale comprises seven items that assess an individual's ability to understand others' perspectives and take them into account when forming judgments or making decisions, as for example, "When I see someone being taken advantage of, I feel kind of protective toward them." Participants indicated their level of agreement with each item on a 5-point Likert scale, ranging from 1 (does not describe me well) to 5 (describes me very well).

In this study, we aimed to measure cognitive empathy, specifically the ability of students to take the perspectives of others. Therefore, we excluded the Fantasy subscale of the Interpersonal Reactivity Index, which shows an individual's tendency to imagine themselves in fictional scenarios and experience the feelings and actions of those characters.

Quality of Collaboration: To assess the quality of participation, the conversations conducted by students in the PyramidApp setting were extracted and coded to analyze aspects related to discussion orientation (Cognitive and Socialization). Each message was coded as one unit. However, if a student sent two or more incomplete messages that together expressed a single idea, these were counted as one unit instead of two.

The messages were coded following the coding scheme of Velamazan et al. [21]. This coding scheme entails messages into two primary categories: those oriented towards the task (Content and cognitive side) and those oriented toward socialization (Social and emotional side). Building on the categorization presented in Velamazan et al. [21], we've refined the classification of spam messages within our study. Previously, these messages fell under the broad category of 'social and emotional'. To enhance clarity, we've separated them and created a new umbrella category: "Non-Task Related Messages." This category encompasses messages that deviate from the core task objective. Within "Non-Task Related Messages," we've further defined two subcategories:

Off-Task Messages: These messages stray from the task at hand and don't contribute to a focused learning environment during collaboration.

Rude Messages: This subcategory captures messages that are disrespectful or disruptive.

Moreover we have included a new subcategory under the messages oriented to socialization category to capture greetings and positive communication messages.

Greetings/Positive Communication: This subcategory captures messages that are oriented towards greeting each other in an attempt to foster a sense of community.

These distinctions allow for a more nuanced understanding of the types of spam messages encountered during the collaborative activities of our study (see Table 1 for final coding scheme).

2.4 Data Analysis

As part of the data analysis, the study followed a mixed method approach which combined the analysis of students' self-reports on Empathic Concern and Perspective Taking, and the qualitative analysis of students' interactions in the PyramidApp tool. The measurement of Empathic Concern and Perspective Taking scales facilitated the calculation of mean values for both variables while students' interactions were coded through a content analysis based in the proposed coding scheme. The data was coded by the authors ($a = .78$) of this paper and compiled with the self-reports of students into a unique dataset. It is important to note that an initial analysis on the individual level has not shown any significant correlation with individual communication behaviors. Indicating that these types of studies need to be analyzed on the group level to encompass the overall interactions that happened during collaboration as reported by previous studies [11].

Therefore in the present study, the data analysis strategy included the observation of students' collaboration within groups and the minimum unit of analysis was set as the PyramidApp conversations (Chat Rooms). A total of 48 collaborative chat rooms were included in the initial analysis.

The final dataset consisted of 41 groups (Brazil N = 12, 29.2% Spain N = 29, 70.7%). While off-task messages are a recognized aspect of collaboration within CSCL environments (e.g., [19, 20, 25]), we excluded seven groups that exhibited a predominant focus on such messages. This decision was made to ensure our analysis focused on groups

Table 1. Coding scheme utilized to code students conversations within the CSCL environment based on Velamazan et al. [21]'s coding scheme.

Oriented to Task messages that are primarily focused on the task at hand and the content being discussed	**Ideas/proposals:** A message that represents any kind of initiative to solve, push forward, iterate or offer a solution to improve or solve a task, or that displays some kind of planning or a strategy to continue a task
	Feedback/answers: Messages that refer to any type of dis/agreement with another message, typically an idea or a proposal
	Questions/doubts: Messages that request any kind of clarification, ask for an opinion or point to a lack of information, precision or any kind of misunderstanding
Oriented to Socialization messages that focus on fostering social connections and maintaining a positive learning atmosphere	**Humour/jokes:** Messages that try to make others laugh but do not disturb or distract from the content of the topic of conversation. They usually create a better atmosphere and/or ease tense situations
	Support/motivation: Messages in support of the team that uphold a good atmosphere and/or ease tense situations
	Regulation of group behavior: Messages about group regulation and time management or those that praise other members' suggestions
	Greetings/positive communication: Messages greeting each other and attempting to identify each other
Non-Task Related messages that diverge from the primary objectives of task completion and maintaining a productive learning atmosphere	**Off-task messages:** Messages that are not aimed at fulfilling a task or maintaining a learning focused atmosphere during collaboration
	Rude messages: Messages that are not related to the task or do not aim to keep a positive social environment

actively collaborating towards the task at hand. Therefore, groups that exhibited less than 10% of task oriented discussion were excluded from the analysis.

A descriptive analysis checked the distribution and normality of the observed variables. Affective empathy and perspective-taking scores were averaged for each group, with minimum and maximum values noted to standardize the values in the variable [32]. As the second step of the analysis, several Pearson correlation tests were conducted to assess linear relationships between variables, specifically between the mean affective empathy and perspective taking scores per group and the frequency of each message type per group. The correlation coefficient "r" ranges from −1 to 1, signifying strength and direction: 1 denotes perfect positive correlation, −1 perfect negative, and 0 no correlation.

3 Findings

In this section we present the key findings from our study to better understand the role of empathy in student collaboration. During this study, students sent a total of 975 messages (mean = 23.8, max = 58, min = 8). These messages can be categorized as follows: 37% task-oriented (mean = 8.7, max = 26, min = 1), 41% social-oriented (mean = 8.3, max = 22, min = 2), and 22% off-task (mean = 6.7, max = 23, min = 0) (see Table 2 for detailed information on subcategories).

Table 2. Frequency of messages being sent per subcategory.

		Total msgs	Mean per group	Max per group	Min per group
Oriented to Task	Ideas/Proposals	113	2.75	14	0
	Feedback/Answers	143	3.48	12	0
	Questions/Doubts	102	2.48	10	0
Oriented to Socialization	Humor/jokes	8	0.19	2	0
	Support/Motivation	9	0.22	1	0
	Group-Regulation	105	2.6	10	0
	Greetings	220	5.36	14	1
Non-Task Related	Off-Tasks Messages	232	5.65	18	0
	Rude	43	1	5	0

The groups exhibited varying levels of empathy, as measured by perspective-taking (mean = 3.10, SD = 0.34) and empathic concern (mean = 3.28, SD = 0.39). Groups with higher empathic concern were: G19 with 4.33, and G28 with 4.03. Whilst groups with lowest empathic concern were: G14 with 2.32, and G13 with 2.61. Groups with higher perspective taking were: G21 with 3.92, and G17 with 3.76. Whilst groups with lowest perspective taking were: G14 with 2.24, and G13 with 2.43. The frequency of type of messages being sent per group can be seen in Fig. 2.

The type of collaboration students engaged in showed significant positive correlations with the number of messages produced and the different message categories identified in our coding scheme (see Table 3). Notably, a strong positive correlation emerged between group regulation messages and the total number of messages sent (r = .778, p < .01).

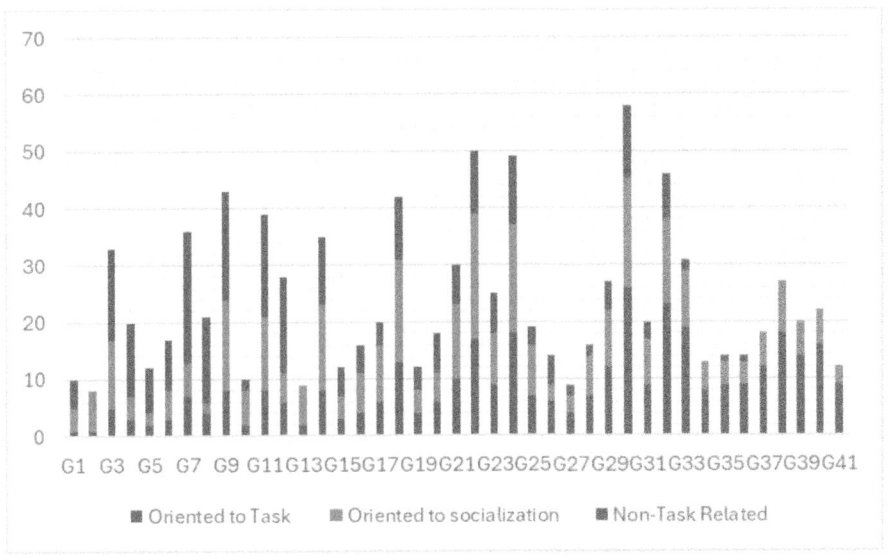

Fig. 2. Frequency of type of messages being sent per group

Table 3. Correlations for coded discussion categories with average group values of perspective taking and empathy concern (* (p < 0.05), ** (p < 0.01)).

		Messages Produced	Perspective Taking	Empathy Concern
Oriented to Task	Ideas/Proposals	.633**	−.072	.185
	Feedback/Answers	.567**	.001	.012
	Questions/Doubts	.332*	−.050	.240
Oriented to Socialization	Humor/jokes	.430**	.284*	.240
	Support/Motivation	.064	.206	.194
	Group-Regulation	.778**	.218	.059
	Greetings	.736**	−.271*	−.090
Non-Task Related	Off-Tasks Messages	.645**	−.067	−.142
	Rude	.333*	−.017	−.240

Our first hypothesis predicted a positive association between students' cognitive empathy, specifically perspective-taking abilities, and task-oriented messages exchanged within a CSCL environment. The findings offer mixed support for this hypothesis. While positive correlations emerged between perspective-taking and social behaviors like humor (r = .28, p < .05), surprisingly, a negative correlation was found with greetings (r = −.27, p < .05) (Table 3). However, the relationship with task-oriented messages was less clear.

Interestingly, groups with a higher max value under perspective-taking abilities (indicating that a student within that group possessed high perspective-taking abilities) displayed a positive influence on collaboration through messages promoting group regulation (r = .34, p < .05) (Table 4). However, the direct association between perspective-taking and task-oriented messages such as proposing ideas (r = −.072), raising doubts (r = −.050) or giving feedback/answers (r = .001) was weak and not statistically significant.

Table 4. Correlations for coded discussion categories with max group values of perspective taking and empathy concern.

		Perspective Taking	Empathy Concern
Oriented to Task	Ideas/Proposals	0.12	0.33*
	Feedback/Answers	0.05	0.10
	Questions/Doubts	0.11	0.31
Oriented to Socialization	Humor/jokes	0.27	0.19
	Support/Motivation	0.19	0.28
	Group-Regulation	0.34*	0.14
	Greetings	−0.07	0.07
Non-Task Related	Off-Tasks Messages	0.09	−0.03
	Rude	0.06	0.01

Our second hypothesis predicted a positive association between students' affective empathy and positive social behaviors within the CSCL environment. The results provided limited support for this hypothesis. While we observed some positive correlations between average group empathy and social behaviors like humor and support (e.g., humor/jokes: r = .240, support/motivation messages: r = .194), these relationships were not statistically significant.

Interestingly, a different pattern emerged when we examined the highest empathy score within each group. While a positive correlation existed with supportive messages (r = .28), it wasn't statistically significant, suggesting a potential, but unconfirmed, link to social behavior.

However, the results for task-oriented messages revealed a positive association. Groups with a member demonstrating high empathic concern (indicated by the max value) displayed a positive association with messages proposing ideas during collaboration (r = .33, p < .05). A similar trend was also observed for asking questions and expressing doubts, although these correlations were weaker and not statistically significant (r = .31).

4 Discussion

This study explored the influence of empathy on collaboration quality within a CSCL environment. While our hypotheses yielded mixed results, the findings offer valuable insights into the interplay between perspective-taking, empathy, and overall collaboration quality.

Our findings suggest a link between perspective-taking and positive social behaviors within collaborative groups. Groups with higher average scores on perspective-taking measures exhibited positive correlations with aspects of social participation, such as using humor. Our findings also revealed suggestive, though not statistically significant, relationships between perspective-taking and positive social behaviors through messages offering support and regulating group dynamics.

The results also uncovered a negative correlation between perspective-taking and students sending greetings and identification messages. This result is rather unexpected and raises the need for further analysis. Even though one might assume that groups with higher perspective taking would have focused on more task oriented discussions and would not engage in socialization behaviors this was not supported by our findings. Further research is needed to explore the potential influence of the CSCL environment design, the specific task requirements, and the overall classroom dynamics on this observed relationship.

In regards to task oriented messages, we found no associations with perspective taking and messages that propose ideas, provide feedback, or ask questions contradicting previous findings [10, 11]. This could be explained by the specific context of the CSCL task and the situations that arose during collaboration. Prior research suggests perspective-taking is particularly crucial when managing negative emotions [21]. If the task lacked significant emotional complexity, students with high perspective-taking might not have needed to utilize their abilities for task-oriented problem-solving.

A secondary analysis revealed further relations. Groups with a higher max value under perspective-taking abilities showed a positive correlation with messages related to group regulation. This suggests that the presence of a student with strong perspective-taking abilities might have a subtle influence on overall group regulation similarly to assigning a highly empathetic leader [9]. This finding has potential implications for the design and development of CSCL grouping mechanisms, as it highlights the potential benefit of including students with strong perspective-taking skills.

Our findings related to H2 did not reveal strong associations between students' empathic concern and positive social behaviors within the collaborative groups. While the analysis of average group empathic concern showed some suggestive, non-significant relationships with humor and motivational messages, these connections were not statistically significant.

Interestingly, a similar pattern emerged with task-oriented messages. Groups with higher average empathic concern scores exhibited a non-significant positive correlation with messages related to asking questions about the task. This suggests a potential link between empathic concern and both social interaction and task engagement, although further research is needed to solidify these findings.

A secondary analysis focusing on the highest empathic concern score within each group (max value) revealed a different pattern. Groups with a student possessing the highest empathic concern score displayed a positive correlation with messages promoting group regulation. Additionally, a suggestive, though non-significant, relationship was observed between the group's max empathic concern and messages expressing questions or doubts. The contextual influence of the task, which centered around cyberbullying a topic closely related to empathy, could potentially have played a role in these observed results. The task's focus may have facilitated the heightened performance of empathetic groups, contributing to their enhanced social interactions and task engagement.

We must acknowledge several limitations that may have affected our findings. One key limitation is the relatively small sample size of the study. While the study sheds light on potential relationships between empathy and collaboration quality in a CSCL environment, the generalizability of these findings may be limited due to the sample size. Future research with larger and more diverse samples is necessary to confirm these initial findings and draw more definitive conclusions.

Moreover, the coding of the CSCL messages focused solely on socialization and task orientation, potentially limiting the depth of analysis. Different scales can offer a further focus on aspects such as positive/negative socioemotional messages [33]. Additionally, the anonymous approach employed in this study might have influenced results, as we observed a high number of students attempting to identify their peers during the collaborative process. This focus on identifying classmates could have potentially detracted from their primary goal of solving the assigned task.

Furthermore, for this study we have decided to exclude groups where task oriented messages were less than 10% of the overall discussion taking place. While excluding these groups allows for a clearer analysis of task-focused collaboration, it does raise intriguing questions about the factors influencing such behavior. While our sample size limited this exploration, future research could delve deeper into these outliers to understand the potential causes and implications.

Lastly, while this study focused on perspective-taking and affective empathy, other factors like gender [12] and emotional intelligence [22] might also play a role in shaping collaborative behaviors within CSCL environments. Future research that explores a wider range of factors alongside perspective-taking and empathy could provide a more comprehensive understanding of how these elements influence collaboration in CSCL settings.

5 Conclusion

This study explored how affective (Empathic Concern) and cognitive empathy (Perspective-Taking) can influence collaboration quality within a CSCL environment. While statistically significant correlations were limited due to the sample size, some interesting trends emerged, suggesting potential relations that warrant further investigation with larger datasets.

Findings under this study demonstrated that students with higher perspective-taking abilities exhibited a tendency to exchange more humorous messages, suggesting a more positive and socially-oriented communication style. Furthermore, a deeper analysis revealed that groups with a higher max value under perspective-taking abilities showed a positive association with messages focused on group regulation, potentially indicating a focus on maintaining a productive collaborative environment. Similarly, groups with a higher max value under empathic concern seemed to be associated with messages related to the proposal of ideas. Further non significant relations suggested potential relations with messages offering support and motivation to peers.

While these findings are suggestive, the small sample size limits the generalizability of these initial insights. Future research on this topic should aim to replicate this study with a larger and more diverse sample size. This would allow for more robust statistical analysis to confirm or refute the potential relationships identified here. To gain a more comprehensive understanding of how empathy shapes collaboration within CSCL environments, future research could explore a wider range of collaboration behaviors and interaction patterns. Additionally, considering student characteristics such as gender, age, and cultural background could provide further valuable insights into how these factors interact with empathy and potentially influence collaboration.

Acknowledgments. This work was supported by the National Research Agency of the Spanish Ministry (PID2020-112584RB-C33/MICIN/AEI/10.13039/501100011033, MDM-2015-0502), the Volkswagen Foundation (COURAGE project, nos. 95567 and 9B145), and the Department of Research and Universities of the Government of Catalonia (SGR 00930). D. Hernández-Leo (Serra Húnter) acknowledges the support by ICREA under the ICREA Academia programme.

Disclosure of Interests. The authors have no competing interests to declare that are relevant to the content of this article.

References

1. Decety, J., Jackson, P.: The functional architecture of human empathy. Behav. Cogn. Neurosci. Rev. **3**, 71–100 (2004). https://doi.org/10.1177/1534582304267187
2. Davis, M.H.: A multidimensional approach to individual differences in empathy. JSAS Catalog Sel. Doc. Psychol. **10**, 85 (1980)
3. Preston, S., Waal, F.: Empathy: its ultimate and proximate bases. Behav. Brain Sci. **25**, 1–20 (2002). Discussion 20. https://doi.org/10.1017/S0140525X02000018
4. Eisenberg, N., Strayer, J.: Critical issues in the study of empathy. In: Eisenberg, N., Strayer, J. (eds.) Empathy and its Development, pp. 3–13. Cambridge University Press (1987)
5. Davis, M.H.: Empathy: A Social Psychological Approach, 1st edn. Routledge, London (1996). https://doi.org/10.4324/9780429493898
6. Rosenberg, M.B., Chopra, D.: Nonviolent Communication: A Language of Life: Life-Changing Tools for Healthy Relationships, 3rd edn. Puddle Dancer Press (2015)
7. Johnson, D.W.: Effectiveness of role reversal: actor or listener. Psychol. Rep. **28**(1), 275–282 (1971). https://doi.org/10.2466/pr0.1971.28.1.275
8. Krznaric, R.: Empathy: A Handbook for Revolution. Random House (2014)
9. Wei, X., Jing, X.: Research on grouping strategies of online collaborative learning based on empathy. In: Proceedings of the 2020 3rd International Conference on Education Technology Management (ICETM 2020), pp. 1–6. Association for Computing Machinery (2021). https://doi.org/10.1145/3446590.3446591

10. Falk, D., Johnson, D.: The effects of perspective-taking and egocentrism on problem solving in heterogeneous and homogeneous groups. J. Soc. Psychol. **102**, 63–72 (1977). https://doi.org/10.1080/00224545.1977.9713241
11. Mouw, J., Saab, N., Gijlers, H., Hickendorff, M., Paridon, Y., van den Broek, P.: The differential effect of perspective-taking ability on profiles of cooperative behaviours and learning outcomes. Frontline Learn. Res. **8**, 88–113 (2020). https://doi.org/10.14786/flr.v8i6.633
12. Prinsen, F., Volman, M.L.L., Terwel, J.: The influence of learner characteristics on degree and type of participation in a CSCL environment. Br. J. Edu. Technol. **38**(6), 1037–1055 (2007). https://doi.org/10.1111/J.1467-8535.2006.00692.X
13. Reis, R.C.D., et al.: Step towards a model to bridge the gap between personality traits and collaborative learning roles. IxD&A **28**, 124–144 (2016)
14. Silva, U., Ferreira, D.: Emotional aspects for productive dialogues in computer-supported collaborative learning: a systematic literature review. JUCS **27**, 303–322 (2021). https://doi.org/10.3897/jucs.66389
15. King, S., Holosko, M.J.: The development and initial validation of the empathy scale for social workers. Res. Soc. Work. Pract. **22**(2), 174–185 (2012). https://doi.org/10.1177/1049731511417136
16. Hernández-Leo, D., Theophilou, E., Lobo, R., Sánchez-Reina, R., Ognibene, D.: Narrative scripts embedded in social media towards empowering digital and self-protection skills. Paper presented at the Sixteenth European Conference on Technology Enhanced Learning, 20–24 September 2021, Bozen, Italy (2021)
17. Börsting, J., et al.: An Empathy Training for Sensitizing Adolescents for Cyberbullying on Social Media: A Cross-National Study. [Manuscript submitted for publication, currently under review] (Submitted)
18. Manathunga, K., Hernández-Leo, D.: Authoring and enactment of mobile pyramid-based collaborative learning activities. Br. J. Edu. Technol. **49**(2), 262–275 (2018)
19. Theophilou, E., Sanchez-Reina, R., Hernandez-Leo, D., Odakura, V., Amarasinghe, I., Lobo-Quintero, R.: The effect of a group awareness tool in synchronous online discussions: studying participation, quality and balance. Behav. Inf. Technol. (2023). https://doi.org/10.1080/0144929X.2023.2200543
20. Velamazán, M., Santos, P., Hernández-Leo, D., Vicent, L.: User anonymity versus identification in computer-supported collaborative learning: comparing learners' preferences and behaviors. Comput. Educ. **203**, 104848 (2023). https://doi.org/10.1016/j.compedu.2023.104848
21. Gerace, A., Day, A., Casey, S., Mohr, P.: An exploratory investigation of the process of perspective taking in interpersonal situations. J. Relat. Res. **4**, e6 (2013). https://doi.org/10.1017/jrr.2013
22. Löffler, C.S., Greitemeyer, T.: Are women the more empathetic gender? The effects of gender role expectations. Curr. Psychol. **42**, 220–231 (2023). https://doi.org/10.1007/s12144-020-01260-8
23. Isohätälä, J., Näykki, P., Järvelä, S., et al.: Social sensitivity: a manifesto for CSCL research. Int. J. Comput.-Support Collab. Learn. **16**, 289–299 (2021). https://doi.org/10.1007/s11412-021-09344-8
24. Slof, B., Nijdam, D., Janssen, J.: Do interpersonal skills and interpersonal perceptions predict student learning in CSCL environments? Comput. Educ. **97**, 49–60 (2016). https://doi.org/10.1016/j.compedu.2016.02.012
25. Vogler, J.S., Munsell, S.E., Knutson, D.: LOLsquared: when laughing-out-loud and learning-on-line intermingle in a computer-mediated classroom discussion. Comput. Educ. **140**, 103597 (2019). https://doi.org/10.1016/J.COMPEDU.2019.103597
26. Geller, S.M., Greenberg, L.S.: Therapeutic Presence: A Mindful Approach to Effective Therapy. American Psychological Association (2012)

27. Baron-Cohen, S., Wheelwright, S.: The empathy quotient: an investigation of adults with Asperger syndrome or high functioning autism, and normal sex differences. J. Autism Dev. Disord. **34**(2), 163–175 (2004). https://doi.org/10.1023/b:jadd.0000022607.19833.00
28. Vollberg, M.C., Gaesse, B., Cikara, M.: Activating episodic simulation increases affective empathy. Cognition **209**, 104558 (2021)
29. Rosenberg, D., Sillince, J.A.A.: Verbal and nonverbal communication in computer-mediated settings. Int. J. Artif. Intell. Educ. **11**, 299–319 (2000). (hal-00197332)
30. Nocentini, A., Calmaestra, J., Schultze-Krumbholz, A., Scheithauer, H., Ortega, R., Menesini, E.: Cyberbullying: labels, behaviours and definition in three European countries. Aust. J. Guid. Couns. **20**, 129–142 (2010). https://doi.org/10.1375/ajgc.20.2.129
31. Hinduja, S., Patchin, J.W.: Bias-based cyberbullying among early adolescents: associations with cognitive and affective empathy. J. Early Adolesc. **42**, 1204–1235 (2022). https://doi.org/10.1177/02724316221088757
32. Cohen, B.H., Lea, R.B.: Essentials of Statistics for the Social and Behavioral Sciences. Wiley, New York (2004)
33. Gorse, C., Emmitt, S., Lewis, M., Howarth, A.: Interaction process analysis: a methodology for researching construction communication. In: Emmitt, S. (ed.) Detailing Design - Towards a Joined-Up Industry: Proceedings of Detail Design in Architecture, vol. 3, pp. 41–49 (2001)

Interpreting Arrows in Mobile Robot-Human Encounters: The Influence of Spatial Context and Presentation Timing

Yo Kuwamiya[✉], Atsuto Kurokochi, and Minoru Kobayashi

Meiji University, 4-21-1 Nakano, Nakano-ku, Tokyo, Japan
{yo.kuwamiya,atsuto.kurokochi}@koblab.org, minoru@acm.org

Abstract. Several studies have proposed that mobile robots can indicate their movement direction by displaying arrows to facilitate smooth passing of humans. However, the interpretation of these arrows can be ambiguous, as they are also commonly used as guiding signs. The way arrows are presented on the robot's body may lead people to perceive them as indicating either the robot's direction of movement or the direction passers-by should move. This study aims to develop arrows into clear and unambiguous non-verbal communication method for robot-human interactions. We investigate how the spatial context and timing of arrow presentation influence people's perception of the arrow's meaning. Building upon our previous experiment, we explore two key aspects: 1) differences in arrow perception based on the spatial context of symmetric and asymmetric corridors, and 2) the influence of presentation timing on perception when varying the mobile robot's speed. We conducted a virtual passing experiment using first-person perspective videos of encounters with a mobile robot. The findings suggest that the corridor's spatial characteristics play a significant role in how people perceive the arrow's meaning. Furthermore, our results indicate that the meaning of the arrow may be determined by the interaction between the spatial context and the presentation timing. Our research highlights the importance of considering the spatial context and presentation timing when using arrows for non-verbal communication in human-robot interactions.

Keywords: Arrow presentation · Mobile robot · Non-verbal communication

1 Introduction

Mobile robots, such as autonomous mobile robots and telepresence robots, are gradually becoming more integrated into human environments. As a result, the challenges surrounding collaboration between robots and humans are attracting increased attention. "Robot-human passing" is a scenario that carries the risks of collisions and can make humans feel uneasy, so ensuring safety and giving people a sense of security are crucial. To achieve this, designing safe navigation paths for robots is not enough. During passing encounters, mobile robots must also communicate their intentions to passers-by in advance to give reassurance.

In spaces where mobile robots are introduced, passing encounters between robots and humans occur frequently. Given the short duration of these encounters, non-verbal communication methods are preferred to convey intentions. Therefore, using arrows to indicate the direction of movement has been proposed and discussed in various studies. These studies use arrows as signs to indicate the robot's direction of movement. However, arrows are also commonly used to guide people's behavior and attention. When a mobile robot displays an arrow on its attached display, as shown in Fig. 1, the interpretation of the arrow may become ambiguous. Specifically, some people interpret the arrow in Fig. 1 as meaning "the robot is moving to the right," while others interpret it as "the passing pedestrian should move to the right." Our previous research [1] has demonstrated this split in interpretation through virtual passing experiments.

Fig. 1. Passing by a mobile robot presenting an arrow.

Our primary objective is to develop arrows into an unambiguous non-verbal communication technique for robot-human interactions. We aim to ensure that the meaning conveyed by the arrows is unambiguous while maintaining their simplicity. This is especially crucial for non-humanoid robots, which often lack human-like features that could assist in communication. To achieve this goal, we investigate how people perceive arrows presented by mobile robots in various situations. Our study focuses on the two key aspects: the spatial context and the presentation timing. In a previous experiment [1], we examined the perception of arrows presented by a mobile robot moving at 0.5 m/s in an asymmetric corridor. The findings revealed that when the arrow was presented 2.5 m ahead of the person, they were more likely to avoid the robot in the direction indicated by the arrow compared to when the arrow was presented 6.5 m ahead. This suggests that presenting the arrow just before the passing moment makes it more likely to be interpreted as "move in the direction of the arrow". However, the previous study had two limitations. First, the experiment was conducted in an asymmetric corridor, which may have influenced the results. Second, it was unclear which specific factor, the distance between the robot and the person at arrow presentation or the time from arrow presentation to passing.

Objectives. This study has two main objectives:

Objective 1: Investigate how the perception of arrows changes based on the spatial context. - This is examined using passing scenarios in a symmetrical corridor.

Objective 2: Investigate changes in arrow perception when varying the robot's speed. - The analysis focuses on how the interpretation of the arrow differs when the robot's speed is set to 0.4 m/s, 0.5 m/s, and 0.6 m/s. This enables us to investigate the influence of two factors: the distance at which the arrow is presented (presentation distance) and the time from the arrow presentation to the passing (presentation time).

Experiment Results. We conducted a web-based questionnaire experiment using first-person perspective videos of passing encounters with a mobile robot. The results showed that:

1. In a symmetrical corridor, participants' avoidance direction was split under all conditions.
2. The arrow's interpretation results in two possible directions based on the presentation distance and time, leading to a divided direction of avoidance due to diverse interpretations.

Contributions. The key contributions of this study are:

1. Demonstrating that the interpretation of arrows is influenced by the spatial context, by comparing arrow perception in symmetrical and asymmetrical corridors.
2. Showing that while ambiguity in the arrow's meaning cannot be eliminated, people make various interpretations based on the presentation distance and time.

2 Related Works

This chapter clarifies the significance and position of this research in relation to existing studies on methods of indicating the direction of movement for mobile robots, particularly those using arrows. We also present the efforts made in previous research and highlight the challenges addressed in this study.

2.1 Intention Communication of Mobile Robots

Mobile robots can be classified into humanoid and non-humanoid robots. Humanoid robots has a human-like structure. This makes it easy for people to understand their direction of movement. In contrast, non-humanoid robots have a mechanical and inorganic appearance, as they are often designed to perform specific tasks. This makes it challenging for people to predict the robot's direction of movement. To address this issue, some studies have explored various methods to facilitate smooth passing between humans and non-humanoid robots by using non-verbal signs.

It is known that people rely on gaze [2] and face orientation [3] to determine the direction in which others are moving. Inspired by this, some studies have investigated methods of conveying a robot's direction of movement through its gaze and face orientation [4–7]. Other approaches have been to apply the rules of turn signals to robots [7–9]. These studies aim to make the robot's intended direction more intuitive for humans to understand. Additionally, research on visualizing robot movements has not been limited to ground-based mobile robots; some studies have also explored ways to display the movements of drones [10].

However, the effectiveness of these methods in clearly conveying the robot's direction of movement can vary. Fernandez et al. [11] found that people could not immediately understand the meaning of turn signals attached to a robot. The researchers proposed conducting a demonstration before the robot and human pass each other. We think that the success of using common signaling methods from other moving objects on mobile robots is heavily influenced by the robot's appearance and design.

2.2 Arrow Presentation by Mobile Robots

Arrow is a non-verbal communication method that can convey intentions without relying on commonsense such as turn signals. Several studies have proposed and discussed the use of arrows as signs to indicate the movements of mobile robots. These studies have shown different ways to display arrows, such as projecting them on the floor [9,12] or showing them on a screen above the robot [13]. When arrows are displayed on the floor or on a surface parallel to the ground, they can point straight ahead, defining arrow's meaning. However, the visibility of these displays can be reduced by factors like floor conditions, ambient light, and the angle from which they are viewed. To improve visibility and make the arrows more noticeable, it is better to display them on a surface that is perpendicular the floor.

Shrestha et al. [8] conducted a study to help human-robot smooth passing using arrows with a perpendicular display and turn signal rules. In their experiments, the arrows were used to guide people passing by the robot. However, participants mentioned that they were "confused about whether the arrow showed the direction the robot was moving or the direction passers-by should move".

Arrows can be used to show a robot's movements and to guide people around the robot. However, because arrows are used in many different situations, their meaning can be misunderstood. If the meaning of arrows can be made clearer, we think they can be used more effectively for non-verbal communication by non-humanoid robots. Therefore, it is important to study how people understand arrows presented by mobile robots and to remove any uncertainty about their meaning.

2.3 Investigation of Perception Based on Presentation Timing in Asymmetric Environments

Arrow-based non-verbal communication requires concise expressions. In a previous study [1], we explored how "presentation timing" of arrows affects their interpretation. Figure 2 shows images from a web-based questionnaire experiment in the study. Participants chose from five options (left, relatively left, I cannot judge, relatively right, right) to indicate their preferred avoidance direction after watched the first-person perspective videos. In these videos, mobile robots approached at 0.5 m/s. The robot presented an arrow at one of five timings, with the robot-person distance ranging from 2.5 m to 6.5 m at 1 m intervals. Figure 3 presents the mean weighted responses, with positive values indicating avoidance by moving in the arrow's direction and negative values indicating the opposite (range: 2 to -2). Figure 4 shows the response percentages for each condition. A Friedman test for each arrow direction revealed a significant difference for the right-pointing arrow, and the Bonferroni post-hoc test found a significant difference between 2.5 m and 6.5 m. The results suggest that:

- Interpretation become more divided with earlier presentation timings.
- Presenting the arrow closer to the passing moment makes it more likely to be interpreted as "move in the direction of the arrow."

However, the experiment had two limitations:

1. The corridor was asymmetric, with space on one side (see Fig. 2). To ensure consistency, all videos showed the arrow pointing toward the side with space.
2. It is unclear whether the presentation timing refers to the "distance at presentation" or the "time from presentation to passing." The experiment conflated these two factors. If distance is the key factor, the finding would be "presenting the arrow when close feels more like an instruction compared to presenting it from far away." If time is key factor, the finding would be "people are more likely to avoid by moving in the arrow's direction when the time between the arrow's presentation and the avoidance action is shorter." Conflating these factors may lead to inconsistent findings depending on the robot's speed.

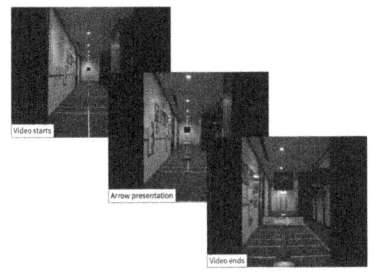

Fig. 2. Captured images of experimental video in previous study.

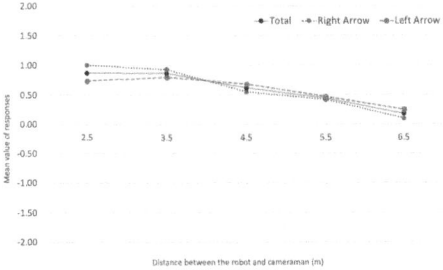

Fig. 3. Mean value of the weighted responses in previous experiment (n = 20).

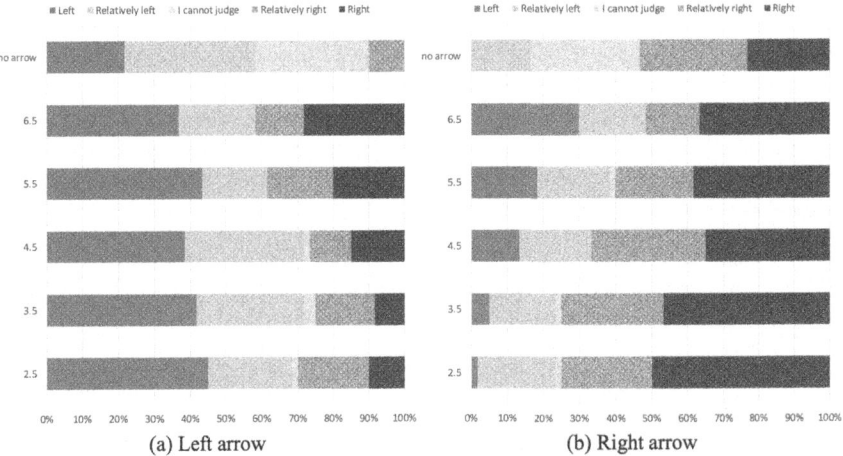

Fig. 4. Percentage of responses in previous experiment (n = 20).

3 Research Subject

This study has two objectives:

Objective 1. Investigate how the perception of arrows changes based on the spatial context.

Objective 2. Investigate changes in arrow perception when varying the robot's speed.

3.1 Corridor Symmetry

Our previous study investigated how people perceive arrows in an asymmetric corridor, using videos filmed in an environment with open space on one side (Fig. 2). However, comments from participants suggested that the corridor's asymmetry affected how they interpreted the arrows (P means participants number):

P4: *"I thought the width of the path next to the robot would influence the direction of avoidance."*

P8: *"I avoided by moving in the direction of the arrow or the side with more open space. I was glad the arrow didn't point toward the wall."*

These comments led us to believe that studying arrow perception in a symmetrical environment could help us determine whether the spatial context influences how people interpret the arrows.

3.2 Presentation Timing: Presentation Distance and Presentation Time

In the previous study, the experiment investigated how people perceived arrows presented by a robot moving at 0.5 m/s at five different timings. The presentation timing has two aspects: the distance at arrow presentation (presentation distance) and the time from the arrow presentation until passing occurs (presentation time). Both factors could influence the interpretation based on human-robot interaction and people's thought processes regarding arrows. Here are the reasons:

Presentation Distance. The distance at which the arrow is presented may change the perception of "for whom" the arrow is presented. For instance, when presented from a distance, people may see it as a signal to an unspecified group, including themselves. However, when presented nearby, people may feel more strongly that the arrow is a signal specifically for them. This idea of "for whom" the arrow is intended can influence how people interpret the arrow's meaning.

Presentation Time. In daily life, there are few situations where an arrow approaches and time to interpret it is limited. When people have less time to interpret the arrow, meaning the presentation time is short, they may rely on their intuition to understand its meaning. In everyday life, arrows are often used to guide people's gaze and behavior, such as on signboards. The thought process of following the direction of the arrow is simple and leads to intuitive actions. However, when the presentation time is longer, more complex thoughts become possible. In other words, an unusual thought process, such as "the arrow indicates the robot's direction of movement", can occur. Therefore, in the previous study, it can be inferred that the longer the presentation time, the more divided the interpretations became. This influence of the thought process based on presentation time can influence how people interpret the arrow's meaning.

4 Experiment

To tackle the objectives, we performed a virtual passing experiment using first-person perspective videos of encounters with a mobile robot. For Objective 1, which focuses on the influence of the spatial context, we conducted an experiment using passing videos in a symmetrical corridor. This allows us to compare the results with our previous study, which used an asymmetrical corridor, and determine how the environment affects people's perception of the arrows. For Objective 2, which aims to investigate the impact of the robot's speed on arrow perception, we prepared three different robot speeds: 0.4 m/s, 0.5 m/s, and 0.6 m/s. Additionally, we tested six different presentation distances, ranging from 2 m to 7 m, with 1.0 m intervals. By combining these factors, we could examine how people interpret the arrows at each presentation timing for each speed. In the following sections, we will provide more detailed information about the experiment.

4.1 Experimental Details

Participants. 21 persons (13 males and eight females).

Experimental Environment. Participants responded to a form created using Microsoft Forms [14] on their personal computers.

Robot. We used a mobile telepresence robot, Beam [15]. Users can control the robot from a PC, allowing them to move it freely and communicate with people around the robot. Although the robot was originally designed to display the user's face on the screen at the top, we covered this with black paper to eliminate the possibility that the face and the user's line of sight might influence the participant's judgment of the robot's direction of movement. We equipped the robot with an LED panel display to present an arrow. Figure 5 shows the robot used in the experiment.

Experimental Videos. Figure 6 shows captured images of the experimental video, and Fig. 7 illustrates the content of the video recordings. The videos were recorded in a corridor with a width of 2 m and a length of 9 m. We created a symmetrical corridor using partitions. The partitions had gaps to allow for the operation of the robot and the arrow from the side, but the gaps were equal on both sides. Additionally, the robot and the camera operator moved along the centerline, ensuring an almost completely symmetrical experimental design. The mobile robot and the camera operator approached at the same speed (0.4 m/s, 0.5 m/s, or 0.6 m/s) and presented an arrow at one of six timings when the distance between them was 2 m to 7 m (at 1.0 m intervals). The videos ended when both parties were 1.2 m apart. Participants were told in advance that the mobile robot would start to avoid the person at the end of the video.

Instructional Contents. We provided the following instructions to explain the situation in the experimental video:

- You will pass a mobile robot.
- When the robot reaches a certain distance from you, it will show an arrow (There are also videos without an arrow).
- The arrow may be "pointing in the direction you should move", or it may be "pointing in the direction the robot will move."

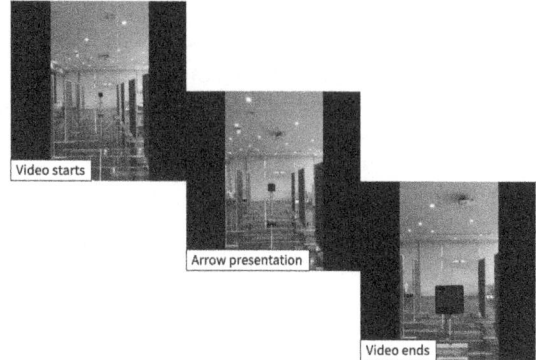

Fig. 5. The robot used in the experiment.

Fig. 6. Captured images of the experimental video.

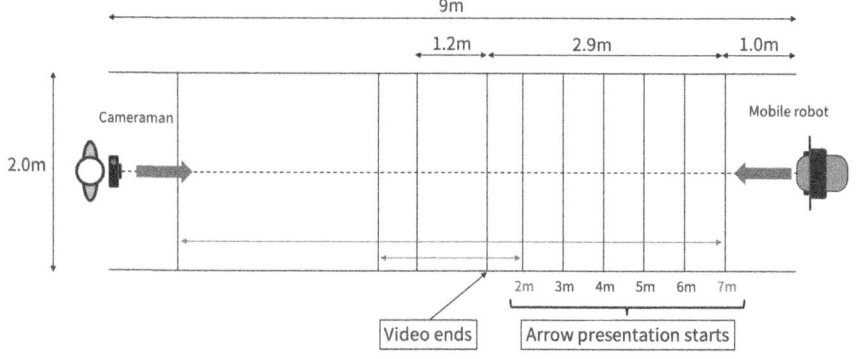

Fig. 7. Content of the experimental video.

– After the video ends, the robot passes you.

Additionally, participants were shown third-person perspective videos of the passing scenario, corresponding to the distances in the first-person perspective videos used in the experiment. This was done to help participants grasp the objective sense of distance between the robot and the person passing by in the first-person perspective videos.

In this experiment, we did not provide any specific instructions about the robot's role or the situational context. The reason for this was that we wanted to investigate participants' perception of the arrows in a state completely free from preconceptions such as "The robot in this situation would likely behave in such and such a way."

Experimental Procedure. We conducted the experiment as follows:

1. Participants watched the experimental videos, which were presented in a random order for each participant.

2. Participants were asked to choose which direction they wanted to go to avoid the robot from five options: "left", "relatively left", "I cannot judge", "relatively right" or "right".
3. There were six videos with a right-pointing arrow, six videos with a left-pointing arrow, and one video without an arrow for each robot's speed. Since there were three different speeds for the mobile robot, participants randomly viewed a total of 39 videos. After the passing experiment, they answered the following questions in the descriptive response section. *Q1: "In what situations did you decide to avoid the robot by moving in the direction of the arrow?". Q2: "In what situations did you decide to avoid the robot by moving in the opposite direction of the arrow?". Q3: Free description.*

Evaluation Method. The responses were assigned values by weighting them on a scale from 2 to −2 (in increments of 1), with positive values for responses indicating avoidance in the direction of the arrow and negative values for responses indicating avoidance in the opposite direction. The mean value of these weighted responses was calculated. Additionally, the percentage of responses for each presentation condition was determined.

4.2 Results

The mean values of the responses are presented in Fig. 8. Graphs (a) to (c) show the mean values for each speed of the mobile robot, with right-pointing arrows, left-pointing arrows, and the sum of both arrows. Graphs (e) and (f) compare the results for the right and left arrows at different moving speeds, while (d) compares the combined results for both arrows. Table 1 shows the percentage of responses for each condition.

Figure 8 (a) to (c) show the results for each speed, but the mean values are close to 0 for all distances. Graphs (e) and (f) show the comparison of mean values for each speed by the presented arrow. Graph (d) shows the combined results for both arrows, here too, the mean values are close to 0 for all distances.

A two-way repeated measures ANOVA was conducted for each arrow direction, with speed and distance as factors and the weighted value as the dependent variable. For the right arrow, the main effect of speed was not significant ($F(2,40) = 0.959$, $p = 0.392$, $\eta_{G^2} = 0.001$), the main effect of distance was not significant ($F(5,100) = 1.145$, $p = 0.342$, $\eta_{G^2} = 0.014$), and the interaction was not significant ($F(10,200) = 1.192$, $p = 0.298$, $\eta_{G^2} = 0.012$). Similarly, for the left arrow, the main effect of speed was not significant ($F(2,40) = 0.096$, $p = 0.909$, $\eta_{G^2} = 1.614 \times 10^{-4}$), the main effect of distance was not significant ($F(5,100) = 0.868$, $p = 0.505$, $\eta_{G^2} = 0.009$), and the interaction was not significant ($F(10,200) = 1.115$, $p = 0.353$, $\eta_{G^2} = 0.012$).

Although the mean values were close to 0 for all presentation conditions, Table 1 shows that this was not because many participants chose "I cannot judge." Instead, the interpretations were divided. In fact, the results for passing a mobile robot without an arrow (Fig. 9) show that "I cannot judge" and "Relatively right/left" were more frequently selected, indicating that participants were interpreting the arrow and deciding on the direction to avoid.

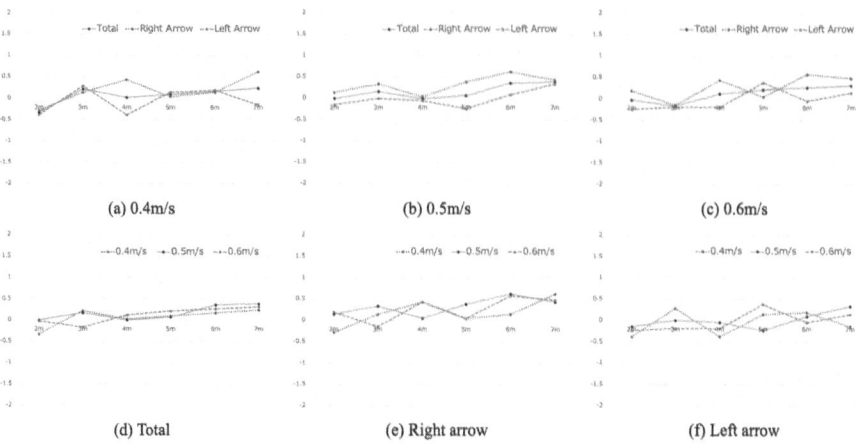

Fig. 8. Mean value of responses. The responses were assigned values by weighting them on a scale from 2 to −2, with positive values for responses indicating avoidance in the direction of the arrow and negative values for responses indicating avoidance in the opposite direction.

Table 1. Percentage of responses by the presentation distance.

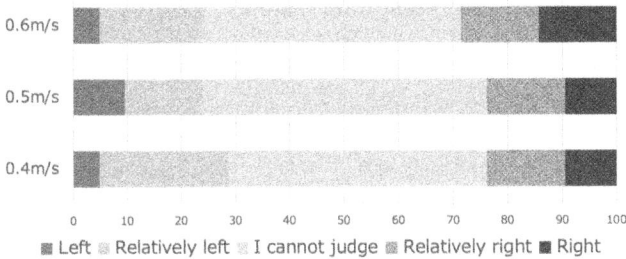

Fig. 9. Percentage of responses for passing a mobile robot without an arrow.

5 Consideration

In this chapter, we discuss the two objectives of this research based on the results of the experiment described in Sect. 4.

5.1 Objective 1: Investigate How the Perception of Arrows Changes Based on the Spatial Context

Conclusion. In a symmetrical corridor, the interpretation of arrows is divided regardless of the presentation timing. In other words, the spatial context of the corridor influences how people perceive the meaning of the arrows.

When comparing the results of the experiment in a symmetrical corridor (Fig. 8) to the findings from the previous study conducted in an asymmetric corridor (Fig. 3), it becomes evident that the interpretations were not biased in either direction in the symmetrical setting. Instead, the interpretation remained divided regardless of the presentation timing. This suggests that spatial context, such as corridor's layout and characteristics, plays a crucial role in shaping people's understanding of the arrow's meaning.

Moreover, the results of previous study showed that the interpretation of arrows changed with the presentation timing, indicating that people do not solely rely on the arrow itself to determine whether it represents the "direction of movement" or the "direction of guidance." Instead, they appear to interpret the arrow's meaning based on a combination of factors, including the environment and the timing of the arrow presentation.

5.2 Objective 2: Investigate Changes in Arrow Perception When Varying the Robot's Speed

Conclusion. The interpretation of arrows based on presentation distance and time is diverse, and the interpretation remains ambiguous under all conditions.

The results of the experiment suggest that the interpretation of arrows does not become consistent based on the presentation timing of the arrows. However, in the descriptive response section, many participants interpreted the meaning of the arrows based on the presentation distance and time. Table 2 shows some examples:

Table 2. Examples of descriptive responses.

	Q1: "In what situations did you decide to avoid the robot by moving in the direction of the arrow?"	Q2: "In what situations did you decide to avoid the robot by moving in the opposite direction of the arrow?"
P1	"When the arrow was displayed for a relatively long time"	"When the arrow was visible for only a short time within the visible range"
P2	"When displayed just before passing"	"When displayed well in advance, it felt like the robot's intention"
P9	"When the distance was far, it felt like a message saying, 'Please avoid by moving this way'"	"When the distance was close, it felt like the robot was indicating 'then I (the robot) will proceed this way'"
P14	"When the arrow was displayed from a far distance, I felt instructed to proceed in that direction. Also, when the arrow was displayed just before a potential collision, I thought I should move in the direction of the arrow at that moment"	"When the arrow was displayed as it approached, I felt that the machine had detected the person and was trying to avoid them"
P20	"When the arrow was presented just before passing"	"When the arrow was presented from a distance"

Numerous participants interpreted the meaning of the arrows based on a certain distance or time. However, the way they interpreted the arrows varied among participants. Some participants decided to avoid the robot by moving in the direction of the arrow when the distance was far, while others decided to avoid it by moving in the opposite direction. Such differences in interpretation existed for each criterion used to judge whether the distance was far or close, or whether the time was long or short. Consequently, we consider that the interpretation of the arrows remained ambiguous under all presentation conditions.

6 Discussion

In this chapter, we further discuss the interpretation of arrows based on the experimental results, and then describe the limitations of the experiment and future prospects.

6.1 Interaction Between Original Intention and Arrows

In the experiment, a few participants reported that their decision on the direction to move to avoid the robot before recognizing the arrow influenced their interpretation of the arrow's meaning. Here are some examples:

P6 (free description response): *"I usually tend to move to the right at an early stage to avoid colliding, so I had a strong desire to avoid the robot by moving to the right in all cases. When the arrow pointing to the right was presented, I often judged it conveniently, but when the arrow pointing in the direction to move to avoid the robot was presented, I felt anxious that it might come this way."*

P15 (Q1 response): *"When the arrow to the right was presented after I decided to avoid the robot by moving to the right."*

P15 (Q2 response): *"When the robot presented the arrow before I moved."*

P17 (Q1 response): *"I avoided the robot by moving in the direction indicated by the arrow when the presentation of the arrow was late and the direction I was thinking of moving avoiding coincided with the direction of the arrow."*

These responses confirm that when participants had already chosen a direction to avoid the robot before the arrow appeared, they found it easier to move in the direction of the arrow if it pointed in the same direction. This observation can be applied to the results under the asymmetric conditions in the previous study. Figure 3 shows that when people decide to avoid the robot by moving towards the open space and an arrow pointing in that direction is presented, more people moved towards the open space. This suggests that when the arrow is presented just before the avoidance action, people are more likely to interpret it as "guidance."

6.2 Limitations of the Experiment

Although the experiment in this study yielded various findings, there are limitations to their generalizability. This is because the experimental method is a virtual passing encounter using first-person perspective videos. There are significant differences in the perception of the robot's approach and the sense of distance to the arrow when viewed in a video compared to actual passing scenarios. In this experiment, we instructed the participants to compare their experiences with an objective viewpoint, but this approach has its limitations.

Moreover, as discussed in the previous section, the interpretation of the arrow may differ depending on the original intention of the person passing by. In addition to simply moving straight ahead, there are many possible behaviors, such as people who avoid the robot by moving to one side in advance, people who stop, and people who make a large detour. We believe it is necessary to increase the degree of freedom of the passing person's behavior.

6.3 Future Prospects

As mentioned in Sect. 6.1, the previous study and the descriptions in this study suggest that if the arrow is presented in a predetermined direction before it is presented, it is more likely to be interpreted as "guiding". To clarify the arrow's meaning as guiding signs, it may be effective to influence people to consider avoiding the robot by moving in a specific direction before the arrow is presented. For example, the robot's movements could be used to bias people's avoidance direction, or the arrow could be pointed towards the wider side of the corridor or the direction with less pedestrian traffic. However, such biasing methods can be complex and may contradict the need for "maintaining simplicity", which is the motivation of this study. In some cases, it may be faster and more effective to inform people verbally to "please avoid the robot by moving this way." Therefore, future experiments should evaluate intuitiveness and comfort of arrow-based communication while comparing with verbal methods.

7 Conclusion

Several studies have proposed and discussed the use of arrows to indicate the robot's direction of movement. However, arrows are used in various ways and can be interpreted as having a guiding meaning. The motivation of this study is to make arrows an unambiguous non-verbal communication method. We aim to achieve this by investigating the perception of arrows under various presentation conditions and deepening our understanding of people's perceptions of arrows. In this study, we focused on the corridor symmetry in which arrows are presented and the timing of presentation (presentation time or presentation distance). A previous study suggested that in an asymmetric corridor with space on one side, presenting an arrow on the side with space just before passing makes it easier to avoid the robot by moving in the direction of the arrow. Therefore, in this study, we conducted passing encounters in a symmetrical corridor and varied the robot's moving speed in three patterns to investigate the following two objectives:

Objective 1. Investigate how the perception of arrows changes based on the spatial context.

Objective 2. Investigate changes in arrow perception when varying the robot's speed.

The results of a virtual passing experiment using videos of passing encounters with a robot presenting arrows at six distances showed that interpretations were divided under all presentation conditions, and no main effects of moving speed or distance were confirmed. However, many participants mentioned presentation time or presentation distance as the basis for their judgment. Therefore, the conclusions concerning the objectives are as follows:

Conclusion 1. In a symmetrical corridor, the interpretation of arrows is divided regardless of the presentation timing. In other words, the spatial context of the corridor influences how people perceive the meaning of the arrows.

Conclusion 2. The interpretation of arrows based on presentation distance and time is diverse, and the interpretation remains ambiguous under all conditions.

Furthermore, from the descriptive responses and the findings of the previous study, it was suggested that when a passing person has already decided on the direction to move to avoid the robot, presenting an arrow pointing in that direction makes it easier to interpret it as "guiding". Therefore, future plans include investigating the interpretation of arrows when a bias in the direction to move to avoid the robot is given based on the robot's movements and the environment in which the arrows are presented.

Acknowledgments. This work was supported by JSPS KAKENHI Grant Number 22H03635 and 23K24891.

References

1. Kuwamiya, Y., Imagawa, T., Kobayashi, M.: "I'm Going Right" or "Please Go to the Right": disambiguation in arrow display on mobile robots to avoid collision with passersby. In: 17th International Workshop on Informatics (IWIN2023), pp. 189–197. Informatics Society, Hokkaido (2023)
2. Nummenmaa, L., Hyönä, J., Hietanen. J.K.: I'll walk this way: eyes reveal the direction of locomotion and make passersby look and go the other way. Psychol. Sci. **20**(12), 1454–1458 (2009)
3. Ueda, S., Kitazaki, M.: Collision avoidance affected by walker's head direction in a virtual environment. In: Stephanidis, C. (eds.) HCI International 2013 - Posters' Extended Abstracts, HCI 2013. CCIS, vol. 374, pp. 727–731. Springer, Heidelberg (2013). https://doi.org/10.1007/978-3-642-39476-8_146
4. Matsumaru, T., Iwase, K., Akiyama, K., et al.: Mobile robot with eyeball expression as the preliminary-announcement and display of the robot's following motion. Auton. Robot. **18**, 231–246 (2005). https://doi.org/10.1007/s10514-005-0728-8
5. Yamashita, S., Ikeda, T., Shinozawa, K., Iwaki, S.: Evaluation of robots that signals a pedestrian using face orientation based on moving trajectory analysis. In: 2019 28th IEEE International Conference on Robot and Human Interactive Communication (RO-MAN), pp. 1–8, New Delhi (2019)
6. Lyu, J., Mikawa, M., Fujisawa, M., Hiiragi, M.: Mobile robot with previous announcement of upcoming operation using face interface. In: 2019 IEEE/SICE International Symposium on System Integration (SII), pp. 782–787, Paris (2019)
7. May, A.D., Dondrup, C., Hanheide, M.: Show me your moves! Conveying navigation intention of a mobile robot to humans. In: 2015 European Conference on Mobile Robots (ECMR), pp. 1–6, Lincoln (2015)
8. Shrestha, M.C., et al.: Exploring the use of light and display indicators for communicating directional intent. In: 2016 IEEE International Conference on Advanced Intelligent Mechatronics (AIM), pp. 1651–1656, Banff (2016)
9. Hetherington, N.J., Croft, E.A., Van der Loos, H.M.: Hey robot, which way are you going? Nonverbal motion legibility cues for human-robot spatial interaction. IEEE Robot. Autom. Lett. **6**(3), 5010–5015 (2021)
10. Szafir, D., Mutlu, B., Fong, T.: Communicating directionality in flying robots. In: 2015 10th ACM/IEEE International Conference on Human-Robot Interaction (HRI), pp. 19–26, Portland (2015)
11. Fernandez, R., et al.: Passive demonstrations of light-based robot signals for improved human interpretability. In: 2018 27th IEEE International Symposium on Robot and Human Interactive Communication (RO-MAN), pp. 234–239, Nanjing (2018)
12. Matsumaru, T.: Mobile robot with preliminary-announcement and display function of forthcoming motion using projection equipment. In: ROMAN 2006 - The 15th IEEE International Symposium on Robot and Human Interactive Communication, pp. 443–450, Hatfield (2006)

13. Matsumaru, T.: Mobile robot with preliminary-announcement and indication function of forth-coming operation using flat-panel display. In: 2007 IEEE International Conference on Robotics and Automation (ICRA 2007), ThA4.4, pp. 1774–1781, Rome (2007)
14. Microsoft Forms. https://forms.office.com/. Accessed 31 May 2024
15. Beam. https://suitabletech.com/. Accessed 31 May 2024

Quantitative Observation to Explore the Turn-Changing Mechanisms of Conversations in Remote Meetings Accompanying Supplemental Materials

Kenta Ohnaka[1(✉)], Taketo Imagawa[1], Kazuyuki Iso[2], Masayuki Ihara[3], and Minoru Kobayashi[1]

[1] Meiji University, 4-21-1, Nakano, Nakano-Ku, Tokyo, Japan
{kenta.ohnaka,taketo.imagawa}@koblab.org, minoru@acm.org
[2] Tokyo Information Design Professional University, 2-7-1, Komatsugawa, Edogawa-Ku, Tokyo, Japan
iso@tid.ac.jp
[3] RIKEN, 2-1, Hirosawa, Wako-Shi, Saitama, Japan
ihara@acm.org

Abstract. This study investigates turn-taking mechanisms in remote meetings involving supplemental materials, such as document browsing and chat tools, by comparing them with collocated meetings. We acquired multimodal datasets, including data on gaze, head movements, pupil size, speech audio, and utterance content, and analyzed gaze behavior during turn-taking and turn-giving instances. Our findings suggest that in collocated meetings, participants tend to gaze at the shared document during turn-changing, while in remote meetings, this tendency is weaker, and participants' attention is more dispersed. Furthermore, we observed that participants are less likely to engage in document browsing in remote meetings than in collocated meetings where unintentional eye contact is likely to occur. Based on these results, we propose four hypotheses regarding turn-changing mechanisms in remote meetings accompanying supplemental materials. This study contributes to the understanding of turn-changing mechanisms in remote meetings by providing insights into the relationship between gaze, turn-taking, and the role of supplemental materials. We discuss the implications of our findings and outline future work.

Keywords: Remote meeting · Turn-taking · Gaze Analysis

1 Introduction

Remote meetings are still widely used, even though the impact of COVID-19 is gradually lessening. There are some apps for remote meetings such as Zoom and Microsoft Teams which allow not only the sharing of videos and audio but also chats and reactions for smooth communication even in remote locations.

However, there are some issues with remote meetings. Compared to collocated meetings, it is more difficult to grasp where other participants are looking and the timing when to start talking. What is worse, participants need to pay attention to the use of chats, reaction buttons and sharing or browsing the shared documents. This multi-tasking will make it more difficult to understand the other participants' reactions and make eye contact, even if the participants keep their eyes on the video images. Furthermore, when participants are required to check the documents or chats, it is tough to be attentive to both video images and the documents or chats, which makes turn-changing hard.

To solve this problem, in this paper, we put a spotlight on the turn-changing mechanism in remote meetings where participants would pay attention not only to the video image but also the supplemental materials such as the shared documents. We recorded meetings and considered the participants' gaze, the content of their speech, and movements of the head to clarify the turn-changing mechanism. From the analyses of one of the recorded meetings, we developed four hypotheses related to the gaze and turn-changing mechanism.

2 Related Work

2.1 The Role of Gaze in Turn-Changing

In this study, the process through which a speaker acquires the right to speak, maintains it, and transfers it to the next speaker is collectively described as "turn-changing". In this context, taking the right to speak is expressed as "turn-taking", and passing the right to speak is expressed as "turn-giving". Also, a person who has been speaking before the speaker is called the "previous speaker", and a person who starts speaking after the speaker is called the "next speaker".

Gaze information is crucial in understanding turn-changing [1–4]. Kendon [1] reported that people tend to gaze at their interlocutor for a long time when listening and look away when speaking. Additionally, Richardson et al. [2] showed that in situations where the roles of the speaker and listener are clearly defined, the closer the listener's gaze is to the speaker's gaze, the better their comprehension of what the speaker said. They also mentioned the importance of having a shared focus of attention, as guiding the speaker's gaze leads to increased comprehension. According to Vertegaal et al. [3], in dyadic conversations, the number of turns taken increases when the interlocutor's gaze information is available. Furthermore, Jokinen et al. [4] reported that turn-taking becomes more complex when there are three participants. They investigated the relationship between smooth speaker changes and gaze in multi-party collocated meetings with three participants and stated that gaze tends to function as a cue indicating that the interlocutor will continue speaking or is preparing to speak.

From the above, it is clear that there is a close relationship between gaze and the turn-changing mechanism. Gaze information has been shown to serve as a cue for taking the floor and as a signal for giving the floor to the speaker.

2.2 Difficulties in Conveying Gaze Cues in Remote Meetings

However, it is difficult to obtain this gaze information in remote meetings. Grayson et al. [5] conducted a test on the ability to judge the direction of a person's gaze in a desktop video conferencing environment. The results showed that the horizontal direction has a particularly large impact, and when the camera is positioned directly above the interlocutor's face image, it is easier to perceive that one is being looked at.

Chen [6] investigated the relationship between camera position and eye contact and stated that eye contact becomes difficult when the interlocutor's face image and the camera position are far apart. He showed that it is difficult to perceive eye contact when the direction of gaze is shifted horizontally, while it is easier to perceive eye contact when the direction of gaze is downward. Boland et al. [7] also mentioned that audio delay in remote meetings affects turn-taking in conversations. When comparing response times to simple questions and answers between remote and local conditions, they found a significant increase in the remote condition, indicating that there is a cognitive load on the timing of speaker changes that does not occur in face-to-face interactions.

In this way, gaze information, which is smoothly transmitted and received in collocated meetings, becomes difficult to transmit and receive properly in remote meetings due to the positional relationship between the input and output of the video image and the problem of delay. As a result, it is considered that taking turns is more difficult in remote meetings compared to collocated meetings.

2.3 The Effect of Multitasking During Remote Meetings

Furthermore, multitasking is also seen as a problem that contributes to the lack of attention toward remote participants. According to a survey by Cao et al. [8], 29% of participants regularly engage in light email work during remote meetings. In addition to email, there are many tools that can be used in parallel with meetings, and due to the proliferation of such tools, there is a possibility that the gaze information necessary for smooth conversation progress may be overlooked if attention is not directed toward the interlocutor. In fact, Brubaker et al. [9] reported that 45% of people are concerned about whether other participants are concentrating during remote meetings. Ansah et al. [10] also investigated the degree of influence of other tasks in remote meetings and showed that when a phone task was given during the meeting, it promoted the group's idea generation, but in non-divergent tasks, it took longer to reach a consensus. Marlow et al. [11] conducted an experiment in which participants watched a video of a person during a remote meeting and evaluated their behavior, reporting that it was impolite and unacceptable. In part of their experiment, they showed that even when taking notes related to the conversation using a mobile device during multitasking, there is a tendency for it to be misunderstood as doing something unrelated to the conversation.

In this way, in remote meetings, attention is not necessarily devoted to the other participants' video images or audio, but rather to chat or document browsing. However, it is difficult to strictly judge whether remote participants are doing other work or work related to the meeting, which may cause concern among meeting participants and decrease meeting productivity. In such situations, information such as gaze is likely to be further overlooked, which is thought to have a significant impact on the turn-changing mechanism.

In this study, the term "supplemental material" is used to refer to the additional activities that participants engage in during remote meetings in parallel with their video and voice communication. These activities include tasks such as document reading and chatting. The presence of a supplemental material may distract participants from the main conversation, making it difficult for them to contribute effectively to the turn-taking process.

3 Purpose of This Study

3.1 Purpose of This Study

The overarching purpose of the study is to discover a method to facilitate turn-changing in remote meetings which include supplemental materials such as documents. In comparison with collocated meetings, it is said that turn-changing in remote meetings is more difficult because it is hard to comprehend the participants' status such as where the participants are looking or who they are speaking to, and because of the abstraction of nonverbal information such as gestures or facial expressions. In addition, supplemental materials make turn-changing more complex as the information necessary for turn-changing is overlooked by participants. To investigate and resolve these matters, we investigated remote meetings which include supplemental materials and examine where the participants are looking during the turn-changing.

3.2 Approach

In order to get a clue to the reasons why turn-changing is tough in remote meetings which include supplemental materials, we took an approach to conduct and compare both remote meetings and collocated meetings with a similar core communication space and supplemental materials. We believe that turn-changing in collocated meetings is easier than in remote ones. For instance, it is complicated to make eye contact, and feel a set of eyes in remote meetings, whereas it is uncomplicated to do so in collocated meetings. Consequently, by observing these differences, we consider that we could get a clue to a smooth turn-changing mechanism.

We analyzed the turn-changing mechanism in remote and collocated meetings based on the gaze since it has a significant influence on the turn-changing mechanism. For example, when one of the participants is about to start speaking, he/she looks at other participants to determine when to speak, or when asking other participants for their opinion, he/she naturally pays attention to that person. Thus, this paper focuses on gaze during turn-changing and analyzes the relationship between gaze and turn-changing.

Therefore, this study's goal is to discover methods for effortless turn-changing in remote meetings which include supplemental materials by comparing remote and collocated meetings. To work out the methods, in this paper, we examine and compare the turn-changing mechanism in both remote and collocated meetings based on the gaze and aim to formulate a hypothesis that addresses gaze and turn-changing.

4 Recording a Multimodal Meeting Dataset

4.1 Purpose

The purpose of the experiment is to design both collocated and remote meetings that include supplemental materials (shared document), to collect a wide range of data that may affect the turn-changing mechanism, and to develop hypothesis influencing the turn-changing mechanism.

4.2 Data Collection Setup

Participants

The participants consisted of 16 individuals, ranging in age from 25 to 47 (eight males, eight females). We selected participants who were familiar with remote meeting tools such as Zoom and had basic computer skills. For precise eye-tracking measurements, we selected those with corrected vision of 0.7 or greater (20/28 or better, log MAR 0.15 or less), excluding those wearing hard contact lenses or glasses. Reflecting true-to-life business settings, we deliberately chose employed individuals over students for the study. The meetings were conducted with four groups, each consisting of four participants who had not met each other before.

Meeting Design

Each group conducted both collocated and remote meetings once. In this experiment, supplemental materials were represented by shared document. Participants progressed through the meetings using shared document prepared in advance by the researchers. Details of the document are elaborated upon in the "Shared Document" section (Fig. 1).

The meeting topics were prepared as Topic 1 "Deciding on a theme for the new cafeteria" and Topic 2 "Planning an internal health promotion event." These topics were chosen with consideration for the employment status of the participants to minimize bias from prior knowledge. During the meetings, participants were allowed to use a browser to search for information as needed. Each meeting was limited to 15 min, within which time participants were to decide on one of the predetermined options A to D. This setup was designed to necessitate the viewing of the document in the supplemental material, simulating a natural meeting environment.

Moreover, all participants were required to reach a consensus on one option. A two-minute time slot was set aside for presenting the chosen option and the reasons behind it, to encourage active and meaningful participation in the meeting. Thus, participants also had to choose a representative to give the presentation during this two-minute period.

Shared Document

The shared document consists of eight pages in total, covering "Meeting Guidelines" (p1–2), "Meeting Topics" (p3), "Options A to D" (p4–7), and "Access to Shared document" (p8).

The "Meeting Guidelines" contains the information shown in the "Meeting Details" section above. In addition, it includes a note that the participants' gaze is recorded by the eye tracker and that screen sharing is allowed if necessary. For collocated meetings,

Fig. 1. Examples of shared documents

Fig. 2. Experimental meeting setup, with collocated configuration on the left and remote configuration on the right.

a projector and screen could be used, and for remote meetings, Zoom's screen-sharing function is possible.

In the "Meeting Topics" section, one topic is designated for each shared document. We have two topics for two different types of meetings: collocated and remote. Topic 1: "Deciding on a theme for the new cafeteria" and Topic 2: "Planning an internal health promotion event."

Each of the "Options A to D" is presented on a single page. To ensure the meeting concludes within 15 min, preliminary information about each option is provided in the document. The information consists of estimated cost per meal, operating hours, number of seats, advantages, and disadvantages. An example slide is shown in Fig. 1.

"Access to Shared Documents" shows that the PDF of the shared document is pinned to Google Docs in the browser of the participant's operating PC. This is the same for both collocated and remote meetings.

Apparatus and Setup

Figure 2-left shows the setup for the collocated meetings. To prevent participants from forgetting each other's names and affecting the flow of the meeting, the participants chose their own nicknames and placed triangular nameplates on the desks. One operator was present in the same room to ensure the eye-tracking device was functioning properly. The camera for measurement was placed 45 degrees behind the participants at 1 m, and it was set up to capture all the participants in the frame. Figure 2-right also illustrates the remote meeting setup. Zoom was used as the communication platform to share audio and video. As in collocated meetings, one operator per participant was stationed in the same room to monitor eye-tracking and handle any issues. The camera for measurement was placed in front of each participant to record their actions.

4.3 Procedure and Meeting Order

Figure 3 shows the flow of the experiment and the order of meetings for each group. In this experiment, there were four variations of meetings: collocated and remote meetings, and meetings on two topics (Topic 1 and Topic 2). We designed the order of the meetings, taking into account that the participants were meeting for the first time.

First, we held an ice-breaker session for each group to encourage natural conversation among participants, considering that they were meeting for the first time.

Next, the meetings took place. For example, Group 1 first had a collocated meeting on Topic 1, followed by a remote meeting on Topic two. Details are shown in Fig. 3. Following each meeting, there was a session questionnaire to gather feedback, and an overall survey was administered to all participants. After all meetings and questionnaires were completed, we carried out a post-experiment interview with the participants to gain more insight into their experiences and opinions.

4.4 Collected Dataset

The measured dataset and the devices used for the experiment are shown in Table 1. Although not used for the measurement, participants used a PC for Zoom and viewing documents. The PC (13–14 inch.) was prepared for the participants. To eliminate the effect of unfamiliarity with the operating system, participants could select Mac or Windows.

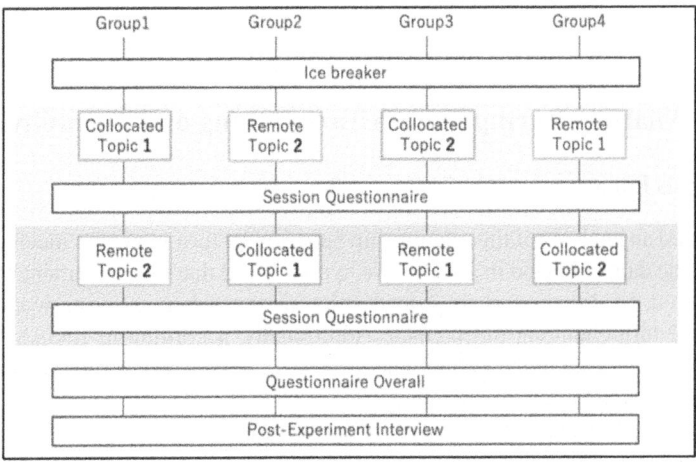

Fig. 3. Experimental flow and meeting order for the four groups, including icebreakers, collocated and remote sessions on two topics, and the concluding questionnaires and interviews.

Table 1. Details of the collected multimodal meeting dataset

Data Type	Collection Method	Details
Gaze	• Tobii Pro Glasses 2 (1 unit) • Tobii Pro Glasses 3 (3 unit) [12]	• Sampling rate: 100 Hz [15] • gaze direction (normalized coordinates)
Pupil Size	• Tobii Pro Glasses 2 • Tobii Pro Glasses 3	• Sampling rate: 100 Hz • Includes pupil position (mm), pupil diameter (mm)
Head Movement	• Tobii Pro Glasses 2 • Tobii Pro Glasses 3	• Sampling rate: 100 Hz • Includes gyro rotation (degrees/s), accelerometer (m/s^2), and magnetometer data
Audio	• Built-in camera of Tobii Pro Glasses • iPhone camera (4 units)	• Tobii Pro Glasses: captures wearer's own voice • iPhone: captures voices of all meeting participants
Video	• Built-in camera of Tobii Pro Glasses • iPhone camera	• Tobii Pro Glasses: first-person perspective of the wearer • iPhone: third-person perspective of the wearer, angle capturing all meeting participants
Mapping Images	• iPhone camera	Collocated meetings: 240° panoramic image covers the range of participants' gaze movements
Utterances	• Transcribed from two types of video recordings	Utterances recorded as text data
Questionnaire	• Google Forms	Conducted online after the meeting

5 Gaze Analysis During Speech Turn-Taking and Turn-Giving

5.1 Analysis Purpose

We conducted an analysis of the relationship between the turn-changing mechanism and gaze using the data collected in Sect. 4. We hypothesized that the fundamental behavior of focusing on the direction of the conversation partner when speaking would greatly influence the turn-changing mechanism. Additionally, according to Jokinen [5], gaze plays an important role in indicating when the next speaker ends a turn. Therefore, we focused on turn-taking and turn-giving.

To investigate the characteristics of gaze during turn-taking, we set two type intervals: "Before" and "Just Before". "Before" refers to the interval from when a speaker takes a turn until another participant takes a turn, while "Just Before" refers to the 1,000 ms interval prior to a speaker taking a turn. Details are shown in Fig. 4. The 1,000 ms time window was chosen based on previous research suggesting that the next speaker can be predicted from gaze information 1,000 ms before their turn [15].

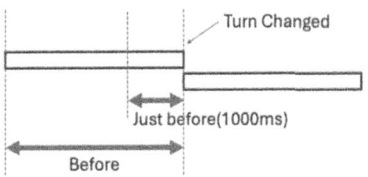

Fig. 4. Time intervals

Considering the types of turn-changes (turn-taking, turn-giving) and the time intervals for aggregating gaze measurements (Before, Just Before), we conducted four types of analyses:

Analysis 1-1: Where is the next speaker looking before taking a turn (turn-taking)?

Analysis 1-2: Where is the next speaker looking just before taking a turn (turn-taking)?

Analysis 2-1: Where is the previous speaker looking before giving a turn (turn-giving)?

Analysis 2-2: Where is the previous speaker looking just before giving a turn (turn-giving)?

5.2 Analysis Methods

Data Preparation

First, for each gaze dataset, we mapped the data onto a single image. The recorded data was auto-mapped using Tobii Pro Lab [13]. We reviewed the mapping results and manually corrected any areas that were not appropriately mapped.

Next, we manually selected the speech intervals. We marked the moments when turns changed. If there was a silent interval of more than two seconds, we considered the turn to have changed even if the speaker did not change. Two independent raters evaluated the timing of turn-changes, and the timing difference between the two raters was within one second for all marks. The average of the two raters' timings was used as the turn-change timing in the experiment.

Then, we defined Areas of Interest (AOIs). For collocated meetings, we set four AOIs: each of the three participants' entire body and the screen of the PC used by the gaze-tracked participant (Fig. 5-top-left). For remote meetings, we set five AOIs: the images of the four participants displayed on Zoom within the PC screen used by the participant, and the area showing the shared document (Fig. 5-bottom left).

Data Formatting

The gaze data was exported to a Comma Separated Value (CSV) file in the above format. Please refer to the Tobii Pro Lab manual for details on the exportable data [14]. The sampling rate was 100 Hz.

For each gaze sample over time, we excluded intervals that were not correctly measured. Specifically, if more than 50% of the samples in the "Before" or "Just Before" interval were "Eyes Not Found", we considered the gaze data for that interval to be incorrectly measured and excluded the data for that interval.

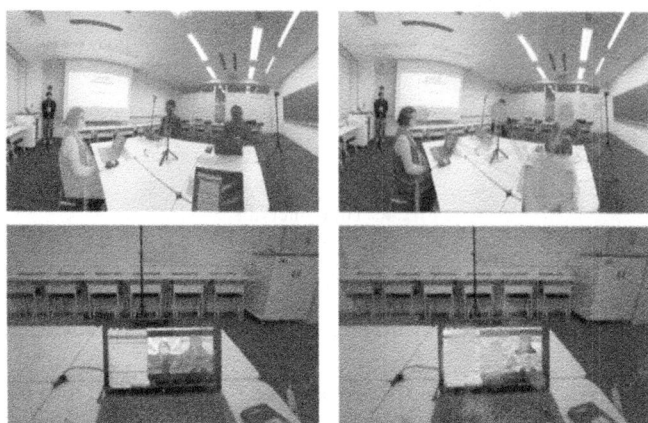

Fig. 5. Example of AOI and gaze overlay. Collocated meeting with AOI (top-left), Collocated meeting with gaze overlay (top-right). Remote meeting with AOI (bottom-left), Remote meeting with gaze overlay (bottom-right)

Furthermore, among the gaze samples counted in the AOIs, we only counted those with an "Eye movement type" of "Fixation". The "Eye movement type" can take values such as "Fixation", "Saccade", or "Unclassified", but in this analysis, we considered "Fixation" to be the appropriate eye movement for human information recognition, so we only counted "Fixations."

5.3 Turn-Taking Analysis

Result

Figure 6 shows the results of turn-taking analysis. "Just Before" indicates what the participants were looking at immediately before taking a turn, while "Before" shows what they were looking at prior to taking a turn. The total for each participant is shown, with AOIs classified as "Previous Speaker," "Document," and "Others." "Others" includes other participants (excluding the next speaker), the table, walls, etc. The numbers below the graph represent the number of turn-taking instances where gaze was correctly detected.

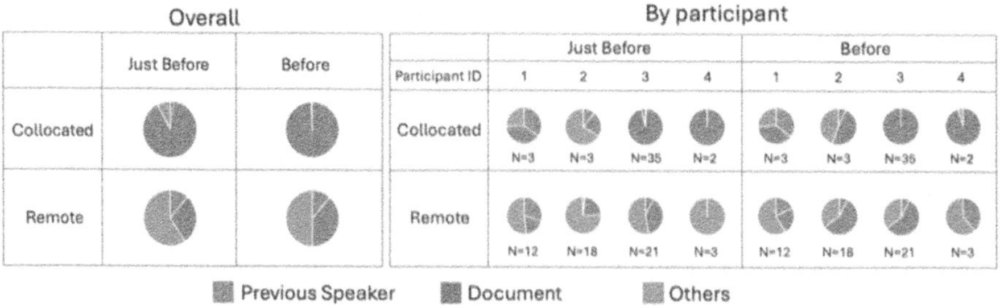

Fig. 6. Results of turn-taking analysis

From Fig. 6-left, it is evident that in collocated meetings, the proportion of time spent looking at the document is high in both the "Just Before" and "Before" intervals. Compared to collocated meetings, in remote meetings, gaze is not only on the document but also on the current speaker and "others" in both time intervals. There was no clear difference between the "Before" and "Just Before" intervals.

Figure 6-right shows the results of Fig. 6-left divided by participant. There was a noticeable difference in the number of turns taken, with Participant 3 taking an exceptionally high number of turns. Among them, Participant 1 gazed equally at the next speaker, document, and "others" in both time intervals during collocated meetings. On the other hand, while Participant 3's gaze was focused on the document in both time intervals during collocated meetings, it tended to be dispersed and not focused on the document in remote meetings. Additionally, comparing the "Just Before" and "Before" intervals of Participant 4, it was found that in collocated meetings, gaze was focused on the document in both intervals, while in remote meetings, there was a tendency for gaze to be directed toward the next speaker.

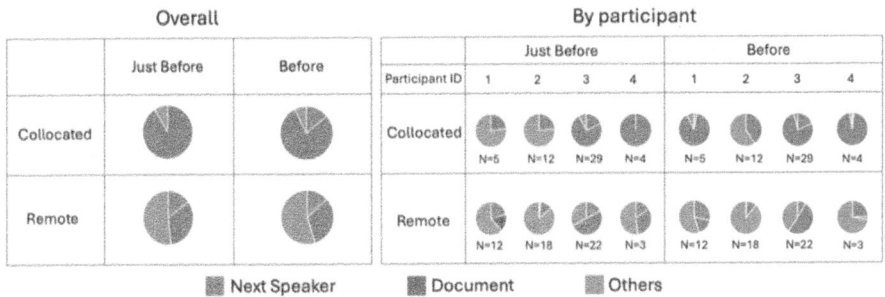

Fig. 7. Results of turn-giving analysis

Discussion

Regarding turn-taking, regardless of the "Just Before" or "Before" interval, participants spent more time looking at the document in collocated meetings compared to remote meetings. One possible reason for this is that since the participants were meeting for the first time, they may have felt reluctant to look at "others" during the collocated meetings. They might have been looking at the document to avoid unintentionally making eye contact and sharing signals such as "Is it my turn to start speaking next?" In this case, the situation would vary depending on whether they intended to speak at that moment. On the other hand, in remote meetings, even if participants were looking at "other" participants, their intention to take a turn was not conveyed, so document browsing was not used as an escape from gaze, and attention may have been dispersed.

5.4 Turn-Giving Analysis

Result

Figure 7-left shows the results of turn-giving analysis. The "Just Before" and "Before" intervals are the same as in Sect. 5.3. The AOIs are classified as "Next Speaker", "Document," and "Others." "Others" includes other participants (excluding the next speaker), the table, walls, etc. The numbers below the graph represent the number of turn-giving instances where gaze was correctly detected.

From Fig. 7-left, it is evident that in collocated meetings, the proportion of time spent looking at the document is high in both the "Just Before" and "Before" intervals. Compared to collocated meetings, in remote meetings, gaze tends to be not only on the document but also on the next speaker and something else in both time intervals. Additionally, in collocated meetings, there was a difference in gaze distribution between the "Just Before" and "Before" intervals. The proportion of participants looking at the next speaker in the "Before" interval was larger compared to the "Just Before" interval.

Figure 7-right shows the results of Fig. 7-left divided by participant. Comparing the time intervals in collocated meetings for Participants 1 and 2, it was found that gaze was more often directed toward something else in the "Before" interval than in the "Just Before" interval. On the other hand, for Participants 1 and 2 in remote meetings, there was no difference between the time intervals. Furthermore, for Participant 4 in the "Just Before" interval, while gaze was concentrated on the document in collocated meetings, it tended to be distributed to the next speaker and something else in remote meetings.

Discussion

Like the gaze distribution in turn-taking shown in Sect. 5.3, in turn-giving, regardless of the "Just Before" or "Before" interval, gaze was more concentrated on the document in collocated meetings compared to remote meetings. Considering the first-time meeting condition, one possible reason for this is that participants tried to avoid designating the next speaker by directing their gaze toward a specific person and instead attempted to speak equally to everyone. On the other hand, in remote meetings, the reason why gaze was not concentrated on the document but directed at the next speaker and something else could be that participants were aware that their gaze was not being conveyed to the other party, and they naturally directed their gaze toward the person who would have spoken next under normal circumstances.

6 Hypotheses on the Relationship Between Gaze and the Turn-Changing Mechanism

In this section, based on the results of the analysis, we formulate hypotheses for remote meetings which include supplemental materials.

H1: In collocated meetings, those who take a turn are more likely to browse documents, but in remote meetings, they are less likely to browse documents.

H2: In collocated meetings, those who give a turn are more likely to browse documents, but in remote meetings, they are less likely to browse documents.

H3: In remote meetings, participants' attention is dispersed rather than focused on documents.
H4: In remote meetings, there is less unintentional eye contact with other participants, and there is less browsing of documents to avoid eye contact.

The results of the analysis suggest that, in both turn-taking and turn-giving, there is a strong tendency to browse the documents in collocated meetings, while the tendency in remote meetings is weaker (H1 and H2). Furthermore, it is suggested that in remote meetings, compared to collocated meetings, participants do not concentrate on a single target and the gaze is equally directed towards the next speaker and other gaze targets (H3). Additionally, we believe that the reason for the weaker tendency to browse documents in remote meetings and the stronger tendency to browse documents in collocated meetings is related to avoiding eye contact by browsing the documents. In remote meetings, even if participants look at the other person's video image, the other person cannot receive their gaze, but in collocated meetings, participants can sense eye contact. Therefore, since unintentional eye contact seems to occur in collocated meetings, the tendency to browse documents is higher than in remote meeting in order to avoid eye contact. On the other hand, we assumed that browsing documents to avoid eye contact seems unlikely to occur in remote meetings (H4).

7 Limitation

The current analyses are limited to the relationship between the gaze and turn-changing mechanisms; without considering the content of utterances. Since the content of the speech is an important factor related to the gaze, future analysis should consider not only the relationship between gaze and turn-changing but also the details of speech, the gaze and turn-changing. To give an example of the relationship between speech and gaze, if a participant is called by name, he/she will look at the person who called his/her name.

Furthermore, it is necessary to factor in individual differences based on the characteristics of the participants. We assumed that there are individual differences in the number of utterances and behavior before utterances. As an example, Participant 3 had more utterances. We also reviewed the video images and found that Participant 2 was more likely to look between the people sitting in front of him during collocated meetings. We believe that by carrying out follow-up experiments and obtaining more data, the effects of individual differences can be reduced as much as possible.

Additionally, the results obtained from this experiment need to be considered in a cultural context. The subjects in this experiment were Japanese, and we cannot ensure that similar results would be found in other cultures.

Also, there were differences among participants in the percentage of correctly tracked gaze depending on the performance of the eye-tracking device. Specifically, for Participant 2's gaze in the collocated meeting, of the 16 manually assigned order-taking counts from the recordings, the measurement rate per unit time exceeded 50% only about four times. Therefore, the experimental design needs to be improved in terms of how the eye-tracking device is worn and the instructions given during the collocated condition.

Moreover, the number and placement of participants in this experiment also need to be carefully considered. Although there were four participants in this experiment, in the collocated condition, the ease of eye movement may physically differ between those sitting in front and those sitting to the side. In the same way, in remote meetings, the ease of directing one's gaze may differ between a person whose image is displayed closer to the on-screen document and a person whose image is displayed farther away from the document. Future analysis should include examination of the relationship between the position of other participants and the ease of directing the participants' gaze.

In addition, the participants in this experiment were meeting for the first time. We conducted an ice-breaker so that the participants could learn each other's names and participate in the meeting without feeling nervous, however, we cannot rule out the possibility that they felt embarrassed to look at the others' faces or that their speech was restricted. As a result, their gaze may have been focused on the document. We plan to conduct additional experiments within the same laboratory and among colleagues at work to investigate the reasons why the gaze tends to be focused on the document.

8 Future Work

8.1 Analyzing Other Groups and Validating Hypotheses

In this paper, we obtained four hypotheses regarding the relationship between turn-changing and gaze by analyzing one of four groups. In the future, we plan to perform similar analyses on the remaining three groups and validate the hypotheses obtained. Furthermore, while this paper focused on the gaze and turn-changing of the participants, we will investigate the relationship between gaze and turn-changing by analyzing AOIs in more detail. For example, it is possible that when taking a turn, the speaker would gaze at each participant individually before speaking. To facilitate such investigations, we are considering a visualization that would provide a chronological overview of the four gaze targets.

8.2 Incorporating Additional Data for a Comprehensive Analysis

Although our analysis was limited to gaze and turn-changing, we also collected data on head movements, pupil size, speech audio, and utterance content in the experiment. By comprehensively capturing these data points, we aim to further clarify the mechanism of turn-changing in remote meetings with supplemental materials.

8.3 The Need for Additional Experiments to Address Insufficient Experimental Conditions

Moreover, it is necessary to investigate the degree of influence that supplemental materials have on discussions. In the current experiment, the participants discussed the topic based on the shared document; however, we need to conduct other experiments such as without the documents, in other words, without supplemental materials to survey the effects of supplemental materials on turn-changing. Furthermore, while this experiment only used documents as supplemental materials, in real-world meetings, it is conceivable that chat tools may be used in addition to document browsing. In such cases, gaze distribution and comprehending the other participants' intention to speak may become even more challenging. Therefore, in additional experiments, we will also vary the number of supplemental materials to elucidate the mechanism of turn-changing.

9 Conclusion

The purpose of this paper was to clarify how turn-changing occurs in remote meetings involving supplemental materials such as document browsing. We monitored both remote and collocated meeting data and analyzed them by comparing the participants' gaze during turn-taking and turn-giving. The present research makes three contributions:

- We designed the setup for acquiring multiple data points from remote meetings with supplemental materials, such as participants' gaze, the context of speech, video images, etc.
- We collected and analyzed data focusing on gaze and turn-changing, and gained insights for future experiments and data analysis.
- We derived four hypotheses related to turn-changing in remote meetings with supplemental materials.

As indicated in the Future Work section, we will analyze not only one group but also other groups in order to verify the hypotheses. Moreover, we will explore the characteristics of turn-changing by combining gaze with head movements and utterance content. Furthermore, by varying the degree of influence and the number of supplemental materials, we will investigate the mechanism of turn-changing in remote meetings with supplemental materials. Based on these results, our goal is to create a system that enables smooth progression in remote meetings while utilizing document browsing and chat tools.

Acknowledgments. We thank several members of the Kobayashi Laboratory at Meiji University for their cooperation as operators in the experiments. This work was supported by JSPS KAKENHI Grant Number JP22H03635 and 23K24891.

References

1. Kendon, A.: Some functions of gaze-direction in social interaction. Acta Psychol. **26**, 22–63 (1967)
2. Richardson, D.C., Dale, R.: Looking to understand: the coupling between speakers' and listeners' eye movements and its relationship to discourse comprehension. Interact. Stud. **8**(3), 509–543 (2007)
3. Vertegaal, R., van der Veer, G. Vons, H.: Effects of gaze on multiparty mediated communication. In: Proceedings of the SIGCHI Conference on Human Factors in Computing Systems, pp. 294–301 (2000)
4. Jokinen, K., Nishida, M., Yamamoto, S.: On eye-gaze and turn-taking. In: Proceedings of EGIHMI 2010, pp. 118–123 (2010)

5. Grayson, D.M., Monk, A.F.: Are you looking at me? Eye contact and desktop video conferencing. ACM Trans. Comput.-Hum. Interact. **10**(3), 221–243 (2003)
6. Chen, M.: Leveraging the asymmetric sensitivity of eye contact for videoconference. Proc. CHI **2002**, 49–56 (2002)
7. Boland, J.E., Fonseca, P., Mennelstein, I., Williamson, M.: Zoom disrupts the rhythm of conversation. In: Proceedings of the 31st Annual Meeting of the Cognitive Science Society, pp. 134–139 (2009)
8. Cao, H., et al.: Large scale analysis of multitasking behavior during remote meetings. In: CHI Conference on Human Factors in Computing Systems, pp. 1–13 (2021)
9. Brubaker, J.R., Venolia, G., Tang, J.: Focusing on shared experiences: moving beyond the camera in video communication. In: Proceedings of the Designing Interactive Systems Conference, pp. 96–105 (2012)
10. Ansah, A.A., et al.: "I need to respond to this" – Contributions to group creativity in remote meetings with distractions. In: Proceedings of the 1st Annual Meeting of the Symposium on Human-Computer Interaction for Work (CHIWORK'22), pp. 1–12 (2022)
11. Marlow, J., Everdingen, E.E., Avrahami, D.: Taking notes or playing games?: Understanding multitasking in video communication. In: Proceedings of CSCW 2016, pp. 1726–1737 (2016)
12. Tobii Pro Glasses 3. https://www.tobii.com/products/eye-trackers/wearables/tobii-pro-glasses-3. Accessed 21 Apr 2024
13. Tobii Pro Lab. https://www.tobii.com/products/software/behavior-research-software/tobii-pro-lab. Accessed 21 Apr 2024
14. Tobii Pro Lab – Data Export information. https://go.tobii.com/Tobii-Pro-Lab-data-export-info. Accessed 21 Apr 2024
15. Ishii, R., Otsuka, K., Kumano, S., Yamato, J.: Prediction of who will be the next speaker and when using gaze behavior in multiparty meetings. In: ACM Transactions on Interactive Intelligent Systems (TiiS) - Special Issue on Multimodal Affective Interaction, vol. 6, no. 1, Article 4, pp. 1–31 (2014)

Engagement Analysis of Speech Text from Activity Reports of a Distance Project-Based Learning

Kosuke Sasaki[1,2] and Tomoo Inoue[3]

[1] Graduate School of Library, Information and Media Studies, University of Tsukuba, Ibaraki, Japan
ksasaki@slis.tsukuba.ac.jp
[2] Faculty of Global Management, Chuo University, Tokyo, Japan
[3] Institute of Library, Information and Media Science, University of Tsukuba, Ibaraki, Japan
inoue@slis.tsukuba.ac.jp

Abstract. This study aims to support Project-Based Learning (PBL) in a distance environment in which teachers provide feedback to learners to facilitate learning. However, in distance PBL, it is difficult for teachers to grasp learners' learning status, and it is difficult for them to provide appropriate feedback. In this study, to assist teachers in providing feedback to learners whose learning status is not good, we estimate engagement, which is one of the mental indicators of their positive attitude toward learning, using activity reports submitted by the learners. In this paper, we analyzed the content of activity reports from perspectives other than the occurrence of negative words, which has been reported on previously. The results of the analysis suggest the possibility of estimating learner engagement and learning status through sentiment estimation using a widely used sentiment analysis program, indicating that activity reports are useful in assisting teachers in providing feedback.

Keywords: Activity report · Learner engagement · Distance PBL

1 Introduction

Distance learning has become increasingly popular. This is because it has various advantages, including the possibility of taking classes from home without having to attend in-person school [7] or using on-demand videos of classes that allow students to learn at the pace of their own lives [1,9].

Among distance learning methods, this study focuses on project-based learning (PBL), a learner-centered learning method that integrates knowledge acquisition with activities aimed at solving real-world problems. In PBL, teachers provide feedback to learners and learners receive feedback from their teachers to further their learning [3]. For teachers to help learners accomplish PBL smoothly, it is necessary to provide feedback. The feedback that teachers should provide to learners has been described in various studies (e.g., [13, 23, 34]). In this study, we focus on the unique problems of PBL in a distance environment (distance PBL), where it is difficult for teachers to monitor the learning status of all learners because of the reduced opportunities for communication due to the distance environment [17, 22] and because one teacher is teaching multiple learners. Because of these problems, it is difficult for teachers to identify learners who need help and subsequently provide feedback in distance PBL.

Therefore, this study aims to support distance PBL and create a framework for teachers to provide appropriate feedback to learners seeking help.

In this study, activity reports were used to obtain the necessary information for providing appropriate feedback. Activity reports, which are part of learning activities, are used by teachers to understand the progress of learners' activities and by learners to consult with teachers. Activity reports also allow learners to reflect on their learning and revise their plans.

In addition, a method for estimating learners' learning status by estimating engagement, which is an indicator of a person's positive mental state toward a task, from activity reports has been studied [15]. In PBL, which is the focus of this study, learners need to not only complete the tasks given by teachers but also find their tasks and promote their learning activities with the support of teachers [21]. By detecting a decrease in engagement, we expect teachers to find that learners are not having a positive PBL experience and that they may have problems with learning activities.

According to a previous study, to estimate engagement from activity reports, especially in studies using activity reports exchanged in video format, it is possible to estimate engagement according to the amount and length of learners' filled or silent pauses in their reports; further, the appearance of negative words in the text transcribed from video activity reports is associated with lower learner engagement [26].

However, there have been no analyses of the content of video activity reports in terms of anything other than the occurrence of negative words and phrases. In addition, it is not known how the occurrence of negative words and phrases relates to the learners' learning status. In other words, there is a lack of useful information for teachers to provide feedback to learners based only on previous findings. While estimating their learning status, it is desirable to do so based on a variety of information rather than focusing only on the presence of negative words and phrases.

Therefore, this paper presents findings on the relationship between learning status and learner engagement obtained by analyzing the speech content of video activity reports. The contributions of this paper are as follows.

First, we investigated the relationship between engagement and third-person estimation of learning progress based on the transcripts of video activity reports, classifying them into three groups: good, poor, and neither (neutral). The results showed that learner engagement was relatively high when they submitted activity reports that were estimated to be neutral in their learning progress. This suggests that the results of engagement estimation can be used to estimate learners' learning status.

Second, we used an existing sentiment analysis program to automatically estimate the sentiments of video activity reports and investigate the relationship between the results of classifying them into three groups (positive, negative, and neutral) and the learner engagement. The results showed that when an activity report classified as positive through sentiment analysis was submitted, the learner was in a state of high engagement. The results suggest that learner engagement can be estimated using programs that run automatically.

Combined with previous findings, these results suggest that analyzing the content of video activity reports using multiple methods and perspectives can provide information from multiple perspectives to enable teachers to provide appropriate feedback in distance PBL. In particular, the results of this study indicate that engagement related to learners' learning status can be estimated not only by focusing on the occurrence of negative words and phrases but also through existing sentiment analysis programs. In other words, this study revealed that video activity reports can be used to support teachers in providing feedback to learners, which is the goal of this study.

2 Related Work

2.1 Activity Reports

The usefulness of activity reports in higher education has been reported on previously. Chickering and Gamson argued that encouraging student-teacher contact and providing quick feedback in undergraduate education can help improve teaching in higher education [8]. In a study on undergraduate education, Etkina and Harper confirmed that assigning weekly reports to students in college classes can help students solve problems quickly, reflect on their daily learning, and help teachers adapt their teaching to the students' needs [11]. Ito et al. assigned weekly reports in informatics classes and demonstrated the possibility of assessing students' learning status from the words used in their reports [16]. These studies have shown that activity reports are often used in educational settings.

Text-based activity reports are commonly used [20]. However, we used video activity reports in this study. Videos are expected to more easily convey mental information, such as emotions [6,33].

2.2 Engagement

Engagement is a measure of a person's mental state [12,18,29] and indicates how positively a person engages in a task when immersed in it [2]. Engagement has been defined in numerous ways in many fields, including education and psychology [4]. In this study, we used the definition of engagement given by Schaufeli et al., which has been studied in the context of the Computer Supported Cooperative Work. Engagement was originally used in the context of work, as proposed by Schaufeli et al. [29]. However, Schaufeli et al. showed that the proposed concept of engagement is meaningful for students. In particular, they showed that higher vigor, a component of engagement, indicates higher academic performance.

As engagement is an abstract concept, questionnaires were used to measure it. Schaufeli et al. developed the Utrecht Work Engagement Scale (UWES) to measure engagement, which consists of 17 questions focusing on the three components of vigor, dedication, and absorption [29]. Based on the UWES, Schaufeli et al. also developed a UWES for students: the UWES-S [28], the UWES-9 [27], which reduces the number of questions to nine and thus the effort required to answer them, and the UWES-3 [30], which further reduces the number of questions to three.

A common problem with these engagement measurement methods is that it is difficult to capture changes in engagement, because they are measured using questionnaire surveys. Engagement is said to change daily [5,32]. However, engagement surveys are often conducted only periodically, such as once a year, which makes it difficult to track changes in engagement [31].

2.3 Estimating Engagement

Some studies have examined methods other than questionnaires for estimating engagement. Kajiwara et al. proposed a method for estimating worker engagement at work using a wearable device to acquire body and eye movements and pulse rates [19]. Qi et al. proposed a method for estimating engagement in educational settings based on eye gaze, facial expressions, and learner movement by acquiring videos of students taking online classes [25]. Yue et al. also estimated engagement by acquiring the facial expressions, gaze, and body movements of students taking online classes using a camera, eye tracker, and mouse movements [35]. As these studies have demonstrated, methods other than questionnaire surveys can be considered to estimate engagement.

One study estimated engagement by using learners' activity reports. Sasaki et al. investigated the relationship between video activity reports submitted by learners and learner engagement. They found that engagement was lower when filled pauses in learners' speech were frequent or longer or when silent pauses were infrequent or shorter in video activity reports submitted by learners. They also focused on the content of transcribed reports and showed that the appearance of negative words was associated with lower engagement [26].

Learners' activity reports have been shown to be useful for estimating engagement. However, the previous study only focused on whether negative words or phrases were included in the report contents. Sufficient information necessary to support teachers' feedback, which is the goal of this study, was not obtained.

3 Objectives

This study aims to support distance PBL. Since it is difficult for teachers teaching in PBL to monitor the progress of all learners, we aimed to create a framework to assist in providing feedback to learners who need help. To understand the learners' learning status, we used their submitted activity reports. From the activity reports, we measured engagement, which is one of the mental indicators of positive attitudes toward learning activities. PBL requires spontaneous learning. Therefore, learning may fail if learner engagement decreases. Decreased learner engagement is a problem that needs to be avoided. However, engagement, an abstract concept, has traditionally been measured using questionnaire surveys, and the surveys have often been conducted at long intervals. To quickly detect a decline in engagement and inform teachers of possible problems in learners' learning activities, this study examined a method for estimating engagement during a short period using daily activity reports.

Previous studies have examined methods for estimating learner status based on engagement using video activity reports submitted by learners [15, 26]. However, while focusing on the content of video activity reports, previous studies have only analyzed content based on the occurrence of negative words and phrases. With only information on the presence or absence of negative phrases, teachers lack information about the learners' situation in order to provide feedback; that is, it cannot sufficiently support teachers to provide feedback.

Therefore, this paper focuses on the transcribed text of the content of video activity reports to present teachers with richer information about learners during feedback. First, we investigated the relationship between the estimation of the learners' learning status based on the text of the report and learner engagement. In other words, we posed the following research question.

RQ1: How does a third person's estimation of learning status from a learner's video activity reports relate to their actual reported engagement?

If the results of the estimation of learning based on reported content are related to engagement, then estimating engagement will lead to an understanding of the learning situation. Therefore, we conducted sentiment estimation using an existing sentiment analysis program with textual information transcribed from the content of the video activity report. To investigate the relationship between the results of emotion estimation and learner engagement, the following research question was posed.

RQ2: How does the result of the sentiment estimation of the content of the video activity report by an existing program relate to learner engagement?

If the results of learning status estimation and engagement are related and if the results of emotion estimation are related to engagement, it may be possible to estimate a learner's learning status by automatically estimating engagement.

4 Method

In this paper, we examine what kind of information can be obtained about feedback from teachers in distance PBL by analyzing activity reports from perspectives different from those employed in a previous study [26]. In this section, we explain the method used to collect the analyzed data and the method used to analyze the video activity reports.

Table 1. Participants of the study

Participant	Age	Gender	Nationality	# of submitted reports/Actual trial days
P1	23		Chinese	56/63
P2	25		Chinese	23/24
P3	25		Chinese	33/36
P4	25		Chinese	33/34
P5	23		Chinese	37/37
P6	24		Chinese	16/16
P7	26		Chinese	16/16
P8	23	Male	Japanese	18/26

4.1 Data Collection

Based on a previous study [15], we describe the method used to collect the video activity reports analyzed in this study and the data collected for engagement estimation.

Participants of the Video Activity Report Collection. With the approval of the Ethics Committee on Library, Information and Media Studies at University of Tsukuba (No. 20-32), video activity reports were collected from learners engaged in distance PBL whose primary learning activity was research. Learners were recruited through snowball sampling using a social media (WeChat[1]) and messenger application (LINE[2]). The participants asked to submit video activity reports were eight graduate students (all male) between the ages of 23 and 26, as shown in Table 1. All learners were supervised by the same teacher. Each learner conducted their research activities individually and was aware of their goals and prospective due dates, which were discussed and agreed upon with the teacher. Once a week, each learner had the opportunity to individually meet with the teacher to report and discuss their research activities.

As all learners were engaged in research activities in an environment where the use of Japanese is common, the language used for the video activity report in this study was Japanese. For learners whose native language was not Japanese, we confirmed in advance that they could speak Japanese at a level equivalent to or higher than N2 of the Japanese-Language Proficiency Test (JLPT)[3] and could report their activities in Japanese without difficulty.

---

[1] WeChat - Free messaging and calling app, https://www.wechat.com/ (Visited on April 21, 2024).
[2] LINE always at your side., https://line.me/en/ (Visited on April 21, 2024).
[3] JLPT Japanese-Language Proficiency Test, https://www.jlpt.jp/e/) (Visited on April 21, 2024).

Table 2. Questionnaire items

No.	Factor	Content
1	Vigor	When I'm doing my work as a student, I feel like I am bursting with energy.
2	Dedication	I am enthusiastic about my studies.
3	Absorption	I am immersed in my studies.

The learners were asked to submit a video activity report and answer a questionnaire to measure their daily engagement. Only when they submitted both the video activity reports and answers to the questionnaire were they considered to have submitted data, and they were paid 100 yen per day. In Table 1, "# of submitted reports" refers to the number of times data were submitted during the collection period of the video activity reports. The "Actual trial days" refers to the period during which each learner participated in the collection of video activity reports. Video activity reports were collected between August 2020 and November 2020.

Engagement Score. To measure engagement, we used the UWES-3 proposed by Schaufeli et al. [30] because we chose an index with the fewest number of questions, so that daily questionnaire surveys would be as less burdensome for the learners as possible. In addition, because the UWES-3 was originally designed for use with workers in companies, the wording of some questions in the UWES-3 was changed with reference to the UWES-S [28], which is a UWES for students. The questions presented to the learners are listed in Table 2.

Learners responded to each question on a 7-point scale from 0 (never) to 6 (always). The average of the scores of the three responses was defined as the engagement score for the day and was used in the analysis.

Procedure. Learners were asked to submit video activity reports and answer a questionnaire on weekdays during the collection period of the video activity reports, excluding holidays. The following instructions were provided to the learners when they submitted video activity reports.

- Your video activity report should be taken using a laptop, smartphone, or any other device with a microphone and camera.
- You should not wear any objects that mask your face and should take a bust shot. (Figure 1(a) shows a screenshot of the submitted video.)
- You should report on what is related to your study or research, such as what you learned in the day's lectures, how you prepared your reports, and the progress of your research in each video.
- There is no limit to the length of each video. We expected that each video would be approximately 30 s long, but it would be acceptable for the video to be shorter or longer than 30 s.

– There are no restrictions on where you take the video, but try to record in a place that is as quiet as possible and ensure that your voice is clear.

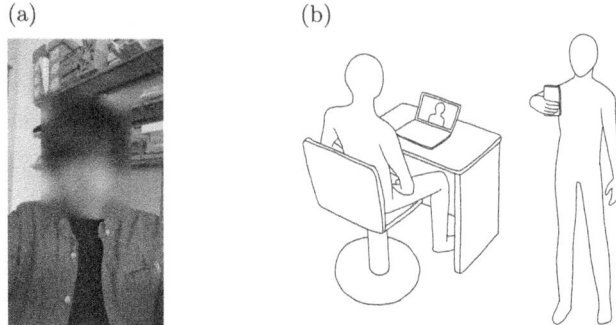

Fig. 1. (a) Screenshot of a video activity report. (b) Illustrations of a participant when recording a video activity report using a laptop (left) and using a smartphone (right).

This procedure was based on a previous study in which similar video activity reports were collected [14]. The authors assumed that a video activity report would be taken in the style shown in Fig. 1(b) and that participants generally took their videos in the same way.

Asking for an activity report once a day has also been done in other studies (e.g., [20,24]). We asked the participants to record a video once a day because engagement may vary from day to day, as argued by Breevaart et al. and Sonnentag et al. [5,32].

We set a guideline of 30 s as the length of one video activity report, according to the result of the experimenter's trial of recording a video activity report in advance, which showed that a learner was able to report a day's activity in approximately 30 s.

Learners recorded a video activity report every weekday and completed a questionnaire after the recording. The video activity reports were uploaded to cloud storage once a month. The engagement score was calculated based on the responses to the questionnaire and was collected together with the video activity report submitted on the same day.

When obtaining consent for the collection of video activity reports, learners were asked to cooperate for at least four weeks. Four weeks after the start of the collection, the learners were free to withdraw from cooperation at any time.

Speech Content Extraction. Speech content in the video activity reports was obtained using Google Cloud Speech-to-Text API[4], so as to transcribe the collected video activity reports into Japanese. The experimenter manually corrected the incorrect transcripts.

---

[4] Speech-to-Text AI: speech recognition and transcription — Google Cloud, https://cloud.google.com/speech-to-text (Visited on April 21, 2024).

4.2 Classifying Activity Reports

For the analysis in this paper, we used video activity reports and the engagement score for the day on which each activity report was submitted, as described in Sect. 4.1 (N=232). Video activity reports were analyzed in RQ1 based on the results of classification by a third person and in RQ2 based on the results of classification by an automatic sentiment analysis program.

Third-Person Classification. The learners who submitted the video activity reports were mainly engaged in research activities. Therefore, the contents of the reports were mainly related to the progress of their research. Two labelers independently reviewed the textual information transcribed from the activity reports and classified the video activity reports as follows: "Research progress is **good**," "Research progress is **poor**," or "Research progress is **neutral** (neither good nor poor)." The labelers were given only the instruction "Classify the reports into one of the following three categories: 'good' for a report of good research progress, 'poor' for a report of poor research progress, or 'neutral' for neither of the 'good' nor 'poor'," without providing detailed classification criteria. By not specifying the classification criteria, we attempted to estimate learning status independently of the PBL context.

Classification by Sentiment Analysis Program. To compare the results of the automatic programmatic sentiment estimation and engagement, we classified the video activity reports into three groups (positive, negative, and neutral) using an existing sentiment analysis program.

The sentiment analysis program used BERT, a natural language model widely used in natural language processing [10]; cl-tohoku/bert-base-japanesewholeword-masking[5], a pre-trained Japanese BERT model as a tokenizer to tokenize words for input into BERT; and koheiduck/bert-japanese-finetuned-sentiment[6], a fine-tuned Japanese sentiment analysis model. This sentiment analysis model can classify sentences as **POSITIVE**, **NEGATIVE**, or **NEUTRAL** based on the highest probability. Results were obtained by inputting the transcribed text of each video activity report as an argument for the program.

5 Results

5.1 Classification Results

The results of the estimation of research progress conducted by the two labelers, based on the transcripts of video activity report are shown in Table 3. The number of cases in which the two labelers' estimates of "good," "poor," and "neutral"

---

[5] https://huggingface.co/tohoku-nlp/bert-base-japanese-whole-word-masking (Visited on April 21, 2024).

[6] https://huggingface.co/koheiduck/bert-japanese-finetuned-sentiment (Visited on April 21, 2024).

Table 3. Results of third-person classifications

		Labeler B			
		Good	Poor	Neutral	Total
Labeler A	Good	28	1	12	41
	Poor	3	9	8	20
	Neutral	30	5	136	171
	Total	61	15	156	232

Table 4. Results of automatic classification based on sentiment analysis

Estimated sentiment	Number of classified activity reports
POSITIVE	128
NEGATIVE	13
NEUTRAL	91
Total	232

matched was 173 (agreement rate 74.6%, $\kappa = 0.44$). The low agreement rate, even though there were only two labelers, was probably due to the classification of the three patterns, while the classification criteria were ambiguous.

The classification results based on the automatic sentiment analysis are shown in Table 4.

5.2 Relationship Between Classification Results and Engagement Score

We analyzed the relationship between engagement and classification of video activity reports by third persons and automatic classification based on sentiment analysis.

To analyze the relationship between the results of third-person classification and engagement, we used the data of the 173 cases in which the classification results of the two labelers were consistent. The engagement scores for the activity reports in which the two labelers consistently estimated that the research progress was good, poor, or neutral are shown in Fig. 2.

A one-way ANOVA with one factor (classification result) and three levels (good, poor, and neutral) showed no difference in engagement scores for each group ($F(2, 170) = 2.00$, $p = .14$, $\eta^2 = 0.02$). However, although the small number of activity reports classified as poor (N=9) should be considered, there was a 0.7-point difference in engagement scores between activity reports classified as poor and neutral, and the effect size based on *Cohen's d* was relatively large (*Cohen's d* $= 0.55$). Although no significant difference was found, it is possible based on Fig. 2 that the engagement score was somewhat higher when the

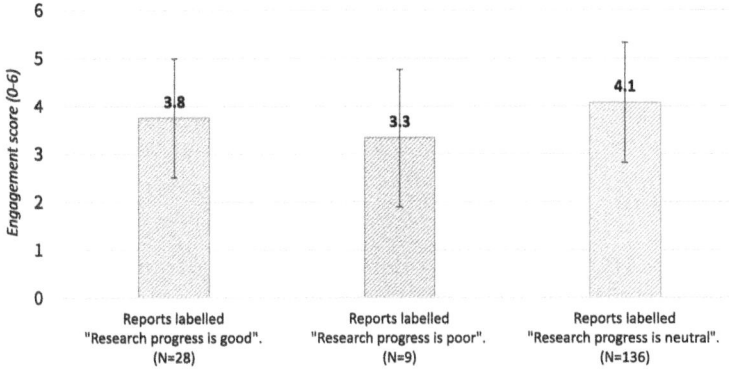

Fig. 2. Relationship between third-person estimates of research progress and engagement scores

research progress was estimated to be neutral, especially compared with when it was estimated to be poor.

The results of the subsequent analysis of the relationship between activity reports and engagement scores, based on automatic classification, are shown in Fig. 3. A one-way ANOVA with one factor (classification result) and three levels (POSITIVE, NEGATIVE, and NEUTRAL) revealed significant differences in the engagement scores for each group ($F(2, 229) = 4.35$, $p = .01 < .05$, $\eta^2 = 0.04$). We then performed multiple comparisons using Welch's t-test with Bonferroni's correction as a posteriori test. The results showed a significant difference between activity reports classified as POSITIVE and NEUTRAL ($t(215) = 2.86$, $p = .01 < .05$, Cohen's $d = 0.38$). In addition, engagement scores for NEGATIVE reports were lower than those for NEUTRAL reports. Although no significant difference was found, a relatively large effect size

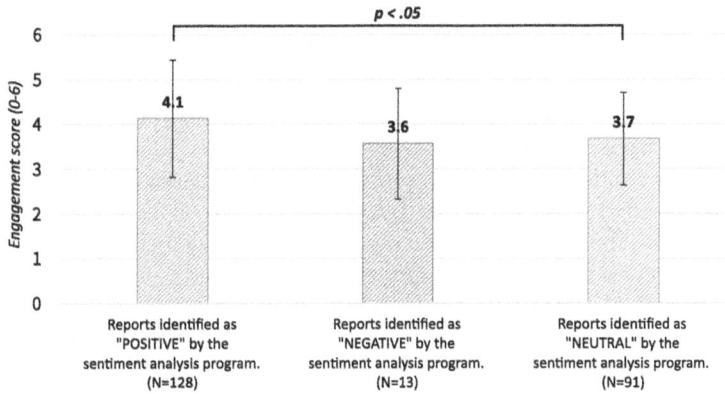

Fig. 3. Relationship between sentiment estimation and engagement scores by automated sentiment analysis program.

was found for the difference between the POSITIVE and NEGATIVE reports ($t(15) = 1.56$, $p = .14$, $Cohen's\ d = 0.43$). These results suggest that the classification of video activity reports based on sentiment analysis can categorize cases of relatively high engagement and cases of relatively low engagement.

6 Discussion

First, we discuss **RQ1**, "How does a third person's estimation of learning status from a learner's video activity reports relate to their actual reported engagement?". Comparing engagement scores based on classification results of the study progress by a third person showed that there was no clear relationship between the three classification results and engagement scores, as shown in Fig. 2. However, the engagement score for each classification result showed that the score was lowest when the activity report was submitted with the estimated poor research progress, which was lower than the engagement score (3.4) when the "activity report contains negative words," which has been reported in a previous study [26]. Comparing the engagement score when research progress was estimated to be neutral and the engagement score when research progress was estimated to be poor showed that the effect size was relatively large, although there was no significant difference. Therefore, there may be a non-negligible difference in engagement when research progress is estimated to be poor and when research progress is estimated to be neutral.

Based on the instructions given to the labelers, the research progress was estimated to be neutral when it was neither good nor poor. This could be perceived by a third person as steady and safe progress of the research activity, and the progress could thus not be judged as particularly good or bad based on the activity report. In this case, we can infer that the engagement score was relatively high. This is because the learners were able to engage in learning in a relatively positive manner, and they did not have much trouble with the progress of their research since the research activities were progressing without any major problems.

Alternatively, learners who identify themselves as putting sufficient effort into their research activities may have higher levels of dedication (high identification), which is a component of engagement. Despite high dedication, if progress in research activities is not estimated as good or poor, the results may not match the effort. Poor academic performance can result in burnout [28].

A more detailed analysis of the relationship between neutral estimates of research progress based on activity reports and engagement requires further investigation to determine an appropriate interpretation.

Next, we consider **RQ2**, "How does the result of the sentiment estimation of the content of the video activity report by an existing program relate to learner engagement?". Analysis of the relationship between the classification results based on sentiment analysis and engagement showed that engagement tended to be higher when activity reports classified as POSITIVE by sentiment analysis were submitted than when activity reports classified as NEGATIVE or

NEUTRAL were submitted. Essentially, engagement is measured using the three factors of vigor, dedication, and absorption and not by a person's thoughts and feelings, as estimated by sentiment analysis. However, engagement and emotion have in common that they both indicate a person's mental state. Therefore, high engagement can be estimated by detecting a positive state through sentiment analysis.

We also discuss the estimation of video activity reports using sentiment analysis from a different perspective. Although we did not modify the sentiment analysis model used in this study, we believe that more accurate classification results can be obtained by training the model according to the PBL context. However, according to the relationship between the engagement scores, the activity report classified as POSITIVE had the highest engagement score and the activity report classified as NEGATIVE had the lowest engagement score, despite the use of a model that was not pre-trained for this research context. This suggests that using a sentiment analysis program based on a widely available model can yield plausible results. Therefore, it may be possible to use sentiment estimation of video activity reports using existing sentiment analysis programs to estimate engagement independent of the PBL context.

In addition, we deal with the occurrence of negative words and phrases in the video activity reports, as reported in a previous study. A relationship was found between the existence of negative words in video activity reports and a decrease in engagement [26]. Figure 2 also shows that learner engagement may be somewhat higher when a third person infers that their learning and research progress is neutral based on the video activity reports. In addition, Fig. 3 shows that learner engagement was relatively high when activity reports classified as positive by sentiment analysis were submitted. Using these results, we can adopt a multifaceted view on when teachers should provide feedback based on learner engagement.

The following examples can be considered. If a third person infers from an activity report that the learner is making poor progress in learning or research or if the activity report is classified as negative by the sentiment analysis, the learner may be less engaged and it may be desirable to give feedback, even if the activity report does not contain any negative words or phrases. Alternatively, although the activity report contains negative words, if the progress of the learning activity is estimated by a third person to not be poor and the activity report is classified as positive by the sentiment analysis, then the learner's learning activity may not be problematic.

The findings of this study can also be applied to a system that assists teachers in providing feedback to learners, such as the following. Learners summarize their daily learning progress in a video activity report and upload it to the system. The system analyzes the content of these videos and detects the learners whose engagement is estimated to decline. The system then notifies teachers that they should provide feedback to learners whose engagement is declining. With such a system, teachers can easily identify learners who are less engaged and may have problems with their learning activities, without having to pay constant attention to them.

The results of this study confirmed several relationships between activity reports and learner engagement. Although it needs to be investigated whether PBL can proceed more smoothly if feedback is given when engagement decreases, it is possible that information about learners can be obtained from multiple perspectives using activity reports. Multifaceted information is expected to present appropriate information to teachers for feedback, thus facilitating distance PBL.

7 Conclusion

This study aims to support distance PBL. In distance PBL, teachers need to provide appropriate feedback to learners; however, it is difficult for them to track their learning status. This study focuses on engagement, a mental indicator that shows that learners are positively engaged in learning activities. When learning activities do not progress well, learner engagement may decline. Therefore, we examined whether a decline in engagement can be detected based on activity reports. A previous study [26] showed that engagement decreases when activity reports contain negative words or phrases. In this paper, we analyzed the content of activity reports from different perspectives and investigated the relationship between content and engagement. The results showed that (1) learner engagement was relatively high when they submitted activity reports where the learning progress was estimated by a third person to be neutral, and (2) learner engagement was higher when they submitted activity reports that were classified as positive by an automated sentiment analysis program than when they submitted other activity reports. This indicates that by analyzing activity reports from different perspectives and in different ways, teachers can obtain the information they need to provide feedback from multiple perspectives.

References

1. Adnan, M., Anwar, K.: Online learning amid the covid-19 pandemic: students' perspectives. Online Submission **2**(1), 45–51 (2020)
2. Afflerbach, P., Harrison, C.: What is engagement, how is it different from motivation, and how can i promote it? J. Adolesc. Adult Literacy **61**(2), 217–220 (2017)
3. Almulla, M.A.: The effectiveness of the project-based learning (PBL) approach as a way to engage students in learning. SAGE Open **10**(3), 2158244020938702 (2020). https://doi.org/10.1177/2158244020938702
4. Azevedo, R.: Defining and measuring engagement and learning in science: conceptual, theoretical, methodological, and analytical issues. Educ. Psychol. **50**(1), 84–94 (2015). https://doi.org/10.1080/00461520.2015.1004069
5. Breevaart, K., Demerouti, E., Hetland, J.: The measurement of state work engagement a multilevel factor analytic study. European J. Psychol. Assessm. **28**, 305 (2012). https://doi.org/10.1027/1015-5759/a000111
6. Bänziger, T., Grandjean, D., Scherer, K.: Emotion recognition from expressions in face, voice, and body: the multimodal emotion recognition test (MERT). Emotion (Washington, D.C.) **9**, 691–704 (2009). https://doi.org/10.1037/a0017088

7. Chen, Z., et al.: Learning from home: a mixed-methods analysis of live streaming based remote education experience in Chinese colleges during the covid-19 pandemic. In: Proceedings of the 2021 CHI Conference on Human Factors in Computing Systems, pp. 1–16 (2021)
8. Chickering, A.W., Gamson, Z.F.: Seven principles for good practice in undergraduate education. AAHE Bull. **3**, 7 (1987)
9. Cojocariu, V.M., Lazar, I., Nedeff, V., Lazar, G.: Swot anlysis of e-learning educational services from the perspective of their beneficiaries. Procedia Soc. Behav. Sci. **116**, 1999–2003 (2014)
10. Devlin, J., Chang, M.W., Lee, K., Toutanova, K.: BERT: pre-training of deep bidirectional transformers for language understanding. In: Proceedings of the 2019 Conference of the North American Chapter of the Association for Computational Linguistics: Human Language Technologies, Volume 1 (Long and Short Papers), pp. 4171–4186. Association for Computational Linguistics, Minneapolis, Minnesota (2019). https://doi.org/10.18653/v1/N19-1423
11. Etkina, E., Harper, K.A.: Weekly reports: student reflections on learning. J. Coll. Sci. Teach. **31**(7), 476–480 (2002)
12. Harter, J.K., Schmidt, F.L., Hayes, T.L.: Business-unit-level relationship between employee satisfaction, employee engagement, and business outcomes: a meta-analysis. J. Appl. Psychol. **87**(2), 268 (2002)
13. Hattie, J., Timperley, H.: The power of feedback. Rev. Educ. Res. **77**(1), 81–112 (2007). https://doi.org/10.3102/003465430298487
14. He, Z., Dai, X., Yamakami, T., Inoue, T.: Preliminary utility study of a short video as a daily report in teleworking. In: Nolte, A., et al. (eds.) CollabTech 2020. LNCS, vol. 12324, pp. 35–49. Springer, Cham (2020). https://doi.org/10.1007/978-3-030-58157-2_3
15. He, Z., Sarcar, S., Inoue, T.: Exploring the feasibility of video activity reporting for students in distance learning. In: Data Science, Human-Centered Computing, and Intelligent Technologies, pp. 44–55 (2022)
16. Ito, K., Kizuka, A., Oba, M.: A trial utilization of weekly reports to evaluate learning for system development PBLS. In: 2016 5th IIAI International Congress on Advanced Applied Informatics (IIAI-AAI), pp. 1064–1067. IEEE (2016)
17. Johnson, B., Zimmermann, T., Bird, C.: The effect of work environments on productivity and satisfaction of software engineers. IEEE Trans. Software Eng. **47**, 736–757 (2021)
18. Kahn, W.A.: Psychological conditions of personal engagement and disengagement at work. Acad. Manag. J. **33**(4), 692–724 (1990)
19. Kajiwara, Y., Shimauchi, T., Kimura, H.: Predicting emotion and engagement of workers in order picking based on behavior and pulse waves acquired by wearable devices. Sensors **19**(1), 165 (2019)
20. Lu, D., Marlow, J., Kocielnik, R., Avrahami, D.: Challenges and opportunities for technology-supported activity reporting in the workplace. In: Proceedings of the 2018 CHI Conference on Human Factors in Computing Systems, pp. 1–12 (2018)
21. Markham, T.: Project based learning a bridge just far enough. Teacher Librarian **39**(2), 38–42 (2011)
22. Mulki, J.P., Bardhi, F., Lassk, F.G., Nanavaty-Dahl, J.: Set up remote workers to thrive. MIT Sloan Manag. Rev. **51**(1), 63 (2009)
23. Narciss, S.: Feedback strategies for interactive learning tasks. In: Handbook of Research on Educational Communications and Technology, pp. 125–143. Routledge (2008)

24. Pogorilich, D.A.: The daily report as a job management tool: a publication of the American Association of Cost Engineers. Cost Engineering **34**(2), 23 (1992)
25. Qi, Y., Zhuang, L., Chen, H., Han, X., Liang, A.: Evaluation of students' learning engagement in online classes based on multimodal vision perspective. Electronics **13**(1), 149 (2023)
26. Sasaki, K., He, Z., Inoue, T.: Using video activity reports to support remote project-based learning. JUCS - J. Univ. Comput. Sci. **29**(11), 1336–1360 (2023). https://doi.org/10.3897/jucs.113266
27. Schaufeli, W.B., Bakker, A.B., Salanova, M.: The measurement of work engagement with a short questionnaire: a cross-national study. Educ. Psychol. Measur. **66**(4), 701–716 (2006)
28. Schaufeli, W.B., Martinez, I.M., Pinto, A.M., Salanova, M., Bakker, A.B.: Burnout and engagement in university students: a cross-national study. J. Cross Cult. Psychol. **33**(5), 464–481 (2002)
29. Schaufeli, W.B., Salanova, M., González-Romá, V., Bakker, A.B.: The measurement of engagement and burnout: a two sample confirmatory factor analytic approach. J. Happiness Stud. **3**(1), 71–92 (2002)
30. Schaufeli, W.B., Shimazu, A., Hakanen, J., Salanova, M., De Witte, H.: An ultra-short measure for work engagement. Eur. J. Psychol. Assessm. (2017)
31. Shami, N.S., Muller, M., Pal, A., Masli, M., Geyer, W.: Inferring employee engagement from social media. In: Proceedings of the 33rd Annual ACM Conference on Human Factors in Computing Systems (CHI 2015), pp. 3999–4008. Association for Computing Machinery, New York (2015). https://doi.org/10.1145/2702123.2702445
32. Sonnentag, S., Dormann, C., Demerouti, E., et al.: Not all days are created equal: the concept of state work engagement. In: Work Engagement: A Handbook of Essential Theory and Research, pp. 25–38 (2010)
33. Veinott, E.S., Olson, J., Olson, G.M., Fu, X.: Video helps remote work: speakers who need to negotiate common ground benefit from seeing each other. In: Proceedings of the SIGCHI Conference on Human Factors in Computing Systems (CHI 1999), pp. 302–309. Association for Computing Machinery, New York (1999). https://doi.org/10.1145/302979.303067
34. Wiliam, D.: Assessment: the bridge between teaching and learning. Voices Middle **21**(2), 15 (2013)
35. Yue, J., et al.: Recognizing multidimensional engagement of e-learners based on multi-channel data in e-learning environment. IEEE Access **7**, 149554–149567 (2019). https://doi.org/10.1109/ACCESS.2019.2947091

Work in Progress Papers

Exploring Interest Similarity Features and Their Combinations for Friendship Recommendation Without Cold Start

Ana Beatriz Pires Quelhas[1], Natsuki Oka[2], and Kazuaki Tanaka[1](✉)

[1] Kyoto Institute of Technology, Kyoto, Japan
d3821003@edu.kit.ac.jp, k_tanaka@kit.ac.jp
[2] Miyazaki Sangyo-keiei University, Miyazaki, Japan
oka@mail.miyasankei-u.ac.jp

Abstract. While people-to-people recommendation often relies on collaborative filtering, which suffers from cold-start issues, this study intends to propose methods of interest similarity that can provide recommendations with only user-provided data, thus circumventing cold-start issues. Participants in a data collection experiment provided personal data about themselves and information about the type of people they would like to become friends with based on a summary of interests and personal information. This data was used to devise several methods of comparing the users' interests and information to determine their potential friendship success. The interests were represented as word embeddings and used in both vectorial and image forms. An original score that calculates similarity based on information about desired friends collected from the users' data is proposed in order to capture interest similarity information based on the users' perception. These inputs were used both separately and combined to train several neural network models, as well as ensemble models. The proposed methods show an improvement in recommendation quality when compared to the established baseline, particularly when used in ensembles.

Keywords: Word Embedding · Recommendation System · Neural Networks · Similarity · People-to-people Recommendation

1 Introduction

Human beings are a social species. Social isolation has been shown to have adverse effects on mental health [2], which may propagate to physical health as well [10]. When placed in situations where face-to-face interaction becomes difficult, the lack of ability to establish meaningful relationships can lead to declining mental health [5].

To facilitate the connection between people, services like dating applications have been gaining traction in recent years. The use of machine learning in such services has also been increasing, in areas such as collaborative filtering with decision trees [1] or content-based filtering [13]. Collaborative filtering suffers from cold start issues, in which recommendations for a user can't be established until they have previously engaged with the system and data about their interactions is collected.

When considering what makes two people compatible with one another, users value similarity as a metric of potential friendship [3], which only relies on user-provided data, in addition to personal and demographic data. Word embeddings such as word2vec [9] can determine similarity between words by representing their meaning in a multi-dimensional vector.

In order to effectively use user-given data, we developed three methods. An original fitness score, which calculates the similarity between hobbies based on previously observed ratings, and two word embedding-based methods, using vector sums and images. These methods of interest similarity are aimed at using user-provided data for reliable recommendations from the very first one, without cold-start issues.

The paper is organized as follows. Section 2 provides an overview of related studies. Section 3 details the experiment through which data was collected. Section 4 describes the methods used for determining interest similarity. Section 5 provides the obtained results, with a discussion of these results taking place in Sect. 6. Section 7 describes approaches for future work, while Sect. 8 outlines the conclusion.

2 Related Works

We focused on social recommendation, word embeddings, and methods of extracting interest similarity as key points of our study. We did not find papers that covered these topics while also focusing on solving the cold start problem of recommender systems.

While most of the research presented in this section is already a few years old, we believe that the problem we propose to solve is still relevant, as many countries are facing an increasing problem of dwindling fertility and birth rate [12].

Recommender systems have been applied to people-to-people recommendation in a variety of ways. There are studies in reciprocal systems [11, 15] that attempt to model an interaction to be successful on both sides. Our method focuses instead on determining interest similarity, which has been shown to be a valuable metric to users when seeking friends.

Word embedding-based approaches have been used for the recommendation of movies [14] using the calculation of cosine similarity based on word embedding vectors. There have also been studies on the learning of word embeddings based on item features for recommendation [6] as well as post recommendation in social media based on word embedding based semantic analysis of user post content [4]. These approaches consider word embedding vectors for item (or post) recommendation rather than for people-to-people recommendation.

Interest similarity is a key concept of social recommendation as a way of determining the compatibility between people. Studies have been conducted into the correlation of interest similarity and the formation of social groups [7], further showing the importance of the determination of interest similarity in this matter.

3 Data Collection

A data collection experiment was conducted using a website designed to look like a social media website. The purpose of this website was to gather the opinions and personal data of the users. The total number of participants was 28 (13 female, 15 male) between the ages of 18 and 55.

To avoid potential issues with interaction between users, aside from the anonymized nature of the website, the recommendation targets shown were selected from 1000 dummies generated with data similar to the input provided by a human user. The participants were not informed that the recommendation targets were not real people. However, participants consented to the collection of their data for academic purposes.

Participants were asked to provide information about themselves: initials, age, gender, prefecture of residence, and their choice of hobbies from a provided list of 143 different interests. After choosing their hobbies, a participant's compatibility coefficient with each dummy is calculated using the Jaccard index, which calculates the similarity between two sets.

Users were presented with the age, gender, prefecture of residence, and hobbies of each dummy, with hobbies in common being highlighted. Then, users were asked to rate whether they would like to become friends with a selected dummy. Users could also provide a written reason for their selection.

4 Method

Features used for interest similarity are explained further along this section. To provide context as to why these features were chosen, and what data is used for each feature, we first explain some analysis that was conducted from the data collection results.

After analysis of users' written justifications, the following information was also provided to the neural network to accommodate points of user discomfort:

- Age difference.
- Residential distance: Distance between the user and the recommendation target.
- Number of common hobbies.
- Number of different hobbies
- Hobby amount difference: Difference between the user and the target's number of hobbies.

Hobbies were also grouped into different categories for ease of selection by users. These could also be considered groupings that attribute similarity to the hobbies:

- Common category hobbies: Number of user's hobbies in which the category was selected by both the user and the target.
- Different category hobbies: Number of user's hobbies in which the category was not selected by the target.

Due to the age and demographic of most of the participants in this data collection experiment, there is a significant number of users who selected interests from the Games category.

4.1 Fitness Score

This score was calculated per possible hobby combination in the training data. The formula used to calculate fitness scores for any hobby combination is as follows:

$$f(h1, h2) = \sum_{U with h1 \in H(U)} \sum_{T with h2 \in H(T)} \frac{r(U,T)}{\|H(U)\| \cdot \|H(T)\|} \quad (1)$$

where f(h1,h2) is the fitness score for a given hobby h1 and hobby h2 combination, r(U,D) is the rating given by user U to target T (1 if the rating was positive, -1 if the rating was negative, or 0 if the rating does not exist), H(U) is user U's interest hobby list, and H(T) is target T's interest hobby list. This is repeated for every user and target combination in the training data. Whether the score updated is added or subtracted depends on whether the user's opinion of the target was positive or negative (respectively). The score for one user and target pair is then calculated as follows:

$$f(U, T) = \frac{\sum_{h1 \in H(U)} \sum_{h2 \in H(T)} f(h1, h2)}{\|H(U)\| \cdot \|H(T)\|} \quad (2)$$

where f(U,T) is the fitness score for the pair consisting of user U and target T, f(h1,h2) is the fitness score of their corresponding hobby pairs, H(U) is U's interest hobby list, and H(T) is T's interest hobby list.

The idea behind the inclusion of this fitness score is that users will be more likely to positively rate dummies with hobbies they consider similar to theirs.

4.2 Word Embedding Vector Sums

We determined that the usage of a pre-trained Japanese word2vec would be more efficient than to train from scratch. Out of several models surveyed, the chiVe model [8] was selected.

Considering that a single word vector has 300 dimensions and that a single user can have dozens of hobbies, a concatenated hobby vector would have too many dimensions to train adequately, so the word embedding vector used as input for each user consisted of the sum of their individual hobby vectors.

4.3 Pixel-by-Pixel Difference

This is a visual representation using principal component analysis to reduce the dimension of the embedding vectors for each hobby from 300 to 2 and mapping a user's hobbies using a grayscale luminance distribution, with kernel density estimation being used for smoothing. Six different amounts of smoothing were used.

For each user and recommendation pair, each pair of luminance distributions with the same value of smoothing was used to calculate the pixel-by-pixel difference between the two images. Both the absolute value of the difference and the squared value of the difference were used, for a total of 12 values calculated per user-target pair.

4.4 Neural Network Specifications

For the neural network, different structures were used depending on the inputs. The network is a multilayer perceptron using ReLU as the activation function and sigmoid as the output layer activation function. Table 1 provides an overview of each model.

Model size 1 refers to a network consisting of 2 layers of 64 and 16 neurons, size 2 to a network consisting of 3 layers of 256, 64, and 16 neurons, and size 3 to a network consisting of 4 layers of 2048, 512, 256, and 64 neurons.

Table 1. Neural network specifications for each model chosen through cross-validation.

Model	I	II	III	IV	V	VI	VII	VIII	IX
Epochs	57	125	175	180	163	110	127	111	185
Model size	3	1	2	3	2	3	3	3	3

5 Results

The performance of the neural network was evaluated by F-score with a chosen β of 0.5. The models were trained on data consisting of 18 users, with 5 users being used as validation data, in total consisting of 23 users and 416 data entries. Evaluation was then performed on a set consisting of 5 users and 141 data entries. Due to the small amount of data, the validation set was fixed. The obtained results can be seen in Table 2.

Table 2. Use of different inputs for each neural network and corresponding results. Models are enumerated from I to IX, with each model using different features. The highest obtained result is highlighted. The features used in each model are as follows. A: Age difference and residential distance. B: Common and different hobbies, as well as hobby amount difference. C: Common and different category hobbies. D: Fitness score. E: Pixel-by-pixel image difference. F: Word embedding vector sums.

Model	I	II	III	IV	V	VI	VII	VIII	IX
A	✓	✓	✓	✓	✓	✓	✓	✓	✓
B		✓	✓	✓	✓	✓	✓	✓	✓
C					✓	✓	✓	✓	✓
D		✓			✓			✓	✓
E		✓					✓		✓
F				✓		✓	✓	✓	✓
F-score	41.6	52.5	60.8	64.1	65.5	61.6	71.4	67.9	69.4

A hard majority vote approach was also considered, in which each model "votes" on the classification of a particular example, and the classification with the most votes is decided as final.

The results can be observed in Table 3, which shows the composition of each ensemble, based on the models it included (described by the Roman numerals used in Table 2), as well as the obtained F-score of each ensemble. Models were selected for inclusion based on individual performance and cross-validation results.

Table 3. Use of different combinations for majority voting and corresponding results. Ensembles are named from E1 through E5, with each being composed of different combinations of models. The highest obtained result is highlighted.

Ensemble	II	III	IV	V	VI	VIII	F-Score
E1	✓	✓	✓				63.5
E2			✓		✓	✓	71.8
E3		✓		✓		✓	67.6

6 Discussion

Compared to the baseline of input I (with a score of 41.6), word embedding vector sums provided the highest improvement, followed by the fitness score.

Regarding combinations between different features, models using word embedding vectors have a higher score than those without, showing this as a feature that provides useful similarity information. This can also be stated about most models containing the fitness score, showing its overall value, since it is a feature that is simple to obtain and calculate. While the collected data was restricted to a certain demographic, this shows the possibility that, used in a larger dataset, it could be a useful feature for determining hobbies that the users involved consider similar.

Additionally, the model with the highest score features pixel-by-pixel difference as well, which shows that the generated images can have value when providing information about interest similarity.

Ensemble E2 reaches a score of 71.8, which is the highest score obtained overall. This ensemble contains models which use both word embedding vector sums and the fitness score.

Despite only having a slight improvement in score compared to the best individual model (71.8 as compared to 71.4), the fitness score is a feature that is faster to calculate than the pixel-by-pixel difference (since it only consists of simple calculations, rather than scanning every pixel pair in two separate images).

7 Future Work

Several approaches can be considered in order to overcome some of the limitations of this work. In particular, considering the overall usage of word embedding vectors in this paper, it's important the word embeddings be extremely accurate to the intended meaning from the users. In order to overcome any unclear or dubious potential meanings from a single word embedding implementation, it may be possible to use the averages of multiple word embeddings instead.

8 Conclusion

Three methods to determine interest similarity between users were proposed: word embedding vector sums, a pixel-by-pixel difference of word embedding-based images of two users, and an original fitness score that calculates similarity based on already-existing interactions of all users in the data. Unlike the remaining features, which are based on the pre-learned word embedding vectors, fitness score was proposed in order to use a feature taking into account the perception of the existing users regarding the similarity between their hobbies.

The results showed the most improvement in the recommendation quality provided by the word embedding vector sums and the original fitness score individually when compared to the baseline input. Additionally, the combination of methods using word embedding vector sums and pixel-by-pixel difference achieved even more significant improvement. Using majority voting, the ensemble of models containing word embedding vectors and fitness score provided the highest overall success, further showing the usefulness of fitness score as a feature.

Since the method proposed relies only on user-provided data, there is no need for additional user or target behavior data to enhance the quality of recommendations. By doing so, it can provide appropriate recommendations right from the outset of service usage. Consequently, users may receive more useful recommendations and eventually forge a greater number of meaningful and lasting connections.

Acknowledgments. This study was supported by JSPS KAKENHI Grant Number JP22K12126.

Disclosure of Interests. The authors have no competing interests to declare that are relevant to the content of this article.

References

1. Cai, X., et al.: A deployed people-to-people recommender system in online dating. Assoc. Adv. Artif. Intell. AI Magaz. **36**(3), 5–18 (2015). https://doi.org/10.1609/aimag.v36i3.2599
2. Erzen, E., Çikrikci, Ö.: The effect of loneliness on depression: a meta-analysis. Int. J. Soc. Psychiatry **64**(5), 427–435 (2018). https://doi.org/10.1177/0020764018776349

3. Jensen, C., Davis, J., Farnham, S.: Finding others online: reputation systems for social online spaces. In: Proceedings of the SIGCHI Conference on Human Factors in Computing Systems (CHI 2002), pp. 447–454. Association for Computing Machinery, New York (2002). https://doi.org/10.1145/503376.503456
4. Jiang, L., Liu, L., Yao, J., Shi, L.: A hybrid recommendation model in social media based on deep emotion analysis and multi-source view fusion. J. Cloud Comput. **9**, 57 (2020). https://doi.org/10.1186/s13677-020-00199-2
5. Killgore, W., Cloonan, S., Taylor, E., Dailey, N.: Loneliness: a signature mental health concern in the era of COVID-19. Psychiatry Res. **290**, 113–117 (2020). https://doi.org/10.1016/j.psychres.2020.113117
6. Krishnamurthy, B., Puri, N.: Learning vector-space representations of items for recommendations using word embedding models. Procedia Comput. Sci. **80**, 2205–2210 (2016). https://doi.org/10.1016/j.procs.2016.05.380
7. Ma, H.: On measuring social friend interest similarities in recommender systems. In Proceedings of the 37th International ACM SIGIR Conference on Research and Development in Information Retrieval (SIGIR 2014), pp. 465–474. Association for Computing Machinery, New York (2014). https://doi.org/10.1145/2600428.2609635
8. Manabe, H., Oka, T., Umikawa, Y., Takaoka, K., Uchida, Y., Asahara, M.: Japanese word embedding based on multi-granular tokenization results (in Japanese). In: Proceedings of the Twenty-fifth Annual Meeting of the Association for Natural Language Processing (NLP2019), 13–15 March 2019, Nagoya. The Association for Natural Language Processing, Kyoto NLP2019-P8-5 (2019)
9. Mikolov, T., Chen, K., Corrado, G., Dean, J.: Efficient estimation of word representations in vector space. arXiv preprint arXiv:1301.3781 (2013)
10. Ohrnberger, J., Fichera, E., Sutton, M.: The relationship between physical and mental health: a mediation analysis. Soc. Sci. Med. **195**(2017), 42–49 (2017). https://doi.org/10.1016/j.socscimed.2017.11.008
11. Pizzato, L., Rej, T., Akehurst, J., Koprinska, I., Yacef, K., Kay, J.: Recommending people to people: the nature of reciprocal recommenders with a case study in online dating. User Model. User-Adap. Inter. **23**, 447–488 (2013). https://doi.org/10.1007/s11257-012-9125-0
12. Sobotka, T., et al.: Pandemic roller-coaster? Birth trends in higher-income countries during the COVID-19 pandemic. Popul. Dev. Rev. (2023). https://doi.org/10.1111/padr.12544
13. Troya, I., Gaur, M., Zejnilovic, L., Han, Q., and Ji, M.: A hybrid recommender system for patient-doctor matchmaking in primary care. In: 2018 IEEE 5th International Conference on Data Science and Advanced Analytics (DSAA), Turin, pp. 481–490 (2018). https://doi.org/10.1109/DSAA.2018.00062
14. Nguyen, L., Nguyen, T., Jung, J.: Content-based collaborative filtering using word embedding: a case study on movie recommendation. In: Proceedings of the International Conference on Research in Adaptive and Convergent Systems (RACS 2020), pp. 96–100. Association for Computing Machinery, New York (2020). https://doi.org/10.1145/3400286.3418253
15. Xia, P., Liu, B., Sun, Y., Chen, C.: Reciprocal recommendation system for online dating. arXiv preprint arXiv:1501.06247 (2015)

Stimulating Creative Hypothesis Discovery by Future Human-AI Teaming

Soichiro Iga[1(✉)], Susumu Takatsuka[2], and Hiroki Tetsukawa[2]

[1] XPARC LLC., 2-33-27 Tsukushino Machida, Tokyo, Japan
soichiro.iga@xparc.co.jp
[2] Sony Group Corp., 1-7-1 Konan Minato-ku, Tokyo, Japan
{Susumu.Takatsuka,Hiroki.Tetsukawa}@sony.com
https://xparc.co.jp/

Abstract. We propose Human-AI teaming to enhance hypothesis discovery creation (HDHAT), envisioning a future where humans and AI collaborate as teams in more creative activities. Our preliminary qualitative experiment on creativity among people extracted implications for supporting creative activities in future Human-AI teams, highlighting the importance of dynamic creative processes and strategy sharing.

Keywords: Human-AI Teaming · Creativity Support · Hypothesis Discovery · Qualitative Research · Conversation Analysis

1 Introduction

Recent Artificial Intelligence (AI) advancements have profoundly impacted society, especially in research fields like Human-Computer Interaction (HCI) and Computer Supported Cooperative Work (CSCW). These areas now require new research agendas to address the changing dynamics between humans and AI. AI now performs higher-order cognitive tasks, exemplified by OpenAI's ChatGPT or Google's Gemini, which is widely used across various domains.

AI's role has shifted from replacing routine tasks to enhancing human creativity and productivity through collaboration, known as Human-AI teaming (HAT). HAT involves shared goals, proactive task management, and joint progress tracking, treating AI as a cognitive partner in problem-solving and decision-making by combining AI's data processing with human creativity and judgment.

2 Toward Hypothesis-Discovery Creative Activities by Human-AI Teaming

In the following sections, we introduce the concept of teaming between humans and AI to stimulate creative hypothesis discovery in a complementary way. Prior to that, we will organize several pieces of background information.

2.1 Human-AI Teaming

The relationship between humans and AI technology is evolving from mere interaction to collaboration, which involves mutual goal understanding, joint task management, and progress sharing [1].

A key paradigm in this trend is Human-AI teaming (HAT), where AI functions as a teammate rather than just a tool. Xu conceptualizes HAT's AI systems as autonomous cognitive systems in a framework called Human-AI joint cognitive systems, aimed at enhancing collaboration in problem-solving and decision-making by leveraging the strengths of both humans and AI [2].

In the context of more creative activities between humans and AI, especially in the context of collaborative discovery of problems and hypotheses, we believe that the capabilities and design of AI are still unknown, and that it is necessary to support research on human-to-human creativity.

2.2 Kawakita's W-Shaped Problem-Solving Framework

Japanese cultural anthropologist Jiro Kawakita introduced the "W-shaped problem-solving framework" [3]. It comprises two stages: hypothesis discovery (field science) and hypothesis verification (experimental science). Initially, relevant information is gathered, leading to the discovery of hypotheses. Then, experiments are conducted to test these hypotheses, concluding the process.

Similarly, the Double Diamond Model by the UK Design Council divides the design process into discovering the right problem and finding the right solution, emphasizing the distinction between hypothesis discovery and verification [4].

2.3 Nonaka's SECI Model

The SECI model, proposed by Japanese management scholar Ikujiro Nonaka, is a knowledge management framework focusing on knowledge creation (Fig. 1) [5]. It distinguishes between tacit knowledge (subjective, experiential) and explicit knowledge (documented, articulated).

The model involves transforming individual tacit knowledge into shared explicit knowledge through four phases: socialization, externalization, combination, and internalization, creating a knowledge spiral that fosters higher-level knowledge creation.

3 Concept: Human-AI Teaming in Hypothesis-Discovery Creative Activity (HDHAT)

We aim to provide insights into future research challenges for Human-AI teams based on Kawakita's W-shaped problem-solving framework and Nonaka's SECI model. We propose that understanding and supporting the process of "socialization" in hypothesis-discovery activities are essential future research challenges for Human-AI teaming (HDHAT).

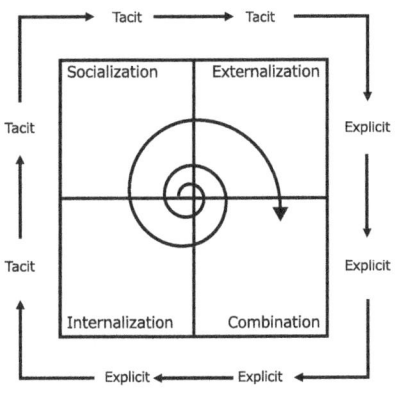
- **Socialization:** Sharing tacit knowledge through shared experiences.
- **Externalization:** Converting tacit knowledge into explicit forms (e.g., language, diagrams).
- **Combination:** Linking explicit knowledge to integrate it into operational processes.
- **Internalization:** Incorporating organizational knowledge back into individual tacit knowledge.

Fig. 1. Nonaka's SECI model [5]

In traditional search and recommendation systems, network data is aggregated and organized, similar to the SECI model's "combination" process. Users internalize this knowledge. Generative AI and LLMs also aggregate data, paralleling "internalization" on the AI side, and generate outputs for human hypothesis verification.

Currently, AI supports the "externalization" of human knowledge, partially realizing the SECI model's "externalization" and "combination" phases. However, the "socialization" phase, crucial for knowledge creation, is lacking in Human-AI Teams (HAT). Achieving "socialization"-where humans and AI share creative strategies and knowledge-could enhance HAT to HDHAT. Understanding and engineering this process is essential.

4 Related Work

Finke's Creative Cognitive Approach and the Geneplore model focus on the interplay between generating and exploring mental images [6]. This approach has been widely used to study human creativity, but it often overlooks the sharing of tacit knowledge, which is vital for creativity.

Research on interactions between humans and robots/agents explores how these entities can influence human decision-making and choice structures [7]. Understanding human-human interactions [8] can provide insights into designing autonomous social robots and agents for creative collaboration.

Estimating the potential and limits of future AI technologies is challenging at present. Of course, in the domain of problem solving, the use of AI is already progressing. However, in the area of hypothesis discovery, we believe that an approach that elucidates and supports the mechanism of human-human collaboration will be effective. In studying the collaborative creativity between humans and AI, it is deemed important to understand the strategies for collaborative creative activities between humans.

5 Experiment

We believe that an important research target for future creative activities between humans and AI as a team is to explore collaboration in hypothesis-discovery situations where the problem space is not fixed at the initial stage.

In order to understand a portion of the exploratory process in hypothesis-discovery, we attempted a preliminary experiment using a qualitative approach, aiming to derive implications for the collaboration between humans and AI.

5.1 Design of Experimental Methods

Kawakita notes that in early creative endeavors like research, hypothesis discovery involves exploratory thinking, where people explore, observe, and organize information, leading to the emergence of ideas. Boden identifies three elements of creativity: novelty, surprisingness, and value [9]. Applying Nonaka's SECI model, sharing implicit knowledge leads to its formalization, generating value. The study uses "Story Cubes," [10] a game where players interpret dice pictures to create stories, to observe creative and hypothesis-discovery processes akin to Nonaka's model and Kawakita's framework.

5.2 Experimental Design

The study had two settings: one where participants worked alone and another where they worked in pairs. Alone, they focused on forming hypotheses and understanding how they discovered them, while in pairs, they aimed to understand their strategies and how they shared ideas. They used two sets of images labeled as Patterns X and Y, without any repeated images within each set.

In the individual setting, participants narrated their thought process aloud while crafting stories. In the paired setup, participants collaborated and conversed to develop a story together.

The experiment was conducted online using commercial tools available on the network(Zoom and Miro).

5.3 Participants

The study involved 10 working professionals, aged between 30 and 40, comprising 6 males and 4 females. They had varied occupations but were accustomed to generating ideas regularly. None had prior experience with the game used in the experiment.

5.4 Task

The experiment involved participants creating a coherent story using 9 dice with different images, writing at least one sentence per die. Common images were used in both individual and pair conditions to observe content-sharing dynamics. Each session lasted 20 min or until completion, followed by 15-min interviews and a 15-min questionnaire. The order of individual/pair conditions alternated, with different image patterns used in alternating trials (Pattern X: trials 1, 2, 4; Pattern Y: trials 3, 5).

6 Results

6.1 Obtained Stories and Data

From Trials 1 to 5, 15 stories were collected, including two individual condition trials per participant and one pair condition trial each. The average total character count for all 9 dice combined was 261.4 Japanese characters ($\tau = 83.1$). A t-test (Welch's test) showed no significant differences in character count per die order (adjusted p-value using Bonferroni correction: $p = 0.0056$). Thus, the study suggests that text was consistently generated for each die, with the order of dice having minimal impact on the quantity of text produced.

The study employs both categorical and structural approaches to analyze data, considering behaviors as both fixed entities (categorical) and sequences over time (structural). It combines Finke's Geneplore model with Ishii's extension [11], integrating mental and external operations in analyzing idea generation. Video data, segmented into 955 activities, reveals 19 elements, 16 for individual (Table 1(a)) and 3 for pair conditions (Table 1(b)). Interview audio data complements the video analysis.

6.2 Similarity of Stories

The study utilized a similarity measure proposed by Shrivastava to quantify surprise and novelty in hypothesis-discovery [12]. Dissimilar stories were considered creative. To assess similarity between stories, nouns, verbs, and adjectives were extracted and cosine similarity computed. Clustering based on Euclidean distances visualized story similarity using dendrograms. Figure 2 illustrates clustering results, with vertical axis indicating Euclidean distances during clustering.

Different dice patterns, Patterns X and Y, led to distinct clusters in Trials 1, 2, and 4 (Pattern X) versus Trials 3 and 5 (Pattern Y), showing participants' reliance on these patterns. Within Cluster X, relatively dissimilar stories indicating creativity were found in individual conditions 2b and 4a, and pair conditions 2p and 4p. Similarly, Cluster Y contained relatively dissimilar stories, notably individual condition 5a and pair condition 5p. For example, the story from pair condition 2p, displaying low similarity, is depicted in Fig. 3.

6.3 Comparison of Activity Elements Between Low/high Similarity

We investigated differences in activity elements between low and high similarity groups. Elements with absolute proportion differences exceeding the average (Individual $|\mu| = 3.60$, Pair $|\mu| = 3.82$) were considered. In individual

Table 1. Elements of activities

(a) Individual condition		
Operation	Activity Element	Description
Mental	Interpretation	Reading and describing the interpretation of images
	Heterogeneity	Attention to images that differ from others
	Approach	Variation in interpreting images
	Association	Assigning meaning between multiple images
	Discovery	New associations or metaphors
	Reinterpretation	Reinterpreting images on a certain perspective
	Setting	Consideration of scenes and characters
	Composition	Consideration involving the overall story structure
	Strategic Planning	Ways of thinking to advance creation
	Discussion	Other creative concerns and tweaks
External	Arrangement	Rearranging the position of dice
	Classification	Grouping similar images
	Preparation	Operation of tools (sticky notes and texts)
	Text	Text input related to the story
	Elaboration	Add text expression for scenes, emotions
	Readability	Organizing visual elements (aligning/color-coding)
(b) Pair condition		
Operation	Activity Element	Description
Mental	Strategic Sharing	Sharing of ideas for advancing creation
	Content Sharing	Reference to previously created stories
External	Communication	Dialogue not directly related to creation

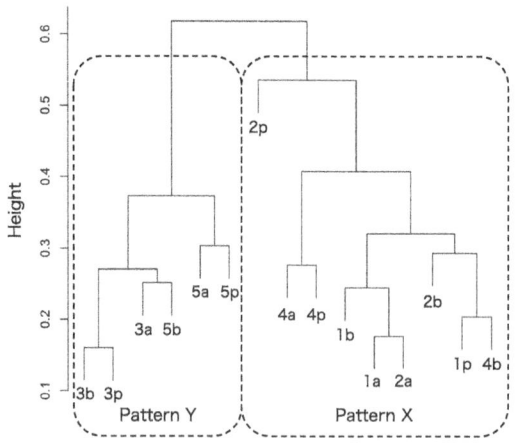

Fig. 2. Dendrogram of Similarities of Stories

(a) Screen shot   (b) Story (English translated)

Monday: Physical labor dominates my work. Tuesday: More physical labor, sometimes leading to injuries. Wednesday: Mid-week training is a must. Thursday: It's a day of relentless digging. Friday: Curious about this week's paycheck. Saturday: Relaxing with my baseball hobby. Sunday: Enjoy a cherished date with my girlfriend, holding hands and creating happy memories before a new week starts.

Fig. 3. Story of Pair Condition 2p

conditions, trials with lower similarity had a higher proportion of "discovery/reinterpretation/examination/writing" activity elements compared to high similarity trials. In pair conditions, lower similarity trials showed a higher proportion of "composition/examination/preparation/readability" elements compared to high similarity trials.

6.4 Pair-Specific Activity Elements

In our study, we defined three activity elements for pairs: "strategy sharing," "content sharing," and "communication." Analyzing all pair trials, a significant difference was found between content sharing and communication ($p = 0.014$).

In trial 1p, content sharing exceeded strategy sharing due to participant 1b's slow narration. Excluding 1p, significant differences were noted between strategy sharing and content sharing ($p = 0.048$), and between content sharing and communication ($p = 0.041$), indicating more time spent on strategy sharing than content sharing.

In pairs, each participant's screen representation strategy was independent. The final story's representation followed the primary strategy of the participant contributing to the story outline.

7 Implications for Future Human-AI Teaming

This section outlines the key implications from our experiment for enhancing the hypothesis-discovery creative process through Human-AI teaming.

Assistance to the Dynamism of Activity Elements: To supplement Sect. 6.3, providing "perspectives" in low similarity trials fosters associations and metaphors through "discovery". Activity patterns differ between individuals and pairs: individuals tend to move from "discovery → reinterpretation," while pairs follow "discovery → construction." Recognizing these differences is crucial for supporting hypothesis-discovery activities in Human-AI teaming (HDHAT).

Strategy Sharing in Creative Activities with AI: Section 6.4 shows strategy sharing takes longer in pair-specific activities than content sharing. In

Human-AI collaborative creativity, AI should offer adaptable strategies instead of fixed ones. Technologies adjusting information based on user context, like cognitive load, are promising [13], crucial for effective HDHAT.

Necessity of Adjusting Strategy Progression by AI: Section 6.4 discusses how individual leadership in story creation can affect the pair's content. While children benefit from positive robot engagement [14], our study suggests AI leadership may not always boost collaborative creativity. Thus, mechanisms are needed to balance human-AI activities, ensuring collaborative strategy progression.

8 Conclusion

In this paper, we introduced the concept of creative hypothesis-discovery activities through future Human-AI teaming (HDHAT) and derived implications from an initial experiment for supporting hypothesis discovery. However, this research is limited by its qualitative nature, focusing solely on human interactions. Future research will involve advancing dialogue studies using actual AI. Moreover, an in-depth analysis of the creative processes observed in the Kawakita and Nonaka model in comparison to the actual hypothesis-discovery creative processes in AI teaming remains a subject for future research.

Disclosure of Interests. The authors have no competing interests to declare that are relevant to the content of this article.

References

1. Wang, D., et al.: From human-human collaboration to human-AI collaboration: designing AI systems that can work together with people. In: ACM CHI EA 2020, pp. 1–6 (2020)
2. Xu, W., Gao, Z.: Applying HCAI in developing effective human-AI teaming: a perspective from human-AI joint cognitive systems. ACM Interactions **31**(1), 32–37 (2024)
3. Kawakita, J.H.: [Abuduction Method], Chuokoronsha (1967) (in Japanese)
4. Design Council UK. The Double Diamond. https://www.designcouncil.org.uk/our-resources/the-double-diamond/. Accessed 24 Mar 2023
5. Nonaka, I., Takeuchi, H.: The Knowledge Creating Company: How Japanese Companies Create the Dynamics of Innovation. Oxford University Press, New York (1995)
6. Finke, R.A., Ward, T.B., Smith, S.M.: Creative Cognition. The MIT Press (1992)
7. Yamada, S., Ono, T.: Mind Interaction. Kindai Kagaku (2019) (in Japanese)
8. Plurkowski, L., Chu, M., Vinkhuyzen, E.: The implications of interactional repair for human-robot interaction design. In: IEEE/WIC/ACM International Conferences on Web Intelligence and Intelligent Agent Technology, pp. 61–65 (2011)
9. Boden, M.A.: The Creative Mind: Myths and Mechanisms. Routledge (2003)
10. Rory's Story Cubes. https://www.storycubes.com/en/. Accessed 24 Mar 2024

11. Ishii, N., Miwa, K.: Interactive processes between mental and external operations in creative activity. Cognit. Stud. **10**(4), 469–485 (2003) (in Japanese)
12. Shrivastava, D., Ahmed, C.G.S., Laha, A., Sankaranarayanan, K.: A machine learning approach for evaluating creative artifacts. In: SIGKDD Workshop on Machine Learning for Creativity (2017)
13. Lindlbauer, D., Feit, A.M., and Hilliges, O.: Context-aware online adaptation of mixed reality interfaces. In: ACM UIST 2019, pp. 147–160 (2019)
14. Ali, S., Moroso, T., Breazeal, C.: Can children learn creativity from a social robot? In: ACM C&C 2019, pp. 359–368 (2019)

Using Word Games as Facilitator to Awareness Raising Communication in Public Spaces

Shinya Nishide[1,2(✉)] and Takeshi Nishida[1]

[1] Graduate School of Intercultural Studies, Kobe University, Kobe, Japan
215c304c@stu.kobe-u.ac.jp
[2] Senri International School of Kwansei Gakuin, Osaka, Japan

Abstract. In public spaces, where individuals with diverse values converge, discrepancies in the perception of acceptable behavior, such as appropriate speaking volumes, are common. Creating a common understanding requires continuous and proactive communication, including outreach to those unfamiliar, which can impose a significant psychological burden. This study proposes an awareness communication method that facilitates forming a common understanding in public spaces through participatory word games. The paper explores the potential of the proposed method by implementing a prototype in a library setting, leading to system design and implementation.

Keywords: Public Space · Word Games · Awareness-Raising Communication

1 Introduction

In public spaces, such as libraries, waiting rooms, and trains, where individuals with diverse values gather, discrepancies often arise in perceptions regarding acceptable behavior, such as the appropriate volume for conversation. Creating a common understanding requires continuous and proactive communication, including reaching out to those with whom one is not familiar, which can impose a significant psychological burden [1].

Communication encompasses various difficulties. One primary challenge is the reluctance to engage in discussions due to the fear of judgment or criticism from others. This fear may result in individuals either refraining from expressing their opinions in the face of dissent or conforming to the opinions of others [2]. Diversifying communication methods and mediums has increased the freedom of choice, which, in turn, has led to a greater diversity in the challenges associated with communication. Especially among younger demographics, there is a tendency to perceive face-to-face conversations, which necessitate sharing time and space, as burdensome and to be avoided.

To make things much more complex, individuals perceive communication difficulty very differently, with some finding it trivial. The existence of individuals who consider communication easy exacerbates the situation for those who find it challenging. For the latter, the inability to communicate effectively can lead to embarrassment and a pessimistic outlook on the possibility of mutual assistance and cooperation.

Traditional research on computer-mediated communication has focused on developing methods to lower the barriers to communication difficulties and reduce the psychological burden on participants [3]. However, making communication appear easier may actually increase pressure, especially for those who still find it difficult even with assistance. Conversely, the assistance may undermine motivation for those who perceive communication as easy in the first place.

We propose an approach contrary to traditional methods by deliberately making communication difficult by using word games, which act as playful constraints on what participants can say. By raising barriers to a level that all participants find challenging, we aim to lower the risk of standing out and feeling embarrassed alone, ultimately reducing their psychological burden. Concurrently, if participants manage to overcome these challenges, they may receive admiration from their peers. We anticipate that this will enhance motivation to participate in communication, leveraging the dynamics of challenge and achievement to foster engagement.

Incorporating the proposed method of using word games in public spaces makes it possible to bring forth topics that participants may have found difficult to voice or deem too trivial to mention. While conflicting opinions among participants may also be visualized, including game elements is expected to facilitate the visualization of a common understanding in a manner that minimizes confrontations.

In this work-in-progress paper, we conducted a design exploration study in a school library to observe if it actually facilitates communication in public space and building common understanding. Based on the lessons learned through the study, we designed and implemented a prototype communication system which we plan to evaluate through deployment experiment in future work.

2 Related Work

Our work builds from prior work on providing support for communication in public spaces, and work on the resolution of group communication difficulties through the incorporation of game elements.

2.1 Providing Support for Communication in Public Spaces

Studies have been conducted to encourage active participation in discussions and to investigate the use of public displays for civic engagement in urban environments [4]. These studies have involved the installation of physical systems in public spaces that utilize technology to enable citizens to post opinions and participate in surveys. They have also researched the effects of data visualization and the provision of immediate feedback [5]. Immediate feedback shows individuals how their thoughts compare with others and offers an opportunity to consider how their views differ from the collective [6]. A limitation of these studies is that the system only allows for multiple-choice answers based on pre-determined questions through physical selectors like sliders or toggle switches, which may limit the reflection of free opinions and potentially inhibit the development of discussions.

2.2 Resolving Challenges in Group Communication Using Game Elements

There are studies that address the difficulties in group communication by visualizing each participant's contributions. These studies propose methods to encourage participation from passive individuals and reduce biases among participants [7, 8]. These efforts are based on research in Group Decision Support Systems (GDSS) [9, 10]. Furthermore, numerous methods have been observed that use competitive game elements to enhance motivation for participation as a solution to alleviate group communication challenges [11]. In contrast to prior work using competitive game elements to facilitate group communication, our proposed method is designed to foster group cooperation through engaging participants in challenging word games.

3 Facilitating Awareness Communication Using Word Games

We propose a method to encourage awareness raising communication in public spaces using word games as a facilitator. Specifically, we use word games where participants create compositions from the acronyms of a given theme, such as "Acrostic." For example, in a library, hosting a word game with the theme "Phrase what people are feeling in this library starting with the letter 'S'" would encourage users to submit entries such as "Seeking Silent Space" or "Shh!". By having users vote on submissions and sharing the results, it is expected that users are given opportunity to reflect on what others might be thinking, potentially leading to a common understanding among the community members.

Compared to simpler methods such as setting up bulletin boards where users of public spaces can freely post their opinions, soliciting opinions through constrained games is expected to have the following advantages. Even for opinions that are difficult to express directly, submitting messages through the creative filter of word games is expected to reduce the psychological burden by allowing "difficulty due to the game constraints" to serve as an excuse. While anonymity is often employed as a means of reducing stress, anonymous communication in public forums carries the potential for negative behaviors like "flaming" or "trolling," and a decrease in accountability [12]. Thus, the ability to reduce psychological burden without relying solely on anonymity is a major advantage.

Incorporating constraints through word games and guiding discussions, along with providing feedback on the state of the public space's environment, are methods designed to direct participants' attention towards the surroundings. Without any guidance, the focus may not land on the "environment" of the public space, leading to situations where individuals merely express their own opinions without broader consideration. This approach aims to ensure that the communication within public spaces remains relevant to the shared environment and encourages thoughtful participation.

In this paper, we ran a design exploration study hosting a series of word games in a real public space setting, to investigate the possibility of the proposed method and to draw insights on the design of a communication system based on the proposed concept.

4 Design Exploration Study

We conducted exploratory experiments in a school library to facilitate communication through word games. The library, which serves both a Japanese combined middle and high school (Senri International School of Kwansei Gakuin) and an international school (Osaka International School of Kwansei Gakuin), was chosen as the public space for experimentation. This location is characterized by the gathering of individuals from diverse backgrounds, making it prone to discrepancies in perception and potentially leading to noisy conditions.

For the word games, a Japanese "あいうえお(aiueo) composition," which is a form of acrostic poem using the Japanese syllabary, was employed. In this experiment, the theme was set to "Compositions starting with 'し(shi)', about what everyone is currently thinking," utilizing the Japanese syllabary. The choice of starting with "し(shi)" aimed to elicit the commonly held perception that "しずかにすごす(one should spend time quietly in the library)."

Participants were provided with pens and sticky notes to jot down their ideas as submissions, and boards for posting these submissions were placed in a public space accessible to everyone (Fig. 1). This was to act as public displays through which the ideas of the game participants could inform others about the current sentiments in the public space. If viewers found a submission they resonated with, they were able to express their empathy by placing a round sticker on the sticky note of that submission.

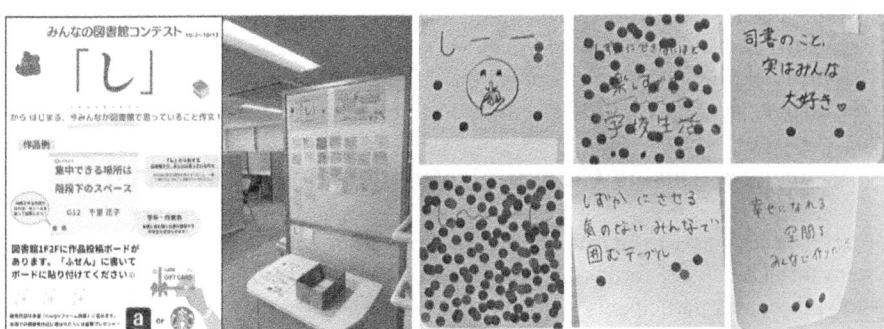

Fig. 1. Word games works submission board (left) and example submissions (right).

Before the experiment commenced, a meeting was held with the library staff to ensure that, during the experiment period, minimal reminders were provided, and the staff were asked to focus primarily on observation.

As a device to direct attention towards environmental factors, a noise meter was installed inside the library where it could be easily seen by the library users. This was in anticipation that merely setting up the word games might not adequately induce communication about appropriate behaviors in that space.

4.1 Results and Lessons Learned

In a nine-day observational study session of a word game themed "Compositions about What Everyone is Thinking in the Library, Starting with the letter 'し(Shi)'", 78 works were pinned up. Distribution of the works visualized the conflicting opinions among users, categorizing them into those who wish for silence in the library and those who want to enjoy it as a group. Additionally, several messages of gratitude towards the library staff were also posted.

We selected 10 works that received the most empathy stickers and conducted a voting via Google Forms where every student at the school could vote for the work they resonated with most (one vote per person). The submission with the highest number of votes was "し〜〜〜し(Shee!)", followed by "しずかな図書館はいつくるのか?(When will a quiet library be achieved?)". Results were announced to all participants via email.

Following the first session, we hosted a second round word game session to observe if it could serve as a channel to resolve the conflicting situation revealed through the first round session. In the second round, we divided the board into two-sides so that participants can choose which side they support when posting their work. The second round of the word game resulted in 11 submitted works, which was fewer in comparison to the first round.

Insights obtained from the study can be summarized as follows:

- Word game effectively visualized what people are thinking in a public space, and also revealed a conflicting situation in public space.
- Word game failed to resolve the conflicting situation in the second round; instead of trying to resolve a conflict in one leap, we should have started from visualizing what people took from the revealed collection of thoughts in public space. In other words, the conflict should have been discovered and brought out by the community.

5 Awareness Raising Communication Facilitation System

Based on the lessons learned from the design exploration study, we developed a prototype system to facilitate the formation of a common understanding in public spaces. This prototype enables participants in public spaces to visualize their current thoughts and opinions through word game based submissions.

5.1 Design Concept

The system provides a two-phase approach to encourage the natural emergence of opinions among participants in public spaces. The first is the word game phase, where the participants spontaneously generate various opinions and conflicts. This stage empowers participants to be the primary source of contributions.

Next, participants will make subcollections of opinions to propose possible different views emerging from the diverse set of opinions submitted in the first phase. This second phase is designed inspired by the "party building" feature which is popular in role-playing games. For example, one can choose an opinion wishing for a quiet library as a "Sage" and an opinion wishing to enjoy chatting in a library as "Warrior", to express a well-balanced party. We expect this feature to playfully promote well-balanced, creative reflection on the first phase and possibly lead to constructive discussion in public space.

The second phase is a process of grouping and categorizing opinions, which is an essential process for fostering a common understanding in public spaces. To further facilitate this process including discovering new insights and learning from the insights of others, the system allows the participants to chat and vote for the parties created.

Moreover, as indicated in previous studies, presenting these results on public displays can be expected to play a role in promoting interaction among participants and fostering shared understanding within public spaces.

Traditional methods like the "KJ method" have been commonly used to organize opinions to a single agreed-upon perspective through a group process; however, our system is different in that it is designed to first make participants work independently, and then facilitate a collaborative process afterwards. This is based on the recognition coming from the exploration study that forming a common understanding cannot be achieved instantaneously, and the system should not be designed to visualize a single answer to the situation.

5.2 Prototype Implementation

We implemented a prototype system as a web application that operates in conjunction with the most popular messaging application in Japan ('LINE' App). To participate in this system, users are required to register an account; however, anonymity is maintained among participants. We plan to extend the application to integrate with public displays installed in public spaces.

The general flow of the system is outlined in the following Step 1 to 2.

Step 1 (Fig. 2)

- Posting: Participants post their word game creations aligned with the theme via the "Post" menu.
- Push Notifications: Participants receive push notifications approximately twice a day, which prompt them to vote on the submissions posted in the 'LINE' App chat room.

Step 2 (Fig. 3)

- Naming: Once a sufficient number of submissions have been accumulated, a push notification delivers the "Name the Party" menu to the chat room. Participants then select submissions that best fit the roles of "Warrior," "Sage," or "Wizard," and assign a name to that group.
- Voting on Named Parties: Push notifications are sent at variable times, averaging approximately twice a day, inviting participants to vote in the 'LINE' App chat room for the named party with which they most resonate.

To make the concept of collecting well-balanced opinions more intuitive for a diverse range of users, we plan to implement templates based on various entertainment concepts, such as sports teams and musical ensembles.

Fig. 2. Screenshots of the prototype application (Step 1: posting word game creations).

Fig. 3. Screenshots of the prototype application (Step 2: naming the party).

6 Conclusion

We proposed a participatory "word games" approach to facilitate awareness-raising communication in public spaces, fostering the formation of a common understanding. Based on the lessons learned from the design exploration study conducted in a school library, we designed a prototype communication system that encourages the visualization and shaping of a common understanding in a public space through a participatory game. It is our future work to employ an "Awareness Raising Communication Facilitation System" in the library where the experiment was conducted, to verify the effectiveness of this process in the public space.

Acknowledgments. This work was supported by JSPS KAKENHI Grant Number JP19K12062.

References

1. Brignull, H., Rogers, Y.: Enticing people to interact with large public displays in public spaces. In: INTERACT 2003 (2003)
2. Edmondson, A.: Psychological safety and learning behavior in work teams. In: Administ. Sci. Quart. **44**(2), 350–383 (1999)
3. Walther, J.B., Burgoon, J.K.: Relational communication in computer-mediated interaction. Human Commun. Res. **19**(1), 50–88 (1992)
4. Du, G., Degbelo, A., Kray, C.: Public displays for public participation in urban settings: a survey. In: Proceedings of the PerDis 2017, pp. 1–9 (2017)
5. Koeman, L., Kalnikaité, V., Rogers, Y.: "Everyone is talking about it!" A distributed approach to urban voting technology and visualisations. In: Proceedings of the CHI 2015, pp. 3127–3136 (2015)
6. Golsteijn, C., Gallacher, S.G., Capra, L., Rogers, Y.: Sens-us: designing innovative civic technology for the public good. In: Proceedings of the DIS 2016, pp. 39–49 (2016)
7. Joan Morris, D., Katherine, J.H., Anna, P., Walter, B.: The impact of increased awareness while face-to-face. Human-Comput. Interact. **22**(1), 47–96 (2007)
8. Dimicco, J.M., Pandolfo, A., Bender, W.: Influencing group participation with a shared display. In: Proceedings of the CSCW 2004, pp. 614–623 (2004)
9. Nunamaker, J.F., Dennis, A.R.: Valacich, J.S., Vogel, D., George, J.F.: Electronic meeting systems. Commun. ACM **34**(7), 40–61 (1991)
10. Neale, D.C., Carroll, J.M., Rosson, M.B.: Evaluating computer-supported cooperative work: models and frameworks. In: Proceedings of the CSCW 2004, pp. 112–121 (2004)
11. Koivisto, J., Juho, H.: The rise of motivational information systems: a review of gamification research. In: IJIM 45, pp. 191–210 (2019)
12. Takeshi, N., Takeo, I.: Bringing round-robin signature to computer-mediated communication. In: Proceedings of the ECSCW 2007, pp. 219–230 (2007)

Enabling Mixed Genetic Algorithm for Automatic Group Formation System

Changhao Liang[✉], Izumi Horikoshi, and Hiroaki Ogata

Kyoto University, Kyoto 606-8501, Japan
liang.changhao.8h@kyoto-u.ac.jp

Abstract. Group formation plays a crucial role in designing collaborative learning activities, as the success of the group largely relies on the makeup of its members. While numerous algorithms exist, many group formation systems tend to adopt a single grouping strategy, such as either heterogeneous or homogeneous grouping, limiting their ability to address diverse student characteristics simultaneously. In this paper, we propose an integrated approach utilizing a mixed genetic algorithm within a data-driven learning platform, which considers both homogeneous and heterogeneous characteristics concurrently. Through an exploratory implementation in a university course, we examined the algorithm's performance using authentic log data under various grouping strategies in classroom settings. We also highlight the potential of interpretability in group formation results, particularly through the composition panel, enabling teachers to make informed interventions and thereby enhancing overall class performance.

Keywords: Group formation · Genetic algorithm · Grouping strategy · Group composition · Classroom implementation

1 Introduction

When conducting collaborative learning teachers tend to spend considerable time on group formation tasks due to their limited familiarity with students, resulting in biased groupings [15]. Using learning log data available in digital platforms, automated group formation techniques can streamline this process and facilitate optimized group compositions. These algorithms can address multiple student characteristics to allocate them homogeneously or heterogeneously [9]. As the prevalence of automatic group formation in educational settings, evidence from learning outcomes and teacher insights suggests that exclusively homogeneous or heterogeneous groupings for all characteristics can be inadequate. The necessity for a combination of homogeneous and heterogeneous groupings concurrently emerges [7]. Theoretically, advancements in genetic algorithms offer promise in meeting this requirement [12]; however, existing studies lack a user-oriented system tailored for educational practitioners. To narrow the gaps, this paper introduces a mixed genetic algorithm integrated into a widely used learning platform and presents an exploratory study to implement the system in an authentic university classroom setting.

2 Research Background

2.1 Group Formation with Genetic Algorithms

There are various computer-supported techniques for creating suitable groups, and many of them concentrate on a single grouping strategy, such as either heterogeneous or homogeneous grouping, and a specific learner characteristic for group formation [9]. The genetic algorithm emerges as a prominent solution due to its ability to incorporate multiple input variables, ensure balanced group sizes to avoid orphan students, produce diverse groups despite identical input parameters, and utilize fitness values to interpret group compositions efficiently.

The key concept of the genetic algorithm for group formation involves identifying grouping candidates with optimized fitness values through iterations (see Fig. 1). The candidate consists of a set of students allocated in a set of groups (G), and the fitness values are determined by functions based on a 0–1 scaled student characteristic matrix (C) to select the optimal candidate as output. Characteristics of C come from recorded learning behaviors in digital learning platforms, such as reading logs, quiz scores, and peer ratings [6]. Previous functions have focused on either inter-group differences for balanced grouping [10] or intra-group compositions [3]. Moreover, for intra-group focus, the method can handle non-numeric indicators by converting overlapped annotations into sub-characters in the student matrix for active reading contexts [7].

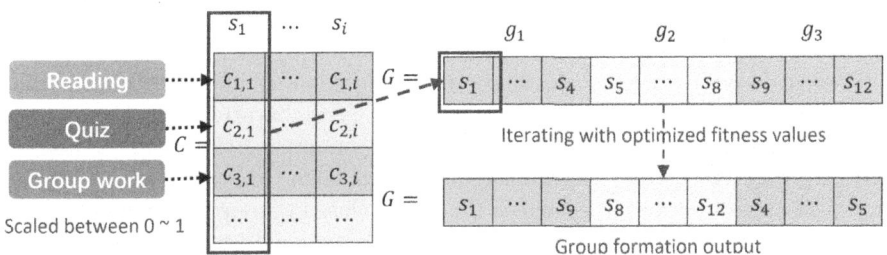

Fig. 1. Characteristic matrix (C) and candidates (G) for the genetic algorithm.

However, as for intra-group compositions, employing a monotonic grouping strategy for all input variables may not suffice. For instance, in active reading classes where students read with different types of markers, [7] shows that groups with heterogeneous difficulty markers facilitate peer assistance, while homogeneous highlighting markers may foster communication based on shared interests. To overcome this gap, [12] introduced a mixed genetic algorithm and evaluated its performance in terms of time cost with varying population sizes. While its empirical study still focuses on evaluating two monotonic strategies, pedagogical implications for the mixed method are still unexplored. Moreover, compared to controlled experiments that incorporate manually collected data from questionnaires like [12], a user-oriented system is absent for educational practitioners and cases using authentic data. This gap leads to further research to bridge the divide between theoretical advancements in group formation algorithms and their practical implementation.

2.2 Group Composition and Criteria in Learning Practice

Besides grouping algorithms, it is also crucial to inspect the characteristics to be taken into account and the appropriate criteria when creating groups with different objectives. Two significant factors to consider are knowledge and engagement, with groups typically being either homogeneous or heterogeneous [9].

Knowledge is often the primary factor to consider, as disparities in knowledge levels provide a basis for peer assistance [5]. Studies like [4] indicate that undergraduate students with complementary incomplete prior knowledge perform better than those with complete knowledge, supporting the heterogeneous strategy. Homogeneous strategy often focuses on non-cognitive issues like personalities or interests, and for less-challenging works [13]. Though we cannot compare high and low for personal traits [12], studies like [2] found that in higher education, homogeneous groups consisting of students with high prior knowledge outperform others in collaborative problem-solving. However, these studies primarily address the effectiveness of individual teams rather than the division of an entire classroom into groups. Consequently, questions remain regarding the overall learning outcomes of the entire class, especially with regard to the equitable treatment of homogeneous low-ability groups that should not be isolated [14].

In cases where cognitive resources are less required, desirable group dynamics also rely on the participation of all members. The engagement levels observed in antecedent learning tasks, such as e-book interactions [1], and individual preparation [8], can mirror the quality of subsequent collaborative learning. During classroom implementations, teachers can intervene during the group orchestration phase to assist groups exhibiting low engagement levels, thereby fostering improved overall performance across the entire class in group learning activities. This intervention strategy can be reinforced through interpretable scaffolding, suggesting avenues for future research.

3 System Design

The Learning and Evidence Analytics Framework (LEAF) serves as an overarching technical framework that consolidates multiple learning log data sources, implemented in over 100 schools globally, with more than 1,000 student users of Japanese public schools [11]. Within the LEAF-enhanced environment, Group Learning Orchestration Based on Evidence (GLOBE) provides a framework and instantiated systems to support group learning with data-driven designs across four phases: formation, orchestration, evaluation, and reflection [6]. Data sensors incorporated in LEAF and other GLOBE modules enrich the group formation module with a diverse data pool (see Fig. 2).

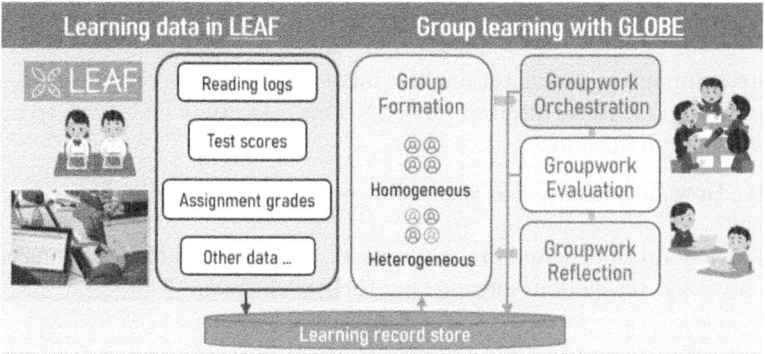

Fig. 2. Iterative use and update of learner model with group work implementations under GLOBE.

Utilizing the fitness function (1) for each group g in the genetic algorithm depicted in Fig. 1, where $\overline{x}_{j,g}$ represents the average value of characteristic j within the group, the group formation module enables the adoption of homogeneous or heterogeneous grouping strategies. The final fitness value (F), obtained by summing all F_g values of all groups, enables the determination of homogeneous groups with a small F or heterogeneous groups with a large F.

$$F_g = \sum_{i=1}^{S} \sum_{j=1}^{C} (c_{j,i} - \overline{x}_{j,g})^2 \tag{1}$$

The latest version of the group formation system integrates the mixed method from [12], leveling a playground for empirical research with routine data. As described in Eq. (2), the mixed method partitions input variables into homogeneous and heterogeneous components, calculating the fitness value for each. The group fitness function F'_g is determined by subtracting the fitness value of the homogeneous part (where smaller values are preferable) from that of the heterogeneous part (where larger values are preferable). A larger resultant value indicates a more favorable grouping candidate.

$$F'_g = \sum_{i=1}^{S} (\sum_{j=1}^{C_{hetero}} (c_{j,i} - \overline{x}_{j,g})^2 - \sum_{k=1}^{C_{homo}} (c_{k,i} - \overline{x}_{k,g})^2) \tag{2}$$

Embedded with the mixed algorithm, the group formation system also features an automatic grouping panel pre-configured with settings on input variables derived from previous evidence for C matrix and grouping strategies, alleviating teachers from the burden of overwhelming parameter adjustments. Additionally, it provides detailed composition panels illustrating group compositions through bars for teachers (see Fig. 5), along with evaluation panels to grade each group and check dynamics through formative peer evaluations [6].

4 System Implementation in a University Course

As a predominant implementation, the mixed method was employed in a university course on Human Interface in 2023. This case study endeavors to address the following two questions.

- **RQ1**: How does the mixed algorithm perform in an authentic educational setting?
- **RQ2**: How do the created groups perform, and how can the group formation system assist teachers in interpreting their performance?

4.1 Learning Context, Course Design, and Data Collection

The system was implemented in a 4-week session instructed by the same lecturer on the basic concepts of human interface design. 40 students enrolled in the course, most of them were beyond sophomore. Each week in this session followed the same workflow shown in Fig. 3.

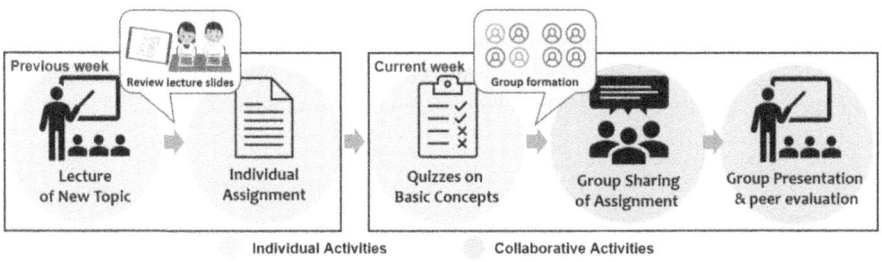

Fig. 3. Workflow of the course.

To examine the impact of the mixed group formation strategy, we implemented two conditions in the final two weeks of the session, as students need to acclimate to the workflow in the preceding weeks and minimize potential learning effects. Condition A utilized homogeneous engagement and heterogeneous knowledge, while Condition B employed heterogeneous engagement and homogeneous knowledge. Each condition consisted of six groups (A1–A6 and B1–B6), with 31 students participating in A and 25 in B due to absences. The tasks involved applying learned concepts to write and present a report, with only subtle differences between weeks. Condition A was based on the lecturer's experience teaching STEM classes, anticipating that groups with high homogeneous engagement would be self-regulated and active, while low engagement groups might need more teacher intervention. Condition B served as a contrasting condition to evaluate the algorithm's performance.

The group formation considered engagement and knowledge indicators to construct the matrix C in Fig. 1. The individual reading engagement was operationalized through the total reading time and operation times logged in the e-book containing the lecture slides for each week, scaled into the range of 0–1 using percentage rank transform $((rank - 1) / (n - 1))$. Knowledge was assessed through five quizzes developed by the lecturer based on the lecture content. All these data points were collected from LEAF systems.

Weekly peer evaluations assessed learning outcomes for presentations based on completion (basic), concept application (knowledge), and additional commendations (extra). The teacher grading used the same criteria but with separate assessments for each construct.

4.2 Result and Discussion

Regarding RQ1, the density plots in the upper part of Fig. 4 illustrate the heterogeneity of each group based on squared difference. Overall, the system effectively generated groups with varying within-group differences based on the selected algorithm. A clear disparity is observed in two engagement indicators between the two conditions. Though the expected lower F values for quiz scores were not achieved, as most students scored above half points, resulting in minimal variance, two typical groups (B2 and B3) had B2 with identical scores. Despite using uniform scales to construct matrix C, the quiz score indicator performed poorly in the algorithm. This finding underscores the challenge of obtaining high-variance indicators for group formation in real-world settings.

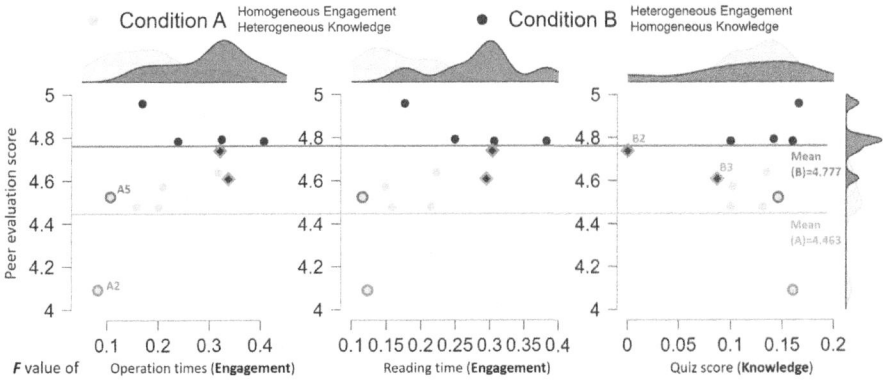

Fig. 4. Interval plots of peer evaluation score.

As for RQ2, we examined peer evaluation scores and teacher's grading. Overall, Condition B outperforms Condition A, indicated by both peer evaluation and teacher grading. We can see Group A2 received the lowest peer rating score in Condition A, with teachers also assigning low ratings in the knowledge construct; and Group B3 obtained the lowest score in Condition B. Regarding teacher grading, all groups across both conditions met the two basic criteria. However, Groups A2 and A5 failed both items in the knowledge construct, and Group B2 failed in item 3 of the knowledge construct.

When comparing the grouping strategies of two conditions, Condition B outperforms Condition A in group presentations, as indicated by both peer evaluation and teacher grading. This finding suggests that the combination of homogeneous engagement and heterogeneous knowledge, inspired by the lecturer, may not be appropriate for this particular learning context. This observation may be partially attributed to the difficulty of the course material, which requires low cognitive resources to understand, but only engagement in reading the slides. In STEM subjects with higher cognitive load, where the deviation in knowledge proficiency is more pronounced, the Condition A strategy may be more suitable, leading to further research. Therefore, employing a heterogeneous strategy for all groups remains a desirable choice for the current scenario.

To interpret the underperforming groups in Fig. 4, we examined the detailed panel of the system (Fig. 5) to understand their compositions. In Fig. 5, each row represents one student, with the color of the bar changing based on the indicator's value: green signifies high, yellow medium, and red low values. Groups A2 and A5 exhibit high levels of engagement homogeneity despite disparities in engagement levels, while Groups B2 and B3 rank as the top two in knowledge homogeneity in Condition B. These findings suggest a potential relevance between undesirable performance and homogeneous group compositions. Rather than facilitating negotiation with surplus cognitive resources [2], homogeneity hinders the spread of ideas within new social communities, which conflicts with the lecturer's expectations [14]. Through the system, teachers can identify such groups like A2 and allocate additional attention to them during class sessions to ensure the overall performance of the entire class.

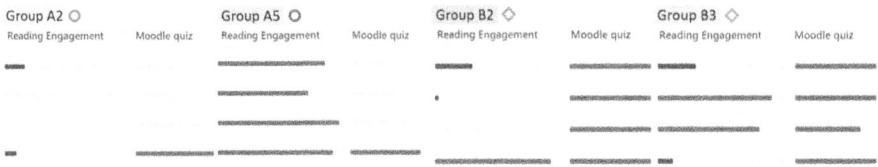

Fig. 5. Interpretation of low-performance groups from the system.

5 Conclusion

In this paper, we introduce a mixed genetic algorithm that incorporates both homogeneous and heterogeneous characteristics simultaneously. We implement this algorithm in a face-to-face university course as part of an exploratory study. Our findings demonstrate that the mixed method can effectively form groups based on the assigned grouping strategy. Based on the group formation system, teachers can examine the composition of these groups, enabling them to intervene promptly to enhance overall classroom performance. Future research could explore grouping strategies across various learning contexts, particularly in STEM subjects with higher cognitive loads of knowledge.

Acknowledgements. This research was partly supported by CSTI SIP Program Grant Number JPJ012347 and JSPS KAKENHI Grant Numbers JP22K20246 and JP24K16751.

References

1. Abou-Khalil, V., Ogata, H.: Homogeneous student engagement: a strategy for group formation during online learning. In: Hernández-Leo, D., Hishiyama, R., Zurita, G., Weyers, B., Nolte, A., Ogata, H. (eds.) CollabTech 2021. LNCS, vol. 12856, pp. 85–92. Springer, Cham (2021). https://doi.org/10.1007/978-3-030-85071-5_6
2. Cai, H., Gu, X.: Factors that influence the different levels of individuals' understanding after collaborative problem solving: the effects of shared representational guidance and prior knowledge. Interact. Learn. Environ. **30**(4), 695–706 (2022)
3. Flanagan, B., Liang, C., Majumdar, R., Ogata, H.: Towards explainable group formation by knowledge map based genetic algorithm. In: 2021 International Conference on Advanced Learning Technologies (ICALT), pp. 370–372. IEEE (2021)
4. Han, J., et al.: Utilizing online learning data to design face-to-face activities in a flipped classroom: a case study of heterogeneous group formation. Education Tech. Research Dev. **68**(5), 2055–2071 (2020)
5. Janssen, J., Kirschner, P.A.: Applying collaborative cognitive load theory to computer-supported collaborative learning: towards a research agenda. Education Tech. Research Dev. **68**(2), 783–805 (2020)
6. Liang, C., Gorham, T., Horikoshi, I., Majumdar, R., Ogata, H.: Estimating peer evaluation potential by utilizing learner model during group work. In: Wong, L.H., Hayashi, Y., Collazos, C.A., Alvarez, C., Zurita, G., Baloian, N. (eds.) Collaboration Technologies and Social Computing, CollabTech 2022. LNCS, vol. 13632, pp. 287–294. Springer, Cham (2022). https://doi.org/10.1007/978-3-031-20218-6_20
7. Liang, C., Toyokawa, Y., Majumdar, R., Horikoshi, I., Ogata, H.: Group formation based on reading annotation data: system innovation and classroom practice. J. Comput. Educ. 1–29 (2023)
8. Lyu, Q., Chen, W., Su, J., Heng, K.H.: Collaborate like expert designers: an exploratory study of the role of individual preparation activity on students' collaborative learning. Internet High. Educ. **59**, 100920 (2023)
9. Maqtary, N., Mohsen, A., Bechkoum, K.: Group formation techniques in computer-supported collaborative learning: a systematic literature review. Technol. Knowl. Learn. **24**, 169–190 (2019)
10. Moreno, J., Ovalle, D.A., Vicari, R.M.: A genetic algorithm approach for group formation in collaborative learning considering multiple student characteristics. Comput. Educ. **58**(1), 560–569 (2012)
11. Ogata, H., Majumdar, R., Flanagan, B., Kuromiya, H.: Learning analytics and evidence-based K12 education in Japan: usage of data-driven services for mobile learning across two years. Int. J. Mobile Learn. Organ. **18**(1), 15–48 (2024)
12. Revelo Sanchez, O., Collazos, C.A., Redondo, M.A.: Automatic group organization for collaborative learning applying genetic algorithm techniques and the big five model. Mathematics **9**(13), 1578 (2021)

13. Sanchez-Anguix, V., Alberola, J.M., Del Val, E., Palomares, A., Teruel, M.D.: Comparing computational algorithms for team formation in the classroom: a classroom experience. Appl. Intell. **53**(20), 23883–23904 (2023)
14. Srba, I., Bielikova, M.: Dynamic group formation as an approach to collaborative learning support. IEEE Trans. Learn. Technol. **8**(2), 173–186 (2014)
15. Wang, C., Xu, Y.: Who will work together? Factors influencing autonomic group formation in an open learning environment. Interact. Learn. Environ. 1–19 (2023)

Make-Up FLOW: A Beauty YouTubers' Video Recommendation Method Based on Make-Up Flowcharts

Sayaka Takano(✉) and Satoshi Nakamura

Meiji University, 4-21-1 Nakano-ku, Tokyo, Japan
takano.s.fms@gmail.com

Abstract. Due to the vast number of makeup videos online, finding a suitable one is challenging. To develop a makeup video recommendation service, we must establish a method for calculating the similarities between the makeup process. This paper proposes a Make-up FLOW system, which represents makeup procedures using a flowchart style structure. We evaluated its effectiveness in recommending videos from 103 tutorial videos based on process similarities. The findings showed a weak correlation using the Levenshtein distance in the first half of the process, suggesting that the process similarity may help recommend multiple information and sort search results.

Keywords: Make-up · Make-up process · Flowchart · Beauty YouTuber

1 Introduction

Beauty information and makeup tutorials are becoming increasingly popular on social network services (SNS). Many people use SNS to research new cosmetics and makeup methods [1, 2]. In addition, several studies have clarified that beauty influencers' reviews significantly impact cosmetics purchases [3–5].

However, finding a suitable makeup video among the over 65 million available online using conventional text-based searches is challenging. Additionally, since makeup involves many processes (refer to Table 1 in Sect. 3) and many people have unique methods of makeup [6], it's easier to adopt new methods from videos that resemble their process rather than entirely different ones. Despite many studies recommending cosmetics or techniques based on users' facial and cosmetic attributes [7–9], none focus on process similarities, forcing users to sift through numerous videos manually. Such a recommendation method using process information can also be used for the previously proposed support methods for makeup techniques [10, 11] and for increasing the variation of makeup [12, 13]. Creating a makeup video recommendation service demands a system that calculates the similarities between a user's routine and the process shown in video content.

Makeup involves applying many products to different face parts. For example, the same item may be applied to different parts or layered with different textures. Flowcharts visualize complex processes and are used in various fields beyond programming, such as culinary arts, medicine, and educational research [14–16]. However, makeup application varies significantly based on time, place, occasion, and individual preferences. Creating a standardized makeup flowchart with general services is problematic due to the diverse techniques and preferences.

This paper proposes a Make-up FLOW system that represents the makeup process using a flowchart format. We also developed a prototype system and created flowcharts from makeup tutorials by beauty YouTubers. To explore the feasibility of a video recommendation service based on flowchart similarities, we evaluate the effectiveness of recommendations based on the process similarities.

The contributions of our paper are as follows:

- We proposed the Make-up FLOW system, which stores and visualizes the user's makeup process using a flowchart and defines an appropriate format.
- We created a makeup flowchart dataset based on 103 makeup tutorial videos by 53 beauty YouTubers and the makeup processes of 34 female college students.
- We proposed a method to calculate makeup process similarities among users by representing these processes as strings of characters.

2 Make-Up FLOW

2.1 Basic Survey on the Makeup Process

Before implementing Make-up FLOW, we conducted a foundational study to determine suitable flowchart formats for the makeup process.

First, we collected makeup flowcharts using draw.io [17], an existing flowcharting service. We recruited 20 female university students to independently create a flowchart of their typical makeup process. The participants used three nodes: a start/end node, a makeup node (indicating a process always performed), and a makeup branch node (indicating a process sometimes not performed). Considering that an individual's motivation level can influence their routine, we introduced a motivation branch node.

Analysis of the flowcharts showed variations in process division and notation among participants. For instance, one participant broke down the eyebrow makeup process into separate steps for each texture, while another consolidated it into one step. We also observed differences in terminology (e.g., face powder vs. powder) and the level of detail provided. These discrepancies pose challenges for analyzing flowcharts and offering makeup support. Predefining process names that users can select in the system would ensure consistency in notation. In some cases, participants applied the same item to various face parts or used items with different textures on the same part. To address this, makeup nodes must explicitly include the item name, application area, and texture.

Next, we conducted a questionnaire survey about makeup routines to choose the type of branch node. From the survey, we selected the presence or absence of motivation, time spent on makeup, length of time out of the house, and seasonal differences as the branches of a Make-up FLOW flowchart.

2.2 Implementation of the Prototype System

We implemented a prototype system of Make-up FLOW. Figure 1 shows a screenshot of the system, with each area delimited by a light blue border and numbered.

The makeup node displays an icon of the facial part where makeup is applied, the item's name, and the texture name in brackets if the item has multiple textures. The system generates a makeup node automatically when the user selects elements from the pull-down menu in the area (3). Users can choose 30 items listed in a category from a well-known cosmetics information website. The branch node includes four conditions: motivation level, makeup time, outdoor time, and seasonal changes. An illustrative face (Fig. 2), shown in area (2), helps users visualize their daily makeup routine by updating with each new process added. Users create a makeup flowchart by dragging and dropping nodes from area (4) to (5) and connecting them.

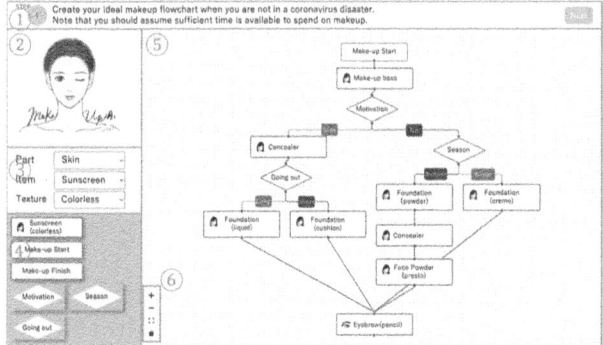

Fig. 1. Make-up FLOW system. (Color figure online)

Fig. 2. Changes in facial illustration with the addition of the make-up process

3 Dataset

At first, we recruited 34 female university students to use the Make-up FLOW system. Then, our system collected over 150 makeup flowcharts from them. Figure 3 shows three examples from the collected flowcharts, demonstrating that the complexity of the flowchart, including the number of processes and branches, varies from user to user.

In addition, to verify the effectiveness of recommending makeup videos based on process similarities, we created a beauty YouTubers flowchart dataset from tutorial videos of Japanese beauty YouTubers with over 50,000 subscribers. To ensure various makeup processes, we included anyone regularly posting beauty videos as a beauty YouTuber, regardless of their primary occupation.

We recruited four participants with over six months of experience using our system. We asked them to create flowcharts while watching the videos using our system. We instructed them to make flowcharts for two genres of makeup videos posted in the past year. Examples of keywords for videos in each genre are as follows.

- Everyday makeup: Everyday, Time reduction.
- Unique makeup: Enhance, Look good, Popular, Scam, Live concert, and Party.

We obtained 103 makeup flowcharts from 53 YouTubers, averaging 706,000 subscribers. Three YouTubers had not posted any unique makeup videos in the past year, resulting in 53 everyday makeup' and 50 unique makeup' flowcharts.

Table 1 shows the statistics of the maximum number of process routes in the flowcharts of 53 YouTubers and 34 female university students created during the same period. This indicates that YouTubers had more processes than general female university students.

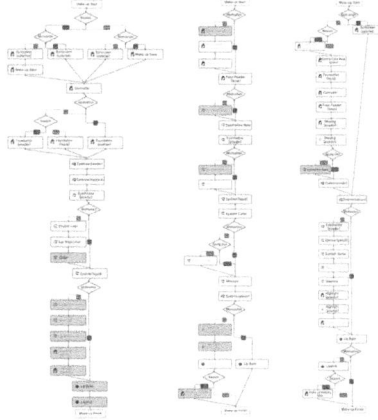

Fig. 3. Example of make-up flowcharts by 3 female university students

Table 1. Statistics on the maximum number of process routes for each category

	Min	Max	Average	Std. Dev.
Female university students	5	29	16.0	5.7
Beauty YouTubers	9	42	19.5	6.5

4 Experiment with Recommending Makeup Videos

We conducted an experiment that analyzed the similarities between the makeup process of participants and beauty YouTubers and recommended videos based on these similarities. Participants were told to create a makeup flowchart in advance. We then calculated the similarities between participants and YouTubers using the Levenshtein distance and the cosine similarity based on N-gram frequency. Based on the classification described in Sect. 4.1, we selected two videos with high and slightly low similarities for each calculation method. Each participant watched eight different videos. After viewing each video, participants completed a questionnaire evaluating aspects such as the video's helpfulness. We recruited five female university students.

4.1 Calculating the Process Similarities Between Participants and YouTubers

Using the dataset constructed in Sect. 3, we calculated the process similarities between participants and beauty YouTubers. We used string similarity calculation methods, specifically the standardized Levenshtein distance and cosine similarity based on N-gram frequency. Each makeup route in the flowchart was represented as a string, and process similarities were calculated based on these strings.

1. We encoded the makeup node's part, item, and texture information with alphabet characters, symbols, and numbers (e.g., "A$2" for A: skin, $: foundation, and 2: liquid). This method is referred to as compound notation. Alternatively, converting the three characters representing a makeup node into a single unique character is called substitution notation.
2. We arranged and concatenated strings of makeup nodes in the sequence of the makeup process. This order reflects the sequence of application in the makeup route.

For the part, a total of five types (e.g., skin and eyebrows) are indicated by A to E. For the item, 30 types (e.g., foundations and eye shadows) are indicated by symbols such as "$" and "%." For the texture, up to seven types (e.g., liquid and powder) are represented by 0 to 6. Figure 4 shows an example of a makeup route converted into a string of characters in compound notation. We focused on the most detailed makeup routes—those with the maximum number of processes—as these are most beneficial for users. The median similarity was 1.20 using the Levenshtein distance and 0.05 for the N-gram frequency. Based on previous research, the part-only distance and the item-and-texture distance were summed to calculate the Levenshtein distance, resulting in a maximum value of 2.00. Consequently, any value less than half of that maximum was considered short. Distances longer than the median were considered slightly long. For cosine similarity, where the maximum value is 0.50, values above 0.20 were considered high similarities, while those below 0.06 were considered slightly low.

4.2 Results

To determine which similarity calculation method better recommends videos, we analyzed the relationship between each method's similarity scores and the video ratings from the questionnaire. We calculated each participant's similarities to beauty YouTuber videos and ranked them according to their similarity scores. We then calculated Spearman's correlation coefficients (ρ).

The analysis used three evaluation criteria from the questionnaire: the helpfulness of the videos, the willingness to adopt the techniques introduced, and the subjective similarity of the process between the participants and the video. Although the participants' flowcharts contained branch nodes and the YouTubers' flowcharts contained only one route, participants judged the similarity level by considering only their main makeup route. The effect of this difference on the subjective similarity was considered small. We first calculated ρ for each evaluation criterion. The results showed no correlation for all evaluation criteria (correlation range: -0.11–0.27).

Next, we calculated a weighted average of the evaluation criteria that maximized the ρ and ranked the videos from 1 to 8. The results showed that the Levenshtein distance had a weak correlation (0.26) when assigning a weight of 0.1 to helpfulness, 0.4 to willingness to adopt techniques, and 0.5 to perceived similarity. N-gram frequencies were uncorrelated (0.08) when assigning a weight of 0.0, 0.5, 0.5.

The first half of the makeup process involves essential elements like base makeup, while the second half creates eye and lip makeup moods. Therefore, we calculated similarities based on the first or second-half processes and determined the weights that maximized the ρ. Table 2 shows the results of each calculation method. The numbers in brackets indicate the weighting of the evaluation criteria (helpfulness: willingness to adopt techniques: perceived similarity). This reveals a weak correlation when the first half is used to calculate the Levenshtein distance. These weight values were intuitive since the most critical factor was whether the video was helpful to the user. However, the N-gram frequencies consistently showed no correlation. Table 3 presents the ρ for each participant and indicates that some participants strongly correlate with the Levenshtein distance. When we asked Participant C why she rated the video with high similarities low, she explained, "I did not gain any new knowledge; the beauty of her true face was remarkable."

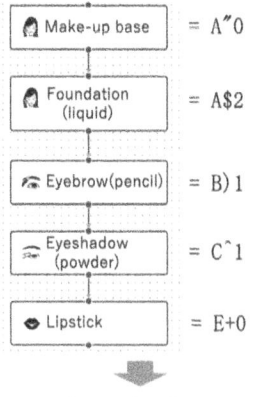

Fig. 4. Example of replacing a cosmetic root with a string in compound notation

Table 2. ρ for each similarity calculation method

	Leven's ρ	N-gram's ρ
First half of process	0.38 (0.6: 0.2: 0.2)	0.08 (0.0: 0.1: 0.9)
Second half of process	0.21 (0.1: 0.7: 0.2)	0.14 (0.5: 0.3: 0.2)

Table3. ρ for each similarity calculation method per participant

	A	B	C	D	E
Leven's ρ	0.32	0.64	−0.07	0.12	0.88
N-gram's ρ	0.28	0.40	−0.37	−0.48	0.22

5 Discussion and Conclusion

We found that the highest correlation was obtained using the Levenshtein distance in the first half of the process. However, the overall correlations were low. The cosine similarity based on the N-gram frequency consistently showed no correlation, indicating that it was unsuitable for recommending makeup videos.

Participants' comments for low-rated videos included, "She discussed the topics I already knew, or that were unsuitable for me." and "My usual process is quite similar, so I felt I was not learning any new techniques." Conversely, comments for high-rated videos included, "She described items I had never used before." and "Though the process was different, she explained tips for effective makeup application in great detail." Trust in beauty Influencers is essential when watching their videos; Ding et al. [5] found that trust in beauty YouTubers was related to their expertise in makeup and appearance. Rasmussen [4] noted that popular beauty YouTubers used professional lighting and sound. Therefore, factors beyond process probably influenced the videos' evaluation, weakening the overall correlation when recommendations were based solely on process similarities.

We initially believed that recommending makeup videos based on the similarities in the process would be effective. However, considering other factors, such as the items used, explanation quality, and video composition, may be essential. In such cases, if it is possible to automatically recognize YouTube videos, it would be better to automatically calculate the similarities to the flowchart created by the user and display recommendations for videos with high similarity on Make-up FLOW. Another application of the process similarities is in sort functionality. For example, allowing users to perform a keyword search on YouTube, analyze the process of the top videos, and then sort them based on their similarities can help users find videos that are easy to follow and practice. In the future, we plan to clarify the factors in evaluating makeup videos and investigate support methods that effectively utilize process information. Based on our findings, we aim to develop a new system that recommends and searches for makeup flowcharts and beauty YouTubers' videos. This system would help users improve and diversify their makeup routines.

References

1. PowerReviews. https://www.powerreviews.com/research/beauty-shopper-digital-expectations-2022/. Accessed 7 Apr 2024
2. Harvard Business School. https://hbswk.hbs.edu/item/lipstick-tips-how-influencers-are-making-over-beauty-marketing. Accessed 7 Apr 2024
3. Chen, J., Dermawan, A.: The influence of YouTube beauty vloggers on Indonesian consumers' purchase intention of local cosmetic products. Int. J. Bus. Manag. 15(5), 100–116 (2020)
4. Rasmussen, L.L.: Parasocial interaction in the digital age: an examination of relationship building and the effectiveness of YouTube celebrities. Soc. Media Soc. 7(1), 280–294 (2018)
5. Ding, W., Henninger, C.E., Blazquez, M., Boardman, R.: Effects of beauty vloggers' eWOM and sponsored advertising on Weibo. Social Commerce, pp. 235–253 (2019)
6. Kajita, M., Nakamura, S.: Basic research on how to apply foundation makeup evenly on your own face. In: 20th IFIP TC14 International Conference on Entertainment Computing (IFIP ICEC 2021), pp. 402–410 (2021)
7. Alashkar, T., Jiang, S., Fu, Y.: Rule-based facial makeup recommendation system. In: 2017 12th IEEE International Conference on Automatic Face & Gesture Recognition (FG 2017), pp. 325–330 (2017)
8. Nguyen, T.V., Liu, L.: Smart mirror: intelligent makeup recommendation and synthesis. In: Proceedings of the 25th ACM International Conference on Multimedia (MM 2017), pp. 1253–1254 (2017)
9. Liu, L., et al.: "Wow! You are so beautiful today!" ACMTrans. Multimed. Comput. Commun. Appl. 11(1s), 1–22 (2014)
10. Treepong, B., Mitake, H., Hasegawa, S.: Makeup creativity enhancement with an augmented reality face makeup system. Comput. Entertain. 16(4), 1–17 (2018)
11. Nishimura, A., Siio, I.: IMake: eye makeup design generator. In: Proceedings of the 11th Conference on Advances in Computer Entertainment Technology (ACE 2014), pp. 1–6 (2014)
12. Nakagawa, M., Tsukada, K., Siio, I.: Smart makeup system: supporting makeup using lifelog sharing. In: Proceedings of the 13th International Conference on Ubiquitous Computing (UbiComp 2011), pp. 483–484 (2011)
13. Truong, A., Chi, P., Salesin, D., Essa, I., Agrawala, M.: Automatic generation of two-level hierarchical tutorials from instructional makeup videos. In: Proceedings of the 2021 CHI Conference on Human Factors in Computing Systems (CHI 2021), pp. 1–16 (2021)
14. Malmaud, J., Wagner, E., Chang, N., Murphy, K.: Cooking with semantics. In: Proceedings of the ACL 2014 Workshop on Semantic Parsing, pp. 33–38 (2014)
15. Miura, F., et al.: TG13 flowchart for the management of acute cholangitis and cholecystitis. J. Hepatobiliary Pancreat. Sci. 20, 47–54 (2013)
16. Bamidele, E.F., Oloyede, E.O.: Comparative effectiveness of hierarchical, flowchart and spider concept mapping strategies on students' performance in chemistry. World J. Educ. 3, 66–76 (2013)
17. draw.io. https://app.diagrams.net. Accessed 7 Apr 2024

Active Participation vs. Directed Observation in Collaborative 3D Virtual Museums

Gustavo Zurita[1](✉) [iD], Joaquín Uribe[2], Nelson Baloian[2], and Valentina Aravena[2]

[1] FEN, Departamento de Control de Gestión y Sistemas de Información, Universidad de Chile, Santiago, Chile
gzurita@fen.uchile.cl

[2] Departamento de Ciencias de la Computación, Universidad de Chile, Santiago, Chile
valentina.aravena.p@ug.uchile.cl

Abstract. This study examines the effects of active participation versus directed observation in collaborative 3D virtual museums on collaboration, learning, and usability. Using a virtual reality setup, 11 engineering students from the Universidad de Chile interacted with digital replicas of Armenian khachkars. Participants either manipulated the objects directly or observed as one member manipulated them. The experiment assessed teamwork quality, usability, and learning outcomes through questionnaires. Results showed that directed observation led to higher teamwork quality and slightly better usability scores, suggesting it provided a more structured and predictable environment. Both modalities achieved high levels of detail attention and personal reflection in learning outcomes, though active participation encouraged slightly greater understanding and engagement. The findings underscore the potential of collaborative virtual 3D museums to enhance educational experiences, indicating that structured observation can facilitate teamwork and usability. Active participation may boost personal engagement with content. Further research with larger samples is needed to confirm these results and optimize collaborative activities in virtual settings.

Keywords: Collaborative 3D Virtual Museum · Active participation · Directed Observation

1 Introduction

Virtual reality and the metaverse have sparked much interest in industry, commerce, and education [1]. Virtual reality has been used in many ways in the latter area, one of the most frequent and oldest being the 3D virtual museum [2]. Today's technologies make it possible to create highly realistic digital twins that are presented to the museum user in an environment where they can interact with the objects on display. Learning linked to virtual museums in which the learner interacts with objects has often been linked to a constructivist learning style, as it promotes the critical aspects of this learning approach [2]. It allows active engagement by providing a platform for users to navigate through exhibits, view artifacts from different angles, and access additional information through multimedia elements like videos, audio guides, and interactive simulations. It allows personalized learning by offering various pathways for exploration, enabling users to choose what exhibits to visit, which artifacts to examine closely, and how deeply to delve into related information. It also offers hands-on exploration by providing interactive features such as virtual tours, 3D models, and exhibits, allowing users to manipulate objects and observe cause-and-effect relationships. Social Interaction can be implemented by incorporating features for collaboration, such as discussion forums, multiplayer activities, and opportunities for sharing insights and interpretations with peers. Finally, reflection and meaning-making can be offered by providing reflection opportunities, such as journaling prompts or guided questions, to encourage users to relate their observations to prior knowledge and experiences. Based on this principle, we can propose that in a virtual museum, the visitor builds an exhibition with the objects that the virtual museum has available and shares it with other visitors. Authors have long discussed enhancing virtual museum visits through collaborative actions among visitors [3]. Collaboration can occur during the three lifecycle stages: design and planning, construction (programming), and operation. Yet, examples of implementing such activities between visitors or with curators are sparse [4]. This scarcity may stem from unclear methodologies for effective interaction. What are the most effective modalities for fruitful interaction in virtual museums?

The [4] authors present a proposal for incorporating collaborative elements into a single-user implementation of a virtual museum. In this work, we revisit that work in which the multiuser feature has already been integrated, and we go further in evaluating how the collaborative construction of an exhibition can be organized for a small group of participants by comparing the approaches of **active participation** vs. **directed observation**. A first evaluation of the effect on learning that interaction with the museum has on users concerning the exhibition's theme is also carried out.

2 Background and Previous Work

Active participation (AP) in a collaborative 3D virtual museum implies that all group members can move and interact with the digital objects in the exhibition; everyone can select, reposition, and manipulate the objects in the virtual environment. This modality allows a) direct **interaction**, as each member interacts with the objects independently, allowing personalized exploration [1]; b) **autonomy**, since members have individual control over the objects and follow their interests over the elements of the exhibition [5]; c) **active collaboration**, as each member can contribute to the common task, in a shared environment that encourages discussion and collaboration among members [1]; and d) **active engagement**, as active learning is promoted where all participants are committed to the task [6]. AP's benefits include promoting personalized exploration and experimentation, increasing information retention by linking learning to each member's actions, and fostering a more profound learning experience [7]. **Directed observation (DO)** In a collaborative 3D virtual museum environment, on the other hand, it implies that a single person is responsible for manipulating the objects while the other members actively participate by giving directions for the person to move the objects, i.e., they may be actively involved in discussions or decisions. This modality allows a) a **focal**

point, as a leader controls the display and manipulation of objects, directing the group's attention to specific aspects of each piece [8]; a **guided structure**, as the leader can plan and execute a strategy for exploring the exhibit, which can help maintain the team's focus and ensure that all critical aspects are covered [8]; c) greater **communicational participation** of members who are unable to move objects [9]; and d) more **reflective observation** as participants have the opportunity to observe more closely without the burden of manipulating objects, which can facilitate a deepening of reflection and analysis [10]. The benefits of this modality are that they are effective for large groups where individual manipulation would be impracticable [11], the leader can guide participants through a coherent narrative or critical learning topics [12], and can foster a group dynamic where some members may prefer to participate as active observers [7].

3 Problem Statement and Research Hypothesis

The choice between AP and DO in a collaborative 3D virtual museum environment for small groups can directly affect how teams collaborate (individual engagement, perception of control, etc.), usability given the way they interact in the environment, and ultimately, learning. Collaboration between members is reflected in communication, coordination, balance of contributions, mutual support, effort, and cohesion [13]. A virtual environment supporting effective collaboration can lead to more successful outcomes and meaningful learning [14].

The usability of the collaborative 3D virtual museum is crucial to ensure that users can interact with the content seamlessly, which could directly influence their ability to collaborate and learn [15]. If the system is not user-friendly, participants could become frustrated, which would decrease their motivation and the quality of their teamwork [16]. The learning outcomes may vary according to the choice of one or the other modality, introducing advantages and disadvantages. AP could foster more profound understanding and greater personal reflection, indicative of increased motivation and good collaboration. However, DO can offer a more structured and cohesive learning experience, which could benefit team coordination and consistency. Likewise, in terms of general comprehension and attention to detail, the modality of AP may foster greater autonomy and personal exploration, leading to a richer and more diverse understanding of the contents presented [17]. However, this can also result in uneven experiences within the group, depending on the individual's ability to handle and explore virtual objects.

On the other hand, DO can provide a more structured and uniform approach. Still, it could limit the learning experience to the leader's perspective, reducing personal autonomy and motivation [8]. Regarding personal reflection, AP can foster greater emotional connection than direct observation, which is crucial for meaningful learning and long-term retention [12, 18].

Then, the balance between directed control and autonomy in virtual environments is crucial to maximizing educational benefits and user satisfaction in collaborative 3D virtual museums and their impact on learning. An approach that does not consider individual needs and group dynamics can compromise the effectiveness of collaborative learning and the overall user experience. This issue is particularly relevant given the increasing use of virtual technologies in education and the need for effective methods that foster collaboration and individualized learning in rich and complex environments such as virtual museums. Considering these aspects, and based on current research, it is essential to develop strategies that balance these two modes of interaction to improve the effectiveness of collaborative learning in virtual environments.

The **research question** is: how do the modalities of AP versus DO influence teamwork, usability, and collaborative learning within virtual environments of collaborative 3D virtual museums?

4 Method

Participants. The participants were 11 students from the Faculty of Engineering of the Universidad de Chile. Five were 17 to 20 years old, five were 21 to 25, and one was 30. Seven participants identified themselves as male, four as female, and one as non-binary (Fig. 1).

Fig. 1. On the left, participants of Group 1. On the right, aerial views of their 3D virtual museum.

Activity. The activity was carried out using the implementation of a collaborative 3D virtual museum, where users can set up exhibitions of Armenian cross-stones called "khachkars," which are archeological objects used for commemorating important events or as tombstones. The museum presents a workspace scenario in which there is an exhibition of 5 khachkars arranged on the left side of a church (Fig. 1), accessed by up to three users who can work collaboratively. Users can select stones from a list of 30 and then place them in a place in the scenario. Users can also choose a khachkar, access its metadata, and move, rotate, and delete it from the exhibition. In addition, users can change the point of view from which they approach the virtual museum. There are two participation modalities: in one, each user can use all available functionalities described above; in the other, only one user can change the exhibition objects, and the others can only observe. The activity consisted of the participants making a mirror copy of the exhibition in the right area of the scenario (in Fig. 1, the replicas of the exhibition of the four groups are seen on the right). To do this, they had to select the correct khachkars from a list and add them at an equivalent position and direction from the one on the left side of the church.

Next, we describe the questionnaires evaluating teamwork quality, usability, and collaborative learning for collaborative 3D virtual museum environments under AP and DO modalities.

Collaborative Questionnaire (CQ). We used the constructs proposed by the Teamwork Quality (TWQ) [13] to set up a questionnaire for evaluation collaboration under the two modalities tested in this work. These are **communication** (there was sufficiently frequent, informal, direct, and open communication); **coordination** (the efforts of each of the team members were well structured and synchronized); **balance of members' contributions** (all team members were able to make contributions); **mutual support** (team members helped and supported each other in carrying out their tasks); **effort** (team members devoted all their possible efforts to the team's tasks); and **cohesion** (Team members were motivated to get the job done together). The questions associated with these constructs will be measured with a 5-point Likert scale: 1 - totally disagree, 2 - disagree, 3 - neutral, 4 - agree, and 5 - totally agree. The questions proposed for each of these constructs (Table 1) come from two previous studies where different teamwork approaches were evaluated, and the questions were validated. The first study was validated within a sample of first-year university students; the main focus was to obtain an instrument to measure teamwork-related competencies [19]. The second corresponds to a validated study within project teams, where the relationship between teamwork quality items and success within innovative projects is observed [13]. Finally, the questions chosen between these two studies correspond to observable criteria within the 20-min activity the participants carried out with the collaborative 3D virtual museum. The score obtained corresponds to the value of the Likert scale in each of the questions.

Usability Questionnaire (SUS) [15]. The standard SUS usability questionnaire consisting of 10 questions with a 5-point Likert scale will be applied, where 1 means "Strongly disagree" and 5 means "Strongly agree". In terms of interpretation, a score above 68 is considered above average in terms of usability, a score below 68 is considered below average, and a score around 50 indicates average usability.

Learning Questionnaire (LQ). Questions to measure the learning experience are based on constructs of general comprehension, interpretation and meaning, attention to detail, personal reflection, and reproduction accuracy. Table 2 shows the questions associated with their constructs and a description of each construct.

To evaluate the answers to the LQ questions from P1 to P5, each answer is rated with values 1, 3, or 5 according to the following criteria: **General comprehension:** 1- no adequate or relevant description provided 3- a basic description provided with some correct elements; 5- clear and detailed description. **Interpretation and meaning:** 1 - shows little understanding of cultural symbolism or meaning, 3 - identifies some basic symbolism correctly, and 5 - shows a deep and detailed interpretation of cultural meaning. **Attention to detail:** 1 - mentions few or no specific details, 3 - describes some details but lacks depth, and 5 - detailed and complete description of geometric features, colors, and sizes. **Personal reflection**: 1 - does not express any personal reflection or is irrelevant, 3 - represents a basic reflection on what caught your attention, and 5 - deep and personal reflection on what you find significant or striking. To evaluate question P6 and determine how much they have learned about khachkars after the participants observed

Table 1. Teamwork Quality Questionnaire (CQ) by Construct.

Construct	Question
Communication	**P1.** Communication with the team was open and honest [13, 19]
	P2. The information shared by the team was useful [19]
Coordination	**P3.** Clear and structured objectives are presented among team members [19]
	P4. I had a clear understanding of my tasks during the activity [19]
Balance of members' contributions	**P5.** The team worked with flexibility allowing adaptation to the challenges posed [13, 19]
	P6. The team recognizes the potentials of each member [13]
Mutual support	**P7.** The team helps each other to achieve the objectives [13, 19]
Effort	**P8.** Team members took the initiative to solve the problems presented [19]
	P9. I am satisfied with the final outcome of the activity [13]
Mutual support	**P10.** I felt heard when I wanted to share the information I knew [13]
	P11. My contributions were valued by the rest of the team [13]

around 30 different models in the collaborative 3D virtual museum, an evaluation rubric of 5 dimensions and sub-dimensions and scores was applied, being evaluated by an expert in Armenian culture: **Accuracy of primary structure**: up to 5 points if the stone has a recognizable shape that matches the typical proportions of a khachkar. Five points if the cross is centered and is the focal point of the khachkar, as is traditional. Five points if additional structural elements, such as the base or capital, are included if present in the models. Ten points, if the spatial distribution of the elements follows the patterns observed in the khachkars presented in the museum. **Design Complexity:** 10 points if it includes intricate details such as rosettes, intertwined leaves, or geometric motifs. Ten points if there is an attempt to incorporate the density and complexity of the designs seen in the models. Five points if details are symmetrical and uniform where appropriate. **Fidelity of the ornamental elements:** 15 points if specific decorative elements such as crosses, rosettes, and grape motifs are recognizable. Ten points if the decorative aspects are correctly proportioned to the central cross. **Creative interpretation:** 15 points if the drawing shows originality while staying true to the fundamental characteristics of the khachkars. **Overall presentation and effort:** 5 points if the drawing is clean and well presented. Five points if perceived that the user dedicated time and effort to complete the draw. The sum of all points reflects how close the drawing is to the khachkars shown

Table 2. Learning Questionnaire (LQ) and its constructs.

Construct	Question	Description
Communication	P1. Describe what khachkars are in your own words	Assesses participants' general understanding and ability to express the concept in their own terms
Interpretation and meaning	P2. What do you think khachkars represent?	Evaluate whether the cultural or spiritual significance of the khachkars is perceived
Attention to detail Coordination	P3. Describe with the highest degree of detail the geometric, colors and sizes of khachkars	It measures attention to detail and precise observation
	P4. Describe the ornaments of the khachkars	Assesses recognition and understanding of specific details in khachkars
Personal reflection	P5. What catches your attention the most about khachkars?	Evaluates the perception of personal reflection
Visual accuracy	P6. Based on what you saw in the virtual museum, make a sketch of a khachkar	Assess the precision each participants reproduces the details of the objects

and how much the student has learned about them; 90–100 points can be considered exceptional, 70–89 points are good, 50–69 points are acceptable, and below 50 points indicate that more study and practice are required.

Procedure. Participants were recruited via the faculty forum at the Universidad de Chile's Computer Science Department and received a chocolate bar as compensation. Each session lasted one hour and took place over two weeks (Fig. 1). The experiment began with a brief 20-min introduction to khachkars, describing them as Armenian sculptures or memorial stones before participants accessed the museum's application. All 11 participants reported no prior knowledge of khachkars. They then attempted to replicate a given presentation within a 30-min limit; completion times were 19, 13, 14, and 9 min for groups 1 through 4, respectively. Afterward, participants completed the CQ, SUS, and LQ questionnaires and provided drawings illustrating the main characteristics of the khachkars.

5 Results

This section presents the inventory results used to evaluate the activity under its two modalities regarding the quality of teamwork, usability, and collaborative learning within virtual environments of collaborative 3D virtual museums.

Collaborative Questionnaire (CQ). A higher average score is observed in the DO modality (with a score of 4.8) than in the AP modality (with a score of 4.2), see Table 3.

Likewise, it is observed that the coordination construct has the lowest average score in both modalities, with 3.5 in AP and 4.58 in DO. It is also seen that the group with the weakest results corresponds to group 3, which consisted of two participants, unlike the 3 participants of the rest of the groups, having lower results in most of the constructs except for communication.

Table 3. CQ Results by Modality, Group, Questions, and Construct.

Construct	Question	Group 1			Group 3		AP	Group 2			Group 4			DO
		M1	M2	M3	M1	M2	Avg	M1	M2	M3	M1	M2	M3	Avg
Communication	P1	5,0	4,0	5,0	5,0	4,0	4,6	5,0	5,0	5,0	5,0	5,0	5,0	5,0
	P2	5,0	4,0	5,0	5,0	4,0	4,6	5,0	4,0	4,0	5,0	5,0	5,0	4,7
	Avg	5,0	4,0	5,0	5,0	4,0	4,6	5,0	4,5	4,5	5,0	5,0	5,0	4,8
Coordination	P3	5,0	4,0	5,0	1,0	2,0	3,4	5,0	4,0	5,0	4,0	5,0	5,0	4,7
	P4	5,0	5,0	5,0	1,0	2,0	3,6	5,0	4,0	4,0	5,0	5,0	4,0	4,5
	Avg	5,0	4,5	5,0	1,0	2,0	3,5	5,0	4,0	4,5	4,5	5,0	4,5	4,6
Balance of members' contributions	P5	5,0	5,0	5,0	3,0	5,0	4,6	5,0	5,0	5,0	5,0	5,0	5,0	5,0
	P6	5,0	5,0	4,0	3,0	5,0	4,4	3,0	5,0	5,0	5,0	5,0	5,0	4,7
	Avg	5,0	5,0	4,5	3,0	5,0	4,5	4,0	5,0	5,0	5,0	5,0	5,0	4,8
Mutual support	P7	5,0	4,0	5,0	3,0	4,0	4,2	5,0	5,0	5,0	5,0	5,0	5,0	5,0
Effort	P8	5,0	5,0	5,0	3,0	3,0	4,2	5,0	4,0	5,0	5,0	4,0	5,0	4,7
	P9	5,0	4,0	5,0	3,0	4,0	4,2	4,0	5,0	4,0	5,0	5,0	5,0	4,7
	Avg	5,0	4,5	5,0	3,0	3,5	4,2	4,5	4,5	4,5	5,0	4,5	5,0	4,7
Cohesion	P10	5,0	5,0	5,0	3,0	3,0	4,2	5,0	5,0	5,0	5,0	5,0	5,0	5,0
	P11	5,0	4,0	5,0	3,0	4,0	4,2	5,0	5,0	5,0	5,0	5,0	5,0	5,0
	Avg	5,0	4,5	5,0	3,0	3,5	4,2	5,0	5,0	5,0	5,0	5,0	5,0	5,0

Notation: Mx = Member number x. Avg = average.

Usability (SUS). Table 4 shows the SUS score for each participant in each group. All SUS scores are above the usability average in the AP modality, except for one participant (M1). In contrast, DO shows usability for everyone consistently above the usability average. Comparatively, DO tends to be more favorable and less variable than AP, potentially influenced by individual differences in learning abilities and preferences; perhaps centralizing actions through a leader makes the experience more predictable and less confusing for participants.

Learning Questionnaire (LQ). Both groups achieved high attention to detail and personal reflection scores, see Table 5. This indicates that, regardless of the work modality, participants were very focused on observing the objects and reflecting on their meaning or personal impact.

Regarding **general understanding**, the DO modality yielded a slightly higher average (3.0) than AP at 2.6, indicating that a single focus point may enhance team focus and improve understanding. Though responses varied, AP averaged higher (3.4) than DO (2.33) for interpretation and meaning. Some individuals in the DO demonstrated deep

Table 4. SUS results by AP and DO modalities.

	AP Avg 76,0		DO Avg 83,5	
	Group 1	Group 3	Group 2	Group 4
M1	95,0	40,0	77,5	87,5
M2	72,5	75,0	80,0	87,5
M3	97,5	--	87,5	80,0
Avg	**88,3**	**57,5**	**81,7**	**85,3**

Notation: Mx = Member number x. Avg = average.

Table 5. LQ results by AP and DO modalities.

Construct	Group 1			Group 3		AP	Group 2			Group 4			DO
	M1	M2	M3	M1	M2	Avg	M1	M2	M3	M1	M2	M3	Avg
General comprehension	3	3	3	1	3	**2,6**	3	5	1	3	3	3	**3,0**
Interpretation and meaning	5	3	1	3	5	**3,4**	1	5	1	1	5	1	**2,3**
Attention to detail	5	5	5	5	5	**5,0**	5	5	5	5	5	5	**5,0**
Personal Reflection	5	5	5	5	5	**5,0**	5	5	5	5	3	5	**4,7**
Visual accuracy	89	91	85	55	65	**72**	82	81	81	84	62	55	**73**

Notation: Mx = Member number x. Avg = average.

understanding, scoring highly, while others showed lesser comprehension. This variation may stem from individual differences in perception and expression rather than from the interaction model. **Visual accuracy** scores were similar between groups but varied significantly among individuals, possibly reflecting varying drawing skills. Nonetheless, feedback from a Khachkar expert suggested substantial learning gains, particularly for participants' first exposure to Khachkars.

6 Conclusions

This initial experience reveals differences between AP and DO modalities to support collaboration in a 3D virtual museum [4], generating different user experiences. The results suggest improvements in collaborative dynamics, particularly favoring the DO modality to strengthen team collaboration. Coordination poses significant challenges in this new dynamic, and it is recommended to conduct activities within three-member groups. Regarding SUS, effective 3D virtual museum design should balance personal exploration and structured guidance to optimize usability and enjoyment. The results emphasize the importance of personalization and adaptability in developing collaborative virtual learning systems. Learning outcomes (LQ) indicate that the chosen modality impacts various learning aspects and perceptions of the collaborative 3D virtual museum. High attention to detail and personal reflection are typical in both modalities, yet understanding and interpretation benefit from structured approaches that ensure collective discussion and interaction. The results show AP promotes better collective understanding and interaction, whereas DO enhances focus and concentration.

Since it has insufficient statistical meaning, we must recognize that the sample size that performed the experiments needs to be more significant to draw general conclusions from its results. This small sample does not allow us to capture a wide variability in technological skills, previous experiences, and group dynamics. Despite this, the results obtained will enable us to gain insights into applying the different modalities, and these can be even improved with a larger sample. This first experience paves the way for designing more meaningful experiments to explore the best ways to organize teamwork in a collaborative 3D virtual museum.

References

1. Johnson, L., Levine, A., Smith, R.: NMC Horizon Report: 2008 Australia-New Zealand Edition. The New Media Consortium (2008)
2. Bada, S.O., Olusegun, S.: Constructivism learning theory: a paradigm for teaching and learning. J. Res. Method Educ. **5**(6), 66–70 (2015)
3. Barbieri, T., Paolini, P.: Co-operation metaphors for virtual museums (2001)
4. Baloian, N., et al.: Exploring collaboration in the realm of virtual museums. In: Gutwin, C., Ochoa, S.F., Vassileva, J., Inoue, T. (eds.) CRIWG 2017. LNCS, vol. 10391, pp. 252–259. Springer, Cham (2017). https://doi.org/10.1007/978-3-319-63874-4_19
5. Smith, B.K., Reiser, B.J.: Explaining behavior through observational investigation and theory articulation. J. Learn. Sci. **14**(3), 315–360 (2005)
6. Prince, M.: Does active learning work? a review of the research. J. Eng. Educ. **93**(3), 223–231 (2004)
7. Chi, M.T., Wylie, R.: The ICAP framework: linking cognitive engagement to active learning outcomes. Educational psychologist **49**(4), 219–243 (2014)
8. Hein, G.: Learning science in informal environments: people, places, and pursuits. Museums Soc. Issues **4**(1), 113–124 (2009)
9. Hmelo-Silver, C.E.: Problem-based learning: what and how do students learn? Educ. Psychol. Rev. **16**, 235–266 (2004)
10. Linn, M.C., Davis, E.A., Bell, P.: Internet environments for science education. Routledge (2013)
11. Eberbach, C., Crowley, K.: From living to virtual: learning from museum objects. Curator: Museum J. **48**(3), 317–338 (2005)
12. Moreno, R., Mayer, R.: Interactive multimodal learning environments: special issue on interactive learning environments: contemporary issues and trends. Educ. Psychol. Rev. **19**, 309–326 (2007)
13. Hoegl, M., Gemuenden, H.G.: Teamwork quality and the success of innovative projects: a theoretical concept and empirical evidence. Organ. Sci. **12**(4), 435–449 (2001)
14. Zurita, G., Nussbaum, M.: Computer supported collaborative learning using wirelessly interconnected handheld computers. Comput. Educ. **42**(3), 289–314 (2004)
15. Brooke, J.: SUS-A quick and dirty usability scale. Usabil. Eval. Ind. **189**(194), 4–7 (1996)
16. Nielsen, J.: Usability Engineering. Morgan Kaufmann, Burlington (1994)

17. Edelson, D.C., Gordin, D.N., Pea, R.D.: Addressing the challenges of inquiry-based learning through technology and curriculum design. J. Learn. Sci. **8**(3–4), 391–450 (1999)
18. Kontra, C., Goldin-Meadow, S., Beilock, S.L.: Embodied learning across the life span. Top. Cogn. Sci. **4**(4), 731–739 (2012)
19. Hebles, M., Yániz-Álvarez-de-Eulate, C., Alonso-Dos-Santos, M.: Teamwork Competency Scale (TCS) from the individual perspective in university students. J. Technol. Sci. Educ. **12**(2), 510–528 (2022)

Generative AI Chatbot in PyramidApp: Students' Behaviors and Design Principles

Aldric Gutiérrez-Ferré(✉) , Davinia Hernández-Leo ,
and J. Roberto Sánchez-Reina

TIDE, ICT Department, Universitat Pompeu Fabra, Barcelona, Spain
aldric.gutierrez01@estudiant.upf.edu

Abstract. Generative Artificial Intelligence (GenAI) offers new opportunities to implement useful features within Computer Supported Collaborative Learning (CSCL) environments. Despite these growing prospects, there is still limited research concerning the application of GenAI in learning environments. This work in progress aims to evaluate the mediation of a masked GenAI chatbot in the setting of the CSCL web application PyramidApp. A quasi-experimental within-subjects study was designed to assess the effect of GenAI chatbot intervention within the environment of PyramidApp. In the setting of 9 online activities, we evaluated the effect of the GenAI chatbot activity in 105 conversational chat rooms. The findings revealed that the GenAI chatbot provides useful feedback as students rate the chatbot's answers higher than their peers' answers ($M_{Chatbot} = 4.11$, $M_{Students} = 3.91$). The presence of the chatbot has an effect on group communication with the length of messages increased in chat rooms where the chatbot was present. Moreover, chatbot behavior to rate the students' answers was correlated with the students' behavior. The present study offers valuable insights into the optimal strategies for integrating a GenAI Large Language Model into educational tools and computer supported learning.

Keywords: Computer-Supported Collaborative Learning · Collaborative Learning Flow Pattern · ChatGPT · Human-AI Collaboration · PyramidApp

1 Introduction

Generative Artificial Intelligence (GenAI) has illuminated the revolution in digital communication. Leveraged by advanced machine learning models, GenAI has enabled unprecedented levels of creativity and innovation in the realms of content creation, conversation, and collaboration online [1]. The study of GenAI in the educational setting is still in development, with much potential for exploration in the context of education and collaborative learning [2, 3].

The fact that the novel approaches in education coupled with an increasing demand for personalized and interactive learning experiences, makes the usage of GenAI especially attractive in online collaborative scenarios [4, 5]. Nevertheless, despite the promising potential of GenAI in education, there remains a significant gap in understanding how to effectively integrate its capabilities to optimize learning outcomes and engagement, particularly in collaborative learning applications.

The present preliminary study aims to explore how a GenAI chatbot can influence the quality and dynamics of student interactions in collaborative settings. Specifically, the study targets to evaluate the mediation of a masked GenAI chatbot in the setting of the web application PyramidApp. By employing the "Wizard of Oz" approach [6] – manually interfacing a simulated AI participant between PyramidApp and ChatGPT, the study identifies opportunities and benefits of integrating a GenAI Large Language Model, addressing the specific research questions: RQ1. How effectively does the GenAI chatbot provide feedback to students? RQ2. Does the GenAI chatbot provide high-quality contributions that facilitate collaborative knowledge building? RQ3. How does the GenAI chatbot modulate students' behaviors in a real-time chat environment?

2 Methodology

We designed a quasi-experimental within-subject study in the setting of two different Engineering courses. The quasi-experimental setting involved 9 collaborative online activities (*Tasks*) supported with the PyramidApp tool. Each task introduced a case study to provide analysis of Computing Engineering problems (e.g. Coding, Non-functional requirements, Ethical code principles). As part of the study design, multiple entities interacted during the execution of the online activities: the researcher, who orchestrated and conducted the online activity; the research assistant who interfaced the AI chatbot between the PyramidApp tool and ChatGPT; and the participant students (N = 291) who completed the activities.

2.1 Materials

PyramidApp is a Computer Supported Collaborative Learning (CSCL) web application created to foster collaborative discussion and debate. As described by its developers, this tool helps to orchestrate and mediate pedagogic activities, following a refined Snowball Learning Flow Pattern, allowing users to interact dialogically to enhance their knowledge building while guiding them through the different stages of the activity [7]. PyramidApp comprises two components: an authoring tool (setup) for teachers to design pyramid activities and a student's interface for users to participate in online discussions. Through the users' interface, participants can join and complete the activity following different steps or phases (see Table 1).

As part of the experimental design, we introduced a simulated GenAI chatbot, assisted by ChatGPT, in the PyramidApp interactive phases (*Submission, Rating,* and *Improvement*). Since the current version of the tool lacks integration with ChatGPT, the mediation of the chatbot was done manually. Hence, we employed a "Wizard of Oz" approach [6] where the researchers would join the activity and go through the same steps as any student – but making use of ChatGPT through its web interface to guide their actions. Table 2 describes the phases where the masked chatbot interacted.

Table 1. PyramidApp activity phases.

#	Phase name and description
0	**Students Join the Activity.** Students join the activity, through a URL
1	**Individual Submission.** Students are asked to formulate an individual answer for an activity/problem statement
2	**Rating.** Participants read and rate the submissions of their upcoming group members
3	**Improvement.** Participants are grouped into virtual "chat rooms", where the previously rated submissions are displayed – sorted by their average rating (which is also shown). As part of this phase, group members engage in a real-time chat, and collaborate on an improved "group answer" through a collaborative text editor
4	**Approval.** Group members vote on whether their new "group submission" is an improvement over the previous individual answers
5	**Debriefing.** At the end of the activity, the collaborative answers are displayed

Table 2. Chatbot intervention in PyramidApp.

#	PyramidApp phases where chatbot interacted
1	**Individual Submission.** An individual submission was AI-generated based on a tailored prompt that included the activity task statement and additional information for the task
2	**Rating.** A separate rating was generated for each of the student's submissions
3	**Improvement.** Several comments for the live chat were AI-generated. The initial comment was meant as feedback on the rated answers. Follow-up comments were generated with the context of the live chat log and, if necessary, the work-in-progress group-submission

2.2 Procedure

As part of the study design, the PyramidApp activities were conducted in the setting of ordinary class sessions. The teacher proposed the activities either as a warm-up reflection or problem-solving analysis. The students accessed the activity through their own laptops and provided identification to join the activity. To complete this step, both students and ChatGPT used alphanumeric pseudonyms to anonymize their names and the presence of the chatbot. As a next step, students provided an individual answer to the task. After the answer submission, the PyramidApp system provided a list of answers and randomly allocated students in small chat rooms (4–6 people). Within the chat rooms, the members had to collaborate to improve the individual answers by arriving at a new consensus solution. During these phases, the simulated GenAI chatbot completed the submission, rated its peer's answers, and joined the chat room discussions.

Masked Chatbot Intervention: A list of prompts was manually prepared to guide the chatbot interactions through the PyramidApp phases. At first, this required copying and pasting text from a template onto ChatGPT's web interface, filling the gaps of the template with student-generated content, sending this as a prompt, getting an output, and using the obtained output for the desired action. As the practice was improved, we created customized GPTs which eased this process. Over the course of the activities, we identified unwanted behaviors of ChatGPT. To this end, it was rarely necessary to manually intervene (e.g. by re-formatting the generated outputs as to emulate a well-behaved GenAI chatbot implementation). Instead, we noted these misbehaviors, which led to iterative improvements of the prompts and our procedure (e.g. dividing the otherwise lengthy live chat contributions of ChatGPT into several smaller bits, like a student would).

3 Measurement

The present study aimed to evaluate the following variables: 1) *Rating Performance.* This variable observed the performance of the AI chatbot in evaluating the students' initial submissions and, likewise, the students' evaluation of the AI-generated answers within the PyramidApp Task. 2) *Students' Chat Behavior.* Similar to prior research within PyramidApp's environment [8, 9], we observed students' interactions in the chat rooms to analyze their contributions and register their interventions by quantitatively measuring their messages and message extensions. The measurement was conducted at three different levels: single message, room member, and chat room. This criterion was defined in order to compare changes in the students' behavior by the presence or absence of the AI chatbot.

3.1 Data Collection and Analysis

The data generated in the PyramidApp activities was collected in data logs and extracted for its analysis. To conduct the analysis, the data was cleaned and coded. A total of 284 individual submissions conformed the rating analysis while the chat room activity was observed in 105 chat rooms. For the analysis of initial submissions, we only considered students that were in groups with the chatbot (i.e. students that for each room rated the same set of answers) (N = 27). A first level of analysis included descriptive statistics and data visualization to check data distribution and normality. A second level of analysis conducted inferential statistics, including hypothesis testing and regression analysis, to examine relationships between variables and assess the significance of findings.

4 Results

4.1 Chatbot Usefulness to Provide Feedback

Average ratings given by the chatbot were consistently lower than the ratings given by students for the same responses ($M_{Chatbot} = 3.48$, $SD = 1.02$; $M_{Students} = 4.22$, $SD = 0.97$, $p < 0.001$). Nevertheless, the Slope T-test revealed that the chatbot's ratings were positively correlated with the students', giving student-like feedback in the evaluation of submissions ($p = 0.025$, Fig. 1).

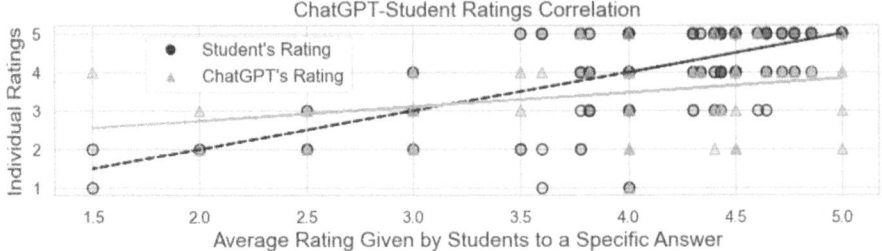

Fig. 1. Scatter plot of how the chatbot rated answers, compared to how students rated the same answers. Answers are sorted increasingly by their average rating as given by students.

4.2 Chatbot Contribution to Quality in Contributions

Chatbot answers reported higher mean ratings in comparison to students' answers ($M_{Chatbot} = 4.11$; $M_{Students} = 3.91$). However, no significant statistical differences were found ($p = 0.330$), Table 3 displays the results for the mean ratings given to chatbot answers.

Table 3. Received ratings for initial submission.

Individual submission ratees	Mean ± SD (N)	P-value
Students (Excluding chatbot ratings)	3.91 ± 1.06 (66)	1.000
Chatbot	4.11 ± 0.84 (37)	0.330

4.3 Chatbot Effects in Chat Room Behavior

By analyzing the produced messages in chat rooms and their extension (message length) (Table 4), the findings revealed that students in rooms with chatbots were more likely to

Table 4. First-level chat room statistics.

	Non-assisted chat rooms (NA-Ch)	Assisted chat rooms (Ch-A)	
Metric	Mean ± SD (N)	Mean ± SD (N)	P-value
Words per Message	3.39 ± 2.60 (1253)	3.82 ± 2.70 (141)	0.057
Messages/Member per Room	5.32 ± 3.21 (60)	3.91 ± 2.82 (13)	0.147
Words/Member per Room	21.75 ± 14.27 (56)	18.62 ± 13.53 (13)	0.474
Short (1–2 words long) Message count per Room Member	2.53 ± 2.03 (209)	1.41 ± 1.56 (32)	0.003
Message count per Room Member	5.83 ± 4.07 (212)	3.90 ± 2.68 (31)	0.011
Message length per Room Member	3.78 ± 1.92 (202)	4.58 ± 2.17 (33)	0.031
Word count per Room Member	23.30 ± 19.59 (205)	16.43 ± 12.83 (30)	0.064

write short messages at most once ($M_{NA-Ch} = 2.53$ vs $M_{Ch-A} = 1.41$, $p = 0.003$). The presence of short messages (i.e. 1–2 word long) was reduced from 46% in NA-Ch to 36% in Ch-A and short message counts were reduced (Fig. 2).

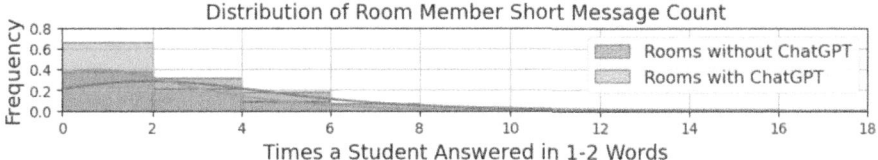

Fig. 2. Distribution of short (i.e. 1–2 word long) message count. In blue, students from rooms without a GenAI chatbot member. In orange, students from rooms with a chatbot member. (Color figure online)

5 Discussion

The present study aimed to evaluate the mediation of a masked GenAI chatbot in the setting of the CSCL web application PyramidApp. Concerning our first research question, our findings revealed that a GenAI chatbot might potentially provide useful feedback to students. As observed in the data analysis, despite the chatbot being likely to rate student answers lower than the students did, the feedback from both aligned in the same direction. Thus, it can be inferred that the chatbot feedback reinforces the students' review of answers. Contrary to similar research [10, 11], the findings suggest that the feedback mechanisms in PyramidApp, do not change significantly with the inclusion of GenAI, maintaining or even reinforcing the established positive aspects of peer reviewing as currently implemented in the web application.

Regarding the second research question, data analysis showed that the GenAI chatbot was able to provide high-quality contributions, facilitating collaborative knowledge building. As observed in the evaluation of initial submissions, chatbot answers received higher ratings compared to those of students; in line with similar research [10, 11], the chatbot mediation was useful either to clarify or refine participants' ideas and increase the clarity and extension of their contributions. Interestingly, one potential drawback is that knowledge building is not necessarily connected to students' learning gains as some students might simply copy chatbot answers to elaborate discussion and "group submission".

Concerning the third research question, the analysis of the GenAI chatbot's ability to modulate students' behaviors, our findings reported that the presence of the chatbot had an effect on how students behaved in the online activity, affecting aspects such as the production of messages and their length. Compared to groups without chatbot intervention, members in GenAI assisted chat rooms wrote longer messages and messages seemed to be of higher quality. In spite of this evidence, the total word count was negatively affected, as less messages were generated. This reduction in message count was especially significant for short messages. However, it is important to consider that quantitatively measuring message extension is not the most reliable metric and other methods could be implemented for Spam detection [12].

Elements of Design for Future Integration in PyramidApp. The presented results inform of ways of effectively implementing a GenAI chatbot in the setting of PyramidApp. The following elements of design are therefore proposed:

Elements for the Individual Submission Phase. The implementation of the GenAI chatbot might feature the generation of high-quality individual submissions to provide key concepts and informational context.

Elements for the Rating Phase. The featured GenAI should give ratings to student submissions to give feedback and guidance. Moreover, the GenAI chatbot could be used to improve decision-making when evaluating tied and/or biased answers.

Elements for the Improvement Phase. The integration of a GenAI chatbot should improve elements of online interaction. For example, the presence of a well-behaved chatbot might reduce spam, improving comprehension and therefore the quality of discussion – contributing to Group Regulation [12]. The GenAI chatbot could also allow for different modes of operation, playing interacting roles in the group discussion [3] to interrogate, challenge, or give input to students. Likewise, the integration of a GenAI chatbot could be beneficial to provide a "debriefing" and additional feedback [13].

6 Conclusions

GenAI offers new opportunities to implement useful features to current and future CSCL applications such as PyramidApp. As observed in the present study, the introduction of an assistant chatbot in the CSCL environment might provide students with useful information and feedback to enhance their contribution and knowledge building, and therefore impact aspects such as online group behavior. The present work has some important limitations. For example, the sample of collected data conditions the generalization of results. Moreover, qualitative research could be implemented to analyze chatbot and students' behaviors and provide contextual data. Future work should explore whether student ratings for initial submissions differ when they are made aware that the answers are AI-generated and, if so, how this affects knowledge building. Along these lines, an evaluation of the quality of chatbot answers is warranted, as well as an assessment of the correctness of the acquired knowledge that is incorporated into group submissions.

Acknowledgments. This work was partially funded by the National Research Agency of the Spanish Ministry (PID2020-112584RB-C33, CEX2021–001195-M) and the Department of Research and Universities of the Government of Catalonia (SGR 00930). The work of D. Hernández-Leo (Serra Hunter) was supported by ICREA under the ICREA Academia program.

Disclosure of Interests. The authors have no competing interests to declare that are relevant to the content of this article.

References

1. Kanbach, D.K., Heiduk, L., Blueher, G., Schreiter, M., Lahmann, A.: The GenAI is out of the bottle: generative artificial intelligence from a business model innovation perspective. Rev. Manag. Sci. **18**(4), 1189–1220 (2024). https://doi.org/10.1007/s11846-023-00696-z
2. Borah, A.R., Nischith, T.N., Gupta, S.: Improved learning based on GenAI. In: 2024 2nd International Conference on Intelligent Data Communication Technologies and Internet of Things (IDCIoT), pp. 1527–1532. IEEE (2024). https://doi.org/10.1109/IDCIoT59759.2024.10467943
3. Sharples, M.: Towards social generative AI for education: theory, practices and ethics. Learn. Res. Pract. **9**(2), 159–167 (2023). https://doi.org/10.1080/23735082.2023.2261131
4. Karpouzis, K., Pantazatos, D., Taouki, J., Meli, K.:. Tailoring education with GenAI: a new horizon in lesson planning. arXiv preprint arXiv:2403.12071 (2024). https://doi.org/10.48550/arXiv.2403.12071
5. Ramadevi, J., Sushama, C., Balaji, K., Talasila, V., Sindhwani, N.: AI enabled value-oriented collaborative learning: centre for innovative education. J. High Technol. Manag. Res. **34**(2), 100478 (2023). https://doi.org/10.1177/00472395241231815
6. Bradley, J., Benyon, D., Mival, O., Webb, N.: Wizard of Oz experiments and companion dialogues. In: Proceedings of HCI 2010, BCS Learning & Development (2010. https://doi.org/10.5555/2146303.2146321
7. Manathunga, K., Hernández-Leo, D.: PyramidApp: scalable method enabling collaboration in the classroom. In: Verbert, K., Sharples, M., Klobučar, T. (eds.) Adaptive and Adaptable Learning, pp. 422–427. Springer, Cham (2016). https://doi.org/10.1007/978-3-319-45153-4_37
8. Theophilou, E., Sanchez-Reina, R., Hernandez-Leo, D., Odakura, V., Amarasinghe, I., Lobo-Quintero, R.: The effect of a group awareness tool in synchronous online discussions: studying participation, quality and balance. Behav. Inf. Technol. **43**(6), 1149–1163 (2024). https://doi.org/10.1080/0144929X.2023.2200543
9. Amarasinghe, I., Hernández-Leo, D., Emily Theophilou, J., Reina, R.S., Quintero, R.A.L.: Learning gains in pyramid computer-supported collaboration scripts: factors and implications for design. In: Hernández-Leo, D., Hishiyama, R., Zurita, G., Weyers, B., Nolte, A., Ogata, H. (eds.) Collaboration Technologies and Social Computing: 27th International Conference, CollabTech 2021, Virtual Event, August 31 – September 3, 2021, Proceedings, pp. 35–50. Springer, Cham (2021). https://doi.org/10.1007/978-3-030-85071-5_3
10. Kyul Kim, H., Nayak, S., Roknaldin, A., Zhang, X., Twyman, M., Lu, S.: Exploring the impact of ChatGPT on student interactions in computer-supported collaborative learning. arXiv e-prints, arXiv-2403 (2024). https://doi.org/10.48550/arXiv.2403.07082
11. Cress, U., Kimmerle, J.: Co-constructing knowledge with generative AI tools: reflections from a CSCL perspective. Int. J. Comput.-Support. Collab. Learn. **18**(4), 607–614 (2023). https://doi.org/10.1007/s11412-023-09409-w
12. Velamazán, M., Santos, P., Hernández-Leo, D., Vicent, L.: User anonymity versus identification in computer-supported collaborative learning: Comparing learners' preferences and behaviors. Comput. Educ. **203**, 104848 (2023). https://doi.org/10.1016/j.compedu.2023.104848

13. Odakura, V., Amarasinghe, I., Hernández-Leo, D., Sánchez-Reina, R., Theophilou, E., Lobo-Quintero, R.: Effects of debriefing in computer-supported collaborative learning pyramid scripts with open-ended task. In: Wong, L.-H., Hayashi, Y., Collazos, C.A., Alvarez, C., Zurita, G., Baloian, N. (eds.) Collaboration Technologies and Social Computing: 28th International Conference, CollabTech 2022, Santiago, Chile, November 8–11, 2022, Proceedings, pp. 23–37. Springer, Cham (2022). https://doi.org/10.1007/978-3-031-20218-6_2

Generative AI Collaboration in the Orchestration of Supervised Classroom Problem Solving

Héctor Florido(✉) and Davinia Hernández-Leo(✉)

Universitat Pompeu Fabra, Barcelona, Spain
hector.florido@estudiant.upf.edu, davinia.hernandez-leo@upf.edu

Abstract. Generative AI has become an all-present tool for high school, vocational, and higher education students. Managing the potential of this AI-driven tool is equally important for teachers, as it facilitates ensuring students use it appropriately. This study centers on gathering data from students' perspectives and their interactions with a web-based problem-solving classroom orchestration tool augmented with generative AI capabilities. Results show that students see potential in the use of GenAI for various classroom scenarios. They have a clear understanding of how their peers also use these tools and how it affects their learning process, both positively and negatively. The findings also indicate that students' engagement with AI chatbots integrated into a devoted tool for classroom orchestration enhances their active participation and provides immediate responses to their doubts, in collaboration with teachers who oversee and complement student support during classroom sessions. Additionally, the results highlight the significance of crafting well-formulated prompts to elicit clear and precise responses. Overall, students have positively recognized the utility of the tool for accessing supplementary examples and explanations, which serve as valuable additions to teacher-led orchestration compensating the additional types of teacher supervision needs (e.g. prompts).

Keywords: Computer-supported collaborative learning · human tutoring · ambient user interface · classroom orchestration · problem solving · artificial intelligence

1 Introduction

Over the past years, advancements in the field of artificial intelligence (AI) have significantly transformed various aspects of our lives, from the way we communicate to how we interact with information and knowledge. One area that has been profoundly influenced by these innovations is the education sector. The convergence of AI, and especially recently Generative AI (GenAI), and education has given rise to a wide spectrum of diverse perspectives, challenges, and opportunities [1].

Learning, teaching, assessment, and administration, the four educational domains [2] have been affected by AI technologies and chatbots, robots and automated assessment in education are clear examples of the impact. These AI-driven technologies have revolutionized traditional approaches within education, offering personalized learning experiences, augmenting teaching methodologies, streamlining assessment processes, and optimizing administrative tasks [3]. Despite its advantages, AI-driven technology cannot entirely replace the pedagogical expertise of teachers, as it lacks the ability to discern the most effective teaching methods for individual students. Ethical concerns, particularly regarding privacy and data collection, pose risks associated with AI implementation in education [4].

Within the field of educational technologies, this paper focuses on orchestration tools, it refers to the management of interactive classrooms in real-time, typically involving collaborative efforts across various social dynamics [5–7]. When working with orchestration tools, soliciting feedback and insights from students regarding their comfort level, perceptions, and more specifically for this paper, their expectations regarding AI technologies, will help us understand their needs in the classroom and the extent to which they engage with these technologies. In this context GenAI, capable of producing content in response to specific commands based on patterns extracted from previous inputs, offers a potential for roles where conversational agents might act as social entities [9] assisting classroom orchestration.

In collaborative digital environments, knowledge creation happens as participants use different tools for communication. These technologies create a transitional space where participants acquire new knowledge and change their identity in the community [8]. Designing new AI-driven collaborative technologies for education involves creating GenAI that respects human rights, values teacher expertise, and supports student diversity. This requires collaboration between AI experts and educators to develop models for collaborative learning [9].

The research questions explored in the paper are: RQ1) Can students derive benefits from GenAI chatbots during classroom sessions? RQ2) Can chatbots play the role of GenAI collaborators, complementing the role of the teacher assisting students, when integrated in classroom orchestration tools for supervised problem solving? RQ3) How effectively can AI-driven tools aid in problem-solving during classroom sessions depending on the prompt used?

To address these research questions, this paper presents a study centered on gathering data from student interactions with a web-based problem-solving classroom orchestration tool augmented with generative AI capabilities. The context for the study is vocational training students' classrooms that usually focus on practice-based problem solving and demand high levels of teacher's attention to address students' technical doubts. These settings are particularly challenging for the teacher to orchestrate due to the large number of students, the practical nature and the complexity of the doubts [10, 11]. The study is structured into distinct phases for data collection: initially, the study group was surveyed to understand their daily usage of AI chatbots in the classroom. Subsequently, classroom sessions were conducted where students interacted with a classroom orchestration AI-driven tool featuring a generative AI chatbot for AI-teacher co-supervised problem solving, and their interactions were recorded. Finally, the recorded interactions were examined from the students' perspective to ascertain the accuracy of doubts sent to the AI-driven tool, the clarity of responses provided, and the significance of well-constructed prompts when engaging with generative AI.

2 Methodology

2.1 Settings and Participants

48 participants involved in the study are aged 18 or older, with none exceeding 30 years old. They are exclusively students enrolled in vocational training programs, specializing in computer science studies.

Every study group participated in one theory session and one practice session in order to collect the necessary data. In both sessions, students were required to use the web-based tool to log their doubts instead of raising their hands. The topic chosen for the sessions was related to databases with an initial explanation of stored procedures provided by the teachers. After the explanation, a range of problems were proposed such as creating stored procedures from scratch and modifying existing ones to incorporate specific functionalities.

Upon receiving a response from the AI chatbot, students were given the option to either present the question to their teachers for more help or withdraw from the queue if the AI chatbot adequately answered their doubts.

Given that all selected study groups were already familiar with utilizing the web-based tool for classroom problem-solving, there was no necessity to allocate session time for explaining its functionality. Instead, the focus remained only on introducing and implementing the new enhancements made for the experimental sessions. These enhancements, which are integrated into the existing tool without requiring any explicit explanation, were designed to operate behind the scenes, ensuring a smooth transition and minimal disruption to the students' workflow.

2.2 Classroom Orchestration Tool

This study used a web-based tool for enhanced supervised collaborative problem Solving [8] that reimplements and extends the "Lanterns" approach by Alavi & Dillenbourg [9]. The web-based tool registers all requests from the students for teacher's assistance when having a doubt during practice sessions focused on problem solving.

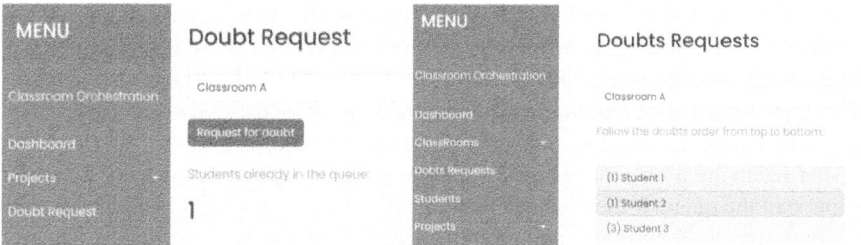

Fig. 1. Web-based Lanterns Orchestration tool for problem Solving. Left: screen when asking for teachers' help. Right: screen for teachers showing the queue.

After students apply for their request (**Fig. 1 - Left**), they are queued and the teachers of the session can check the order (**Fig. 1 - Right**). The web-based tool helps the teachers organize their time in their classroom orchestration, especially when involving attention to student's questions and there is a wish to optimize (reduce) the waiting time of the students [11] and follow a suitable order when addressing students' doubts. The development consists in adding an automatic request to an AI chatbot with the concrete doubt and specifying the context needed for every subject. In this way, students' doubts are reached by both the teacher and an AI agent ready to generate an answer and collaborate with the teacher in providing more immediate answers to the students.

After developing the needed functionalities for the web-based tool, students can request for a doubt by explaining it. Due to the tool adding the subject context, the student doesn't need to specify additional information when requesting for a doubt than the doubt itself.

Fig. 2. Web-based Lanterns Orchestration tool for problem Solving with AI-driven technology behind. Left: Changes applied to the students' side. Right: Response from AI chatbot received and shown to the student.

The web-based tool stills works as a problem solving web-based tool for students where teachers in the session can check and attend to all the doubts students have in a theory or practice session. **Figure 2 - left** shows the modifications applied to the tool with a text area where a description must be specified with at least 20 characters when applying for a doubt.

Teachers don't need to do anything additional than check the list of students that requested for help as seen previously in **Fig. 1 - right**. Behind the students request, a prompt is sent to an AI chatbot with the concrete doubt of the students and an answer is returned to the student. The responses are prepared to use different formats such as formatted text, programming code or structured lists or tables, because of the diversity of the subjects that can be taught in vocational training where the study is focused. Those responses are registered by the tool, so teachers can revise it.

After receiving a response (**Fig. 2 - right**), students are presented with the option to either exit the queue if they believe that the AI's response adequately addresses their query or to remain in the queue and await the teacher's attention for further explanation and resolution, following the usual procedure facilitated by the web tool..

The modified web-based tool was consistently utilized throughout all sessions, including both theory and practice sessions. Comprehensive data logging was implemented, storing all relevant information in a database for subsequent analysis once the sessions concluded across all study groups.

2.3 Data Collection Instruments and Analysis

The research involves surveying student participants about their perceptions and usage of AI tools in the classroom, both personally and within their peers. In a pre-questionnaire, they were asked about the benefits and drawbacks of AI tool integration, their opinions on incorporating AI education into the curriculum, and their confidence in utilizing pre-trained AI tools for problem-solving across theoretical, practical, and exam sessions. Additionally, the study explores students' ideas for integrating AI-driven tools into the classroom environment to enhance learning experiences and facilitate various aspects of classroom activities.

During the sessions, data was meticulously recorded and stored in a database using the classroom orchestration AI-driven tool. Each interaction was logged with timestamps indicating when students queued their queries, along with a brief description containing a minimum of 20 characters. Additionally, details such as the AI chatbot's response, the prompt used to query the AI chatbot, and whether students marked their query as resolved through the AI or still required assistance from teachers were recorded for analysis.

The post-questionnaires were designed to assess the effectiveness of interactions between students and the AI chatbot, focusing on the formulation of queries, the relevance of prompts, and the clarity of responses. The aim of collecting this data from the participating students is to determine whether interactions with the AI chatbot was appropriately formulated, whether queries contained sufficient data for a response, and whether prompts generated by the tool were relevant to the subject matter being queried. This comprehensive analysis provided insights into the quality and appropriateness of interactions between students and the AI chatbot, helping to refine and improve the tool's performance in future iterations.

3 Findings

3.1 Understanding Needs

The pre-questionnaire results showed that over 70% of students reported using AI tools extensively, with a similar percentage believing their peers did too. Notably, a minority claimed to use them very frequently. Despite their usage, students generally viewed AI tools as supplementary aids rather than replacements for traditional learning methods, with almost all supporting their integration into the classroom sessions. Responses regarding the benefits and drawbacks of AI tools highlighted their speed, task facilitation, and quick responses, alongside concerns about dependency and potential hindrance to learning.

From the students point of view, both theory and practice sessions are suitable for integrating AI-driven technology tools. In theory sessions they see AI useful to focus on addressing and providing parallel explanations and reinforcing theoretical concepts with examples apart from the ones used in the classroom. The students needed a way to communicate with the AI and explain their doubt regarding the subject they are working on. Students found that AI-driven tools could help them on problem-solving and as a guidance for understanding the subject concepts.

Thus, students' answers to the pre-questionnaires illustrate that there emerges a notable opportunity for AI-driven technologies to enhance classroom support tools in problem-solving interactions (RQ1). Students indicated their potential to offer detailed explanations, examples, and clarifications, which can sometimes be challenging to obtain from teachers due to the sheer volume of student queries when encountering new concepts. The use of low-cost web based tool channeling this option is explored in the next section.

3.2 Use of the AI-Driven Web Based Tool

Percentage of the correct responses provided by the AI was gathered both from on-site interactions using the web-based tool and from post-questionnaires completed by students after the sessions. These post-questionnaires included a copy of random doubts and responses from other students during theory and practice sessions for them to assess whether these responses were accurate based on context and subject matter. They were also asked to evaluate the clarity of the questions and whether the AI chatbot's responses were helpful in addressing their specific queries (Table 1).

Table 1. Problems solved by the AI-driven tool with and without teacher's help.

Typology	On site students feedback	Post-questionnaire students feedback (to validate doubts were solved)
Doubts solved by the GenAI with no teacher's help	88,24% of the doubts solved	92% of the doubts solved
Doubts not solved by the GenAI so teachers help was required	11,76% of the doubts solved	8% of the doubts solved

The results show that the 88.24% of the queries directed to the AI were successfully resolved (as perceived during the class and later peer-revised in a post-questionnaire). On the "not solved by the AI" side, we included doubts that students couldn't resolve with the AI's response, often due to poorly formulated questions by the students reducing the AI's ability to provide an appropriate response. At this juncture, we assess **RQ2** of our study, concluding that a web-based tool leveraging AI technology, such as a chatbot, can effectively support students to a large but not complete extent in the classroom. The broad range of percentages indicates that students felt assisted by the AI, particularly because the tool provided context relevant to the subject matter. Still, teacher supervision and support is needed.

3.3 Relevance of the AI-Chatbot Prompts Used

The choice of prompt used when querying the AI chatbot proved crucial (Table 1), aligning with the correct context and contributing to accurate response assessment, as indicated by all student groups. They unanimously agreed that the prompt suggested to base their queries to the AI-driven tool facilitated appropriate responses. When asked about the potential benefits of utilizing well formed prompts when asking the AI chatbot, 94% of students expressed agreement that such the initial prompt could enhance the accuracy of responses. They believed even that a pre-trained AI would better contextualize responses and eliminate complex responses not covered in classroom sessions.

Finally, students were asked about their experiences with the AI-driven tool, focusing on the accuracy of the prompts used in every question made, with nearly all reporting that it encouraged them to ask questions and share doubts they might not have raised by raising their hands. They focused on the tool's accuracy in aligning with their knowledge and the promptness of responses as key factors, along with the freedom to ask multiple questions without disrupting or monopolizing teacher attention. After this data analysis and regarding the **RQ3** of the study, an AI-driven tool could be a good option to help students due that with an AI chatbot with a correct initial prompting is rising over the 90% of accurate responses.

4 Conclusions and Future Work

The integration of Generative AI into a classroom orchestration tool aims to reduce the duration students spend waiting for teacher assistance during problem-solving scenarios. The goal is not to eliminate students' access to teachers but rather to provide additional resources such as varied examples and reiterations of the subject matter being covered. Additionally, it aims to offer students a tool to pose questions without the need to raise their hands during ongoing explanations, thereby mitigating potential shyness or reluctance to ask questions in front of their peers. Combining a user-friendly web-based tool integrated into the classroom environment, with the capabilities of AI-driven tools like generative AI chatbots, has proven to be a highlight of the study. The feedback received from students has provided valuable insights into the importance of supplemental resources in the classroom, beyond traditional lectures and example explanations provided by teachers.

The significance of employing well-constructed prompts for AI chatbots is a key factor, as it directly impacts the success of problem-solving sessions in the classroom. Thoughtfully selecting prompts, which include explanations of the context and the study group, as well as introducing the problems students are working on, is crucial in developing an effective AI-driven tool. It's worth noting that initial prompts may be less accurate when introducing pre-trained AIs, as the underlying data is more generalized. However, refining and adapting prompts over time can enhance the accuracy and relevance of AI-driven interactions in the classroom.

Pre-trained AIs are advancing incrementally and hold significant potential for AI-driven tools, particularly in educational settings. By focusing exclusively on content familiar to teachers and understandable to students, pre-trained AIs can effectively address new scenarios. This approach contrasts with relying on internet data, which may be challenging for students to comprehend or contain deprecated information. Introducing a pre-trained AI into the classroom, equipped with teachers' theoretical knowledge and an extensive repository of problems and solutions that can be continually updated, could position an AI chatbot as a helpful tool for classroom orchestration. Yet, progressing towards that direction comes with challenges related to the economic and environmental costs associated with the technology as well as the need to conduct more extensive research reproducing similar studies in larger and discipline-varied contexts. This study shows that, when doing so, studies should follow teacher-AI collaboration and human-centered research processes.

Acknowledgements. This work was partially funded by the National Research Agency of the Spanish Ministry (PID2020-112584RB-C33, PID2023-146692OB-C33, CEX2021–001195-M) and the Department of Research and Universities of the Government of Catalonia (SGR 00930). The work of D. Hernández-Leo (Serra Hunter) was supported by ICREA under the ICREA Academia program.

Disclosure of Interests. The authors have no competing interests to declare that are relevant to the content of this article.

References

1. Chen, L., Chen, P., Lin, Z.: Artificial intelligence in education: a review. IEEE Access **8**, 75264–75278 (2020)
2. Chiu, T.K., Xia, Q., Zhou, X., Chai, C.S., Cheng, M.: Systematic literature review on opportunities, challenges, and future research recommendations of artificial intelligence in education. Comput. Educ. Artif. Intell. **4**, 100118 (2023)
3. Akgun, S., Greenhow, C.: Artificial intelligence in education: addressing ethical challenges in K-12 settings. AI Ethics **2**(3), 431–440 (2022)
4. Klimova, B., Pikhart, M., Kacetl, J.: Ethical issues of the use of AI-driven mobile apps for education. Front. Public Health **10**, 1118116 (2023)
5. Amarasinghe, I., Hernández-Leo, D., Ulrich Hoppe, H.: Deconstructing orchestration load: comparing teacher support through mirroring and guiding. Int. J. Comput.-Support. Collab. Learn. **16**(3), 307–338 (2021)
6. Schwendimann, B.A., Rodríguez-Triana, M.J., Vozniuk, A., et al.: Understanding learning at a glance: an overview of learning dashboard studies. In: Proceedings of the Sixth International Learning Analytics & Knowledge Conference (LAK'16), pp. 532–533. ACM, New York (2016)
7. Van Leeuwen, A., et al.: Orchestration tools for teachers in the context of individual and collaborative learning: what information do teachers need and what do they do with it?. International Society of the Learning Sciences, Inc. [ISLS] (2018)
8. Cuthell, J., et al.: Everyone is an Expert: rhizomatic learning in professional learning contexts. In: Khine, M.S. (ed.) Rhizome Metaphor: Legacy of Deleuze and Guattari in Education and Learning, pp. 25–52. Springer, Singapore (2022). https://doi.org/10.1007/978-981-19-9056-4_3
9. Sharples, M.: Towards social generative AI for education: theory, practices and ethics. Learn. Res. Pract. **9**(2), 159–167 (2023)
10. Florido, H., Hernandez-Leo, D.: Reimagining "The Lantern" as a Web-Based Tool for Enhanced Supervised Collaborative Problem Solving. International Society of the Learning Sciences, Inc. [ISLS] (2024)
11. Alavi, H.S., Dillenbourg, P.: An ambient awareness tool for supporting supervised collaborative problem solving. IEEE Trans. Learn. Technol. **5**(3), 264–274 (2012)

Development and Evaluation of Gamification-Based Addressing Promotion System for Teaching Assistants

Kanato Murobayashi[✉], Takahiro Yoshino, and Hironori Egi

Department of Informatics, Graduate School of Informatics and Engineering,
The University of Electro-Communications, Chofu, Japan
m2430133@gl.cc.uec.ac.jp

Abstract. This study developed a gamification-based address promotion system and analyzed the effects of the proposed system on teaching assistants (TAs). The goal of this study is to develop a system that promotes more TAs to perform active learning support activities like proactive TAs, and to analyze the impact of the system on TAs. The proposed system is based on the game balance concept, with the first stage aimed at enabling TAs to gain experience in proactively addressing students. In the second stage, the TAs are required to perform learning support activities more proactively. Prior to introducing the proposed system for comparison, we observed the behavior of conventional TAs in a first-year programming class of a science and engineering university. Subsequently, we introduced the proposed system and analyzed the system's effect on the TAs. The results demonstrated that all TAs recognized the need to proactively address the students and actively perform learning support activities.

Keywords: Teaching Assistants · Behavior Change · Gamification

1 Introduction

1.1 Gamification and Education

In this study, we developed a gamification-based addressing promotion system for teaching assistants (TAs) to promote active involvement in learning support activities, such as student support and rounds in the classroom. Gamification, which enhances user engagement and experience [1], involves applying game design elements in nongame contexts. This approach suggests that appropriately internalizing extrinsic motivation can facilitate the development of intrinsic motivation [2], which is expected to facilitate changes in both consciousness and behavior.

Gamification has been actively introduced in education and other learning contexts. Gamification in education offers two primary benefits. First, it enhances learner motivation. Game elements provide learners with a sense of achievement and progress, which promotes proactive engagement in the learning process. Second, gamification results in improved learning outcomes. By designing appropriate educational objectives within the games, the learners are guided toward achieving those outcomes [3].

1.2 Isolated Students

In many lectures, there are students who "suffer in silence," and such students are often hesitant to ask questions. This study refers to such students as isolated students, who either do not seek help independently or lack the ability to do so. For example, many students in programming exercise classes experience embarrassment due to their lack of understanding and are hesitant to ask instructors questions [4]. Thus, it is necessary for teachers and TAs to support these isolated students by addressing them proactively. In this study, "addressing" is defined as an attempt to solve problems through proactive interactions between the TAs and isolated students rather than the students raising their hands to ask questions.

However, inexperienced TAs may not be accustomed to addressing students proactively or may not recognize the need to do so. In contrast, some TAs who frequently move through classrooms and proactively interact with students who appear to have questions. In this study, such TAs are referred to as proactive TAs, and other TAs are referred to as novice TAs.

To offer more comprehensive support for isolated students, it is preferable for novice TAs to perform active learning support activities like a proactive TAs.

2 Related Works

Ueno et al. developed a system to display students who should be addressed proactively in programming exercise classes, taking into consideration the students' sense of isolation [5]. This system determines the priority for addressing students based on the results from a loneliness questionnaire administered at each lecture, as well as scores from a review test given at the start of the class. As a result of implementing this system in programming exercise classes, the frequency of addressing by TAs has increased, leading to a reduction in students' feelings of isolation. In that study, the system identified the students who should be addressed by the TAs, and the purpose was to reduce the sense of isolation among students. The current study investigates the effect of introducing gamification into an addressing promotion system on TAs.

3 The Proposed System

We developed the proposed addressing promotion system based on the framework defined by Armond et al. [6]. The proposed addressing promotion system implements five game elements, Game balance, Feedback, Unlock, Quest and

Ranking. Game balance refers to the balance between a game's difficulty and the rewards provided by the game. Feedback involves rewarding users for their actions and choices, as well as visualizing their progress. Unlocking means that restricted content is released when certain conditions are met. Quest refers to a specific goal or task to be accomplished by the user at a given time in a game environment. Ranking refers to a structured evaluation of the user's game performance based on their level and score.

3.1 Game Design

The proposed system was designed based on game balance. As mentioned previously, in the first stage, the TA gains experience in proactively addressing students, and in the second stage, the TA is required to perform learning support activities more proactively.

In the first stage, the system presents the students to be addressed in ascending order of addressing difficulty level. In this study, the degree of the students' desire to be addressed was obtained using a questionnaire, and the degree of class comprehension was identified by conducting and scoring a review test at the beginning of the class. The addressing difficulty level is determined by the students' desire to be addressed and their class comprehension, as shown in Table 1, where each level is expressed by the number of stars.

Table 1. Addressing difficulty level in the first stage

Desire to be addressed \ Comprehension	High	Medium	Low
High(green)	★	★★	★★★
Medium(yellow)	★★★ / ★	★★★ / ★★	★★★ / ★★★
Low(red)	★★★ / ★★★ / ★	★★★ / ★★★ / ★★	★★★ / ★★★ / ★★★

Students with a high degree of desire to be addressed were defined as those with a low addressing difficulty level because such students are considered to be more open to being addressed by the TAs. The proposed system displays the students to be addressed in order from the lowest addressing difficulty level to the highest. If the TA addresses the displayed students, the TA is rewarded with a score corresponding to the addressing difficulty level.

In the second stage, the proposed system does not display the students to be addressed, and the TAs can freely determine which students to address. If the TA chooses to address independently, the TA is rewarded with a score corresponding to the addressing importance level. The addressing importance level was determined based on the students' class comprehension and their desire to be addressed, as shown in Table 2, where each level is expressed by the number of stars.

Table 2. Addressing importance level in the second stage

Comprehension \ Desire to be adressed	High	Medium	Low
High(green)	★	★★	★★★
Medium(yellow)	★★★ ★	★★★ ★★	★★★ ★★★
Low(red)	★★★ ★★★ ★	★★★ ★★★ ★★	★★★ ★★★ ★★★

Students with low desire to be addressed and limited class comprehension are deemed susceptible to be isolated students. Hence, the proposed system was devised to prioritize these students with the highest level of addressing importance. In the second stage, the TAs are required to act more proactively. In other words, they must act independently rather that rely on the recommendations provided by the system. Thus, the rewards in the second stage are larger than those in the first stage.

3.2 System Functions

To activate the TAs' learning support activities, we developed a gamification-based address promotion system. Figure 1 shows the content displayed on the proposed system's screen. The system's display consists of four elements:

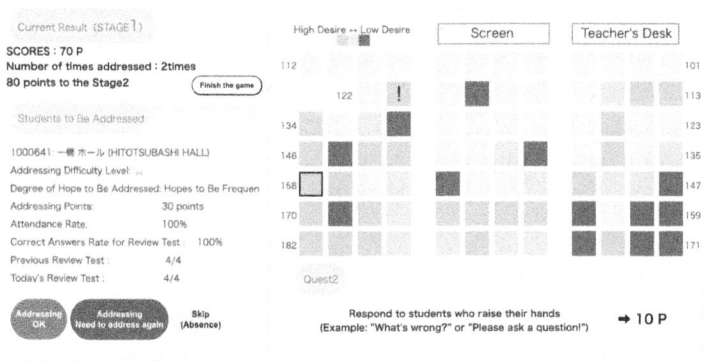

Fig. 1. System presentation details

progress, students to be addressed and their information, seating chart, and quests.

The progress section shows the point value, the number of people addressed, and the score required to advance to the second stage. If the user's score exceeds a certain point value, a button is displayed to advance to the second stage.

The section containing information about the student to be addressed identifies them and presents relevant information, e.g., the student's attendance rate and their score on the review test. When addressing students, the blue OK button, red Re-address button, or yellow Skip button is tapped (Fig. 1).

The seating chart is colored based on the addressing difficulty level and the addressing importance level. Here, the colors are assigned according to the degree of desire to be addressed (in the first stage) and the degree of class comprehension (in the second stage), as shown in Table 1 and Table 2, respectively. The seats of students to be addressed are identified by blinking on the seating chart. In addition, the seats of students who have been addressed previously are identified by a black border (Fig. 1). When a student taps the "Re-address" button after being addressed by the TA, the student's seat is marked with an exclamation mark, as shown in Fig. 1. Tapping the seat of a student who has raised their hands allows the TA to view that student's information. Once the TA have responded to the raised hands, the TA can earn points by tapping either the "Complete" button or the "Respond again" button, simmilar to the addressing task. However, the point value is less than that for the addressing addressing.

The quest section displays goals, i.e., small steps in the game's progress. Note that a corresponding point value is awarded when a quest is completed.

4 Experiment

In a programming exercise class for first-year science and engineering university students (with two TAs per class), experiments were conducted six times across four classes. The class is divided into class time and exercise time due to its flipped classroom format. The experiment consisted of two TA Observation Phases, in which the TAs' activities were observed without the proposed system, and four System Introduction Phases, in which the TAs supported the learning activities using the proposed system.

In the TA Observation Phase, the evaluation criteria included the number of addresses, the ratio of active time, and questionnaire for addressing awarness. This evaluation aimed to determine whether each TA was a proactive TA before the introduction of the system. The TA's ratio of active time is an indicator of the extent to which the TA performed learning support activities during the exercise time. In this study, the ratio of active time(RAT) was calculated as follows.

$$\text{RAT} = \frac{\text{TA's round time} + \text{TA's time to support students}}{\text{Exercise time}} \times 100 \qquad (1)$$

Note that the RAT value can exceed 100% if the learning support activities were conducted outside of the exercise time. Here, a proactive TA is one who moved through the classroom frequently and addressed students with questions proactively. In other words, a TA is proactively TA if he is able to address students, has a RAT value close to 100%, and recognizes the need to address students.

In the System Introduction Phase, the effect of the system on the TAs were evaluated based on the number of addresses, the RAT value, the questionnaire results and interviews. The questionnaire consisted of 30 items rated on a five-point Likert scale, encompassing topics such as game elements, proposed system functions, and motivation for learning support activities, including student engagement. Subsequently, interviews were conducted to delve deeper into the rationales behind the questionnaire responses.

5 Results

The results for each TA in obtained during the TA Observation Phase and the System Introduction Phase are shown in Table 3. The questionnaire to address awareness was based on the following question: "Do you think it is necessary to address students proactively?" The responses were obtained using a five-point Likert scale (1: not applicable; 2: somewhat not applicable; 3: neutral; 4: somewhat applicable; and 5: applicable).

Table 3. Results of TA observation phase and system introduction phase

TA	Indicator	TA Observation		System Introduction	
		Average	Questionnaire	Average	Questionnaire
TA1	Number of addresses	2.50	4	6.25	5
	RAT	97.7%		113.1%	
TA2	Number of addresses	3.50	5	4.75	5
	RAT	86.8%		95.0%	
TA3	Number of addresses	0	3	6.00	5
	RAT	92.3%		99.8%	
TA4*	Number of addresses	1.00	3	1.00	5
	RAT	76.6%		88.8%	
TA5	Number of addresses	0	3	0	4
	RAT	32.5%		48.7%	
TA6	Number of addresses	0	4	4.25	5
	RAT	30.8%		31.7%	
TA7	Number of addresses	1.00	5	5.25	5
	RAT	107.4%		107.7%	
TA8	Number of addresses	1.00	5	2.75	5
	RAT	103.3%		101.8%	

* TA4 was absent for the second and fourth experiment

6 Discussion

6.1 TA Observation Phase

Based on the results, which included the number of addresses, the RAT value, and the questionnaire to address awareness during the TA Observation Phase, we evaluated whether each TA was a proactive TA or a novice TA prior to the System Introduction Phase. We found that TA1, TA2, TA7, and TA8 frequently moved through the classroom before the system was introduced, addressed the students, and recognized the need for proactive addressing. In contrast, TA3, TA4, TA5, and TA6 did not satisfy all the requirements for proactive TAs. Thus, the proactive TAs were identified as TA1, TA2, TA7, and TA8, and the novice TAs were identifyed TA3, TA4, TA5, and TA6.

6.2 System Introduction Phase

We also evaluated the effect of the proposed system by comparing the result shown in Tables 3. By comparing the questionnaire results, we found that most of the TAs (except TA5) answered 5, and TA5 answered 4. In other words, the system made all of the TAs aware of the need to address students proactively. Comparing the results of the number of addresses and the RAT values of the proactive TAs (i.e., TA1, TA2, TA7, and TA8), we found that both the number of addresses and the RAT values increased for TA1, TA2, and TA7, and the number of addresses increased for TA8. In other words, while using the system, the proactive TAs became more active in learning support activities. For the novice TAs (i.e., TA3, TA4, TA5, and TA6), we found that the number of addresses and/or the RAT increased. In other words, the system made novice TAs more active in their learning support activities. In particular, TA6 increased both the number of addresses and the RAT value, and the learning support activities of TA6 during the System Introduction Phase satisfied all three conditions of proactive TAs. Thus, the proposed system to motivated TA6 to engage in active learning support activities like a proactive TA.

Next, we discuss the reasons why the system made all TAs aware of the need to address the students, based on the interview results. TA3, TA4, TA5, and TA7 stated that, as they used the system, they became aware of the large number of students who did not comprehend the subject matter and were made aware of students who desired TA support without raising their hands. These findings suggest that the information displayed by the system promoted a change in consciousness in the four TAs. In addition, both TA6 and TA8 stated that they noticed an unexpectedly large number of students with questions when they actually addressed them, and TA8 pointed out codes that were difficult to read even if the students did not have questions. These findings suggest that TA6 and TA8 better recognized need to address the students as a result of using the proposed system.

Furthermore, we discusses the reasons for each TA's more active learning support activities based on the results of the interviews.

First, we discuss the proactive TAs, i.e., TA1, TA2, TA7, and TA8. TA1 and TA2 stated that he was interested in the game elements; however, he was not dependent on the game and performed learning support activities, independently. In addition, TA7 was more motivated to obtain a high point value than TA1 and TA2; however, TA7 also stated that he became bored when there was nothing new in the game. TA8 also stated that he had little interest in the game element to begin with, and that he originally targeted his learning support activities at students needing help. Despite being less reliant on the game aspect, these TAs expressed appreciation for the system's capacity to present information and identify students to be addressed. Here, the proactive TAs performed active learning support activities even before the system was introduced. Thus, these TAs are likely to have established their own guidelines for learning support activities. Based on the above discussion, the reason the proactive TAs became more active in their learning support activities can be attributed to the fact that the system created an environment for additional active learning support activities, and the TAs utilized the proposed system as an effective support for their own learning support activities.

Among the novice TAs, we discuss TA3 and TA6, whose efforts to address the students was promoted. Both TA3 and TA6 were interested in the game elements implemented in the proposed system, and they stated that they did not become bored with the game during this experiments. The interview results also indicate that the TAs were performing learning support activities according to the game elements, with the quests and the second stage as small steps. It is highly likely that novice TAs have not established personal guidelines for performing learning support activities compared to the more proactive TAs. Based on this discussion, we infer that these TAs became more proactive in carring out learning support activities because the game elements implemented in the proposed system became an effective guideline for learning support activities.

Among the novice TAs, we discuss TA4 and TA5, whose efforts in terms of addressing students was not promoted. For these TAs, only the RAT value increased. In the interview, TA4 stated that, when he attempted to address the students, he did not feel like addressing them because they clearly did not need to be addressed. TA5 indicated that he tried to address them, but was hesitant to suddenly start addressing them, which he had not done before. Based on this discussion, one reason why the number of addresses of these TAs did not increase and only the RAT value increased may be that the TAs actually attempted to start rounds to address the students according to the system but did not feel the need to address the students and/or were unable to address the students.

7 Conclusion

In This study, we developed a gamification-based address promotion system and analyzed the effect of the system on TAs. The experimental results demonstrated that all TAs recognized the need to proactively address students and actively perform learning support activities. However, we found that some TAs did not ehibit increased efforts to engage with students. Thus, in the future, we intend to enhance the promoted system in light of the interview findings and study the effects of introducing the system at the initial stages of the teaching process.

References

1. Deterding, S., Dixon, D., Khaled, R., Nacke, L.: From game design elements to gamefulness: Defining "gamification". In Proceedings of the 15th International Academic MindTrek conference: Envisioning Future Media Environments, pp. 9–15 (2011). https://doi.org/10.3390/App122111214
2. Rutledge, C., Walsh, C.M., Swinger, N., Auerbach, M., Castro, D., Dewan, M., Chang, T.P.: Gamification in action: Theoretical and practical considerations for medical educators. Acad. Med. **93**(7), 1014–1020 (2018). https://doi.org/10.1109/EDUCON.2017.7942927
3. Majuri, J., Koivisto, J., Hamari, J.: Gamification of education and learning: a review of empirical literature. In: Proceedings of the 2nd International GamiFIN Conference, GamiFIN 2018. CEUR-WS (2018)
4. Martínez-Treviño, Y.: InClass Assistant, enhancing student class participation. In: 2016 IEEE Frontiers in Education Conference (FIE), Erie, PA, USA, pp. 1–5 (2016) https://doi.org/10.1109/FIE.2016.7757493
5. Ueno, S., Yoshino, T., Egi, H.: Addressing promotion system based on student data to supportesk-to-desk instruction by teaching assistants, the 13th International Conference on Learning Analytics and Knowledge (LAK 2023) Companion Proceedings, pp. 162–164 (2023)
6. Toda, A.M., et al.: Analysing gamification elements in educational environments using an existing Gamification taxonomy. Smart Learning Environments **6**(1), 1–14 (2019)

Boosting Non-Native Speaker Engagement: Simplifying Text with Large Language Models

Mondheera Pituxcoosuvarn[✉] and Yohei Murakami

Faculty of Information Science and Engineering, Ritsumeikan University, Osaka, Japan
mond-p@fc.ritsumei.ac.jp

Abstract. Effective communication between native and non-native speakers is crucial for intercultural collaboration and successful teamwork. Non-native speakers often struggle to comprehend complex messages, which can lead to miscommunication or exclusion. We explored using Large Language Models (LLMs) to translate complex text into summarized and simplified versions to improve readability and accessibility. We tested this approach with non-native speakers in a controlled experiment, where participants were given both complex and simplified versions of the same text. Although the simplified text was rated as easier to read, there was no significant difference in comprehension accuracy compared to the original text. This suggests that simplification might lead to a loss of critical information, impacting overall comprehension. Our findings suggest that text simplification, while enhancing readability, must be balanced against the risk of reduced comprehension accuracy. This has implications for designing communication tools in diverse and multicultural environments, emphasizing the need for a careful approach to ensure effective communication without compromising essential information.

Keywords: Intercultural collaboration · Non-native communication · Text simplification

1 Introduction

Intercultural cooperation is essential in today's globalized world for international projects, academic research, and business success. Mixed-native and non-native teams face communication issues impacting output, innovation, and team dynamics. Effective communication is crucial for sharing ideas, solving problems, and achieving shared goals.

A major challenge is the comprehension gap when non-native speakers (NNSs) struggle with jargon, complex language, or culturally specific references [2]. This can lead to reduced participation, misunderstandings, and exclusion from important discussions, causing inefficiencies and lack of cohesion in teams.

Large Language Models (LLMs) are effective tools for text generation and processing [1]. They have shown significant potential in text simplification, content summarization, and language translation. LLMs can simplify complex texts, bridging the comprehension gap for NNSs.

We propose using LLMs to simplify complex texts into clear, concise language, enhancing comprehension and conversation among NNSs. This capability can greatly improve inclusivity and ensure all team members can contribute their ideas. Our study examined how LLM-based text simplification affects NNSs' comprehension and engagement in group settings. We conducted a pilot study to explore this strategy's efficacy and its potential to improve communication in diverse teams. By applying LLMs to bridge the comprehension gap, we aim to enhance intercultural collaboration and foster a more inclusive and effective work environment.

2 Related Work

Researchers have explored various methods to support NNS in communication. One study involved NS highlighting key words in conversations with NNS, which reduced NNS workload and improved communication quality, enhancing recall for both NS and NNS. However, this method was tested on participants in the top 10% of the TOEIC test, suggesting it may not suit lower proficiency individuals [7].

Another approach involved a browser extension to improve webpage readability for NNS by enlarging significant text and reducing less important content. This customization aids in reducing cognitive load and facilitates easier comprehension for NNS when reading online content [9].

Automatic Speech Recognition (ASR) systems have been explored as support tools for NNS, transcribing spoken words into text to improve comprehension in audio/video meetings. While real-time transcription significantly enhances understanding, ASR systems face challenges such as high error rates in large vocabulary continuous speech recognition (LVCSR), unclear articulation, varying speaking rates, accents, and background noise. Although manual transcription is more accurate, it is slower and more expensive [5,6].

Machine Translation (MT), particularly neural machine translation (NMT), offers real-time translation to facilitate cross-lingual communication. However, NMT accuracy decreases with longer, complex sentences. Strategies like shortening sentences to improve translation accuracy may hinder language proficiency for NNS by reducing practice opportunities [4].

Summarization has been useful for providing simplified content to NNS. The EUSUM system [8] generates easy-to-understand English summaries by accounting for reading ease, producing clearer summaries compared to other systems. However, this research did not examine the impact on overall communication. Summarization technology has been used to address comprehension issues in lengthy dialogues, aid collaborative writing, and enhance discussion efficiency, benefiting those with cognitive impairments and non-native readers [3].

These approaches offer a spectrum of strategies to support NNS in various communication scenarios, but each has limitations and must be considered based on context and individual proficiency levels.

3 Text Summarization and Simplification with ChatGPT

3.1 Experiment Design

We designed an experiment to assess comprehension among NNSs.

The experiment involved asking NNS participants to read a set of text paragraphs and then answer comprehension questions. To ensure a solid benchmark, we sourced text paragraphs and comprehension questions from the SAT practice test, a widely recognized standardized test in the United States. The SAT is known for its rigorous reading comprehension sections, designed for native English speakers and often used to assess high school students' readiness for college.

The study included 13 participants with diverse backgrounds in age (21 to 62 years, average 36.5), occupation (students, business owners, engineers, sales professionals, baristas, and programmers), and native languages (Thai, Cantonese, Japanese, Chinese, and Indonesian). This diversity provided a comprehensive view of language proficiency across different contexts. English proficiency was self-evaluated, with most participants identifying as intermediate, and others ranging from beginner to advanced. Some participants shared their English test scores, with TOEIC scores between 560 and 705, and TOEFL scores from 72 to 116.

3.2 Prompts

We conducted an experiment with the GPT-4 model. The parameters for the experiment were set with a Temperature of 1 and a Top P of 1.

For summarization, we used the following prompt to guide ChatGPT:

> "You are an assistant who helps English-as-a-second-language (ESL) speakers understand the message. Your task is to generate a summarized version of the input message for ESL speakers."

For simplification, we used a slightly different prompt for ChatGPT:

> "You are an assistant who helps English-as-a-second-language (ESL) speakers understand the message. Your task is to generate a simplified version of the input message for ESL speakers."

These prompts were followed by the original English text for ChatGPT to summarize. These prompts were intended to guide ChatGPT in creating a more accessible and comprehensible version of the test materials for the NNS participants.

3.3 Task

In this experiment, each participant was presented with three tasks, with each task containing a paragraph in one of three formats: original, summarized, or simplified. For each task, one of the following formatted paragraph was shown to each participant. Here are example of comprehension passages given to the participants.

Original In 2007, computer scientist Luis von Ahn was working on converting printed books into a digital format. He found that some words were distorted enough that digital scanners couldn't recognize them, but most humans could easily read them. Based on that finding, von Ahn invented a simple security test to keep automated "bots" out of websites. The first version of the reCAPTCHA test asked users to type one known word and one of the many words scanners couldn't recognize. Correct answers proved the users were humans and added data to the book-digitizing project.

Summarized by GPT-4 In 2007, Luis von Ahn, a computer scientist, was converting printed books into digital format. He noticed that scanners couldn't recognize some distorted words, but humans could. From this, von Ahn created a security test called reCAPTCHA to stop bots from using websites. The test involved typing a familiar word and a word that scanners couldn't recognize. Correct answers showed users were human and helped the book-digitizing project.

Simplified by GPT-4 In 2007, a man called Luis von Ahn was turning books into digital or computer versions. Some words were hard for machines to read, but humans could read them. So, von Ahn made a simple online check, named reCAPTCHA, to prevent bots from accessing websites. If people could write a simple word and a word hard for machines to understand correctly, it was proof they were humans, and it helped in making digital versions of books.

For question and answer choices, all the participants received the same version. An example is shown as follows:

What is the text mainly talking about?

A) von Ahn's creation of reCAPTCHA
B) Explaining how machines that scan work
C) Bringing attention to von Ahn's project of turning books into digital
D) Showing how famous reCAPTCHA is

The order of tasks was randomized to eliminate any pattern or bias, ensuring participants' responses were based on text format rather than sequence. Participants read paragraphs and answered comprehension questions, providing insights into their understanding of the texts.

After completing the tasks, participants rated the reading difficulty of each paragraph on a 5-point scale from "very easy" (0) to "very difficult" (5). This post-task rating allowed comparison of the accessibility of original, summarized, and simplified texts. Analyzing these ratings alongside comprehension responses aimed to reveal the relationship between text simplification and reading difficulty.

4 Experiment Result

4.1 Reading Difficulty

Figure 1(a) presents the average reading difficulty ratings from several participants. This figure compares the perceived difficulty of the original message, the summarized message, and the simplified message. Difficulty is rated on a scale from 0 (very easy) to 5 (very difficult).

Beginner-level participants rated the original message with a difficulty of 3.00, indicating a moderate challenge. The summarized message was found to be somewhat more challenging, with an average difficulty rating of 3.33. In contrast, the simplified message was easier for this group, with an average difficulty rating of 2.33.

Intermediate-level participants rated the original message with an average difficulty of 2.57, suggesting moderate comprehensibility. The summarized message was rated slightly more difficult at 3.14, indicating an increase in complexity for these participants. The simplified message was easier, with an average difficulty of 2.43, suggesting that this format is more accessible for intermediate learners.

Advanced-level participants rated both the original message and the summarized message with an average difficulty of 2.67, suggesting they found them equally comprehensible. However, the simplified message was easier, with an average difficulty of 1.67, indicating that advanced learners also benefit from a simplified format.

Overall, the results indicate that simplified messages tend to be easier to understand across all proficiency levels. Summarized messages, on average, are more challenging for beginners and intermediate learners, while advanced learners find them comparable to the original message. This emphasizes the need for careful text adaptation to match the comprehension abilities of different proficiency levels.

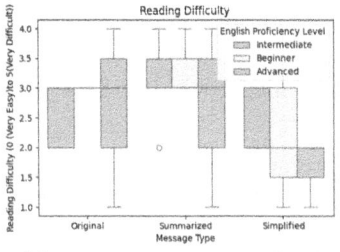

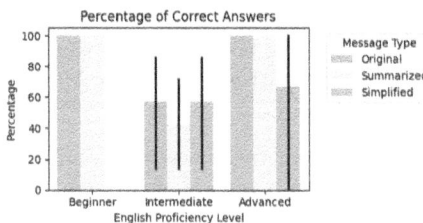

(a) Perceived reading difficulty.   (b) Percentage of correct answer.

Fig. 1. Perceived reading difficulty ratings from participants for each type of message(a) and percentage of correct answer(b).

4.2 Answer Accuracy

The accuracy of answers is illustrated in Fig. 1(b). The results indicated that beginners achieved a 100% success rate with both the original and summarized messages, but their performance dropped to 0% with the simplified message. This suggests that excessive simplification can lead to ambiguity. Among intermediate participants, 57% correctly answered the original and simplified messages, but only 43% answered correctly for the summarized message. This inconsistency implies that summarization may result in a loss of context, which can negatively impact comprehension. Advanced participants performed well with both the original and summarized messages, achieving a 100% success rate in both cases, but their performance dropped to 67% with the simplified message. This decline suggests that oversimplification may cause a loss of nuance, affecting their ability to understand the message accurately.

These results suggest that while summarization and simplification can aid comprehension, they need to be carefully balanced to avoid omitting key information or reducing context, which can impact different proficiency levels in varying ways. While the simplified text was rated as easier to read by participants, it did not necessarily lead to a higher rate of correct answers among NNSs. This suggests that although simplification can make text appear more accessible, it may also lead to a loss of critical information, impacting comprehension accuracy.

4.3 Statistical Significance

We conducted a statistical analysis to determine if there were significant differences in reading difficulty for three types of messages (Original, Summarized, Simplified) and across different English proficiency levels (Beginner, Intermediate, Advanced). To accomplish this, we employed three statistical tests, the results of which are presented in Table 1. McNemar's Test was used to compare the outcomes of the message types, revealing no significant difference in the accuracy of information comprehension between original and summarized messages. Friedman's Test assessed variations in reading difficulty among the three message types within each subject, indicating a significant difference in perceived difficulty. Kruskal-Wallis Test examined reading difficulty across different proficiency levels for each message type, showing no significant differences across varying proficiency levels. These tests provided valuable insights into the relationships between message types, reading difficulty, and proficiency levels.

The results of the analysis present several noteworthy conclusions. Initially, there is no statistically significant disparity in correct response outcomes between participants who received unabridged messages and those who received condensed messages, as indicated by McNemar's Test. This suggests that summarizing messages does not diminish the ability to comprehend information accurately. However, Friedman's Test demonstrated a significant disparity in the perceived reading difficulty across the three message types, emphasizing the impact of summarization and simplification on user experience. Additionally,

Table 1. Statistical Test Results

Test	Results
McNemar's Test	Contingency Table: [[7, 3], [2, 1]]
	p-value: 1.0
Friedman's Test	p-value: 0.017768944609069973
Kruskal-Wallis Test	Original Message: p-value = 0.5771290151656221
	Summarized Message: p-value = 0.8455354066830325
	Simplified Message: p-value = 0.3302293256525736

the Kruskal-Wallis Test did not reveal any significant discrepancies in the perceived reading difficulty across varying proficiency levels, indicating consistency regardless of participants' language proficiency. In summary, while message simplification affects perceived difficulty, it does not impact understanding accuracy, and this effect is consistent across different language proficiency levels.

5 Discussion and Future Direction

The results from our study indicate that while simplified text is perceived as easier to read by NNSs, it doesn't always translate into a higher accuracy rate in answering questions based on that text. This observation suggests that while simplification can improve readability and potentially increase engagement, it may lead to a loss of essential information, thereby impacting comprehension.

Despite the decreased accuracy, the positive response from participants towards simplified text indicates that LLMs can be a useful tool in encouraging NNSs to engage with content written by native speakers (NSs). Participants reported increased confidence and a greater willingness to engage in conversations when the text was simplified, pointing to a subjective improvement in their ability to process the information. This outcome is encouraging for fostering a more inclusive environment, as it suggests that simplification can help overcome initial communication barriers.

Another possible reason for the discrepancy between perceived ease of reading and actual comprehension might lie in the nature of the task itself. Our study employed multiple-choice questions with a mix of different topics, which could have contributed to the lower answer accuracy among NNSs. To better assess comprehension, future studies might consider using open-ended or closed-ended questions without predefined choices, allowing participants to express their understanding in their own words.

6 Conclusion

Our research on the application of LLM for summarizing and simplifying text in intercultural cooperation shows a complicated relationship between readability and comprehension accuracy. Although simplified text was rated as simpler to read by non-native speakers, it did not necessarily result in higher accuracy for understanding the content. This suggests that while simplification enhances accessibility, it can sometimes lead to a loss of crucial information, which can affect comprehension. Nonetheless, our method of using LLMs to create simplified text demonstrates their potential to bridge communication gaps and cultivate inclusivity in diverse settings. The result suggests that while message simplification affects perceived difficulty, it does not impact the accuracy of understanding, and this effect is consistent across different levels of language proficiency.

Acknowledgments. This research was partially supported by a Grant-in-Aid for Scientific Research (A) (17H00759, 2017-2020), a Grant-in-Aid for Scientific Research (B) (21H03561,2021-2024) and a Grant-in-Aid for Early-Career Scientists (21K17794,2021-2024) from the Japan Society for the Promotion of Science (JSPS).

References

1. Chang, Y., et al.: A survey on evaluation of large language models. ACM Trans. Intell. Syst. Technol. (2023)
2. Cox, T.H., Blake, S.: Managing cultural diversity: Implications for organizational competitiveness. Acad. Manage. Perspect. **5**(3), 45–56 (1991)
3. Heuer, H., Glassman, E.L.: Accessible text tools for people with cognitive impairments and non-native readers: Challenges and opportunities, pp. 250–266 (2023). https://doi.org/10.1145/3603555.3603569
4. Ishida, T., Murakami, Y., Lin, D., Nakaguchi, T., Otani, M.: Language service infrastructure on the web: the language grid. IEEE Comput. **51**(6), 72–81 (2018)
5. Kovacs, G.: Smart subtitles for language learning. In: CHI 2013 Extended Abstracts on Human Factors in Computing Systems (CHI EA 2013), pp. 2719–2724. Association for Computing Machinery, New York (2013). https://doi.org/10.1145/2468356.2479499
6. Kovacs, G., Miller, R.C.: Smart subtitles for vocabulary learning. In: Proceedings of the SIGCHI Conference on Human Factors in Computing Systems (CHI '14). pp. 853–862. Association for Computing Machinery, New York, NY, USA (2014). https://doi.org/10.1145/2556288.2557256
7. Pan, M.H., Yamashita, N., Wang, H.C.: Task rebalancing: Improving multilingual communication with native speakers-generated highlights on automated transcripts. In: Proceedings of the 2017 ACM Conference on Computer Supported Cooperative Work and Social Computing (CSCW 2017), pp. 310–322. ACM, Portland, Oregon, USA (2017)
8. Wan, X., Li, H., Xiao, T.: Eusum: Extracting easy-to-understand English summaries for non-native readers. In: Proceedings of the 33rd International ACM SIGIR Conference on Research and Development in Information Retrieval (SIGIR 2010), pp. 491–498. Association for Computing Machinery, New York (2010). https://doi.org/10.1145/1835449.1835532
9. Yu, C.H., Miller, R.C.: Enhancing web page readability for non-native readers. In: Proceedings of the SIGCHI Conference on Human Factors in Computing Systems (CHI 2010), pp. 2523–2532. Association for Computing Machinery, New York (2010). https://doi.org/10.1145/1753326.1753709

Author Index

A
Aadmi-Laamech, Khadija El 45
Álvarez, Claudio 61, 81
Aravena, Valentina 237

B
Baloian, Nelson 237

C
Carrió, Mar 29

E
Egi, Hironori 265

F
Farías, Antonio 61
Florido, Héctor 257
Fujita, Kinya 17

G
Gutiérrez-Ferré, Aldric 248
Gutierrez-Paez, Nicolas 29

H
Haibo, Yu 3
Hernández-Leo, Davinia 29, 45, 129, 248, 257
Horikoshi, Izumi 220
Hoshino, Mizuki 3

I
Ibarra, Javier 81
Iga, Soichiro 203
Ihara, Masayuki 161
Imagawa, Taketo 161
Inoue, Tomoo 177
Iso, Kazuyuki 161

K
Kinoshita, Yuichiro 114
Kobayashi, Minoru 144, 161
Kurokochi, Atsuto 144
Kuwamiya, Yo 144

L
Liang, Changhao 220

M
Michos, Konstantinos 29
Mizumoto, Takeshi 3
Motozawa, Mizuki 97
Murakami, Yohei 97, 274
Murobayashi, Kanato 265

N
Nakamura, Satoshi 114, 229
Nishida, Takeshi 212
Nishide, Shinya 212

O
Odakura, Valguima 129
Ogata, Hiroaki 220
Ohnaka, Kenta 161
Oka, Natsuki 195

P
Pituxcoosuvarn, Mondheera 97, 274

Q
Quelhas, Ana Beatriz Pires 195

R
Recabarren, Matías 81

S
Sánchez-Reina, J. Roberto 129, 248
Santos, Patricia 29, 45

Sasaki, Kosuke 177
Sato, Gen 3
Shiramatsu, Shun 3
Sugisawa, Ryota 17

T
Takaku, Takumi 114
Takano, Sayaka 229
Takatsuka, Susumu 203
Tanaka, Kazuaki 195
Tetsukawa, Hiroki 203
Theophilou, Emily 129

U
Uribe, Joaquín 237

W
Watanabe, Shuhei 3

Y
Yoshino, Takahiro 265
Yunga, Manuel 61

Z
Zurita, Gustavo 61, 237

SPRINGER NATURE

GPSR Compliance

The European Union's (EU) General Product Safety Regulation (GPSR) is a set of rules that requires consumer products to be safe and our obligations to ensure this.

If you have any concerns about our products, you can contact us on ProductSafety@springernature.com

In case Publisher is established outside the EU, the EU authorized representative is:

Springer Nature Customer Service Center GmbH
Europaplatz 3
69115 Heidelberg, Germany

The manufacturer's authorised representative in the EU is Springer Nature Customer Service Centre GmbH, Europaplatz 3, 69115 Heidelberg, Germany. If you have any concerns regarding our products, please contact ProductSafety@springernature.com

Printed and bound by CPI Group (UK) Ltd, Croydon, CR0 4YY

25/03/2026

02078187-0016